Fodor's 2013

MONTRÉAL & QUÉBEC CITY

Fodor's Travel Publications   New York, Toronto, London, Sydney, Auckland
www.fodors.com

FODOR'S MONTRÉAL & QUÉBEC CITY 2013

Writers: Chris Barry, Marcella De Vincenzo, Amanda Halm, Joanne Latimer, Vanessa Muri
Editors: Penny Phenix, Debbie Harmsen, Maria Teresa Hart

Production Editor: Evangelos Vasilakis
Maps & Illustrations: David Lindroth, Inc.; Mark Stroud, Moon Street Cartography, *cartographers*; Rebecca Baer, *map editor*; William Wu, *information graphics*
Design: Fabrizio La Rocca, *creative director*; Tina Malaney, Chie Ushio, Jessica Ramirez, *designers*; Melanie Marin, *associate director of photography*; Jennifer Romains, *photo research*
Cover Photo: Front cover: Jean Heguy/age fotostock [*Description: Montreal History Museum*]. Back cover (from left to right): Comstock Images/Thinkstock; POUTINE! by Patty http://www.flickr.com/photos/zorbs/2790844808/ Attribution License; meunierd/Shutterstock. Spine: Massimiliano Pieraccini/Shutterstock.
Production Manager: Angela L. McLean

ISBN 978-0-89141-939-6

ISSN 1525–5867

SPECIAL SALES

This book is available at special discounts for bulk purchases for sales promotions or premiums. Special editions, including personalized covers, excerpts of existing books, and corporate imprints, can be created in large quantities for special needs. For more information, write to Special Markets/Premium Sales, 1745 Broadway, MD 3-1, New York, NY 10019, or e-mail specialmarkets@randomhouse.com.

AN IMPORTANT TIP & AN INVITATION

Although all prices, opening times, and other details in this book are based on information supplied to us at press time, changes occur all the time in the travel world, and Fodor's cannot accept responsibility for facts that become outdated or for inadvertent errors or omissions. So **always confirm information when it matters,** especially if you're making a detour to visit a specific place. Your experiences—positive and negative—matter to us. If we have missed or misstated something, **please write to us.** Share your opinion instantly through our online feedback center at fodors.com/contact-us.

PRINTED IN COLOMBIA

10 9 8 7 6 5 4 3 2 1

CONTENTS

MAPS

ABOUT THIS GUIDE

Fodor's Ratings

Everything in this guide is worth doing—we don't cover what isn't—but exceptional sights, hotels, and restaurants are recognized with additional accolades. **Fodor's Choice★** indicates our top recommendations; ★ highlights places we deem highly recommended; and **Best Bets** call attention to notable hotels and restaurants in various categories. Care to nominate a new place? Visit Fodors.com/contact-us.

Trip Costs

We list prices wherever possible to help you budget well. Hotel and restaurant price categories from **$** to **$$$$** are noted alongside each recommendation. For hotels, we include the lowest cost of a standard double room in high season. For restaurants, we cite the average price of a main course at dinner or, if dinner isn't served, at lunch. For attractions, we always list adult admission fees; discounts are usually available for children, students, and senior citizens.

Hotels

Our local writers vet every hotel to recommend the best overnights in each price category, from budget to expensive. Unless otherwise specified, you can expect private bath, phone, and TV in your room. For expanded hotel reviews, facilities, and deals visit Fodors.com.

Restaurants

Unless we state otherwise, restaurants are open for lunch and dinner daily. We mention dress code only when there's a specific requirement and reservations only when they're essential or not accepted. To make restaurant reservations, visit Fodors.com.

Ratings		Hotels & Restaurants	
★	Fodor's Choice	🏨	Hotel
★	Highly recommended	🛏	Number of rooms
🌣	Family-friendly	⑪	Meal plans
Listings		✕	Restaurant
✉	Address	🍴	Reservations
📧	Branch address	👗	Dress code
☎	Telephone	⚊	No credit cards
🖷	Fax	⑤	Price
⊕	Website		
✍	E-mail	**Other**	
🎫	Admission fee	⇨	See also
⊙	Open/closed times	🖙	Take note
Ⓜ	Subway	🏌	Golf facilities
⊹	Directions or Map coordinates		

Credit Cards

The hotels and restaurants in this guide typically accept credit cards. If not, we'll say so.

Experience Montréal and Québec City

WHAT'S NEW IN MONTRÉAL AND QUÉBEC CITY

Montréal and Québec City are like France without jet lag, two vibrant centers of European *joie de vivre* within driving distance of major cities in the northeastern United States. They are cities of great contrasts between old and new, quaint and cool. Sidewalk cafés and cobblestone streets are charming backdrops to the latest in high fashion, haute cuisine, and avant-garde art.

Montréal is a forward-thinking, party-loving island metropolis of 1.9 million people that expands to about 3.8 million with its environs. A new art gallery, a new concert hall, refurbished downtown parks, and the return of Formula 1 racing are all signs of Montréal's restored fortunes.

Meanwhile, Québec City brims with new confidence. It has even one-upped Montréal by snagging a deal with the Cirque du Soleil to provide free street entertainment for visitors and locals.

Both cities are defined by the exhilarating extremes of four distinct seasons, picturesque waterfront settings along the St. Lawrence River, and four centuries of history. Montréal and Québec City are easily walkable, with lively downtown cores and friendly, relaxed vibes. You can expect tantalizing French food in both cities, from humble to haute, and good value for hotels and shopping. The U.S. and Canadian dollars are roughly at par, so the big currency discount for Americans is a thing of the past, at least for now.

Montréal Arts in Motion
Culturally, Montréal is in constant motion. A new concert hall for the Orchestre Symphonique de Montréal is the *pièce de résistance* of the Quartier des Spectacles, an effervescent downtown district of more than 80 venues for film, music, theater, dance, visual arts, and comedy.

The Musée des Beaux-Arts de Montréal, one of Canada's oldest museums, has created a new pavilion of Canadian and Québec art in an adjacent church. To the relief of local architectural preservationists, the museum retained the church's magnificent stone exterior and its main nave, which will be used as an auditorium and site for temporary exhibitions. It also rescued the 20 Tiffany stained-glass windows—the largest collection of Tiffany glass outside the United States—from the chapel and remounted them in the nave.

Cirque for Free in QC
Can't afford tickets to the Cirque du Soleil's big shows in Las Vegas? Make a summer visit to Québec's Old City in 2013 for a free taste of the world's most innovative circus. Thanks to a five-year C$30-million deal signed with the Cirque in 2009, the company has been providing free street shows five days a week each summer. A notable success, the contract has been extended until 2015 and might well continue indefinitely.

The mayor is betting the Cirque will continue staving off any recession-driven drop in tourism. And he has to enjoy the discomfort of his city's upstart, upriver rival, Montréal, which, in spite of being the site of the Cirque's world headquarters, has to make do with occasional performances by visiting troupes.

Another wildly creative happening in the city is the monumental Image Mill 3D, which includes a dazzling three-dimensional video projected onto the stark walls of the Old Port's grain silos. This is sound, light, music, and film with a futuristic style.

Refreshed Ritz in Montréal

Even in a city full of chic boutique hotels, the Ritz-Carlton Montréal is something to behold. After a four-year hiatus while major renovations were taking place, this iconic Montréal hotel re-opened in 2012 just in time for its 100th birthday. Even if you can't afford a Ritzy room, this exquisitely restored landmark is the place for celebrity spotting, cocktail sipping, and dining in the new Maison Boulud, home to international star chef Daniel Boulud.

Montréal's Fresh Green Start

At most, Dorchester Square and Place du Canada, which face each other across boulevard René Lévesque, total just a little more than 5 acres, but their location right in the center of downtown make them worthy of the money and care the city has lavished on them in the last few years. In 2010, Montréal reopened Dorchester Square after a restoration project that added new lawns and wide walkways and replanted trees.

In 2012, Place du Canada also benefited from a major facelift. The two neighboring squares with their lawns and mature shady trees play an important part in the lives of Montrealers. If the corner of rues Ste-Catherine and Peel is the heart of downtown, Dorchester and Place du Canada are its lungs.

All Aboard to Charlevoix

The exciting Train du Massif de Charlevoix departs Parc de la Chute-Montmorency outside of Québec City, heading for the superb ski resort of Le Massif de Charlevoix and the artistic village of Baie-Saint-Paul. At the end of the line is the charming cliff-top town of La Malbaie, home of the baronial Hôtel Fairmont Le Manoir Richelieu. The hotel's talented chefs cater the train's gourmet meals. The new railway features restored vintage cars with exceptional interiors and panoramic windows, which are key to taking in the scenery along the route.

Restaurant Week

If you're interested in sampling a wide array of Montréal's many famous restaurants without spending a fortune, then Taste MTL is the ideal solution. In early November, close to 100 dining establishments participate in Montreal's newly established Restaurant Week, offering their table d'hôte menus at the particularly appetizing prices of C$19, C$29, and C$39. Over the course of 11 days Taste MTL not only enables foodies to savor the creativity of the city's top chefs for considerably less money than usual, but to also witness a variety of activities that showcase the fine art of dining. Reservations are mandatory and can be arranged via ⊕ *www.tourisme-montreal. org/tastemtl.*

See the Stars

A state-of-the-art planetarium, due to open in 2013, will add a powerful new element to the natural-sciences district the city is developing in the east end near the Stade Olympique. Built right next to the Biodôme and just across from the Insectarium and the Jardins Botaniques, the Planétarium Rio Tinto Alcan de Montréal will use the latest audiovisual techniques to create a realistic experience for the digital generation.

WHAT'S WHERE

1 Montréal. Montréal and the island on which it stands take their name from Mont-Royal, a stubby plug of tree-covered igneous rock that rises high above the surrounding cityscape. It's a bustling, multiethnic city of neighborhoods, from the historic Old City to the hip Plateau.

2 Québec City. The capital of the province of Québec is widely considered to be the most French city in North America. Québec's Old City (Vieux Québec) is split into two tiers, separated by steep rock against which are more than 25 *escaliers* (staircases) and a funicular. The surrounding cluster of small, low-rise neighborhoods each have their own charm and flavor.

3 The Laurentians. The Laurentians (les Laurentides) encompass thousands of miles of forests, mountains, and lakes, but for many people the draw is Mont-Tremblant and its world-class ski slopes. At just 1½ hours from Montréal, the area has also become a favorite weekend golf destination.

4 The Eastern Townships. Called les Cantons de l'Est in French, the Eastern Townships region has quaint architecture and rolling hills that might remind you of New England. Atop imposing Mont-Mégantic,

you're 3,150 feet closer to the heavens. Far from city lights, the sky here is ideal for star-gazing.

5 Île d'Orléans. Famed for its strawberry crop, Île d'Orléans is called the "Garden of Québec" for its local produce, wine, and cider. Made up of six small villages, this charming island has several bed-and-breakfasts and fabulous farm stands selling local products.

6 Côte de Beaupré. The coast hugged by the St. Lawrence River embraces the thundering Montmorency Falls and the impressive Ste-Anne-de-Beaupré shrine. It leads to Mont-Sainte-Anne, famous for its skiing, golfing, and mountain biking.

7 Charlevoix. The big bang of an ancient meteor created picturesque valleys, cliffs, and mountains that brush the St. Lawrence River. This "Switzerland of Québec" has inspired painters, poets, and musicians for generations.

Mont-Tremblant

THE LAURENTIANS

Lac Saint-Pie

3

Berthierville 40

Saint-Joseph-de-Sorel

15 St Jérôme 25

Le Gardeur Douville

Boisbriand

Oka 20 Montréal Beloeil

1

Candiac Iberville

Salaberry-de-Valleyfield Mercier

MONTÉRÉGIE

CANADA

UNITED STATES

NEW YORK

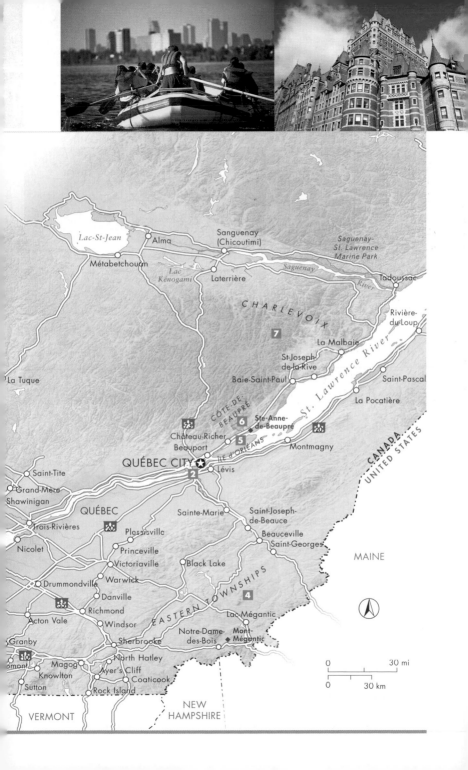

MONTRÉAL & QUÉBEC CITY TOP ATTRACTIONS

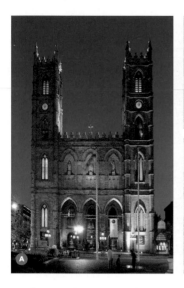

Basilique Notre-Dame-de-Montréal

(A) Everything about Montréal's magnificent basilica is grand, from the 228-foot twin steeples to the 7,000-pipe organ in the loft. The thousands of stars spattered across the vaulted blue ceiling are 24-carat gold and were painstakingly applied by hand. To experience a bit of heavenly Catholic pomp and hear the choir sing and the organ roar, consider attending the 11 am mass on Sunday.

Parc du Mont-Royal

(B) The modest mountain that gives Montréal its name is at the center of a 500-acre park with wooded trails, a trio of chalets, and splendid views from the city's highest point. City-weary people flirt here in spring, picnic in summer, enjoy the colors of autumn, and skate in winter.

Mont-Tremblant

(C) This towering peak of the Laurentian Mountains, northwest of Montréal, has become one of North America's finest ski resorts, with 650 acres of skiable terrain, state-of-the-art snowmaking and lift equipment, first-class lodging, and an on-slope village of shops and restaurants.

La Citadelle

(D) The fascinating star-shaped fortress on Québec City's Cap Diamant is the largest fortified base in North America still occupied by troops. Built in the 1800s to protect the city from a feared American invasion that never came, La Citadelle is currently home to Canada's Royal 22nd Regiment. Every summer morning at 10 am, the regiment turns out in scarlet tunics and bearskin caps for the colorful, ceremonial changing of the guard.

Musée des Beaux-Arts de Montréal

(E) One of Canada's oldest museums has an exceptional collection of Canadian art, from portrayals of pioneer life by Paul Kane to dazzling abstractions by Paul-Émile Borduas, all housed in a former church. The permanent collection

1

features works by such world masters as Rembrandt, Renoir, and Picasso.

Fairmont Le Château Frontenac

(F) The most photographed sight in Québec City, the Fairmont Le Château Frontenac towers above quaint 18th- and 19th-century homes that have been transformed into shops and bistros. At the hotel's base is Terrasse Dufferin, a wide boardwalk with sweeping views of the St. Lawrence River and the Laurentian Mountains.

Tadoussac

This old trading post north of Québec City, situated at the confluence of the St. Lawrence and Saguenay rivers, is now a major whale-watching venue. You may see minke, finback, and even blue whales, but more commonly the southernmost colony of beluga whales. Watch them from shore, or sign up for a cruise to get a closer look.

Montréal's Old Port

In Montréal's Old Port, centuries-old warehouses now house art galleries, ice-cream parlors, and other attractions. It's one of the city's most popular parks: a place to cycle, stroll, or take a boat ride on the Lachine Rapids.

Plains of Abraham

It's a peaceful city park now, full of winding walking paths and bicycle trails, and a favorite in winter of Québec City's cross-country skiers. But on September 13, 1759, it was anything but peaceful, when British troops routed the flower of New France and changed North American history.

MONTRÉAL AND QUÉBEC CITY TOP EXPERIENCES

À la Française

Steeped in the traditions and the language of its mother country, Québec has a distinctly Continental flavor. Where else in North America can you relax on the terrace at a bistro, sipping a café au lait while listening to everyone around you debate politics or popular culture in French?

Québec is a little like the European country next door, the France you can drive to in less than a day from many parts of the United States. It's different from anything just south, or north, or east, or west of its borders. The people who reside in this relatively laid-back part of the world—French, English, and newcomers from around the world—share an approach to life that is uniquely Québecois. Locals are warm, intriguing, and gracious hosts. From the magnificent architecture of the grand basilicas to the trendy terraces lining the bohemian enclaves of Montréal's Plateau district, the French face of Québec is delightfully omnipresent, and one of the most charming elements of this destination.

You can immerse yourself in French culture at several venues. The plays of such prominent Québecois writers as Michel Tremblay command the stages of French-language theaters, including the Théâtre du Nouveau Monde and the historic Monument-National. The stately Grande Bibliothèque Nationale du Québec is home to more than a million books in French and English, with special collections for children and visually-challenged readers. The Université de Montréal houses 18 libraries and several world-renowned research centers. With 60,000 students and a sprawling campus, it's one of the top universities in the French-speaking world.

Savor French and Local Cuisine

The Québecois take their French food very seriously. Traveling through most cities and towns you won't have to look too hard to find a restaurant serving traditional French fare and regional specialties. Many restaurants serve *cuisine du terroir* (food of the region) using ingredients like lamb, veal, bison, caribou, and foie gras. These temples of gastronomy create artful dishes, usually with a contemporary flair. But not everything in Québec is *haute*. A far cry from fine dining is the time-honored and much-cherished *casse croûte* (snack bar), where you can chow down on comfort foods like hot dogs and chicken sandwiches with gravy. Every visitor has to sample *poutine*, a heap of french fries topped with gravy and melted cheese curds. And your best bet for a quick lunch might be a simple ham-and-cheese baguette from a great *boulangerie* (bakery).

Québec is one of the largest maple syrup producers in the world, so a visit to a traditional *cabane à sucre* (maple-sugar shack) is a ritual that comes every spring with the maple syrup harvest. There's no better way to sample the province's wares than by stopping by one of these rural establishments for a home-cooked meal that may include pea soup, baked beans, eggs with ham, and deep-fried pork rinds called *les oreilles de Crisse* (Christ's ears), a nod to the region's Catholic upbringing. But the food here goes way beyond French. Montréal's long-established Jewish community has contributed bagels and smoked meat sandwiches. The city also enjoys a world-beat of national treasures like Arabic shish kebab, Chinese dim sum, Spanish tapas, Vietnamese spring rolls, and Lebanese tabbouleh.

Romp in the Snow

Ice-skating, cross-country skiing, tobogganing—the Québecois embrace winter with enthusiasm. It's the best way to cope with the weather, since from mid-December until mid-April the province is covered in snow and bitterly cold temperatures prevail.

With much of the landscape blanketed in the white stuff for months at a time, it's not surprising that Québec has taken great pains to nurture its reputation as one of the top winter vacation destinations in North America. Fans of winter sports can revel in the thrilling adventures of dog sledding, ice fishing, and kite skiing on frozen lakes. You don't have to worry about staying warm because outfitters provide weatherproof gear. Globe-Trotter Aventure Canada Tours (☎ 888/598–7688 ⊕ www.aventurecanada.com) is one operator that organizes excursions lasting from a few hours to a full week.

With so many mountains, the province has about 75 ski resorts. Skiers and snowboarders can enjoy a day on the slopes for C$40–C$60 a day at Mont-Blanc in the Laurentians, Owl's Head and Mont-Sutton in the Eastern Townships, Le Massif in Charlevoix, and Mont-Sainte-Anne near Québec City. Mont-Tremblant, northwest of Montréal, is a little pricier, but it's Eastern Canada's largest ski area, with a stylish slope-side village, five-star lodgings, and the fancy Casino de Mont Tremblant. Try night skiing at Mont-Saint-Sauveur (northwest of Montréal), Ski Bromont (Eastern Townships), or Mont-Sainte-Anne. The snow takes on a luminescent glow under the lights and the stars provide a little extra sparkle.

For a tamer ride, hop aboard one of the classic horse-drawn sleighs gliding through the streets of Montréal or Québec City.

Shop for Fur and Crafts

People have traveled to Canada to seek out furs ever since the early 1600s. The fur industry still generates about C$800 million annually and employs about 60,000 trappers and 5,000 fur farmers, manufacturers, craftspeople, and retailers. Mink, fox, and chinchilla are the most commonly farmed fur-bearing animals in Canada. Trappers in the wild, many of them Native Canadians, also supply beaver, raccoon, muskrat, otter, bear, seal, and wolf pelts. In Montréal, the best bargains are found in shops near rue Bleury and boulevard de Maisonneuve. However, most furriers have moved north to 9250 rue Parc in the rue Chabanel fashion district. Harricana on rue Atwater is an atelier for unique, stylish accessories like backpacks and boas made from recycled furs. In Québec City, try Richard Robitaille Fourrures in the Old City. You can pick up a toasty fur hat for about C$100 or splurge on a glamorous mink coat for around C$5,000.

Arguably, it was the fur trade that allowed many of Canada's First Nations peoples to live according to the traditions of their ancestors, which explains why Canada has such a rich heritage of native crafts. Québec's best-known crafts are wood carving, weaving, pine cabinetry, leather and bead work, and canoe making. For guaranteed authenticity, look for the Canadian government's igloo symbol on crafts and the Beautifully Canadian logo on furs.

MONTRÉAL AND QUÉBEC CITY LIKE A LOCAL

Visiting Montréal and Québec City is like stumbling upon a little corner of Europe in North America. Soak up the rich French culture by sampling local cuisine, catching a hockey game at a bar, or finding yourself in the midst of some fabulous all-night party.

Try Some Poutine

The legend is that sometime in 1957 a customer walked into Le Café Idéal in the village of Warwick, Québec, and asked owner Fernand Lachance to add a handful of cheese curds to his order of *frites-sauce* (fries and gravy). Lachance served the result while muttering "Quelle poutine!"— roughly translated as "What a mess!"

And so was born what has become Québec's favorite fast food. Poutine is everywhere, even at McDonalds. But it's no longer just hot french fries topped with cheese curds and a ladleful of thick brown gravy, as dozens of high- and lowbrow variations have sprung up.

Top chefs have come up with their own gourmet versions, using duck gravy instead of the usual gelatinous brown sauce or blue cheese instead of curds. Martin Picard at Montréal's Au Pied de Cochon drew rave reviews for his foie gras poutine, and Chuck Hughes of Montréal's Garde-Manger won TV's *Iron Chef* competition with his delectable lobster poutine.

Enjoy Hockey Night

What soccer is to Brazilians and baseball is to Americans, hockey is to the Québecois. It's not a game, it's a religion, and its winter-long rites are celebrated in hundreds of arenas across the province.

On weekend mornings, bleary-eyed parents hunker down in the stands watching their children practice. At 10 pm the beer-sponsored leagues take over the ice—men and women with full-time jobs strap on the skates and pads just for the fun of it.

If you can afford the scalpers' ticket prices (or if you have a friend with connections), catch a Montréal Canadiens game at the Centre Bell. The province's only National Hockey League team hasn't won a Stanley Cup since 1993, but a night watching the Habs—as they're known locally—is an experience to savor.

Attend a Cinq-à-sept

If someone invites you to what sounds like a "sank-a-sett," it has nothing to do with swimming or tennis. It's a *cinq-à-sept*, a cocktail party that's supposed to happen between 5 and 7 pm but that rarely starts before 6 pm and usually ends around 8 or 8:30 pm.

The true 5-à-7 isn't to be confused with the raucous 2-for-1 happy hour. The *cinq-à-sept is* a more refined affair, at which conversation is at least as important as the drinks.

One of the essential skills you should master before attending your first 5-à-7 is the two-cheek kiss. The secret to perfecting this Continental-style greeting is capturing the middle ground between the air kiss and the passionate enthusiastic smack of long-separated lovers. A light cheek brush, something that expresses delight, is just about right.

Embrace the Outdoors

Quebecers are crazy about the great outdoors, no matter what time of year. Cycling trails crisscross Montréal and Québec City, making good use of canal routes, former railway beds, and even major downtown streets. One of the most popular outings is a ride along La Route Verte, a 2,500-mile network of bike trails. **Fitz and Follwell Co.** (☎ *514/754–3691* ⊕ *www.fitzandfollwell.com*)   arranges

delightful tours through Montréal that include hot chocolate, fresh bagels, and a lunch of poutine.

In winter, why try to avoid the weather when it's better to join the frosty fun? In Montréal, try ice-skating in Parc Lafontaine and cross-country skiing, snowshoeing, and snow tubing on Mont-Royal. In Québec City there's ice-skating at Place d'Youville, cross-country skiing on the Plains of Abraham, and tobogganing near the Château Frontenac.

Soak in a Nordic Spa

Quebecers have pioneered the concept of Nordic spas in America. These spas are a hot trend, even in Québec's often-cold climate. Based on a 1,000-year-old Viking tradition, a Nordic spa sojourn consists of alternating between soaking in outdoor hot tubs, baking in saunas, and plunging into icy waters. Add a Turkish steam bath and a Swedish massage and you're cooked.

Also known as thermo-therapy, the experience is gently invigorating yet totally relaxing. Clad in swimsuits, spa-goers dash from a hot whirlpool into an icy pond, then heat up again in a sweltering steam bath and chill out under a cold waterfall. You'll be hot, cold, and hot again, for hours, marinating in the aromas of eucalyptus and pine or the fresh mountain air. It's especially fun in winter when snow banks surround the whirlpools. The pioneer of Québec's Nordic spas is the Polar Bear's Club, which opened about 25 years ago in the Laurentians. Now, with approximately 40 Nordic spas in the province, this watery adventure is *de rigeur* after sports, shopping, or a stressful day. Expect to pay C$45 to C$55 for the experience, including robe, towel, and locker. Massages and other treatments are extra.

Drink Some Beer

Not so long ago, a pint of Ex (Molson's Export Ale) or a tin of Blue (Labatt's Pilsner) were the staples of sports bars, taverns, and brasseries. Things have changed in the Canadian beer world, as microbreweries have entered the beer scene. Their products have taken their place alongside the best beers from Belgium, England, and Germany. In Québec, brewers tend to choose apocalyptic labels like Maudite (Damned) and La Fin du Monde (End of the World).

Linger at Sidewalk Cafés

There's something about surviving the harsh winters—which Québec winters still unquestionably are—that makes it particularly sweet to spend long summer evenings sipping drinks under the open sky. Alfresco dining blooms as early as May, when it still can be quite chilly, especially at night. But when locals have been cooped up indoors for months, a few buds on the trees or a few crocuses in the garden are enough to lure diners outside to sidewalk tables with colorful umbrellas or awnings. These *terrasses* are perfect for watching the passing parade of people.

MONTRÉAL AND QUÉBEC CITY WITH KIDS

There's no shortage of fantastic activities in Montréal and Québec City for kids. Here's just a sampling of what the little ones might enjoy during a visit.

Montréal

Montréal's wildly popular rent-a-bicycle **Bixi** system is a great way for families to see the city. The expanding network of car-free cycling paths now meanders around Parc du Mont-Royal and through Old Montréal, across the island Parc Jean-Drapeau, and along the Lachine Canal.

Kids who've had their fill of churches and museums can expend some pent-up energy at the adjacent **Old Port**, which has boats to pedal, a clock tower to climb, and a maze. There's also a new waterfront beach, but alas, no swimming is allowed.

For culturally adventurous youngsters, there are outdoor dance and theater presentations at **Parc Lafontaine.** Kids can also explore the mysteries of bonsai trees and Chinese gardens at the **Jardin Botanique** and drop into the on-site **Insectarium** to see the world's largest collection of bugs.

Québec City

Ice-cream stands, street performers, and (in winter) a thrilling toboggan run make **Terrasse Dufferin** as entertaining for children as for adults, as do the **Plains of Abraham's** open spaces.

Place Royale in the Lower Town brings the 17th and 18th centuries to life for even the youngest children.

La Citadelle's changing-of-the-guard ceremony, complete with the Royal 22e Régiment's mascot, Batisse the Goat, has lots of kid appeal. The hands-on exhibits at the **Musée de la Civilisation** and the 19th-century jail cells preserved in the **Musée de Québec** are both must-see attractions.

And for a little animal fun, polar bears, seals, and walrus are the stars of the city's **Aquarium du Québec.**

Side Trips from Montréal and Québec City

In the Laurentians, the gentle rides of the **Au Pays des Merveilles** and the **Village du Père Noël** (Santa's Village) are perfect for younger children. There are plenty of thrills at the **Water Parks** at Mont-St-Sauveur in the Laurentians and Bromont in the Eastern Townships.

Montmorency Falls, on the Côte de Beaupré, aren't as grand as Niagara, but they're higher, and crossing the suspension bridge above the spectacular chutes of water is a thrill. Farther along the St. Lawrence coast in **Tadoussac** you can take a boat ride for an up-close encounter with whales (be careful not to get salt water in your camera or phone).

FREE AND ALMOST FREE THINGS TO DO

There might be no such thing as a free lunch in Montréal or Québec City, but plenty of other things are free, or nearly so.

Art

Admission to the permanent collections of Montréal's Musée des Beaux-Arts (⊕ www.mbam.qc.ca) and Québec City's Musée National des Beaux-Arts (⊕ www. mnba.qc.ca) is always free. Every summer the city of Montréal mounts an outdoor exhibit of art or photographs on the sidewalks of avenue McGill College between rues Ste-Catherine and Sherbrooke.

Concerts

Montréal's Christ Church Cathedral (⊠ 635 rue Ste-Catherine Ouest ☎ 514/843–6577), a magnificent neo-Gothic treasure, and Oratoire St-Joseph (⊠ 3800 Chemin Queen-Mary ☎ 514/733–8211) offer free organ recitals on Sunday afternoons at 3 pm throughout the year. And Les Petits Chanteurs du Mont-Royal, one of the finest boys' choirs in North America, sings the 11 am mass at the Oratoire every Sunday from March to December 24. They also perform several free concerts through the year.

Montréal's Festival Internationale de Jazz every June and Québec City's Festival d'Été in July have dozens of free, open-air concerts. These huge happenings bring thousands, and tens of thousands, of revelers to the streets.

Fireworks

From mid-June through July, the sky comes alive with light and color on most Wednesday and Saturday evenings when fireworks teams from around the world compete in the spectacular L'International des Feux Loto-Québec. You can pay for a seat at La Ronde amusement park or join thousands of Montrealers in the Old Port, on the Jacques Cartier Bridge, and in Parc Champlain on the South Shore and watch for free.

Politics

Political junkies can join free guided tours of North America's only French-speaking legislature, the Assemblée Nationale du Québec (☎ 418/643–7239). The parliamentary debates are on Tuesday to Thursday from August to November and February to May.

Science

McGill University's Redpath Museum (⊠ 859 rue Sherbrooke Ouest ☎ 514/398–4086) houses an eclectic collection of dinosaur skeletons, seashells, fossils, minerals, Egyptian mummies, and Stone Age tools in a beautiful 19th-century building. Watch for free lectures.

Sightseeing

For one of the best views of Québec City, take the C$3.10 ferry (⊠ 10 rue des Traversiers ☎ 418/643–8420) for a mini-cruise across the St. Lawrence River to Lévis and back. Or for C$2, ride the Funiculaire du Vieux-Québec (⊠ 16 rue Petit-Champlain ☎ 418/692–1132), the sharply vertical railway that creaks along the cliff from Lower Town to Upper Town.

GREAT ITINERARIES

Montréal and Québec City are perfect for long weekend trips, although if you'd like to see both areas, you could easily spend a week.

Essential Montréal in a Day

Start with a stroll to the peak of Mont-Royal, the city's most enduring natural symbol. Afterward, wander south on avenue du Parc and through McGill University's leafy campus to downtown. The Musée des Beaux-Arts de Montréal, on rue Sherbrooke, was once the bastion of the Anglo-Canadian establishment, and is worth a visit.

For a Francophone perspective, head from Mont-Royal (the mountain) along rue Mont-Royal (the street) to rue St-Denis, home to funky boutiques and a boisterous strip of bars near the Université du Québec à Montréal.

In the late afternoon head down to Old Montréal, and pop into the Basilique Notre-Dame-de-Montréal before getting in some nightlife, as in the summer months the Old City is one of the most popular places to party. There are dozens of restaurants to choose from, as well as clubs and bars.

Day Trips and Overnights from Montréal

If you have only a couple of days for a visit and you need to concentrate on one area, the Laurentians are a good choice. Less than an hour's drive from downtown Montréal, this resort area has recreational options (depending on the season) that include golf, hiking, and superb skiing, both Alpine and cross-country.

Pick a resort town to stay in and use that as a base for visiting some of the surrounding towns. Each town has its own style and appeal: St-Sauveur-des-Monts is lively, Morin Heights is tranquil, and Ste-Adèle is

a center of gastronomy. Mont-Tremblant, a sophisticated ski and golf resort, is worth a trip, particularly for the picturesque gondola ride to the summit.

You can combine a taste of the Eastern Townships with a two-day visit to the Laurentians. After an overnight stay in the Laurentians, head back south of Montréal to the Townships, which extend to the east along the border with New England. Overnight in Granby or Bromont: Granby has a zoo, and Bromont is known for golf, skiing, and its water park.

The next day, you can shop in pretty Knowlton (look for signs to Lac Brome) and explore regional history in such towns as Valcourt. Spend a night or two in the appealing resort town of Magog, along Lac Memphrémagog, or in the quieter North Hatley, on Lac Massawippi. You'll have good dining in either. Save some time for outdoor activities, whether it's golfing, skiing, biking, or hiking.

Essential Québec City in a Day

It's inspiring to start your day in Québec's Lower Town, the earliest site of French civilization in North America. Stroll along the narrow streets of the Quartier Petit-Champlain, visit the Maison Chevalier, and browse the craft stores and boutiques. From there, head to Place Royale, making a stop at the Église Notre-Dame-des-Victoires, and continue on to Terrasse Dufferin. In the afternoon, when the crowds thin out, check out the Musée National des Beaux-Arts du Québec or the Musée de la Civilisation.

Catch a gorgeous sunset from the Plains of Abraham—site of the battle that ended France's colonial dreams in North America and marked the beginning of British rule in Canada—before dining anywhere

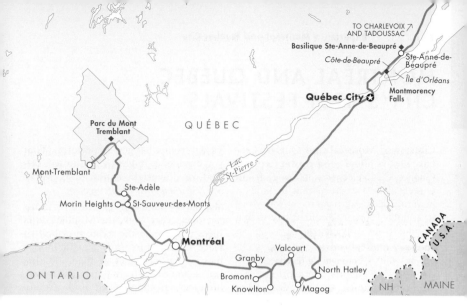

Basilique Ste-Anne-de-Beaupré ◆
Côte-de-Beaupré ◇   ◇ Ste-Anne-de-
                              Beaupré
                          ○ Île d'Orléans
                          Montmorency
                          Falls
Québec City ◎

Parc du Mont
Tremblant ◆   QUÉBEC

Mont-Tremblant ○

                    Ste-Adèle ○   Lac
Morin Heights ○ ○ St-Sauveur-des-Monts St-Pierre

                    Montréal ○
                          Valcourt ○
              Granby ○   ○ North Hatley
ONTARIO   Bromont ○
              Knowlton ○   ○ Magog   NH   MAINE

CANADA
U.S.A.

on rue St-Jean, one of the best streets in the city for restaurants and nightlife.

Day Trips and Overnights from Québec City

If you want to get out of Québec City for a day or two, take a 20-minute drive to Île d'Orléans, a picturesque island called the "garden of Québec." In summer, explore this idyllic island's boutiques, galleries, and food stands, then dine in a vineyard at Panache Mobile. Stay over in a cozy B&B, or continue on Route 138 northeast to Côte de Beaupré. Here you can visit the impressive Montmorency Falls and the ornate shrine at Ste-Anne-de-Beaupré. Don't miss the classic Québec cuisine of roast goose, tourtière, and sugar pie at historic Auberge Baker on Côte-de-Beaupré.

Another option is to take the Train du Massif de Charlevoix, which departs from the spectacular Parc de la Chute-Montmorency outside Québec City. It follows the picturesque St. Lawrence shore and the dramatic mountainous landscapes of Charlevoix. You'll visit the artistic community of Baie St-Paul, the impressive mountain Le Massif, and the cliff-top village of La Malbaie. You can do the rail trip in one day or stay overnight at the castle-like Fairmont Le Manoir Richelieu.

From La Malbaie, it's an hour by car to Tadoussac, at the confluence of the Saguenay and St-Lawrence rivers, where you can hop on a boat for a whale-watching excursion.

Montréal and Québec City over a Long Weekend

Looking for an ideal four-day getaway? It's possible to see the best of both cities without feeling rushed. Here's one expedient itinerary: Fly into Montréal's Trudeau International Airport on a Thursday evening, rent a car, and grab a bite at a late-night bistro like L'Express. Stay at a hotel downtown. Spend Friday seeing the city's top sites, hit Old Montréal in the evening for dinner and nightlife, and enjoy a leisurely brunch on Saturday morning.

By early afternoon, pack up and drive north to Québec City, which takes about three hours. Check into a B&B or boutique hotel in the Old City and spend the rest of the day exploring sites there. Spend Sunday morning in the Old City and dedicate the afternoon to the Fortifications, or take a day trip to the Côte-de-Beaupré or Île d'Orléans. On Monday, fly out of Québec City's Jean Lesage International Airport.

MONTRÉAL AND QUÉBEC CITY'S BEST FESTIVALS

Citizens of Montréal and Québec City have always found good reason to party. Québec City celebrates its long, frigid winters with a carnival that includes a boat race across a frozen river. And Montréal holds February's cold at bay with a sizzling food extravaganza.

January and February

Québec City's **Carnaval de Québec,** a festival of winter-sports competitions, ice-sculpture contests, and parades, spans three weekends. The historic Plains of Abraham are the main stage. ⊕ *www.carnaval.qc.ca*

La Fête des Neiges is Winter Carnival in Montréal. It lasts about two weeks and takes place at Parc Jean Drapeau on the river, across the Port from Old Montréal. ⊕ *www.fetedesneiges.com*

Montréal en Lumière (*Montréal Highlights*). Montréal en Lumière brightens the bleak days of February with fabulous food and cultural activities. Leading chefs from around the world give demonstrations and take over the kitchens of top restaurants for special dinners. ☎ *514/288–9955, 888/477–9955* ⊕ *www.montrealenlumiere.com.*

June

Les FrancoFolies de Montréal. FrancoFolies celebrates the art of French songwriting. Such major Québecois stars as Isabelle Boulay, Paul Piché, and Michel Rivard play at packed concert halls, while lesser-known artists play free outdoor concerts. More than 1,000 musicians, many from France, Belgium, Senegal, and Haiti, perform rock, hip-hop, jazz, funk, and Latin. ☎ *514/876–8989* ⊕ *www.francofolies.com.*

Fringe Festival. Montréal's Fringe Festival is open to playwrights, acting troupes, dancers, comics, and musicians. It all depends on a lottery system—whomever's name is picked from a hat gets to perform. What you experience might be traditional, offbeat, or downright risqué. ☎ *514/849–3378* ⊕ *www.montrealfringe.ca.*

Mondial de la Bière. In Montréal, for five days every June, the Mondial de la Bière transforms the exhibition hall of Place Bonaventure into a giant indoor beer garden serving more than 600 ales, lagers, and ciders from nearly 100 microbreweries from Québec and around the world. ☎ *514/722–9640* ⊕ *www.festivalmondialbiere.qc.ca.*

July

Concours d'Art International Pyrotechnique (*International Fireworks Competition*). Join the thousands heading to Montréal's Jacques Cartier Bridge or the Old Port to watch the free fireworks show most Wednesday and Saturday nights in late June and July. The launch site for this high-in-the-sky show set off by competing international teams is La Ronde, on Île Ste-Hélène. ☎ *514/397–2000* ⊕ *www.montrealfeux.com.*

Festival d'Été de Québec (*Québec City Summer Festival*). Festival d'Été de Québec is an exuberant 11-day music extravaganza in Québec City featuring rock, folk, hip-hop, and world-beat sounds. The main concerts rock nightly in early July on outdoor stages in or near Old Québec, including one on the Plains of Abraham. ☎ *418/523–4540, 888/992–5200* ⊕ *www.infofestival.com.*

Festival International de Jazz de Montréal (*Montréal International Jazz Festival*). The Festival International de Jazz de Montréal attracts more than 1,000 musicians for more than 400 concerts held over a period of nearly two weeks from the end of June through the beginning of July. Past stars have included Count Basie,

Ella Fitzgerald, Lauryn Hill, Wynton Marsalis, Chick Corea, Dave Brubeck, and Canada's most famed singer-pianist, Diana Krall. Many of the free outdoor concerts draw thousands on hot summer nights. You can also hear blues, Latin rhythms, gospel, Cajun, and world music. ☏ 514/790–1245, 855/299–3378 ⊕ *www.montrealjazzfest.com.*

Bell Info-Jazz. Contact Bell-Info Jazz for information about the festival and travel packages ☏ 514/871–1881, 888/515–0515.

Festival OFF. Festival OFF is a sidekick of the Festival d'Été International de Québec, taking to the stage in July at the same time as its big brother. Most of the shows are free and take place in offbeat spaces—in front of Église St-Jean-Baptiste, Bar Le Sacrilèe, and Musée de l'Amérique Française, just to name a few. People of all ages check out this more alternative scene. Folk, alternative, experimental, and everything in between is what you'll find. ⊕ *www.quebecoff.org.*

Juste pour Rire (*Just for Laughs*). Montréal's world-famous Juste pour Rire comedy festival hosts international comics, in French and English, from the second through third weeks of July. ☏ 514/845–2322 ⊕ *www.hahaha.com.*

August

Festival International des Films du Monde (*World Film Festival*). For several days in Montréal every August, the Festival International des Films du Monde presents about 400 films from all over the world. Movie buffs are captivated by feature films, documentaries, shorts, animation, and student productions. This is serious stuff, so no popcorn allowed. ☏ 514/848–3883 ⊕ *www.ffm-montreal.org.*

Fêtes de la Nouvelle France (*New France Festival*). During Fêtes de la Nouvelle France, Québec City's centuries-old heritage comes alive. The streets of Lower Town are transported back in time for this five-day festival in early to mid-August. Events range from an old-time farmers' market to games and music—all done in period costume. ☏ 418/694–3311 ⊕ *www.nouvellefrance.qc.ca.*

St-Jean-sur-Richelieu's Hot-Air Balloon Festival. St-Jean-sur-Richelieu's Hot-Air Balloon Festival is the largest gathering of hot-air balloons in Canada. This colorful airborne event takes flight about 25 minutes southeast of Montréal. The balloons are so vivid and plentiful that you can sometimes see them from downtown. ☏ 450/347–9555 ⊕ *www.montgolfieres.com.*

October

Black and Blue Festival. The Black and Blue Festival, organized by the Bad Boy Club Montréal, started more than 20 years ago as a gay community fundraiser for AIDS charities. It has grown to be a gay and gay-friendly week of intense partying, featuring soirées like the Leather Ball, the Military Ball, and the Black and Blue Ball. These energetic dance galas last from 12 to 15 hours; save time for the Recovery Party. ☏ 514/875–7026 ⊕ *www.bbcm.org.*

Farmers' markets, arts-and-crafts fairs, and weekend hikes are part of the **Festival of Colors**, which celebrates autumn throughout Québec. If you head to a ski resort you can get a bird's-eye view of the splendid fall foliage from the chairlifts.

FLAVORS OF MONTRÉAL AND QUÉBEC CITY

Bistro and brasserie culture is vibrant across the province, with a focus on seasonal, regional, and often organic ingredients.

Cheeses

There are more than 300 varieties of cheese in Québec, made from goat, sheep, and cow milk. Enthusiasts of France's *fromages au lait cru* are thrilled by the province's permissive raw-milk cheese laws, resulting in the delicious Pied-de-Vent from the Magdalene Islands and Au Gré des Champs from the Montérégie region.

Famous among Trappist cheeses is Bleu Ermite, made by Benedictine monks in the Eastern Townships. For organic semi-firm cheese, don't miss Le Baluchon. Equally lauded are Le Migneron from Charlevoix and a washed-rind cheese from the Saguenay region called Kénogami. Prizewinning Cendrillon, an ash-covered goat cheese from St-Raymond-de-Portneuf, is world famous. And the triple-cream Riopelle, named for Québec's influential artist, is a favorite. Tour the province's top 50 *fromageries*, now mapped on a scenic cheese route (⊕ *www.routedesfromages.com*).

Best City Shops: Fromagerie du Marché Atwater, Montréal (☎ 514/932–4653); Yannick Fromagerie, rue Bernard, Montréal (☎ 514/279–9376); La Fromagerie Hamel, Marché Jean-Talon, Montréal (☎ 514/272–1161); Épicerie Européenne (☎ 418/529–4847) and Épicerie J.A. Moisan (☎ 418/522–0685), both on rue Saint-Jean in Québec City.

Best Country Tours: Fromagerie Au Gré des Champs, St-Jean-sur-Richelieu (☎ 450/346–8732); Fromagerie du Ruban Bleu, Montérégie (☎ 450/691–2929); Les Fromages de l'Île d'Orléans (☎ 418/829–0177).

Ice Wine

Québec's climate is ideal for making this sweet but pricey aperitif. Frozen grapes—usually from Riesling, Vidal, Gewürztraminer, and Chardonnay vines planted close together in the Alsatian manner—are harvested by hand once the temperature drops to about 10°C (50°F). Their high acidity is balanced by sweet aromas of apricot, mango, honey, and peach.

Québec's ice wine is aptly compared to wines of Germany and Canada's Niagara region and the Okanagan Valley. And there's a new star beverage called ice cider that hails from the apple orchards of the Montérégie region of the Eastern Townships, and Île d'Orléans.

Best Eastern Township Vineyards: Chapelle Ste-Agnes Vineyard (⊕ *www.vindeglace. com*); Clos Saint Denis (⊕ *www.krugerws. com*); Clos Saragnat (⊕ *www.saragnat. com*); Domaine Pinnacle (⊕ *www. domainepinnacle.com*); La Face Cachée de la Pomme (⊕ *www.lafacecachee.com*).

Best Montréal Area Vineyards: Romance du Vin Vignoble, near Mont Rigaud (⊕ *www. laromanceduvin.ca*); Vignoble du Marathonien, Havelock (⊕ *www.marathonien. qc.ca*).

Best Québec City Area Vineyards: Vignoble de l'Isle de Bacchus, Île d'Orléans (⊕ *www.isledebacchus.com*); Cidrerie Verger Bilodeau (⊕ *www.cidreriebilodeau. qc.ca*); Vignoble Sainte-Pétronille (⊕ *www. vignoblesp.com*).

Meat and Game

Carnivores are well fed in Québec, with the rich selection of bison, duck, lamb, wild boar, and elk—Canadians call it wapiti. Bestsellers include grain-fed quail and pheasant from Drummondville, Kamouraska lamb, Lac Brome duck, and veal from Charlevoix. Venison and caribou are favorites among top chefs. Organic farms supply turkey, guinea hen, and duck prosciutto among other delights. And Québec is home to all the principal foie gras producers in Canada, a steady source for the country's best chefs.

Aux Anciens Canadiens, Québec City. Try the pheasant breast, topped with cheddar and smoked bison, or the grilled stag with cognac red pepper sauce.

Club Chasse et Pêche, Montréal. This warm, sophisticated eatery features roasted wapiti, braised lamb, and boar belly—all from Québec.

La Traite, Québec City. Venison, duck, boar, and rare wild herbs make for inspiring meals in the stylish **Hôtel-Musée Premières Nations.**

L'Orignal, Montréal. True to the chalet-chic decor, the menu features venison, bison, and lamb burgers. Its version of shepherd's pie is pure Québecois.

Toqué! Montréal. Chef Normand Laprise made famous Québec's Boileau venison, regularly flown down to discerning New York chefs. Braised lamb and duck from the region also grace the menu of this trendy eatery.

Contemporary Québec Cuisine

Tucked into boutique hotels and refurbished warehouses, the bistros and fine-dining halls that create modern Québec cuisine are wildly eclectic and French at heart.

From foamy sauces to sheets of potato lattices, the variations are limitless. You'll find tartars, foie gras, and lobster lasagna served with traditional Lac St-Jean *tourtières*—meat pies made with ground pork. Poutine, once a traditional dish of french fries topped with cheese curds and gravy, is now jazzed up with designer toppings.

Laurie Raphaël, Québec City. Chef Daniel Vézina conjures up modern sugar pie topped with a 10-inch swirl of maple cotton candy! While the menu changes with the seasons, Vezina's classic Bellechasse pigeon, infused with chocolate, and his rabbit terrine, which is finely layered with shiitake mushrooms, are especially worth checking out.

Panache, Québec City. Gussying up the staples brilliantly, Panache serves emu tartare in truffle dressing. Panache wows with St. Apollinaire duck, spit-roasted and glazed with maple.

A FOOD-LOVER'S TOUR OF MONTRÉAL

Many Montrealers are true gourmets, or at least enthusiastic gourmands. And, indeed, the city has thousands of restaurants, markets, and food boutiques catering to just about every conceivable taste, from Middle Eastern shish kebab to Portuguese barbecue to Tonkinese soup. Most menus are posted outside, so you can stroll around a neighborhood and leisurely choose whichever sounds most tantalizing.

Downtown

While you can't go wrong starting the day with a bowl of steaming café au lait at **Café Myriade** downtown, for something a little different head over to Chinatown for a dim sum breakfast at the neighborhood institution, **Maison Kam Fung**.

The Plateau

Fortified with filling dumpling dough, walk up through the streets of the Latin Quarter on rue St-Denis and you'll hit Square St-Louis.

Turn west, then north on boulevard St-Laurent and browse through dozens of ethnic food shops and delis, inhaling the aromas from the Caribbean, the Middle East, Asia, and Eastern Europe. If that reanimates your appetite, stop at the iconic **Schwartz's Delicatessen** and split one of the world's best smoked-meat sandwiches, served piled high on rye (it's best slathered with spicy deli mustard), with your walking companion.

Next, work up an appetite for lunch with a walk. Head east along avenue Duluth and take a stroll through Parc Lafontaine. When you leave the park, go northwest on avenue Christophe Colomb until you reach avenue Mont-Royal, a spirited stretch of *terrasses*, tattoo parlors, and thrift shops. Grab a dozen hot and sweet Montréal-style bagels at **St-Viateur Bagel &**

Café. In summer, stop for Montréal's best ice cream at **Le Glacier Bilboquet** on avenue Laurier Est.

Little Italy

Time to cheat. Hop on the métro at Laurier station and head north to the Jean-Talon stop for an afternoon visit to one of Canada's best markets, **Marché Jean-Talon.** You can spend hours browsing fish, sausage, and cheese shops and sampling everything from smoked buffalo to seasonal produce like heirloom tomatoes.

There's no leaving this area without stopping for dinner, so stroll over to boulevard St-Laurent and find a place to eat in Pétite-Italie (Little Italy). Two restaurants to try are **Il Mulino** (was closed temporarily for renovations at time of this writing) and **Bottega Pizzeria**. Finish with a bracing espresso at **Café Italia,** where neighborhood men huddle around the TV to watch soccer.

From here, it's an easy walk back to the Beaubien métro stop for a train back to Old Montréal or Downtown.

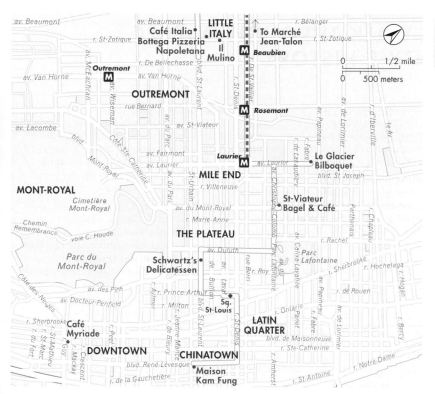

Highlights	A fat smoked meat sandwich at Schwartz's Delicatessen; walking around the Marché Jean-Talon tasting vendors' samples.
Where to Start	Chinatown, located downtown, at the ornately decorated red gate on St-Laurent off boulevard René-Lévesque.
Length	About 5.5 kilometers (3.5 miles) walking, plus the métro from Laurier to Marché Jean-Talon on the Orange Line.
Where to End	Little Italy. From here, you can walk back to the Orange Line that runs through downtown.
Best Time to Go	Busy summer Saturday (the crowds are half the entertainment).
Worst Time to Go	Dull winter Monday.
Editor's Choices	Walking up boulevard St-Laurent, peeking in the delis and offbeat boutiques; the colorful streets of the Plateau; the maple ice cream at Le Glacier Bilboquet.

A WALK THROUGH QUÉBEC CITY'S HISTORY

Exploring Québec City's history can be an all-consuming pastime, and a rewarding one. The walk outlined here takes you through much of it, but feel free to pursue the Old City's inviting little detours.

Outside the Old City

The best place to begin a journey through the history of New France is at the end. Start your tour at the **Wolfe Monument,** on the far west side of the **Plains of Abraham.** It was here in 1759 that British General James Wolfe extinguished France's dreams of a North American empire and set off the English-French divergence that has enriched and plagued Canada's history.

The Plains of Abraham was where the famous battle took place. Today it's a pleasant and expansive city park, with trees, lawns, and meandering paths with sweeping views of the St. Lawrence River.

Make your way over to the Fortifications and the Old City via the northern side of the Plains of Abraham, along the **Grande Allée** and then to the residential neighborhood of **Montcalm,** home to gorgeous 19th-century neo-Gothic and Queen Anne–style mansions and **Hôtel du Parlement.**

The Fortifications

The end of the Grand Allée is Porte St-Louis. Turn right down the Côte de la Citadelle, which leads to **La Citadelle.** Something of a microcosm of Canada's cultural tensions, the fortress is home to the Royal 22e Régiment, a crack military unit that speaks French but dresses in the bearskin hats and red tunics of a British guards unit for ceremonial parades. Don't miss the daily changing of the guard ceremony.

Upper Town

Beyond **Porte St-Louis,** you're in 17th- and 18th-century France. Steep-roofed houses with small windows crowd a tangle of narrow, curving streets and the rattle of horse-drawn carriages on ancient cobblestones adds to the illusion.

The **Maison Jacquet** on rue St-Louis looks exactly as it did when it was built in 1677 and the **Maison Kent** was once the home of Queen Victoria's father, the Duke of Kent. **Le Convent des Ursalines** at 12 rue Donnacona is now a museum featuring an exhibit of magnificent lace embroidery created by Ursaline nuns in the 19th and early 20th century.

Québec City's most famous building, the **Fairmont Le Château Frontenac,** is situated at the beginning of **Terrasse Dufferin,** worth a stroll up and down for sweeping views of the St. Lawrence River before you get on the funicular to reach Lower Town.

Lower Town

Once at the base of this cable-connected elevator, you end up in the 17th-century **Maison Louis-Jolliet,** built before he paddled off to explore the Mississippi River. From here, it's a short walk to **Place Royale,** a square graced by a statue of the Sun King Louis XIV, and considered to be the birthplace of New France. The last jaunt is along **rue du Petit-Champlain,** the oldest street in the city, lined with cafés.

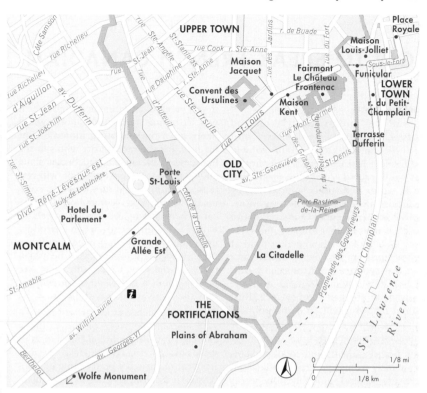

Highlights	Exploring La Citadelle; leisurely strolling along the Terrasse Dufferin; walking along rue du Petit-Champlain in the Old City.
Where to Start	The Wolfe Monument, on the far western side of the Plains of Abraham outside the walls of the city.
Length	About 3 kilometers (2 miles).
Where to End	On rue du Petit-Champlain, in the Lower Town section of the Old City.
Best Time to Go	If you want to avoid crowds in summer, go on a weekday morning.
Worst Time to Go	A cold winter day.
Editor's Choice	Strolling along the tree-lined streets off Grande Allée in Montcalm; riding the funicular from Upper Town to Lower Town; standing in historic Place Royale.

HOW TO SPEAK FRENCH CANADIAN

Français, S.V.P.

As with any foreign country you find yourself visiting, being familiar with the local dialect is only going to win you friends. Just learning a few phrases that you'll probably wind up pronouncing all wrong will still be appreciated by the locals—if only for the novelty value. More than 80 percent of Quebecers claim French as their mother tongue, and while many Québecois are bilingual or have at least a modicum of English under their belts, plenty more don't, especially outside of downtown Montréal and the less touristy areas of the province. Rest assured that you will, at some point in your visit, come across more than a few unilingual Francophones.

As in France, accents and colloquialisms vary widely from region to region. Still, there are several uniquely Québecois words and expressions commonly used throughout the province.

For starters, Montréal's impressive subway system is known as *le Métro*. If you go around asking French Canadians where the closest subway station is you'll likely be greeted with a blank stare followed by a *"Je m'excuse, mais je ne parle pas l'anglais"* ("I'm sorry but I don't speak any English"). Similarly, don't go looking for a "convenience store" when you need some last-minute item. Here, even Anglophones call them *dépanneurs, or "deps"* for short.

Of course many things in Québec, like the menus in most restaurants, will be in both French and English, but you'll impress the waitstaff if you order a *steak-frites avec un verre de vin rouge* when you want steak with french fries and a glass of red wine. Later, when you ask for *la facture* (your bill) and your waiter inquires

if you've enjoyed your meal, tell him it was *écœurant* (wonderful) and you'll likely see a big amused grin come over his face. It's the rare tourist who's in the know when it comes to Québecois slang and/or colloquialisms, so locals will certainly be impressed if they hear you coming out with the occasional *mon char* (my car) when talking about your wheels or *ma blonde* (girlfriend) when introducing somebody to your female significant other, who might just as easily be a brunette, by the way. Conversely, if you're talking about a boyfriend, *mon chum* is how the locals would say it.

Almost all Québecois swear words—aka *sacres*—come courtesy of the Catholic church, so while the literal translation of words like *tabernac* (tabernacle) or *câlice* (chalice) might seem pretty tame or nonsensical in English, here they're the equivalent of the dreaded F-word, and definitely not meant to be used in polite company.

While here you'll probably spend a lot of time in *centre-ville* (downtown) checking out splendid sights like the *Palais de Justice* (not a palace at all, but a courthouse). Except in order to do so you're likely going to need some *l'argent* (money), or better, *un peu de cash*, which is *franglais* (a curious yet distinct local hybrid of French and English) for "a bit of money." And where will you be getting that money? Nowhere if you start asking people for the closest ATM. In Québec a bank machine is called a *guichet* (the *gui* pronounced like guitar, the *chet* like "shea," as in the stadium). One last piece of friendly advice: Be careful with *je t'aime*, which means both "I like you" and "I love you." Getting that one wrong could potentially leave you in a pretty awkward position.

Exploring Montréal

WORD OF MOUTH

"My first choice in neighborhoods is the Plateau area, which is more 'French Montréal' than either the downtown or the Old City. Montréal is wonderful—no matter which area you choose you will love the city!"

—zootsi

WELCOME TO MONTRÉAL

TOP REASONS TO GO

★ **Browse Public Markets:** Marché Atwater, one of the city's oldest public markets, and the bustling Marché Jean-Talon, in Little Italy, are two must-see places.

★ **Check Out the Nightlife:** There's a strong heritage of late-night revelry in this city. Top spots include rue Crescent, boulevard St-Laurent, and rue St-Denis, as well as Old Montréal and the Village, Montréal's gay epicenter.

★ **Get a Dose of Multiculturalism:** Montréal is a melting pot of world culture, yours to experience by exploring ethnic neighborhoods and sampling a range of cuisine.

★ **Celebrate Jazz Fest:** Montréal's biggest party happens every year in late June and early July—and if jazz is your thing it's not to be missed. Reserve early: Hotels book up months in advance.

★ **Stroll Old Montréal:** Old Montréal has it all— cobblestone streets, a great waterfront, fine restaurants and bed-and-breakfasts, and the Old Port, which buzzes with nightlife.

1 Old Montréal. This is the oldest part of the city, rife with historical buildings, horse-drawn carriages, street performers, charming restaurants with terraces.

2 Downtown, Golden Square Mile, and Chinatown. Montréal's center for hustle and bustle, where you can shop on rue Ste-Catherine, take a quick walk over to Chinatown for lunch, and check out the museums' newest exhibition.

3 Latin Quarter and Village. People watching is the order of the day in these two neighborhoods bordering the downtown core. Have a drink at any number of the outdoor terraces lining rue St-Denis.

4 Plateau, Mile End, Little Italy, and Outremont. Come to the cozy Plateau and bordering neighborhoods Mile End and Outremont for Sunday brunch, upscale boutiques, funky resale shops, and art galleries.

5 Parc du Mont-Royal. Home of the mountain that gave Montréal its name, this is where city dwellers come for refuge—and for some of the city's best world cuisine in the Côte-des-Neiges neighborhood.

6 Hochelaga-Maisonneuve. Visit this corner of Montréal to see the site of the 1976 Olympics, explore the universe in the new planetarium, and take in its great parks and gardens, including the lovely Jardin Botanique.

7 The Islands. Île Ste-Hélène and Île Notre-Dame, which together make up Parc Jean-Drapeau, are now a vast playground—from La Ronde amusement park to Casino de Montréal to the Grand Prix's Formula 1 race track.

KEY
M	Métro Stations
🚲	Route Verte Bike Route

GETTING ORIENTED

Montréal is divided by a grid of streets roughly aligned east–west and north–south, though the shape of the island has skewed the compass points. North–south street numbers begin at the St. Lawrence River and increase as you head north; east–west street numbers begin at boulevard St-Laurent.

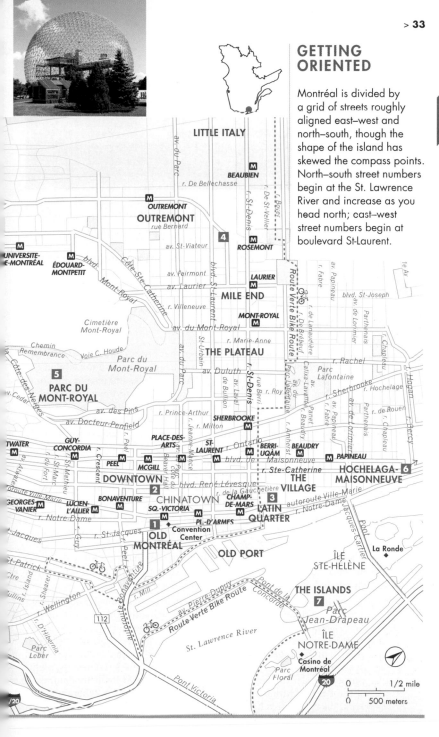

LITTLE ITALY

BEAUBIEN

r. De Bellechasse

OUTREMONT
OUTREMONT
rue Bernard

av. St-Viateur
ROSEMONT

UNIVERSITE-
E-MONTRÉAL
ÉDOUARD-
MONTPETIT

av. Fairmont

av. Laurier
LAURIER

r. Villeneuve
MILE END

Cimetière
Mont-Royal
av. du Mont-Royal
MONT-ROYAL

Chemin
Remembrance
Voie C. Houde
r. Marie-Anne

Parc du
Mont-Royal
THE PLATEAU

av. Duluth

5
**PARC DU
MONT-ROYAL**

av. des Pins

r. Prince-Arthur

av. Docteur-Penfield
r. Milton
SHERBROOKE

TWATER
GUY-
CONCORDIA
PLACE-DES-
ARTS

PEEL
DOWNTOWN
MCGILL
ST-
LAURENT
r. Ontario
BERRI-
UQAM
BEAUDRY
PAPINEAU

blvd. de Maisonneuve

r. Ste-Catherine
**HOCHELAGA-
MAISONNEUVE**

GEORGES-
VANIER
LUCIEN-
L'ALLIER
BONAVENTURE
CHINATOWN
SQ.-VICTORIA
CHAMP-
DE-MARS
blvd. René-Lévesque
r. de la Gauchetière
**THE
VILLAGE**

r. Notre-Dame
PL.-D'ARMES
**LATIN
QUARTER**

r. St-Jacques
**OLD
MONTRÉAL**
Convention
Center
OLD PORT

ÎLE
STE-HÉLÈNE
La Ronde

THE ISLANDS
7
Parc
Jean-Drapeau

St-Patrick
r. Wellington
r. Mill
Route Verte Bike Route

112

Parc
Leber
St. Lawrence River

ÎLE
NOTRE-DAME

Parc
Floral
Casino de
Montréal
20

Pont Victoria

r. De St-Vellier
r. St-Denis
r. De St-Bruel
blvd. St-Laurent
Route Verte Bike Route

r. Fabre
r. Papineau
blvd. St-Joseph
av. de Lorimier
Parthenais
r. Chapleau

r. Rachel
Parc
Lafontaine
r. Sherbrooke

r. Hochelage
av. Papineau
Parthenais
r. de Rouen
r. Chapleau

autoroute Ville-Marie
r. Notre-Dame

0   1/2 mile
0   500 meters

2

4

6

1 **2** **3**

Updated by
Chris Barry

Canada's most diverse metropolis, Montréal, is an island city that favors grace and elegance over order and even prosperity, a city where past and present intrude on each other daily. In some ways it resembles Vienna—well beyond its peak of power and glory, perhaps, yet still vibrant and beautiful.

But don't get the wrong idea. Montréal has always had a bit of an edge. During Prohibition, thirsty Americans headed north to the city on the St. Lawrence for booze, music, and a good time, and people still come for the same things. Summer festivals celebrate everything from comedy and French songs to beer and fireworks, and, of course, jazz. And on those rare weeks when there isn't a planned event, the party continues. Clubs and sidewalk cafés are abuzz from late afternoon to the early hours of the morning. More extraordinarily, Montréal is a city that knows how to mix it up even when it's 20 below zero. Rue St-Denis is almost as lively on a Saturday night in January as it is in July, and the festival Montréal en Lumière, or Montréal Highlights, enlivens the dreary days of February with concerts, balls, and gourmet food.

Montréal takes its name from Mont-Royal, a stubby plug of tree-covered igneous rock that rises high above the surrounding cityscape. Although its height is unimpressive, "the Mountain" forms one of Canada's finest urban parks, and views from the Chalet du Mont-Royal in the Parc du Mont-Royal provide an excellent orientation to the city's layout and major landmarks.

Old Montréal holds museums, the municipal government, and the magnificent Basilique Notre-Dame-de-Montréal within its network of narrow, cobbled streets. Although Montréal's centre-ville, or downtown, bustles like many major cities on the surface, it's active below street level as well, in the Underground City. Residential Plateau Mont-Royal and its surrounding trendy neighborhoods are abuzz with restaurants, nightclubs, art galleries, and cafés. The greener areas of town are composed of the Parc du Mont-Royal and the Jardin Botanique, where you can walk, bike, or take a horse-drawn carriage ride along miles of paths.

MONTRÉAL'S HISTORY

Montréal is the second-largest French-speaking city in the Western world, but it's not only Francophone culture that thrives here. About 14% of the 3.3 million people who call Montréal home claim English as their mother tongue.

The two cultures, however, are not as separate as they were. Chatter in the bars and bistros of rue St-Denis east of boulevard St-Laurent still tends to be French, and crowds in clubs and restaurants on rue Crescent downtown speak, argue, and court in English. But the lines have definitely blurred.

Both major linguistic groups have had to come to grips with no longer being the only players on the field. So-called *allophones*—people whose mother tongue is neither French nor English—make up fully 19% of the city's population.

The first European settlement on Montréal island was Ville-Marie, founded in 1642 by 54 pious men and women under the leadership of Paul de Chomedey, Sieur de Maisonneuve, and Jeanne Mance, a French noblewoman, who hoped to create a new Christian society.

But piety wasn't Ville-Marie's only raison d'être. The settlement's location near the convergence of the St. Lawrence and Ottawa rivers meant a lucrative trade in beaver pelts, as the fur was a staple of European hat fashion for nearly a century.

The French regime in Canada ended with the Seven Years' War—what Americans call the French and Indian War. The Treaty of Paris ceded all of New France to Britain in 1763. American troops under generals Richard Montgomery and Benedict Arnold occupied the city during their 1775–76 campaign to conquer Canada, but their efforts failed and the troops withdrew. Soon invaders of another kind—English and Scottish settlers, traders, and merchants—poured into Montréal. By 1832 the city became a leading colonial capital. But 1837 brought anti-British rebellions, and the unrest led to Canada's becoming a self-governing dominion in 1867.

The city's ports continued to bustle until the St. Lawrence Seaway opened in 1957, allowing ships to sail from the Atlantic to the Great Lakes without having to stop in Montréal to transfer cargo.

The opening of the métro in 1966 changed the way Montrealers lived, and the next year the city hosted the World's Fair. But the rise of Québec separatism in the late 1960s under the charismatic René Lévesque created political uncertainty, and many major businesses moved to Toronto. By the time Lévesque's separatist Parti Québecois won power in Québec in 1976—the same year the summer Olympics came to the city—Montréal was clearly No. 2.

Uncertainty continued through the 1980s and '90s, with the separatist Parti Québecois and the federalist Liberals alternating in power in Québec City. Since 1980 the city has endured two referenda on the future of Québec and Canada. In the most recent—the cliff-hanger of 1995—just 50.58% of Québecois voted to remain part of Canada. Montréal bucked the separatist trend and voted nearly 70% against independence.

MONTRÉAL PLANNER

WHEN TO GO

To avoid crowds and below-freezing temperatures, Montréal's short spring, which typically starts in late April or early May but doesn't end until well into June, is ideal. Fall is gorgeous—and touristy—when the leaves change color, so expect traffic on weekends. Early September after Labor Day is another good time to visit.

PLANNING YOUR TIME

Put Old Montréal and the Old Port at the top of your sightseeing list. Spend a full day walking around this area, head back to your hotel for a late-day break, and return for dinner. Aside from finding several of the city's top restaurants here, City Hall, Marché Bonsecours, and other charming buildings are illuminated at night. Also dedicate a full day to wandering around downtown to visit museums, check out rue Ste-Catherine, and explore Chinatown. Visit the Latin Quarter and the area around McGill University—both have vibrant student life, but shouldn't be dismissed as places where only under-20s frequent. Even if you're too tired to go out on the town, take a nighttime walk down rue Crescent and rue St-Denis for a taste of the city's *joie de vivre.*

For browsing, shopping, and dining out, explore Outremont, Mile End, the Plateau, and Westmount. For kid-friendly activities, check out Hochelaga-Maisonneuve and the Islands for the Biôdôme, La Ronde, and the Jardin Botanique. If it's an ethnic culinary tour you're after, hit the Côte-des-Neiges neighborhood, as well as Little Italy.

GETTING HERE AND AROUND

AIR TRAVEL

Montréal's Trudeau International Airport (also often referred to by its previous name, Dorval) is about 24 km (15 miles) west of the city center.

GROUND TRANSPOR-TATION The easiest way to get in is to take a cab for a fixed fare of C$38 or a limousine for about C$55, unless your hotel provides transportation. The cheapest way to get into town is a 24-hour shuttle service from the airport to the main bus terminal with stops at the Lionel-Groulx métro station and several downtown hotels. The fare is C$8 one-way. Plan on it taking about a half hour outside rush hour to get downtown from the airport.

BICYCLE TRAVEL

An extensive network of bike paths and relatively flat terrain make Montréal ideal for bicycles. For visitors, the Bixi (a contraction of "bicycle" and "taxi") system—with more than 3,000 sturdy aluminum-frame bikes at over 300 credit-card operated stands scattered throughout the city—makes two-wheel exploring easy. For just C$7 you can take as many bike trips as you like, but beware: the system is designed for short hops; keep any one bike for more than 30 minutes, and you'll be charged extra.

CAR TRAVEL

If you're driving in to the city, take I–91 or I–89 from Vermont, I–87 from New York, and Autoroute 20 (also known as Autoroute Jean-Lesage) from Québec City.

MONEY-SAVING TIPS

Even if you happen to be taking a trip to Montréal when the U.S. dollar dips in value below the Canadian dollar, there are several ways to save money during your trip.

If you'll be visiting three or more of the city's museums, consider buying a museum pass. It's available for C$60 for three days, but an even better deal is to purchase a C$65 pass, which also entitles you to unlimited access to Montréal's transportation system, including the métro and buses.

Tourist passes also may be worth your while; one-day passes are C$8 and three-day passes are C$16. Weekly passes are C$23.50, but they're loaded electronically on a special Opus card that costs C$6.

Take advantage of Montréal's fabulous markets, including Marché Jean-Talon and Marché Atwater, to grab provisions for picnics or for snacks to take back to your hotel room.

Hitting the town earlier in the evening is a good way to save as well, by stopping into cafés and bars for food and drink specials offered during cinq-à-sept (5-to-7), Montréal's happy hour.

Having a car downtown isn't ideal—garages are expensive and on-street parking can be a hassle. The city has a diligent tow away and fine system for double-parking or sitting in no-stopping zones during rush hour, and ticket costs are steep. In residential neighborhoods, beware of alternate-side-of-the-street-parking rules and resident-only parking. In winter, street plows are ruthless in dealing with parked cars in their way. If they don't tow them, they'll bury them.

PUBLIC TRANSPORTATION TRAVEL

The Société de transport de Montréal (STM) operates both the métro (subway) and the bus system. The métro is clean and quiet (it runs on rubber tires), and will get you to most of the places you want to visit. For those few places that are more than a 15-minute walk from the nearest métro station, bus connections are available.

Métro hours on the Orange, Green, Blue, and Yellow lines are weekdays 5:30 am to 12:30 am and weekends 5:30 am to 12:30, 1, or 1:30 am (it varies by line). Trains run every three minutes or so on the most crowded lines—Orange and Green—at rush hours. The cash fare for a single ticket is C$3. One- and three-day unlimited-use cards are also available for C$8 and C$16.

TAXI TRAVEL

Taxis in Montréal all run on the same rate: C$3.30 minimum and C$1.60 per kilometer (roughly ½ mile). They're usually easy to hail on the street, outside train stations, in shopping areas, and at major hotels. You can also call a dispatcher to send a driver to pick you up at no extra cost. A taxi is available if the white or orange plastic rooftop light is on.

⇨ *For more information on getting here and around, see Travel Smart Montréal and Québec City.*

OLD MONTRÉAL (VIEUX-MONTRÉAL)

A walk through the cobbled streets of Old Montréal is a lot more than a privileged stroll through history; it's also an encounter with a very lively present—especially in summer, when the restaurants and bistros spill out onto the sidewalks. Jugglers, musicians, and magicians jockey for performance space on the public squares and along the riverfront, and things get turned up a notch at the Old Port, which has become one of the city's hottest spots for nightlife.

Old Montréal, which was once enclosed by thick stone walls, is the oldest part of the city. It runs roughly from the waterfront in the south to ruelle des Fortifications in the north and from rue McGill in the west to rue Berri in the east. The churches and chapels here stand as testament to the religious fervor that inspired the French settlers who landed here in 1642 to build a "Christian commonwealth" under the leadership of Paul de Chomedey, Sieur de Maisonneuve, and the indomitable Jeanne Mance. Stone warehouses and residences are reminders of how quickly the fur trade commercialized that lofty ideal and made the city one of the most prosperous in 18th-century Nouvelle France. And finally, the financial houses along rue St-Jacques, bristling with Victorian ornamentation, recall the days when Montrealers controlled virtually all the wealth of the young Dominion of Canada.

History and good looks aside, however, Old Montréal still works for a living. Stockbrokers and shipping companies continue to operate out of the old financial district. The city's largest newspaper, *La Presse*, has its offices here. Lawyers in black gowns hurry through the streets to plead cases at the Palais de Justice or the Cour d'Appel, the City Council meets in the Second Empire City Hall on rue Notre-Dame, and local shoppers hunt for deals in the bargain clothing stores just off rue McGill.

GETTING HERE AND AROUND

The easiest way to get from downtown to Old Montréal is aboard the 515 city bus shuttle that provides a quick direct link to several sites in the Old City and Old Port. It runs from 7 am to midnight. You can also take the métro orange line to the Place-d'Armes and Square-Victoria stations, or you can walk, but the primary routes from downtown go through some drab and somewhat seedy, although not especially dangerous, areas. If you want the exercise, it's better to rent a Bixi bicycle at a downtown stand and drop it off at one in Old Montréal. Biking

to Old Montréal is a breeze since it's all downhill, but the return trip downtown is a challenging work-out.

Taxis can whisk you here from downtown in about 10 minutes, but it can be hard to find one to take you back downtown late in the evening.

The best way to get around the Old City is on foot, but wear good shoes because some of the cobbled streets can be hard on the feet. A more romantic (and more costly) option is to hire a *calèche* from the stand on south side of Place-d'Armes for a horse-drawn tour of the district. Be aware that the city sets the fares—C$45 for 30 minutes and C$75 for an hour—and you shouldn't be asked for more.

TIMING

Having enough time to see the sights, stroll around, and try some of the area's notable restaurants means dedicating at least one day. If it's your first time in the city and you're only here for an extended weekend, consider staying in one of Old Montréal's auberges or boutique hotels.

EXPLORING

TOP ATTRACTIONS

Fodor's Choice
★

Basilique Notre-Dame-de-Montréal (*Our Lady of Montréal Basilica*). Few churches in North America are as wow-inducing as Notre-Dame. Everything about the place, which opened in 1829, seems designed to make you gasp—from the 228-foot twin towers out front to the tens of thousands of 24-karat gold stars that stud the soaring blue ceiling.

Nothing in a city renowned for churches matches Notre-Dame for sheer grandeur—or noisemaking capacity: its 12-ton bass bell is the largest in North America, and its 7,000-pipe Casavant organ can make the walls tremble. The pulpit is a work of art in itself, with an intricately curving staircase and fierce figures of Ezekiel and Jeremiah crouching at its base. The whole place is so overwhelming it's easy to miss such lesser features as the stained-glass windows from Limoges and the side altars dedicated to St. Marguerite d'Youville, Canada's first native-born saint; St. Marguerite Bourgeoys, Canada's first schoolteacher; and a group of Sulpician priests martyred in Paris during the French Revolution.

For a peek at the magnificent baptistery, decorated with frescoes by Ozias Leduc, you'll have to tiptoe through the glassed-off prayer room in the northwest corner of the church. Every year dozens of brides march up the aisle of **Chapelle Notre-Dame-du-Sacré-Coeur** (Our Lady of the Sacred Heart Chapel), behind the main altar, to exchange vows with their grooms before a huge modern bronze sculpture that you either love or hate.

Notre-Dame is an active house of worship, so dress accordingly (i.e., no shorts or bare midriffs). The chapel can't be viewed weekdays during the 12:15 pm mass, and is often closed Saturday for weddings. ⊠ *110 rue Notre-Dame Ouest, Old Montréal, Montréal* ☎ *514/842–2925, 866/842–2925* ⊕ *www.basiliquenddm.org* ⊠ *Tours C$5, La Lumière Fut C$10* ☉ *July–Sept., daily 8:15–4:30; Oct.–June, weekdays 9–3:30, Sat. 8–3:30, Sun. 12:30–3:30; tours in French and English every ½ hr.* Ⓜ *Place-d'Armes.*

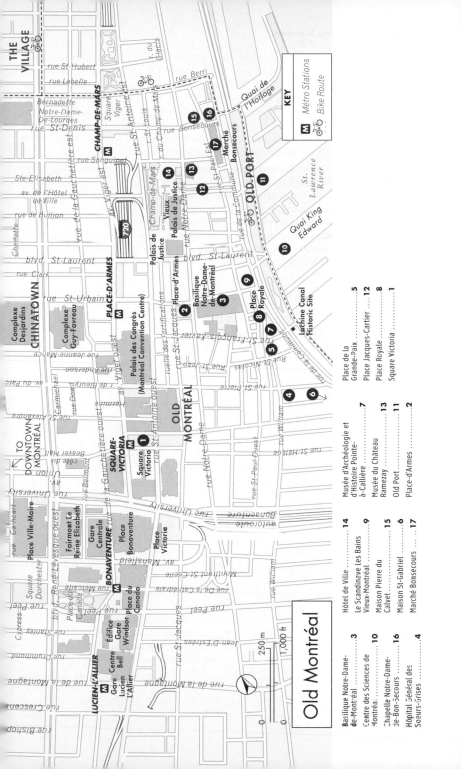

Old Montréal

KEY

Ⓜ Métro Stations
🚲🚲 Bike Route

Basilique Notre-Dame-
de-Montréal **3**

Centre des Sciences de
Montréa **10**

Chapelle Notre-Dame-
de-Bon-Secours **16**

Hôpital Général des
Soeurs-Grises **4**

Hôtel de Ville **14**

Le Scandinave Les Bains
Vieux-Montréal **9**

Maison Pierre du
Calvet **15**

Maison St-Gabriel **6**

Marché Bonsecours **17**

Musée d'Archéologie et
d'Histoire Pointe-
à-Callière **7**

Musée du Château
Ramezay **13**

Old Port **11**

Place-d'Armes **2**

Place de la
Grande-Paix **5**

Place Jacques-Cartier **12**

Place Royale **8**

Square Victoria **1**

250 m
1,000 ft

The stone residence on the west side of the basilica is the **Old Séminaire** (*Old Seminary* ✉ *116 rue Notre-Dame Ouest, behind wall west of Basilique Notre-Dame-de-Montréal, Old Montréal, Montréal* Ⓜ *Place-d'Armes*), Montréal's oldest building. It was built in 1685 as a head-quarters for the Sulpician priests who owned the island of Montréal until 1854. It's still a residence for the Sulpicians who administer the basilica. The clock on the roof over the main doorway is the oldest (pre-1701) public timepiece in North America.

Chapelle Notre-Dame-de-Bon-Secours (*Our Lady of Perpetual Help Chapel*). Mariners have been popping into Notre-Dame-de-Bon-Secours for centuries to kneel before a little 17th-century statue of the Virgin Mary and pray for a safe passage—or give thanks for one. Often, they've expressed their gratitude by leaving votive lamps in the shape of small ships, many of which still hang from the barrel-vaulted ceiling. This is why most Montrealers call the chapel the Église des Matelots (the Sailors' Church), and why many still stop by to say a prayer and light a candle before leaving on a long trip.

These days, the statue of Our Lady of Perpetual Help guards the remains of St. Marguerite Bourgeoys, who had the original chapel built in 1657 and is entombed in the side altar next to the east wall of the chapel. The current chapel dates from 1771; a renovation project in 1998 revealed some beautiful 18th-century murals that had been hidden under layers of paint.

The steep climb to the top of the steeple is worth the effort for the glori-ous view of the harbor, as is the equally steep climb down to the archaeo-logical excavations under the chapel for a glimpse into the history of the chapel and the neighborhood. The dig is accessible through the adjacent **Musée Marguerite Bourgeoys,** which also has exhibits on the life of St. Marguerite and the daily lives of the colonists she served. The chapel is closed mid-January through February except for the 10:30 am mass on Sunday. ✉ *400 rue St-Paul Est, Old Montréal, Montréal* ☎ *514/282–8670* ⊕ *www.marguerite-bourgeoys.com* ✒ *Museum C\$10, museum plus archaeology site with guide C\$12* ⊙ *May–Oct., Tues.–Sun. 10–6; Nov.–mid-Jan., Mar. and Apr., Tues.–Sun. 11–4* Ⓜ *Champ-de-Mars*.

Le Scandinave Les Bains Vieux-Montréal. A bastion of urban chic in his-toric Old Montréal, this spa is especially popular on cold winter days. Inspired by the age-old tradition of public baths, the Scandinave prides itself on offering guests an authentic yet contemporary experience with an accent of privacy and total relaxation. The swish interior of slate, marble, and wood contrasts nicely with the bubbling pools and misty steam rooms. The ultimate meltdown is the zero-stress chamber of absolute quiet and darkness to intensify the peacefulness. All you need to bring along is your bathing suit; the spa provides guests with sandals, bathrobes, and towels. ✉ *71 rue de la Commune Ouest, Old Montréal, Montréal* ☎ *514/288–2009* ⊕ *www.scandinave.com.*

OFF THE BEATEN PATH

Maison St-Gabriel. This little island of New France is well off the beaten path, deep in the working-class Pointe St-Charles neighborhood, but it's certainly worth the 10-minute taxi ride from Old Montréal. Thick stone walls, a steep roof, and mullioned windows mark the Maison

Lachine Attractions

Lachine Canal National Historic Site. If you want to work up an appetite for lunch—or just get some exercise—rent a bike on rue de la Commune and ride west along the 14-km (9-mile) Lachine Canal through what used to be Montréal's industrial heartland to the shores of Lac St-Louis. You could stop at the Marché Atwater to buy some cheese, bread, wine, and maybe a little pâté for a picnic in the lakefront park at the end of the trail. If paddling and pedaling sound too energetic, hop aboard an excursion boat and dine more formally in one of the century-old homes that line the waterfront in Lachine, the historic city borough at the western end of the canal that was once the staging point for the lucrative fur trade.

The Lachine Canal is all about leisure now, but it wasn't always so. Built in 1825 to get boats and cargo around the treacherous Lachine Rapids, it quickly became a magnet for all sorts of industries. But when the St. Lawrence Seaway opened in 1959, allowing large cargo ships to sail straight from the Atlantic to the Great Lakes without stopping in Montréal, the canal closed to navigation and became an illicit dumping ground for old cars and the victims of underworld killings. The area around it degenerated into an industrial slum.

A federal agency rescued the place in 1978, planting lawns and trees along the old canal, transforming it into a long, thin park, or *parc linéaire*. The abandoned canneries, sugar refineries, and steelworks have since been converted into desirable residential and commercial condominiums. The bicycle path is the first link in the more than 97 km (60 miles) of bike trails that make up the **Pôle des Rapides** (☎ *514/364-4490* ⊕ *www.poledesrapides.com*)

Two permanent exhibits at the **Lachine Canal Visitor Services Centre**, at the western end of the canal, explain its history and construction, and the center also has a shop and lookout terrace. You can take a guided boat tour (C$18, plus tax) of the canal from late May to early October (*514/469-7443*). ✉ *500 chemin des Iroquois, Lachine, Montréal* ☎ *514/283-6054* ⊕ *www.pc.gc.ca* ⬚ *Free* ☉ *10-4* Ⓜ *Angrignon*.

At the **Lachine Canal Nautical Centre** (✉ *2985B rue St-Patrick, near Atwater Market, Old Montréal, Montréal* ☎ *877/935-2925, 514/842-1306* ⊕ *www.h2oadventures.ca* ☉ *May and Sept., weekdays noon-8, weekends 9-8; June-Aug., daily 9-9*), open from May to mid-September, you can rent anything from a one-person kayak to a 13-passenger Voyageur canoe and paddle along the canal. Electric boat rentals are also available.

In the waterfront park at the end of the canal, an 1803 stone warehouse has been converted into the **Fur Trade at Lachine National Historic Site** (✉ *1255 boul. St-Joseph, Lachine, Montréal* ☎ *888/773-8888, 514/283-6054* ⊕ *www.pc.gc.ca* ⬚ *Free* ☉ *May 17-Oct. 8, daily 9:30-12:30 and 1-5; Apr.-May 14 and Oct. 12-Nov. 26, open only for group reservations*), a museum that commemorates the industry that dominated Canada's early history.

Old Montréal has winding cobblestone streets, cafés with terraces for eating and drinking outside, and many of the city's top historical sites.

St-Gabriel as one of Montréal's rare surviving 17th-century houses. But it's the interior and the furnishings that will sweep you back to the colonial days when St. Marguerite Bourgeoys and the religious order she founded used this house to train *les filles du roy* (king's daughters) in the niceties of home management. Les filles were young women without family or fortune but plenty of spunk who volunteered to cross the Atlantic in leaky boats to become the wives and mothers of New France. It wasn't an easy life, as the Maison's hard, narrow beds, primitive utensils, and drafty rooms attest—but it had its rewards, and the prize at the end was a respectable, settled life. St. Marguerite also had some state-of-the-art domestic equipment—the latest in looms and butter churns, labor-saving spit turners for roasting meat, and an ingenious granite sink with a drainage system that piped water straight out to the garden. ✉ *2146 pl. Dublin, Pointe-St-Charles, Montréal* ☎ *514/935–8136* ⊕ *www.maisonsaint-gabriel.qc.ca* ✉ *C$10* ⊙ *June 25–early Sept., Tues.–Sun. 11–6 (guided tours every hr); early Sept.–mid-Dec. and Jan. 19–June 19, Tues.–Sun. 1–4:30* Ⓜ *Square-Victoria, Bus 61.*

Fodor's Choice ★ **Musée d'Archéologie et d'Histoire Pointe-à-Callière** (*Pointe-à-Callière Archaeology and History Museum*). The modern glass building is impressive, and the audiovisual show is a breezy romp through Montréal's history from the Ice Age to the present, but the real reason to visit the city's most ambitious archaeological museum is to take the elevator ride down to the 17th century.

It's dark down there, and just a little creepy thanks to the 350-year-old tombstones teetering in the gloom, but it's worth the trip. This is a serious archaeological dig that takes you to the very foundations of the city.

You begin on the banks of the long-vanished Rivière St-Pierre, where the first settlers built their homes and traded with the First Nations inhabitants. From there you climb up toward the present, past the stone foundations of an 18th-century tavern and a 19th-century insurance building. Along the way, filmed figures representing past inhabitants appear on ghostly screens to chat to you about their life and times. A more lighthearted exhibit explores life and love in multicultural Montréal. For a spectacular view of the Old Port, the St. Lawrence River, and the Islands, ride the elevator to the top of the tower, or stop for lunch in the museum's glass-fronted café.

In summer there are re-creations of period fairs and festivals on the grounds near the museum. At this writing, a major expansion to the museum was scheduled to be completed by the end of 2012. ⊠ *350 pl. Royale, Old Montréal, Montréal* ☎ *514/872–9150* ⊕ *www.pacmuseum. qc.ca* ☜ *C$18* ☉ *June 24–early Sept., weekdays 10–6, weekends 11–6; early Sept.–June 23, Tues.–Fri. 10–5, weekends 11–5* Ⓜ *Place-d'Armes.*

Musée du Château Ramezay. Claude de Ramezay, the city's 11th governor, was probably daydreaming of home when he built his Montréal residence. Its thick stone walls, dormer windows, and steeply pitched roof make it look like a little bit of 18th-century Normandy dropped into the middle of North America—although the round, squat tower is a 19th-century addition. The extravagant mahogany paneling in the Salon de Nantes was installed when Louis XV was still king of France. The British used the château as headquarters after their conquest in 1760, and so did the American commanders Richard Montgomery and Benedict Arnold. Benjamin Franklin, who came north in a failed attempt to persuade the Québecois to join the American Revolution, stayed here during that winter adventure.

Most of the château's exhibits are a little staid—guns, uniforms, and documents on the main floor and tableaux depicting colonial life in the cellars—but they include some unexpected little eccentricities that make it worth the visit. One of its prized possessions is a bright-red automobile the De Dion-Bouton Company produced at the turn of the 20th century for the city's first motorist. ⊠ *280 rue Notre-Dame Est, Old Montréal, Montréal* ☎ *514/861–3708* ⊕ *www.chateauramezay.qc.ca* ☜ *C$10* ☉ *June–mid-Oct., daily 10–6; Oct.–May, Tues.–Sun. 10–4:30* Ⓜ *Champ-de-Mars.*

NEED A BREAK? **Musée du Château Ramezay.** Step out the back door of the Musée du Château Ramezay and into 18th-century tranquillity. The *jardins* (gardens) are laid out just as formally as Mme. de Ramezay might have wished, with a *potager* for vegetables and a little *verger*, or orchard. You can sit on a bench in the sun, admire the flowers, and inhale the sage-scented air from the herb garden. ⊠ *280 rue Notre-Dame Est, Old Montréal, Montréal* ☎ *514/861–3708* ⊕ *www.chateauramezay.qc.ca.*

☺ ★ **Old Port** (*Vieux Port*). Montréal's favorite waterfront park is your ideal gateway to the St. Lawrence River. Rent a pedal boat, take a ferry to Île Ste-Hélène, sign up for a dinner cruise, or, if you're really adventurous, ride a raft or a jet boat through the turbulent Lachine Rapids. It you're determined to stay ashore, however, there's still plenty to do, including street performances, sound-and-light shows, art displays, and exhibitions. Visiting warships from the Canadian navy and other countries often dock here and open their decks to the public. You can rent a bicycle or a pair of in-line skates at one of the shops along rue de la Commune and explore the waterfront at your leisure. If it's raining, the Centre des Sciences de Montréal on **King Edward Pier** will keep you dry and entertained, and if your lungs are in good shape you can climb the 192 steps to the top of the **Clock Tower** for a good view of the waterfront and the Islands; it was erected at the eastern end of the waterfront in memory of merchant mariners killed during World War I. You can, quite literally, lose the kids in Shed 16's Labyrinthe, a maze of alleys, surprises, and obstacles built inside an old waterfront warehouse. Every couple of years or so Montréal's Cirque du Soleil comes home to pitch its blue-and-yellow tent in the Old Port. But be warned: when the circus is in town, the tickets sell faster than water in a drought. ⊠ *Old Montréal, Montréal* ☎ *514/496–7678, 800/971–7678* ⊕ *www.quaysoftheoldport.com* Ⓜ *Place-d'Armes or Champ-de-Mars.*

Place Jacques-Cartier. The cobbled square at the heart of Old Montréal is part carnival, part flower market, and part sheer fun. You can pause here to have your portrait painted or to buy an ice cream or to watch the street performers. If you have more time, try to get a table at one of the sidewalk cafés, order a beer or a glass of wine, and watch the passing parade. The 1809 monument honoring Lord Nelson's victory over Napoléon Bonaparte's French navy at Trafalgar angers some modern-day Québec nationalists, but the campaign to raise money for it was led by the Sulpician priests, who were engaged in delicate land negotiations with the British government at the time and were eager to show what good subjects they were. ⊠ *Bordered by rues Notre-Dame Est and de la Commune, Old Montréal, Montréal* Ⓜ *Champ-de-Mars.*

WORTH NOTING

☺ **Centre des Sciences de Montréal.** You—or more likely, your kids—can design an energy-efficient bike, create a television news report, explore the impact that manufacturing one T-shirt has on the environment, find out what it's like to ride a unicycle 20 feet above the ground, create an animated film, or just watch an IMAX movie on a giant screen at Montréal's interactive science center. Games, puzzles, and hands-on experiments make it an ideal place for rainy days or even fair ones. The center also has a bistro serving light meals, a coffee and pastry shop, and a food court. ⊠ *Quai King Edward, Old Montréal, Montréal* ☎ *514/496–4724, 877/496–4724* ⊕ *www.centredessciencesdemontreal. com* ⊡ *Exhibit halls C$11.50, IMAX C$11.50, combined ticket C$19* ⊙ *June 18–Sept. 18, Sun.–Wed. 10–6, Thurs.–Sat. 10–9. Sept. 19–June 17, weekdays 9–4, weekends 10–5.* Ⓜ *Place-d'Armes.*

Hôpital Général des Soeurs-Grises (*General Hospital of the Gray Nuns*). A few jagged stone walls are all that's left of Montréal's first general hospital. The ruins—which once formed the west wing and the transept of the chapel—have been preserved as a memorial to Canada's first native-born saint, Marguerite d'Youville (1701–71), who took over the hospital in 1747 and ran it until a fire destroyed the building in

MONTRÉAL'S BEST WALKING TOURS

Guidatour. You can walk through various historic, cultural, or architecturally diverse areas of the city with a costumed guide, courtesy of Guidatour. Popular tours include Old Montréal, the Underground City, and the elite 19th-century neighborhood known as the Golden Square Mile. Prices start at C$12. ✉ *360 rue St-François-Xavier, Suite 400, Old Montréal, Montréal* ☎ *514/844–4021, 800/363–4021* ⊕ *www.guidatour.qc.ca* ☉ *Office: weekdays 9–5* Ⓜ *Place-d'Armes.*

Circuit des Fantômes du Old Montréal (*Old Montréal Ghost Trail*). From mid-April to mid-November, Circuit des Fantômes du Old Montréal has walking tours through the old city where a host of spirits are said to still haunt the streets. Reservations are required. ✉ *360 rue St-François-Xavier, Old Montréal, Montréal* ☎ *514/844–4021, 800/363–4021* ⊕ *www.fantommontreal.com* ☒ *C$22.00* Ⓜ *Champ-de-Mars.*

Kaleidoscope. A wide selection of guided walking tours explores Montréal's many culturally diverse neighborhoods. Prices range from C$15 to C$20. ✉ *Montréal* ☎ *514/990–1872* ⊕ *www.tourskaleidoscope.com.*

1765. St. Marguerite's life was no walk in the park, as you'll find out if you visit the **Maison de Mère d'Youville** next door to the ruins. Marguerite started looking after the city's down-and-outs after the death of her abusive and disreputable husband. Amused that the widow of a whiskey trader should be helping the town drunks, locals took to calling Marguerite and her Soeurs de la Charité (Sisters of Charity) the Soeurs Grises (Grey Nuns), slang for "tipsy nuns." The Maison has some remarkable reminders of her life, such as the kitchen where she worked, with its enormous fireplace and stone sink. Call ahead for tours of the house. ✉ *138 rue St-Pierre, Old Montréal, Montréal* ☎ *514/842–9411* ⊕ *www.sgm.qc.ca* ☒ *Free* ☉ *By appointment only, Tues.–Sun. 9:30–11:30 and 1:30–4* Ⓜ *Square-Victoria.*

Hôtel de Ville (*City Hall*). President Charles de Gaulle of France marked Canada's centennial celebrations in 1967 by standing on the central balcony of Montréal's ornate city hall on July 24 and shouting "*Vive le Québec libre*" ("Long live free Québec"), much to the delight of the separatist movement and to the horror of the federal government that had invited him over in the first place. Perhaps he got carried away because he felt so at home: the Second Empire–style city hall, built in 1878, is modeled after the one in Tours, France. Free guided tours are available (reservations required). ✉ *275 rue Notre-Dame Est, Old Montréal, Montréal* ☎ *514/872–0077* ⊕ *www.ville.montreal.qc.ca* ☒ *Free* ☉ *Weekdays 8:30–5* Ⓜ *Champ-de-Mars.*

Maison Pierre du Calvet. Merchant Pierre du Calvet was everything that British-ruled Montréal didn't like—a notorious republican, an admirer of Voltaire, a pal of Benjamin Franklin, and a fierce supporter of the American Revolution. But he was also prosperous enough in 1725 to build a fine residence with thick stone walls and multipane casement windows. His home now houses a restaurant and a small but opulent bed-and-breakfast (called Pierre du Calvet AD 1725), where you can enjoy the same hospitality Franklin did in the mid-18th century. ⊠ *405 rue Bonsecours, Old Montréal, Montréal* ☎ *514/282–1725, 866/544– 1725* ⊕ *www.pierreducalvet.ca* Ⓜ *Champ-de-Mars.*

Marché Bonsecours (*Bonsecours Market*). You can't buy fruits and vegetables in the Marché Bonsecours anymore, but you can shop for local fashions and crafts in the row of upscale boutiques that fill its main hall, or lunch in one of several restaurants opening onto the Old Port or rue St-Paul. But the Marché is best admired from the outside. Built in the 1840s as the city's main market, it is possibly the most beautifully proportioned neoclassical building in Montréal, with its six cast-iron Doric columns and two rows of meticulously even sashed windows, all topped with a silvery dome. In fact, the Marché was always too elegant to be just a farmers' market. ⊠ *350 rue St-Paul Est, Old Montréal, Montréal* ☎ *514/872–7730* ⊕ *www.marchebonsecours.qc.ca* Ⓜ *Champ-de-Mars.*

Place-d'Armes. When Montréal was under attack, citizens and soldiers would rally at Place-d'Armes, but these days the only rallying is done by tourists, lunching office workers, calèche drivers, and flocks of voracious pigeons. The pigeons are particularly fond of the triumphant statue of Montréal's founder, Paul de Chomedey, with his lance upraised, perched above the fountain in the middle of the cobblestone square. Tunnels beneath the square protected the colonists from the winter weather and provided an escape route; unfortunately, they are too small and dangerous to visit. ⊠ *Bordered by rues Notre-Dame Ouest, St-Jacques, and St-Sulpice, Old Montréal, Montréal* Ⓜ *Place-d'Armes.*

Place de la Grande-Paix. If you're looking for peace and quiet, the narrow strip of grass and trees on Place d'Youville just east of Place Royale is an appropriate place to find it. It was here, after all, that the French signed a major peace treaty with dozens of aboriginal nations in 1702. It was also here that the first French colonists to settle in Montréal landed their four boats on May 17, 1642. An obelisk records the names of the settlers. ⊠ *Between pl. d'Youville and rue William, Old Montréal, Montréal* Ⓜ *Place-d'Armes.*

Place Royale. The oldest public square in Montréal, dating to the 17th century, was a market during the French regime and later became a Victorian garden. ⊠ *Bordered by rues St-Paul Ouest and de la Commune, Old Montréal, Montréal* Ⓜ *Place-d'Armes.*

Square Victoria. The perfect Montréal mix: an 1872 statue of Queen Victoria on one side and an authentic Parisian métro entrance on the other. Both are framed by a two-block stretch of trees, benches, and fountains that makes a great place to relax and admire the handsome 1920s business buildings on the east side. The art nouveau métro entrance, incidentally, was a gift from the French capital's transit commission. ⊠ *Rue du Square Victoria, between rues Viger and St-Jacques, Old Montréal, Montréal* Ⓜ *Square-Victoria.*

2

DOWNTOWN, GOLDEN SQUARE MILE, AND CHINATOWN

Rue Ste-Catherine—and the métro line that runs under it—is the main cord that binds together the disparate, sprawling neighborhoods that comprise Montréal's **downtown,** or *centre-ville*, just north and west of Old Montréal. It's a long, boisterous, sometimes seedy, and sometimes elegant street that runs from rue Claremont in Westmount to rue d'Iberville in the east end.

The heart of downtown—with department stores, boutiques, bars, restaurants, strip clubs, amusement arcades, theaters, cinemas, art galleries, bookstores, and even a few churches—runs from avenue Atwater to boulevard St-Denis.

Walk even farther north on rue Crescent to the lower slopes of Mont-Royal and you come to what was once the most exclusive neighborhood in Canada—the **Golden Square Mile.** During the boom years of the mid-1800s, baronial homes covered the mountain north of rue Sherbrooke. Many are gone, replaced by high-rises or modern town houses, but there are still plenty of architectural treasures to admire, even if most of them are now foreign consulates or university institutes.

Sandwiched between the downtown and the Old City is bustling **Chinatown,** with a pedestrian street closed to traffic lined with restaurants and gift shops, as well as markets selling everything from hard-to-find Asian produce to dim sum.

And underneath it all—the entire downtown area and then some—is Montréal's **Underground City,** a vast network of more or less anything you'd find on the street above.

GETTING HERE AND AROUND

Getting to and around downtown is easy, thanks to the métro. There are several stations along boulevard de Maisonneuve, which is a block away from and runs parallel to rue Ste-Catherine. Many of them link directly to the **Underground City.** Note that if you're coming from Old Montréal you'll be walking uphill, and streets become steeper beyond downtown toward the Plateau and Mont-Royal. The best way to enter Chinatown is through the ornate gates on boulevard St-Laurent—Place d'Armes is the closest métro station—then head for the hub at rue de la Gauchetière at the intersection of rue Clark. Surrounding streets such

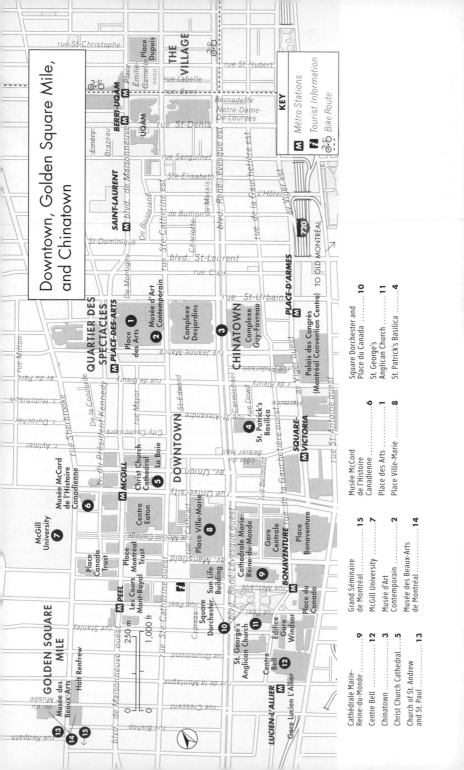

Downtown, Golden Square Mile, and Chinatown

KEY

M Métro Stations

i Tourist Information

o-o Bike Route

The Musée des Beaux-Arts has one of Canada's largest permanent collections of Canadian art, as well as a gallery where you can buy paintings by local artists.

as St-Urbain and St-Laurent also have restaurants and shops, but you won't need an entire day to see it all. To avoid crowds come to Chinatown on a weekday for breakfast or lunch; if you want to experience the crush, come after 10 am on Saturday.

EXPLORING

TOP ATTRACTIONS

Cathédrale Marie-Reine-du-Monde (*Mary Queen of the World Cathedral*). The best reason to visit this cathedral is that it's a quarter-scale replica of St. Peter's Basilica, complete with a magnificent reproduction of Bernini's ornate baldachin (canopy) over the main altar and an ornately coffered ceiling. When Bishop Ignace Bourget (1799–1885) decided to build his cathedral in the heart of the city's Protestant-dominated commercial quarter, many fellow Catholics thought he was crazy. But the bishop was determined to assert the Church's authority—and its loyalty to Rome—in the British-ruled city. Bourget didn't live to see the cathedral dedicated in 1894, but his tomb holds place of honor among those of his successors in the burial chapel on the east side of the nave. ⊠ *1085 rue de la Cathédrale (enter through main doors on boul. René-Lévesque), Downtown, Montréal* ☎ *514/866–1661* ⊕ *www.cathedralecatholiquedemontreal.org* ⊠ *Free* ☉ *Daily 7–6* Ⓜ *Bonaventure or Peel.*

Chinatown. Chinese immigrants first came to Montréal in large numbers after 1880, following the construction of the transcontinental railroad, and there's been a steady influx of peoples from Asia and Southeast Asia—including the Vietnamese—since then. Now the city's Chinatown covers about an 18-block area between boulevard René-Lévesque and

avenue Viger to the north and south, and near rue de Bleury and avenue Hôtel de Ville on the west and east.

The center of the action is at the intersection of rue Clark and rue de la Gauchetière, where part of the street is closed to traffic. On weekends, especially in summer, it's particularly vibrant, crowded with tourists as well as residents shopping in the Asian markets for fresh produce, meat and fish, and health supplements.

Along with the many Cantonese restaurants, there are a few places to get Vietnamese *pho*, a huge bowl of noodle soup with sliced beef. It's also one of the best lunch deals in town for around C$10.

For an inexpensive breakfast or brunch, nothing is more satisfying than a few rounds of dim sum, served at several restaurants here, including **Maison Kam Fung** (✉ *1111 rue St-Urbain* ☎ *514/878-2888*).

■ **TIP➔** This is also a great place to pick up some souvenirs, with a number of tiny shops selling everything from brightly colored silk floral scarves to ornate chopsticks. ✉ *Chinatown, Montréal.*

Christ Church Cathedral. The seat of the Anglican (Episcopalian) bishop of Montréal offers downtown shoppers and strollers a respite from the hustle and bustle of rue Ste-Catherine, with free noontime concerts and organ recitals. Built in 1859, the cathedral is modeled on Snettisham Parish Church in Norfolk, England, with some distinctly Canadian touches. The steeple, for example, is made with aluminum plates molded to simulate stone, and inside, the Gothic arches are crowned with carvings of the types of foliage growing on Mont-Royal when the church was built. The stained-glass windows behind the main altar, installed in the early 1920s as a memorial to the dead of World War I, show scenes from the life of Christ. On the wall just above and to the left of the pulpit is the Coventry Cross; it's made of nails taken from the ruins of Britain's Coventry Cathedral, destroyed by bombing in 1940. ✉ *635 rue Ste-Catherine Ouest, Downtown, Montréal* ☎ *514/843-6577* ⊕ *www.montrealcathedral.ca* ✉ *Free* ☉ *Sun.–Fri. 8–6, Sat. 11–6* Ⓜ *McGill.*

★ **Musée d'Art Contemporain** (*Museum of Contemporary Art*). If you have a taste for pastoral landscapes and formal portraits, you might want to stick with the Musée des Beaux-Arts. But for a walk on the wild side of art, see what you can make of the jagged splashes of color that cover the canvases of the "Automatistes," as Québec's rebellious artists of the 1930s styled themselves. Their works form the core of this museum's collection of 5,000 pieces. One of the leaders of the movement, Jean-Paul Riopelle (1923–2002), often tossed his brushes and palette knives aside and just squeezed the paint directly on to the canvas—sometimes several tubes at a time. In 1948, Riopelle and his friends fired the first shot in Québec's Quiet Revolution by signing *Le Refus Global*, a manifesto that renounced the political and religious establishment of the day and revolutionized art in the province. The museum often has weekend programs and art workshops, some of which are geared toward children, and almost all are free. And for a little romance and music with your art, try the Vendredi Nocturnes on the first Friday evening of every month with live music, bar service, and guided tours of the exhibits.

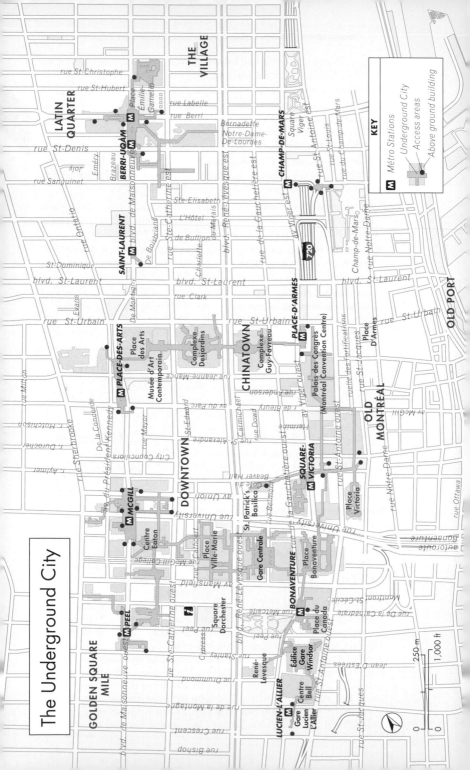

Neighborhood Focus: The Underground City

2

When Place Ville-Marie, the cruciform skyscraper designed by I. M. Pei, opened in the heart of downtown in 1962, the tallest structure of the time also signaled the beginning of Montréal's subterranean city. Montrealers were skeptical that anyone would want to shop or even walk around in the new "down" town, but more than four decades later they can't live without it.

About half a million people use the 30-km (19-mile) Underground City, or *la ville souterraine,* daily. The tunnels link 10 métro stations, seven hotels, 200 restaurants, 1,700 boutiques, and 60 office buildings—not to mention movie theaters, concert halls, convention complexes, the Centre Bell, two universities, and a college. Those who live in one of more than 2,000 connected apartments can buy milk on a February day and never have to put on their coat.

GETTING HERE AND AROUND
Most of the Underground City parallels the métro lines. The six-block sector

of continuous shopping between La Baie (east of the McGill station) and Les Cours Montréal (west of the Peel station) is perhaps the densest portion of the network. The first link in the system is at Place Ville-Marie, which is part of the main hub and a good place to start exploring. From here you could cover most of the main sites—from the Centre Bell to Place des Arts—without ever coming up and without having to take the métro.

WHEN TO GO
There aren't any bad times to visit—of course it's busy at rush hour and during the holiday season—but there are certainly good times, such as during a snowstorm or in the heat of summer. While Montréal is generally a safe city, note that some of the farther reaches of the network can become desolate at night.

Hours for guided tours vary. ✉ *185 rue Ste-Catherine Ouest, Downtown, Montréal* ☎ *514/847–6226* ⊕ *www.macm.org* 🎫 *C$12, free Wed. 5–9* ⊙ *Tues. and Thurs.–Sun. 11–6, Wed. 11–9* Ⓜ *Place des Arts.*

Fodor'sChoice **Musée des Beaux-Arts de Montréal** (*Montréal Museum of Fine Arts*). Not
★ surprisingly, Canada's oldest museum has one of the finest collections of
Canadian art anywhere. In the fall of 2011 the museum moved the works
of such luminaries as Paul Kane, the Group of Seven, Paul-Émile Borduas, and Marc-Aurèle Fortin into a brand new display space, built onto
the back of the neoclassical Erskine and American United Church, one of
the city's most historic Protestant churches. The nave has been preserved
as a meeting place and exhibition hall and also displays the church's 18
Tiffany stained-glass windows, the biggest collection of Tiffany's work
outside the United States. The rest of the Musée's permanent collection,
which includes works by everyone from Rembrandt to Renoir, is housed
in its two other pavilions: the neoclassical **Michal and Renata Hornstein
Pavilion** just across rue de la Musée from the church, and the glittering,
glass-fronted **Jean-Noël-Desmarais Pavilion** just across rue Sherbrooke.
All three are linked by tunnels. The museum also includes the Musée
des Arts Décoratifs, where you can see some fanciful bentwood furniture designed by Frank Gehry, a marvelous collection of 18th-century
English porcelain, and 3,000—count 'em—Japanese snuff boxes collected by, of all people Georges Clemenceau, France's prime minister
during World War I. The museum also has a gift shop, a bookstore, a
restaurant, a cafeteria, and a gallery where you can buy or even rent
paintings by local artists. ✉ *1380 rue Sherbrooke Ouest, Downtown,
Montréal* ☎ *514/285–2000* ⊕ *www.mmfa.qc.ca* 🎫 *Permanent collection
free; special exhibits C$15, C$7.50 Wed. after 5* ⊙ *Tues. 11–5, Wed.
11–9, Thurs. and Fri. 11–7, weekends 10–5* Ⓜ *Guy-Concordia.*

★ **Musée McCord de l'Histoire Canadienne** (*McCord Museum of Canadian
History*). David Ross McCord (1844–1930) was a wealthy pack rat
with a passion for anything that had to do with Montréal and its history. His collection of paintings, costumes, toys, tools, drawings, and
housewares provides a glimpse of what city life was like for all classes
in the 19th century. If you're interested in the lifestyles of the elite,
however, you'll love the photographs that William Notman (1826–
91) took of the rich at play. One series portrays members of the posh
Montréal Athletic Association posing in snowshoes on the slopes of
Mont-Royal, all decked out in Hudson Bay coats and woolen hats.
Each of the hundreds of portraits was shot individually in a studio
and then painstakingly mounted on a picture of the snowy mountain
to give the impression of a winter outing. There are guided tours (call
for schedule), a reading room, a documentation center, a gift shop,
a bookstore, and a café. ✉ *690 rue Sherbrooke Ouest, Downtown,
Montréal* ☎ *514/398–7100* ⊕ *www.mccord-museum.qc.ca* 🎫 *C$14;
free Wed. 5–9* ⊙ *Weekdays 10–6 (to 9 pm on Wed.), weekends 10–5.
Closed Mon. early Sept.–late June* Ⓜ *McGill.*

★ **St. Patrick's Basilica.** St. Pat's—as most of its parishioners call it—is to
Montréal's Anglophone Catholics what the Basilique Notre-Dame is to
their French-speaking brethren—the mother church and a monument
to faith and courage. One of the joys of visiting the place is that you'll

probably be the only tourist there, so you'll have plenty of time to check out the old pulpit and the huge lamp decorated with six 6-foot-tall angels hanging over the main altar. And if you're named after some obscure saint like Scholastica or Aeden of Fleury, you can search for your namesake's portrait among the 170 painted panels on the walls of the nave.

The church was built in 1847, and is one of the purest examples of the Gothic Revival style in Canada, with a high vaulted ceiling glowing with green and gold mosaics. The tall, slender columns are actually pine logs lashed together and decorated to look like marble, so that if you stand in one of the back corners and look toward the altar you really do feel as if you're peering at the sacred through a grove of trees. ⊠ *454 boul. René-Lévesque Ouest, Downtown, Montréal* ☎ *514/866–7379* ⊕ *www.stpatricksmtl.ca* ⊠ *Free* ⊙ *Sept.–June, daily 8:30–6, July and Aug., daily 9–5* Ⓜ *Square-Victoria.*

WORTH NOTING

Centre Bell. The Montréal Canadiens haven't won the Stanley Cup since 1993, and most of the team's fans can't remember the golden 1960s and '70s when *Les Glorieux* virtually owned the trophy. The superstitious blame the team's fallen fortunes on its 1996 move from the hallowed Forum to the brown-brick Centre Bell arena. Still, Montréal is a hockey-mad city and the Habs, as locals call the team, are still demigods here. When they celebrated their 100th season in 2009–10, the city changed the name of the strip of rue de la Gauchetière in front of the Centre Bell to avenue des Canadiens-de-Montréal. Don't miss the square on the west side of the arena, which has been turned into a shrine to the team's glorious history, with plaques commemorating the Canadiens' record 24 Stanley Cups and life-size action statues of such hockey heroes as Maurice "Rocket" Richard and Guy Lafleur. ⊠ *1260 av. des Canadiens-de-Montréal, Downtown, Montréal* ☎ *877/668–8269, 514/790–2525 for hockey tickets; 800/663–6786, 514/932–2582 for other events* ⊕ *www.centrebell.ca* Ⓜ *Bonaventure or Lucien-l'Allier.*

The team opened the 10,000-square-foot **Montréal Canadiens Hall of Fame** (⊠ *1909 av. des Canadiens-de-Montréal, Downtown, Montréal* ☎ *514/925–7777* ⊕ *hall.canadiens.com* ⊠ *C$11* ⊙ *Tues.–Sat. 10–6, Sun. noon–5. On game days doors close two hours before beginning of game* Ⓜ *Bonaventure*) inside the Centre Bell, where you can view relics of the team's past and even visit a replica of the Habs' 1976–77 locker room. The Hall of Fame also organizes tours of the Centre Bell (C$6), complete with a visit to the alumni lounge, press gallery, and, depending on the schedule, the current dressing room. It's wise to call in advance to make sure tours will be operating as they're sometimes postponed on short notice.

Church of St. Andrew and St. Paul. If you want to see the inside of Montréal's largest Presbyterian church—sometimes affectionately called the A&P—you'll have to call the secretary and make arrangements, or simply show up for Sunday services. Either way, it's worth the effort, if only to see the glorious stained-glass window of the risen Christ that dominates the sanctuary behind the white-stone communion table.

It's a memorial to members of the Royal Highland Regiment of Canada (the Black Watch) who were killed in World War I. ⊠ *3415 rue Redpath (main entrance on rue Sherbrooke), Downtown, Montréal* ☎ *514/842–3431* ⊕ *www.standrewstpaul.com* ☒ *Free* ☾ *Sun. service at 11 am, other times by appointment* Ⓜ *Guy-Concordia.*

Grand Séminaire de Montréal. Education goes way back at the Grand Séminaire. In the mid-1600s, St. Marguerite Bourgeoys used one of the two stone towers in the garden as a school for First Nations (Native American) girls while she and her nuns lived in the other. The 1860 seminary buildings behind the towers are now used by men studying for the priesthood. In summer there are free guided tours of the towers, the extensive gardens, and the college's beautiful Romanesque chapel. ⊠ *2065 rue Sherbrooke Ouest, Downtown, Montréal* ☎ *514/935–7775* ⊕ *www.gsdm.qc.ca* ☒ *By donation* ☾ *Guided tours June–Aug., Tues.– Fri. 1 and 3, Sat. 10 and 1.* Ⓜ *Guy-Concordia.*

McGill University. Merchant and fur trader James McGill would probably be horrified to know that the university that he helped found in 1828 has developed an international reputation as one of North America's best party schools. The administration isn't too happy about it, either. But there's no real cause for alarm. McGill is still one of the two or three best English-language universities in Canada, and certainly one of the prettiest. Its campus is an island of grass and trees in a sea of traffic and skyscrapers. If you take the time to stroll up the drive that leads from the Greek Revival Roddick Gates to the austere neoclassical Arts Building, keep an eye out to your right for the life-size statue of McGill himself, hurrying across campus clutching his tricorn hat. If you have an hour or so, drop into the templelike **Redpath Museum of Natural History** to browse its eclectic collection of dinosaur bones, old coins, African art, and shrunken heads. ⊠ *859 rue Sherbrooke Ouest, Downtown, Montréal* ☎ *514/398–4455, 514/398–4094 tours, 514/398–4086 museum* ⊕ *www.mcgill.ca* ☒ *Free* ☾ *Museum weekdays 9–5, Sun. 1–5* Ⓜ *McGill.*

Place des Arts. Montréal's primary performing-arts complex has been undergoing a major renaissance. The center's main lobby was completely refurbished in 2010 and a new 2,000-seat concert hall for the Orchestre Symphonique de Montréal opened on the northeast corner of the site in the fall of 2011, fulfilling a decades-old dream of Montréal music lovers. Place des Arts is also the centerpiece of the city's new Quartier des Spectacles, a square kilometer dedicated to arts and culture, with performance halls, dance studios, broadcasting facilities, and recording studios. The huge plaza in front of the complex is a favorite gathering place for locals and visitors—especially during the Jazz Festival when it's packed for free concerts. Sadly, the complex no longer offers backstage tours. ⊠ *175 rue Ste-Catherine Ouest, Downtown, Montréal* ☎ *514/842–2112 tickets, 514/285–4422 information* ⊕ *www.pda.qc.ca* Ⓜ *Place des Arts.*

Place Ville-Marie. The cross-shape 1962 office tower was Montréal's first modern skyscraper; the mall complex underneath it was the first link in the Underground City. The wide expanse of the building's plaza, just upstairs from the mall, makes a good place to relax with coffee or a snack from the food court below. Benches, potted greenery, and fine views of Mont-Royal make it popular with walkers, tourists, and office workers. ✉ *Bordered by boul. René-Lévesque and rues Mansfield, Cathcart, and University, Downtown, Montréal* ☎ *514/866–6666* ⊕ *www.placevillemarie.com* Ⓜ *McGill or Bonaventure.*

Square Dorchester and Place du Canada. On sunny summer days you can join the office workers, store clerks, and downtown shoppers who gather in these two green squares in the center of the city to eat lunch under the trees and perhaps listen to an open-air concert. If there are no vacant benches or picnic tables, you can still find a place to sit on the steps at the base of the dramatic monument to the dead of the Boer War. Other statues honor Scottish poet Robert Burns (1759–96); Sir Wilfrid Laurier (1841–1919), Canada's first French-speaking prime minister; and Sir John A. Macdonald (1815–91), Canada's first prime minister.

While the squares don't amount to more than a few acres, they're very popular with locals and tourists alike. In 2010, the city completed a major C$9.5-million refurbishment of Square Dorchester, and funds are also being allocated to fix up Place du Canada. ✉ *Bordered by boul. René-Lévesque and rues Peel, Metcalfe, and McTavish, Downtown, Montréal* Ⓜ *Bonaventure or Peel.*

St. George's Anglican Church. St. George's is possibly the prettiest Anglican (Episcopalian) church in Montréal. Step into its dim, candle-scented interior and you'll feel you've been transported to some prosperous market town in East Anglia. The double hammer-beam roof, the rich stained-glass windows, and the Lady Chapel on the east side of the main altar all add to the effect. It certainly seems a world away from Centre Bell, the modern temple to professional hockey just across the street. On the other hand, several prominent National Hockey League players and game announcers regularly drop in for a few minutes of quiet meditation before joining the action on the ice. ✉ *1101 rue Stanley (main entrance on rue de la Gauchetière), Downtown, Montréal* ☎ *514/866–7113* ⊕ *www.st-georges.org* 🎫 *Free* ⊙ *Tues.–Fri. 9–4, weekends 9–3; Sun. services at 9 and 10:30 am* Ⓜ *Bonaventure.*

THE LATIN QUARTER AND THE VILLAGE

The **Latin Quarter** (Quartier Latin), just south of the Plateau, has been a center of student life since the 18th century, when Université de Montréal students gave the area its name, and today it continues to infuse the city with youthful energy. When night falls its streets are filled with multinational hordes—young and not so young, rich and poor, established and still studying.

The Université de Québec à Montréal (UQAM) spreads across the district, along with theaters, restaurants and bars, bookstores, and cinemas. Some area businesses cater to a young clientele and their penchant for the loud and grungy, but the quarter is also home to some of the city's trendiest restaurants and nightspots. In summer, the streets of the Latin Quarter are busy with summer festival events, such as the Just for Laughs Festival in July.

But in late July, it's the Pride Parade in the **Village** (which some residents refer to as the "Gay Village") that many consider the biggest and most outrageous party of the year, attracting more than a million people who come to celebrate diversity.

Montréal has one of the most vibrant gay communities in the world, widely supported by residents of this proudly liberal, open-minded city. In recent years the municipal, federal, and provincial governments have taken it upon themselves to aggressively promote the Village and Montréal's gay-friendly climate as a reason for tourists to visit, including those who wish to wed, but its restaurants, antiques shops (on rue Amherst), and bars make it a popular destination for visitors of all persuasions. The lively strip of rue Ste-Catherine running east of the Latin Quarter is the backbone of the Village.

WORD OF MOUTH

"Les Quebecois are serious about beer and support a range of small breweries.... Here are my choices: L'Amere a Boire (2049 Rue Saint-Denis). A nook on the north edge of the so-called Latin Quarter.... The repertoire of brews is carefully balanced and it is hard to have only one.... Le Saint Bock Brasserie (1749 St-Denis). In the heart of the Latin Quarter. Saint-Bock can turn into a young people's party on weekend nights but always offers a strong range of brews."
—Southam

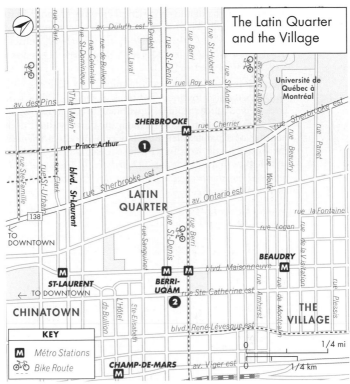

The Latin Quarter and the Village

2

GETTING HERE AND AROUND

The Latin Quarter is concentrated on boulevard de Maisonneuve and rue St-Denis. The busy Berri-UQAM métro station is the closest.

The Village centers on the Beaudry métro station, which has its entrance adorned with rainbow pillars. Its borders are considered rue Ste-Catherine Est from Amherst to de Lorimier, and on the north–south axis from René-Lévesque to Sherbrooke.

TIMING

Both of these neighborhoods have a steady energy during the day, the Latin Quarter busy with students heading to class and sitting hunched over laptops in cafés. But both areas are best explored in the evening—and often the later, the better.

EXPLORING

Chapelle Notre-Dame-de-Lourdes (*Our Lady of Lourdes Chapel*). Artist and architect Napoléon Bourassa called the Chapelle Notre-Dame-de-Lourdes *l'oeuvre de mes amours*, or a labor of love—and it shows. He designed the little Byzantine-style building himself and set about decorating it with the exuberance of an eight-year-old making a Mother's Day card. He covered the walls with murals and encrusted the altar and pillars with gilt and ornamental carving. It's not Montréal's biggest monument to the Virgin Mary, but it's the most unabashedly sentimental. ✉ *430 rue Ste-Catherine Est, Latin Quarter, Montréal* ☎ *514/845–8278* ⊕ *www.cndlm.org* 🎫 *Free* ⊙ *weekdays 11–6, Sat. 10:30–6:30, Sun. 9–6:30* Ⓜ *Berri-UQAM.*

Square St-Louis. The bourgeois families who built their homes around Square St-Louis's fountain and trees in the late 1870s would probably be dismayed to see the kind of people who congregate in their little park today. It's difficult to walk through the place without dodging a skateboarder or a panhandler. But they're generally a friendly bunch, and the square is still worth a visit just to see the elegant Second Empire–style homes that surround it. ✉ *Bordered by av. Laval and rue St-Denis between rue Sherbrooke Est and av. des Pins Est, Latin Quarter, Montréal* Ⓜ *Sherbrooke.*

THE PLATEAU, OUTREMONT, MILE END, AND LITTLE ITALY

Plateau Mont-Royal—or simply the **Plateau** as it's more commonly called these days—is still home to a vibrant Portuguese community, but much of the housing originally built for factory workers has been bought and renovated by professionals, artists, performers, and academics eager to find a place to live close to all the action. The Plateau is always bustling, even in the dead of winter, but on sunny summer weekends it's packed with Montrealers who come here to shop, dine, and observe each other.

The gentrification of the Plateau has pushed up rents and driven students, immigrant families, and single young graduates farther north, following the main thoroughfares of boulevard St-Laurent as well as St-Denis. Above the Plateau and next to Mont-Royal, **Outremont** has long been Montréal's residential Francophone enclave (as opposed to Westmount, always stubbornly English right down to its neo-Gothic churches and lawn-bowling club). It has grand homes, tree-shaded streets, perfectly groomed parks, and two upscale shopping and dining strips along rues Laurier and Bernard. Rue Bernard is particularly attractive, with wide sidewalks and shady trees. The eastern fringes of Outremont are home to Montréal's thriving Hasidic community.

Bordering Outremont is the funky neighborhood of **Mile End,** historically home to Montréal's working-class Jewish community and now full of inexpensive, often excellent restaurants and little shops selling handicrafts and secondhand clothes. In recent years Mile End has become one of the hippest neighborhoods in town. By day it's a great place to take a stroll or sit in a café's *terrasse* to watch its residents—from artsy bohemians to Hasidic Jews—pass by.

Farther north is **Little Italy,** which is still home base to Montréal's sizable Italian community of nearly a quarter of a million people, and though families of Italian descent now live all over the greater Montréal area, many come back here every week or so to shop, eat out, or visit family and friends, and the 30-odd blocks bounded by rues Jean-Talon, St-Zotique, Marconi, and Drolet remain its heart and soul. You'll know you've reached Little Italy when the gardens have tomato plants and grapevines, there are sausages and tins of olive oil in store windows, and the heady smell of espresso emanates from cafés.

Many of the older residences in these neighborhoods have the graceful wrought-iron balconies and twisting staircases that are typical of Montréal. The stairs and balconies, treacherous in winter, are often full of families and couples gossiping, picnicking, and partying come summer. If Montrealers tell you they spend the summer in Balconville, they mean they don't have the money or the time to leave town and won't get any farther than their balconies.

GETTING HERE AND AROUND

Although all four neighborhoods have convenient métro stops, if you already have a car, driving up here is definitely easier and often faster. However, note that on weekends—the most crowded but definitely the best time to visit—it can be difficult to find on-street parking, as most of it's metered. Plan to spend a day exploring these areas, or at least come for a meal or two during your stay.

The Plateau's most convenient métro station is Mont-Royal on the Orange Line. It's a large district, but relatively flat and easy to walk around. If you want to cover more ground without resorting to a taxi, there are several Bixi bicycle stands in the area, and plenty of bike lanes.

The streets of Mile End (Orange Line to Laurier) and Outremont (Blue Line to Outremont) start buzzing the moment restaurants open for brunch. Both the Orange and Blue lines can be taken to get to Little Italy, using the Jean-Talon stop. Once here, shop for produce and cheese at the Marché Jean-Talon or see a wedding party outside the Madonna della Difesa church.

EXPLORING

TOP ATTRACTIONS

Boulevard St-Laurent. A walk along this section of the boulevard St-Laurent is like a walk through Montréal's cultural history. The shops and restaurants, synagogues and churches that line the 10-block stretch north of rue Sherbrooke reflect the various waves of immigrants that have called it home. Keep your eyes open and you'll see Jewish delis, Hungarian sausage shops, Chinese grocery stores, Italian coffee bars, Greek restaurants, Vietnamese sandwich shops, and Peruvian snack bars. You'll also spot some of the city's trendiest restaurants and nightclubs. The first immigrants to move into the area in the 1880s were Jews escaping pogroms in Eastern Europe. It was they who called the street "the Main," as in Main Street—a nickname that endures to this day. Even Francophone Montrealers sometimes call it "Le Main." ⊠ *Plateau Mont-Royal, Montréal* Ⓜ *St-Laurent, Sherbrooke, or Mont-Royal.*

Chiesa della Madonna della Difesa. If you look up at the cupola behind the main altar of Little Italy's most famous church, you'll spot Montréal's most infamous piece of ecclesiastical portraiture. Yes, indeed, that lantern-jaw fellow on horseback who looks so pleased with himself is Benito Mussolini, the dictator who led Italy into World War II on the wrong side. In fairness, though, the mural, by Guido Nincheri

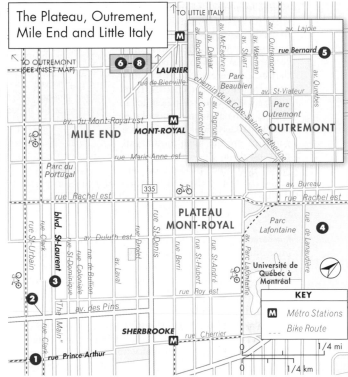

(1885–1973), was completed long before the war and commemorates the signing of the Lateran Pact with Pope Pius XI, one of Il Duce's few lasting achievements. The controversy shouldn't distract you from the beauties of the rest of the richly decorated church. ⊠ *6800 av. Henri-Julien, Little Italy, Montréal* ☎ *514/277–6522* 🖂 *Free* ☉ *Daily 10–6* Ⓜ *Beaubien or Jean-Talon.*

OFF THE
BEATEN
PATH

Église de la Visitation de la Bienheureuse Vierge Marie. You have to ride the métro to its northern terminus at the Henri-Bourassa station, and then walk for 15–20 minutes through some pretty ordinary neighborhoods to reach the Church of the Visitation of the Blessed Virgin Mary, but it's worth the trek to see the oldest church on the island. Its stone walls were raised in the 1750s, and the beautifully proportioned Palladian front was added in 1850. Decorating lasted from 1764 until 1837, with stunning results. The altar and the pulpit are as ornate as wedding cakes but still delicate. The church's most notable treasure is a rendering of the Visitation attributed to Pierre Mignard, a painter at the 17th-century court of Louis XIV. Parkland surrounds the church, and the nearby Île de la Visitation (reachable by footbridge) make for a very good walk. ⊠ *1847 blvd. Gouin Est, Montréal North, Montréal* ☎ *514/388–4050* 🖂 *Free* ☉ *Fri.–Wed. 8–noon and 1–3. Closed Thurs.* Ⓜ *Henri-Bourassa.*

Marché Jean-Talon. If you're trying to stick to a diet, stay away: the smells of grilling sausages, roasting chestnuts, and fresh pastries will almost certainly crack your resolve. And if they don't, there are dozens of tiny shops full of Québec cheeses, Lebanese sweets, country pâtés, local wines, and handmade chocolates that will. Less threatening to the waistline are the huge mounds of peas, beans, apples, carrots, pears, garlic, and other produce on sale at the open-air stalls. On Saturday mornings in particular, it feels as if all Montréal has come out to shop. ⊠ *7070 rue Henri-Julien, Little Italy, Montréal* ☎ *514/277–1588* ⊕ *www.marchespublics-mtl.com* Ⓜ *Jean-Talon.*

> ## WORD OF MOUTH
>
> "I liked the Jean Talon Market better than Atwater (I thought there was more variety, plus many of the vendors were giving out produce samples!). But Atwater has the bonus of being beside the Lachine Canal, which is very pretty."
>
> —Cranachin

★ **Rue Bernard.** If your taste runs to chic and fashionable rather than bohemian and eccentric, there is simply no better street for people-watching than rue Bernard. Its wide sidewalks and shady trees make it ideal for the kind of outdoor cafés that attract the bright and the beautiful. ⊠ *Outremont, Montréal* Ⓜ *Outremont.*

WORTH NOTING

Musée des Hospitalières de l'Hôtel-Dieu. The nuns of the Religieuses Hospitalières de St-Joseph ran Montréal's Hôpital Hôtel-Dieu for more than 300 years until the province and the Université de Montréal took it over in the 1970s. The first sisters—girls of good families caught up in the religious fervor of the age—came to New France with Jeanne Mance in the mid-1600s to look after the poor, the sick, and the dying. The order's museum—tucked away in a corner of the hospital the nuns built but no longer run—captures the spirit of that age with a series of meticulously bilingual exhibits. Just reading the excerpts from the letters and diaries of those young women helps you to understand the zeal that drove them to abandon the comforts of home for the hardships of the colonies. The museum also traces the history of medicine and nursing in Montréal. ⊠ *201 av. des Pins Ouest, Plateau Mont-Royal, Montréal* ☎ *514/849–2919* ⊕ *www.museedeshospitalieres.qc.ca* ⊠ *C$6* ☉ *Mid-June–mid-Oct., Tues.–Fri. 10–5, weekends 1–5; mid-Oct.–mid-June, Wed.–Sun. 1–5* Ⓜ *Sherbrooke.*

Parc Lafontaine. You could say that Parc Lafontaine is a microcosm of Montréal: the eastern half is French, with paths, gardens, and lawns laid out in geometric shapes; the western half is English, with meandering paths and irregularly shaped ponds that follow the natural contours of the land. In summer you can take advantage of bowling greens, tennis courts, an open-air theater (Théâtre de Verdure) where there are free arts events, and two artificial lakes with paddleboats. In winter one lake becomes a large skating rink. The park is named for Sir Louis-Hippolyte Lafontaine (1807–64), a pioneer of responsible government in Canada. His statue graces a plot on the park's southwestern edge. ⊠ *3933*

ART IN THE MÉTRO

Montréal was ahead of the curve in requiring all construction in the métro system to include an art component, resulting in such dramatic works as Frédéric Back's mural of the history of music in Place des Arts and the swirling stained-glass windows by Marcelle Ferron in Champs-de-Mars. The art nouveau entrance to the Square-Victoria station, a gift from the city of Paris, is the only original piece of Hector Guimard's architectural-design work outside the City of Light.

Operating since 1966, the métro is among the most architecturally distinctive subway systems in the world, with each of its 65 stations individually designed and decorated.

The newer stations along the Blue Line are all worth a visit as well, particularly Outremont, with a glass-block design from 1988. Even Place-d'Armes, one of the least visually remarkable stations in the system, includes a treasure: look for the small exhibit of archaeological artifacts representing each of Montréal's four historical eras (Aboriginal, French, English, and multicultural).

av. Parc Lafontaine, Plateau Mont-Royal, Montréal ☎ *514/872–9800* ☉ *Daily 9 am–10 pm* Ⓜ *Sherbrooke or Mont-Royal.*

Rue Prince-Arthur. In the 1960s rue Prince-Arthur was the Haight-Ashbury of Montréal, full of shops selling leather vests, tie-dyed T-shirts, recycled clothes, and drug paraphernalia. It still retains a little of that raffish attitude, but it's much tamer and more commercial these days. The blocks between avenue Laval and boulevard St-Laurent are a pedestrian mall, and the hippie shops have metamorphosed into inexpensive Greek, Vietnamese, Italian, Polish, and Chinese restaurants and neighborhood bars. So grab a table, order a coffee or an *apéro*, and watch the passing parade. ✉ *Plateau Mont-Royal, Montréal* Ⓜ *Sherbrooke.*

PARC DU MONT-ROYAL

Fodor'sChoice
★

In geological terms, Mont-Royal is a mere bump of basaltlike rock worn down by several ice ages to a mere 760 feet. But in the affections of Montrealers it's a Matterhorn. Without a trace of irony, they call it simply *la Montagne* or "the Mountain," and it's easy to see why it's so well loved.

For Montrealers it's a refuge in the middle of the city, a semitamed wilderness you can get to by bus or, if you have the lungs for the climb, simply by walking. It's where you go to get away from it all. And even when you can't get away, you can see the mountain glimmering beyond the skyscrapers and the high-rises—green in summer, gray and white in winter, and gold and crimson in fall.

The heart of all this is Parc du Mont-Royal itself—nearly 500 acres of forests and meadows laid out by Frederick Law Olmsted (1822–1903), the man responsible for New York City's Central Park. Olmsted believed that communion with nature could cure body and soul, so much of the park has been left as wild as possible, with narrow paths meandering through tall stands of maples and red oaks. In summer it's full of picnicking families and strolling couples; in winter cross-country skiers and snowshoers take over, while families skate at Lac aux Castors and ride sleds and inner tubes down groomed slopes. If you want to explore with minimum effort, you can hire the services of a horse-drawn carriage (or sleigh in winter).

Just outside the park's northern boundaries are the city's two biggest cemeteries, and beyond that the campus of the Université de Montréal.

GETTING HERE AND AROUND
If you're in good shape, you can walk up from downtown. Climb rue Peel to the entrance to Parc du Mont-Royal and then wheeze your way up the stairway—completely rebuilt in 2010—to the top of the mountain. Or you can simply take the métro to the Mont-Royal station and catch the No. 11 bus. If you have a car, there's good parking in Parc du Mont-Royal and at the Oratoire St-Joseph (the latter asks for a contribution of $5 per vehicle Monday to Saturday for anyone not attending a service or coming to pray). Biking up the mountain will test your endurance, but the park has an extensive network of scenic trails.

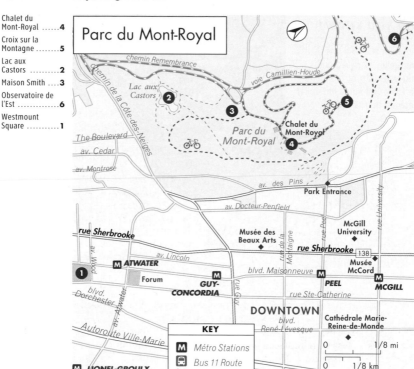

TIMING

Depending on your interest, you could spend anywhere from a few hours—if you simply just want to see the view—to the entire day here. If here for the afternoon, there's a cafeteria in the park for lunch, or pick up picnic provisions before you set out.

EXPLORING

TOP ATTRACTIONS

★ **Chalet du Mont-Royal.** No trip to Montréal is complete without a visit to the terrace in front of the Chalet du Mont-Royal. It's not the only place to go to get an overview of the city, the river, and the countryside beyond, but it's the most spectacular. On clear days you can see not just the downtown skyscrapers, but also Mont-Royal's sister mountains—Monts St-Bruno, St-Hilaire, and St-Grégoire. These isolated peaks, called the Montérégies, or Mountains of the King, rise dramatically from the flat countryside. Be sure to take a look inside the chalet, especially at the murals depicting scenes from Canadian history. There's a snack bar in the back. ⊠ *Off voie Camillien-Houde, Parc du Mont-Royal, Montréal* 🖭 *Free* ☉ *Daily 9–5* Ⓜ *Mont-Royal.*

ALL ABOARD THE EXPORAIL!

You can rattle around Canada's largest railway museum in a vintage tram specially built in the 1950s for sightseeing tours in Montréal when the city still had a streetcar system. The museum has more than 120 train cars and locomotives, but if you're a steam buff, you won't want to miss CPR 5935, the largest steam locomotive built in Canada, and CNR 4100, the most powerful in the British Empire when it was built in 1924. To see how the rich and powerful traveled, take a look at Sir William Van Horne's luxurious private car. Of special interest to the kids will be the car that served as a mobile classroom. The museum is south of the city in the town of St-Constant. In the summer, the Agence métropolitaine de transport, the commuter rail agency, runs train excursions to the museum from the Gare Lucien-l'Allier next to the Centre Bell. Trains depart at 11 am and return at 4 pm. ⊠ *110 rue St-Pierre, St-Constant* ☎ *450/632–2410* ⊕ *www.exporail.org* ☜ *C$19* ⊙ *June–Labor Day, daily 10–6; early Sept.–Oct., Wed.–Sun. 10–5; Nov.–May, weekends 10–5. Outdoor exhibits close an hour earlier.*

WORTH NOTING

Croix sur la Montagne (*Cross atop Mont-Royal*). The 102-foot-high steel cross at the top of Mont-Royal has been a city landmark since it was erected in 1924, largely with money raised through the efforts of 85,000 high-school students. In 1993 the 249 bulbs used to light the cross were replaced with an ultramodern fiber-optic system. ⊠ *Parc du Mont-Royal, Montréal.*

Ⓒ **Lac aux Castors** (*Beaver Lake*). Mont-Royal's single body of water is actually a reclaimed bog, but it's a great place for kids to float model boats in the summertime. In winter, the lake's frozen surface attracts whole families of skaters, and nearby there's a groomed slope where kids of all ages can ride inner tubes. The glass-fronted Beaver Lake Pavilion is a very pleasant bistro that serves lunch and dinner. Skate and cross-country-ski rentals are available downstairs. ⊠ *Off chemin Remembrance, Parc du Mont-Royal, Montréal* Ⓜ *Edouard Montpetit.*

Maison Smith. If you need a map of Mont-Royal's extensive hiking trails or want to know about the more than 180 kinds of birds here, the former park keeper's residence is the place to go. It's also a good spot for getting a snack, drink, or souvenir. The pretty little stone house—built in 1858—is the headquarters of Les Amis de la Montagne (The Friends of the Mountain), an organization that offers various guided walks on the mountain and in nearby areas. ⊠ *1260 chemin Remembrance, Parc du Mont-Royal, Montréal* ☎ *514/843–8240* ⊕ *www.lemontroyal.qc.ca* ⊙ *Daily 9–6 (times may vary slightly by season)* Ⓜ *Mont-Royal.*

Observatoire de l'Est. If you're just driving across the mountain, be sure to stop at its eastern lookout for a view of the Stade Olympique and the east end of the city. Snacks are available. ⊠ *Voie Camillien-Houde, Mont-Royal, Montréal* Ⓜ *Mont-Royal.*

OFF THE BEATEN PATH

Westmount Square. When skylights were cut into the terrace of Westmount Square in 1990, the architectural community was outraged at the "desecration" of the revered Ludwig Mies Van der Rohe's original work. Others deemed it a necessary step to bring some light into the gloomy, high-end mall beneath the square—a complex of three towers, a two-story office building, and a shopping concourse. ⊠ *Corner of av. Wood and boul. de Maisonneuve, Westmount, Montréal* ☎ *514/932–0211* ⊇ *Free* Ⓜ *Atwater.*

WORD OF MOUTH

"I totally understand when people liken Montréal to Paris. Old Montréal certainly has the charm and quaintness of certain areas of Paris, but it's cheaper and easier to explore Montréal and all it has to offer."

—mitchdesja

2

CÔTE-DES-NEIGES

One of Montréal's most-visited sites—the Oratoire St-Joseph (St. Joseph's Oratory)—sits atop the northern slope of Mont-Royal, dominating the surrounding neighborhood of Côte-des-Neiges. More than 2 million people of all faiths visit the shrine every year. The most devout pilgrims climb the staircase leading to the main door on their knees pausing on each of its 99 steps to pray.

Even without the Oratoire (as well as the Cimetière de Notre-Dame-des-Neiges, another site worth seeing), Côte-des-Neiges is a district worth visiting. It's also an area where the dominant languages are neither English nor French.

It's largely working-class immigrants who live here—Filipino, Latin American, Southeast Asian, West Indian, Arab, Jewish, Chinese, and most recently people from Eastern Europe and Africa. It's also home to a sizable student population, many of whom attend the Université de Montréal, as well as other smaller surrounding colleges and universities.

As a result, if you're looking for inexpensive, authentic world cuisine, there's no better place in Montréal to come to than Côte-des-Neiges. It's literally teeming with ethnic shops and restaurants—Thai, Russian, Korean, Indian, Peruvian, Filipino, and more.

GETTING HERE AND AROUND

Côte-des-Neiges is bordered by avenue Decelles to the north and the Cimetière de Notre-Dame-des-Neiges to the south. It's easy to get here by public transit, either the métro to the Côte-des-Neiges station or the 166 Bus from the Guy-Concordia métro station to chemin Queen Mary. If you take a car—not a bad idea if you plan to visit the Parc du Mont-Royal as well—it's usually easy to get a parking space at the Oratoire St-Joseph (a contribution of $5 per vehicle is requested Monday to Saturday, except for those attending services or coming to the Oratoire to pray).

WHEN TO GO

Côte-des-Neiges bustles during the day, but is a little quieter at night.

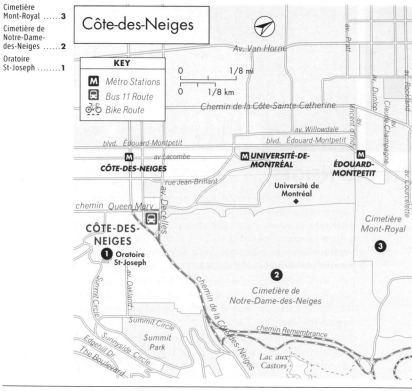

EXPLORING

Cimetière de Notre-Dame-des-Neiges (*Our Lady of the Snows Cemetery*). At 343 acres, Canada's largest cemetery is not much smaller than the neighboring **Parc du Mont-Royal,** and, as long as you just count the living, it's usually a lot less crowded. You don't have to be morbid to wander the graveyard's 55 km (34 miles) of tree-shaded paths and roadways past the tombs of hundreds of prominent artists, poets, intellectuals, politicians, and clerics. Among them is Calixa Lavallée (1842–91), who wrote "O Canada," the country's national anthem. The cemetery offers some guided tours in summer. Phone ahead for details. ✉ *4601 chemin de la Côte-des-Neiges, Côte-des-Neiges, Montréal* ☎ *514/735–1361* ⊕ *www.cimetierenddn.org* ☉ *Daily 8–5* Ⓜ *Université-de-Montréal.*

Cimetière Mont-Royal. If you find yourself humming *Getting to Know You* as you explore Mont-Royal Cemetery's 165 acres, blame it on the graveyard's most famous permanent guest, Anna Leonowens (1834–1915). She was the real-life model for the heroine of the musical *The King and I.* The cemetery—established in 1852 by the Anglican, Presbyterian, Unitarian, and Baptist churches—is laid out like a terraced garden, with footpaths that meander between crab-apple trees and past Japanese lilacs. You can also enter the cemetery through a gate in Parc du Mont-Royal, but it's only open 9–4. ✉ *1297 chemin de la Forêt,*

2

Côte-des-Neiges, Montréal ☎ 514/279–7358 ⊕ www.mountroyalcem. com ⊙ June–Sept., weekdays 8–7, weekends 9–4:30; Oct.–May, week-days 8–5, weekends 9–4:30 Ⓜ Edouard-Montpetit.

Fodor's Choice **Oratoire St-Joseph** (St. Joseph's Oratory). Each year some 2 million peo-
★ ple from all over North America and beyond visit St. Joseph's Oratory.
The most devout Catholics climb the 99 steps to its front door on their
knees. It is the world's largest and most popular shrine dedicated to the
earthly father of Jesus (Canada's patron saint), and it's all the work of
a man named Brother André Besette (1845–1937).

By worldly standards Brother André didn't have much going for him,
but he had a deep devotion to St. Joseph and an iron will. In 1870 he
joined the Holy Cross religious order and was assigned to work as a
doorkeeper at the college the order operated just north of Mont-Royal.
In 1904 he began building a chapel on the mountainside across the road
to honor his favorite saint, and the rest is history. Thanks to reports
of miraculous cures attributed to St. Joseph's intercession, donations
started to pour in, and Brother André was able to start work replacing
his modest shrine with something more substantial. The result, which
wasn't completed until after his death, is one of the most triumphal
pieces of church architecture in North America.

The oratory and its gardens dominate Mont-Royal's northwestern
slope. Its copper dome—one of the largest in the world—can be seen
from miles away. The interior of the main church is equally grand, but
its austerity is almost frigid. The best time to visit is on Sunday for the
11 am solemn mass, when the sanctuary is brightly lighted and the
sweet voices of Les Petits Chanteurs de Mont-Royal—the city's best
boys' choir—fill the nave with music.

The crypt is shabbier than its big brother upstairs but more welcoming.
In a long, narrow room behind the crypt, 10,000 votive candles glitter
before a dozen carved murals extolling the virtues of St. Joseph; the
walls are hung with crutches discarded by those said to have been cured.
Just beyond is the simple tomb of Brother André, who was canonized a
saint in 2010. His preserved heart is displayed in a glass case in one of
several galleries between the crypt and the main church.

High on the mountain, east of the main church, is a garden commemorating the Passion of Christ, with life-size representations of the 14
stations of the cross. On the west side of the church is Brother André's
original chapel, with pressed-tin ceilings and plaster saints that is, in
many ways, more moving than the church that overshadows it. Note:
The oratoire operates a shuttle bus for visitors who aren't up to the steep
climb from the main parking lot to the entrance of the crypt church.
The main church is several stories above that, but escalators and two
elevators ease the ascent. ⊠ 3800 chemin Queen Mary, Côte-des-Neiges,
Montréal ☎ 514/733–8211 ⊕ www.saint-joseph.org ⊠ Free. Parking:
C$5 per vehicle contribution requested (except for those attending ser-
vices or coming to pray) ⊙ Mid-Sept.–mid-May, daily 7 am–8:30 pm;
mid-May–mid-Sept., daily 7 am–9 pm Ⓜ Côte-des-Neiges.

HOCHELAGA-MAISONNEUVE

There's more to see and do in the neighborhood of Hochelaga-Maisonneuve than visit the Stade Olympique, which played host to the 1976 Summer Olympics, and the leaning tower that supports the stadium's roof and dominates the skyline. It's one of the best spots to go if you're craving green space, plus it has one of Montréal's best markets.

It's worth the trip on the Green Line just to see Jardin Botanique (Botanical Garden); the Insectarium, which houses the world's largest collection of bugs; and Parc Maisonneuve, an ideal place for a stroll or a picnic. The rest of the area is largely working-class residential, but there are some good restaurants and little shops along rue Ontario Est.

Until 1918, when it was annexed by Montréal, the east-end district of Maisonneuve was a city unto itself, a booming, prosperous industrial center full of factories making everything from shoes to cheese. The neighborhood was also packed with houses for the almost entirely French-Canadian workers who kept the whole machine humming.

Maisonneuve was also the site of one of Canada's earliest experiments in urban planning. The Dufresne brothers, a pair of prosperous shoe manufacturers, built a series of grand civic buildings along rue Morgan—many of which still stand—including a theater, public baths, and a bustling market, as well as Parc Maisonneuve. All this was supposed to make working-class life more bearable, but World War I put an end to the brothers' plans and Maisonneuve became part of Montréal, twinned with the east-end district of Hochelaga.

GETTING HERE AND AROUND

It's not necessary to drive to the area, as the Pie-IX and Viau métro stops on the Green Line provide easy access to all the sites, including the Insectarium and the Jardin Botanique. For bikers, it's a straight shot across the path on rue Rachel.

TIMING

If traveling with kids, you'll probably want to dedicate more time to exploring the area to see the sites. One of the city's major markets—Marché Maisonneuve—is on the corner of rue Ontario and avenue Bennett, and is well worth a stop.

EXPLORING

TOP ATTRACTIONS

🐞 **Insectarium.** If you're a little squeamish about beetles and roaches, you might want to give the bug-shape building in the middle of the **Espace pour la Vie Jardin Botanique** (Space for Life Botanical Garden) a pass, but kids especially seem to love it. Most of the more than 250,000 insects in the Insectarium's collection are either mounted or behind panes of glass thick enough to minimize the shudder factor—a good thing when you're looking at a tree roach the size of a wrestler's thumb. There is, however, a room full of free-flying butterflies, and in February and May the Insectarium releases thousands of butterflies and moths into the Jardin Botanique's main greenhouse. At varying times during the year the Insectarium brings in chefs to prepare such delicacies as deep-fried bumblebees and chocolate-dipped locusts—protein-rich treats that most adults seem able to resist. ⊠ *4581 rue Sherbrooke Est, Hochelaga-Maisonneuve, Montréal* ☎ *514/872–1400* ⊕ *www. montrealspaceforlife.ca* ⊡ *C$17.55 (includes Jardin Botanique)* ⊙ *Mid-May–Labor Day, daily 9–6; Sept. and Oct., daily 9–9; Nov.–mid-May, Tues.–Sun. 9–5* Ⓜ *Pie-IX or Viau.*

Jardin Botanique (*Botanical Garden*). Creating one of the world's great botanical gardens in a city with a winter as harsh as Montréal's was no mean feat, and the result is that no matter how brutal it gets in January there's one corner of the city where it's always summer. With 181 acres of plantings in summer

and 10 greenhouses open all year, Space for Life Montréal's Jardin Botanique is the second-largest attraction of its kind in the world (after England's Kew Gardens). It grows more than 26,000 species of plants, and among its 30 thematic gardens are a rose garden, an alpine garden, and—a favorite with the kids—a poisonous-plant garden.

You can attend traditional tea ceremonies in the Japanese Garden, which has one of the best bonsai collections in the West, or wander among the native birches and maples of the Jardin des Premières-Nations (First Nations Garden). The Jardin de Chine (Chinese Garden), with its pagoda and waterfall, will transport you back to the Ming Dynasty. Another highlight is the **Insectarium.** ⊠ *4101 rue Sherbrooke Est, Hochelaga-Maisonneuve, Montréal* ☎ *514/872–1400* ⊕ *www.montrealspaceforlife.ca* ✉ *C$17.55 (includes Insectarium)* ☉ *May–Aug., daily 9–6; Sept. and Oct., daily 9–9; Nov.–Apr., Tues.– Sun. 9–5* Ⓜ *Pie-IX.*

Maisonneuve. World War I and the Depression killed early 20th-century plans to turn this industrial center into a model city with broad boulevards, grand public buildings, and fine homes, but a few fragments of that dream have survived the passage of time, just three blocks south of the Olympic site.

The magnificent beaux arts building, site of the old public market, which has a 20-foot-tall bronze statue of a farm woman, stands at the northern end of tree-lined avenue Morgan. Farmers and butchers have moved into the modern building next door that houses the **Marché Maisonneuve**, which has become one of the city's major markets along with Marché Jean-Talon and Marché Atwater. The old market is now a community center and the site of summer shows and concerts.

Monumental staircases and a heroic rooftop sculpture embellish the public baths across the street. The **Théâtre Denise Pelletier,** at the corner of rue Ste-Catherine Est and boulevard Morgan, has a lavish Italianate interior; **Fire Station No. 1,** at 4300 rue Notre-Dame Est, was inspired by Frank Lloyd Wright's Unity Temple in suburban Chicago; and the sumptuously decorated **Église Très-Saint-Nom-de-Jésus** has one of the most powerful organs in North America. The 60-acre **Parc Maisonneuve,** stretching north of the botanical garden, is a lovely place for a stroll. ⊠ *Hochelaga-Maisonneuve, Montréal* Ⓜ *Pie-IX or Viau.*

WORTH NOTING

Biodôme. Not everyone thought it was a great idea to transform an Olympic bicycle-racing stadium into a natural-history exhibit, but the result is one of the city's most popular attractions. Four ecosystems—a

boreal forest, a tropical forest, a polar landscape, and the St. Lawrence River—are under one climate-controlled dome. You follow pathways through each environment, observing indigenous flora and fauna. ■**TIP→** A word of warning: the tropical forest is as hot and humid as the real thing, and the Québec and Arctic exhibits can be frigid. If you want to stay comfortable, dress in layers. ✉ *4777 av. Pierre-de-Coubertin, Hochelaga-Maisonneuve, Montréal* ☎ *514/868–3000* ⊕ *www.biodome. qc.ca* 🎟 *C$16.50* ☉ *Late June–early Sept., daily 9–6; early Sept.–early Mar., Tues.–Sun 9–5, early Mar.–late June, daily 9–5* Ⓜ *Viau.*

Château Dufresne. The adjoining homes of a pair of shoe manufacturers, Oscar and Marius Dufresne, provide a glimpse into the lives of Montréal's Francophone bourgeoisie in the early 20th century. The brothers built their beaux-arts palace in 1916 along the lines of the Petit-Trianon in Paris, and lived in it with their families—Oscar in the eastern half and Marius in the western half.

Worth searching out are the domestic scenes on the walls of the Petit Salon, where Oscar's wife entertained friends. Her brother-in-law relaxed with his friends in a smoking room decked out like a Turkish lounge. During the house's incarnation as a boys' school in the 1950s, the Eudist priests, who ran the place, covered the room's frieze of nymphs and satyrs with a modest curtain that their charges lifted at every opportunity. ⊠ *2929 rue Jeanne-d'Arc, Hochelaga-Maisonneuve, Montréal* ☎ *514/259–9201* ⊕ *www.chateaudufresne.com* ⊠ *C$9* ⊙ *Wed.–Sun. 10–5* Ⓜ *Viau.*

Planetarium Rio Tinto Alcan. In the spring of 2013, Montréal will be blessed with a brand new, ultra-modern planetarium, one of only a handful of planetariums worldwide to have two circular theaters—one for astronomy exhibits and the

> **WORD OF MOUTH**
>
> "The ride up the world's tallest inclined tower was fun, and I spent the time clicking my camera and joining the others saying 'Ohh! Ahh!' At the top is a lookout center giving excellent views of Montréal."
>
> —SandyBlandy

other a high-tech multimedia venue. Built at a cost of C$48 million, this state-of-the-art facility promises a futuristic experience unlike any other. ⊠ *av. Pierre-de-Coubertin, Hochelaga-Maisonneuve, Montréal* ☎ *514/872–4530* ⊕ *www.planetarium.montreal.qc.ca* ⊠ *C$17.75* Ⓜ *Viau.*

Stade Olympique. Montrealers finished paying for their Olympic stadium (dubbed the "Big O") in the spring of 2006—30 years after the games it was built for—but they still call it the Big Owe, and not very affectionately, either. It certainly looks dramatic, squatting like a giant flying saucer in the middle of the east end. But the place is hard to heat, it's falling apart, and the saga of the retractable roof—it worked precisely three times—is a running joke for local comics. Abandoned by the baseball and football teams it was supposed to house, the stadium is now used mostly for trade shows. ⊠ *4141 av. Pierre-de-Coubertin, Hochelaga-Maisonneuve, Montréal* ☎ *514/252–8687* ⊕ *www.parcolympique.qc.ca* ⊠ *Tour of Olympic complex C$9* ⊙ *Daily 11–3:30* Ⓜ *Pie-IX or Viau.*

Tour Olympique. The world's tallest tilting structure—take that, Pisa—is the 890-foot tower that was supposed to hold the Stade Olympique's retractable roof. It looked great on paper, but never worked in practice, and the current roof is a permanent fixture. If you want a great view of the city, however, ride one of the cable cars that slide up the outside of the tower to the observatory at the top. On a clear day you can see up to 80 km (50 miles). ⊠ *4141 av. Pierre-de-Coubertin, Hochelaga-Maisonneuve, Montréal* ☎ *514/252–4141, 877/997–0919* ⊠ *Observation deck C$16; half-hour guided tour of Olympic complex C$9* ⊙ *Mid-June–early Sept., daily 9–7; early Sept.–mid-June, daily 9–5. Closed Jan. 9–Feb. 17* Ⓜ *Pie-IX or Viau.*

THE ISLANDS

The two islands just east of the city in the St. Lawrence River—Île Ste-Hélène, formed by nature, and Île Notre-Dame, created with the stone rubble excavated from the construction of Montréal's métro—are Montréal's indoor-outdoor playground, Parc Jean-Drapeau.

Expo '67—the World's Fair staged to celebrate the centennial of the Canadian federation brought here by the city's mayor, Jean Drapeau—was the biggest party in Montréal's history, and it marked a defining moment in its evolution as a modern metropolis.

The spirit of coming here for excitement and thrills lives on. La Ronde, a major amusement park that has the highest double wooden roller coaster in the world, is on Île Ste-Hélène. On Île Notre-Dame, there's Casino de Montréal, with more than 3,200 slot machines.

For a completely different kind of fun, however, there's much to learn about the Islands' history. At the Stewart Museum at the Old Fort, kids will love watching soldiers in colonial uniforms hold flag-raising ceremonies twice a day, rehearse maneuvers, and even practice drills and fire muskets.

GETTING HERE AND AROUND
Both Île Ste-Hélène and Île Notre-Dame are very accessible. You can drive to them via the Pont de la Concorde or the Pont Jacques-Cartier, take the ferry from the Old Port to Île Ste-Hélène (seasonal), or take the métro from the Berri-UQAM station to Jean-Drapeau.

TIMING
If traveling with kids, there's enough here to keep them occupied for a full day, especially in nice weather. Because the Islands are so easy to get to with the ferry, visiting can be tacked on to time spent in Old Montréal.

EXPLORING

TOP ATTRACTIONS
Biosphère. Nothing captures the exuberance of Expo '67 better than the geodesic dome designed by Buckminster Fuller (1895–1983) as the American Pavilion. It's only a skeleton now—the polymer panels that protected the U.S. exhibits from the elements were burned out in a fire long ago—but it's still an eye-catching sight, like something plucked from a science-fiction film.

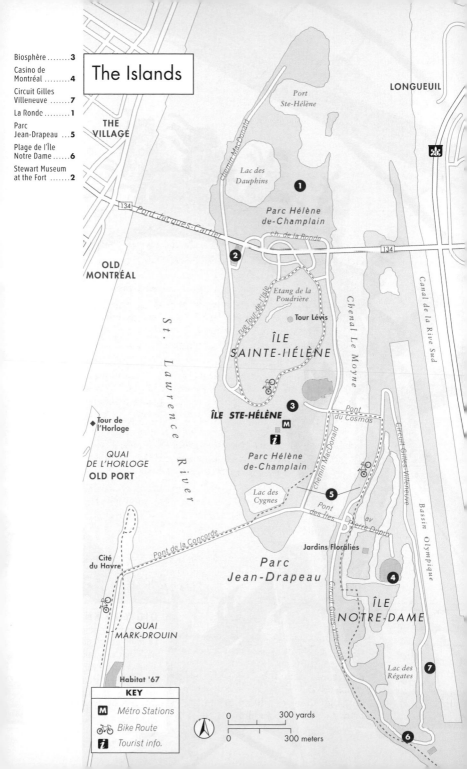

The Islands

LONGUEUIL

*Port
Ste-Hélène*

THE
VILLAGE

134

Pont Jacques-Cartier

*Lac des
Dauphins*

*Parc Hélène
de-Champlain*

ch. de la Ronde

134

OLD
MONTRÉAL

rue Tour-de-l'Isle

*Étang de la
Poudrière*

Tour Lévis

ÎLE
SAINTE-HÉLÈNE

Chenal Le Moyne

Canal de la Rive Sud

Tour de
l'Horloge

ÎLE STE-HÉLÈNE

Pont
du Cosmos

QUAI
DE L'HORLOGE
OLD PORT

*Parc Hélène
de-Champlain*

chemin MacDonald

Circuit Gilles Villeneuve

Bassin Olympique

*Lac des
Cygnes*

Pont
des Îles

av
Pierre-Dupuy

Pont de la Concorde

Jardins Floralies

Cité
du Havre

*Parc
Jean-Drapeau*

ÎLE
NOTRE-DAME

Circuit Gilles Villeneuve

QUAI
MARK-DROUIN

*Lac des
Régates*

Habitat '67

KEY

M *Métro Stations*

Bike Route

Tourist info.

0   300 yards

0   300 meters

2

Science of a nonfictional kind, however, is the special environmental center the federal government has built in the middle of the dome. It focuses on the challenges of preserving the Great Lakes and St. Lawrence River system, but it has lively and interactive exhibits on climate change, sustainable energy, and air pollution. Visitors of all ages—especially kids—can use games and interactive displays arranged around a large model of the waterway to explore how shipping, tourism, water supplies, and hydroelectric power are affected. ⊠ *160 chemin Tour-de-l'Îsle, Île Ste-Hélène, Montréal* ☎ *514/283–5000* ⊕ *www.biosphere. ec.gc.ca* ☐ *C$12* ⊙ *June–Oct., daily 10–6; Nov.–May, Tues.–Sun. 10–5* Ⓜ *Jean-Drapeau.*

Casino de Montréal. You have to be at least 18 to visit Montréal's government-owned casino, but you don't have to be a gambler. You can come for the bilingual cabaret theater or to sip a martini in the Cheval bar or to dine in Nuances, where the prices are almost as spectacular as the views of the city across the river. You can even come just to look at the architecture—the main building was the French pavilion at Expo '67. But if you do want to risk the family fortune, there are more than 3,200 slot machines, a keno lounge, a high-stakes gaming area, and 120 tables for playing blackjack, baccarat, roulette, craps, and various types of poker. ⊠ *1 av. du Casino, Île Notre-Dame, Montréal* ☎ *514/392–2746, 800/665–2274* ⊕ *www.casino-de-montreal.com* Ⓜ *Jean-Drapeau (then Bus 167).*

⟳
Fodor's Choice
★

Parc Jean-Drapeau. Île Ste-Hélène and Île Notre-Dame now constitute a single park named, fittingly enough, for Jean Drapeau (1916–99), the visionary (and spendthrift) mayor who built the métro and brought the city both the 1967 World's Fair and the 1976 Olympics. The park includes a major amusement park, acres of flower gardens, a beach with filtered water, and the Casino de Montréal. There's history, too, at the Old Fort, where soldiers in colonial uniforms display the military methods used in ancient wars. In winter you can skate on the old Olympic rowing basin or slide down iced trails on an inner tube. ⊠ *Île Notre-Dame, Montréal* ☎ *514/872–6120* ⊕ *www.parcjeandrapeau.com* Ⓜ *Jean-Drapeau.*

★
Stewart Museum at the Fort. Housed in the arsenal of Île Ste-Hélène's 1820s Old Fort, the Stewart Museum was completely refurbished in 2011, and now encompasses two floors full of interesting historical artifacts. The permanent collection of original images, displays, maps, and other items, many on display to the public for the first time, documents the history of Montréal, l'Île Ste-Hélène, and the surrounding area, from the early Aboriginals to today. Open year-round, the Stewart Museum is definitely worth a visit for those interested in the history of New France. ⊠ *20 chemin du Tour-de-l'Îsle, Île Ste-Hélène, Montréal* ☎ *514/861–6701* ⊕ *www.stewart-museum.org* ☐ *C$13* ⊙ *Wed.–Sun. 11–5* Ⓜ *Jean-Drapeau, plus 10-min walk.*

WORTH NOTING
Circuit Gilles Villeneuve. In July you can join the glitterati of Europe and America in the Circuit Gilles Villeneuve's grandstand to watch million-dollar Formula 1 cars shriek around the 4.3-km (2.7-mile) track—if

you're lucky enough and rich enough to get a ticket, that is. This is the kind of crowd that uses Perrier water to mop up caviar stains from the refreshment tables. ⊠ *Île Notre-Dame, Montréal* ☎ *514/350–0000* ⊕ *www.circuitgillesvilleneuve.ca* Ⓜ *Jean-Drapeau.*

Ⓒ **La Ronde.** Every year, it seems, La Ronde amusement park adds some new and monstrous way to scare the living daylights (and perhaps your lunch as well) out of you. The most recent addition, is Vol Ultime, an extreme tower ride that will hoist you up a full 148 feet—as high as a 15-story building—where it will then mercilessly spin you around at a speed of 60 km (37 miles) an hour. It began terrifying people in May 2012, joining such other stomach-turning champions as the the Ednor, the Goliath, the Vampire, and the Monstre. For the less daring, there are Ferris wheels, boat rides, and kiddie rides. The popular **International Fireworks Competition** is held here weekends and a couple of weeknights in late June and July. ⊠ *22 chemin Macdonald (eastern end of Île Ste-Hélène), Île Ste-Hélène, Montréal* ☎ *514/397–2000, 800/361–4595* ⊕ *www.laronde.com/larondeen* 🎟 *C$46.99* ⊙ *Late May, weekends 11–7; early June–late June, daily 10–8; late June–late Aug., daily 11–10; Sept., weekends 10–7; Oct., Fri. 5 pm–9 pm, Sat. noon–9, Sun. noon–8. Open later on nights when there are fireworks* Ⓜ *Jean-Drapeau.*

Ⓒ **Plage de l'Île Notre-Dame** (*Île Notre-Dame Beach*). The dress code at the neighboring **Casino de Montréal** might ban camisoles and strapless tops, but here anything seems to go on warm summer days, when the beach is a sea of oiled bodies. You get the distinct impression that swimming is not uppermost on the minds of many of the scantily clad hordes. If you do want to go in, however, the water is filtered and closely monitored for contamination, and there are lifeguards on duty to protect you from other hazards. A shop rents swimming and boating paraphernalia, and there are picnic areas and a restaurant. ⊠ *West side of Île Notre-Dame, Île Notre-Dame, Montréal* ☎ *514/872–4537* 🎟 *C$8* ⊙ *Late June–mid-Aug., daily 10–7; adults only, weekends 7 pm–midnight* Ⓜ *Jean-Drapeau.*

Nightlife

WORD OF MOUTH

"Montreal is a charming city with diverse offerings like museums, parks, festivals and music. It is the city of festivals and one can enjoy these festivals at any time of year."

—daneryland

Updated by
Vanessa Muri

If nightlife in Montréal could be distilled into a cocktail, it would be one part sophisticated New York club scene (with the accompanying pretension), one part Parisian joie-de-vivre (and again, a dash of snobbery), and one part Barcelonan stamina, which keeps the clubs booming until dawn.

Hot spots are peppered throughout the city. There are compact clusters along rue Crescent, boulevard St-Laurent, avenue Mont-Royal, and rue St-Denis. Prominent rue Ste-Catherine plows through town, connecting most of these nighttime niches, and farther east, near Beaudry métro station, it becomes the main drag for the Village, also called Gay Village. For whatever reason, the streets named after saints contain most of the clubs: rue Ste-Catherine, boulevard St-Laurent, rue St-Paul, and rue St-Denis. The Old Port is currently Montréal's hottest neighborhood, with a steady stream of chic venues opening all the time in this cobblestone district.

Montréal's nightlife swings with a robust passion; from the early evening "5 à 7" after-work cocktail circuit, to the slightly later concerts and supperclubs (restaurant-dance club hybrids where people dance on the tables after eating on them), on into the even later dance club scene; all tastes, cultural backgrounds, and legal ages join the melee. Adult clubs abound in this sexually freewheeling city and are often frequented by mixed groups of people seeking a fun night out on the town. Clubbing is, to say the least, huge in Montréal. Some restaurants are even installing discotheques in their basements.

As for what to wear on a Montréal night out: If you have a daring outfit in your closet that you've hesitated to wear—bring it. Montrealers get absolutely decked to go out on the town to bars and clubs, even if the temperature is below freezing. And remember, most club regulars don't even know where they're going until midnight, so don't go out too early.

MONTRÉAL NIGHTLIFE PLANNER

EVENTS INFORMATION

Check out Cult MTL (⊕ *www.cultmontreal.com*), a new webzine born of the old weekly *Mirror* newspaper, updated daily with information on the various goings-on about town. The "Friday Preview" section of the *Gazette* (⊕ *www.montrealgazette.com*), the English-language daily paper, has a thorough list of events at the city's concert halls, clubs, and dance spaces.

3

The following websites provide comprehensive information about Montréal's nightlife scene: ⊕ *www.tourisme-montreal.org,* ⊕ *www.nightlife. ca,* ⊕ *www.montreal-clubs.com, and* ⊕ *www.bestclubsinmontreal.com*.

HOURS

The bars stop serving around 3 am and shut down shortly thereafter (with the exception of sanctioned "after-hour" haunts), and on the weekends expect them to be packed to the gills until closing. The club scene picks up right after the bars close, and then extends until dawn.

LATE-NIGHT TRANSPORTATION

The Montréal métro Line 1 (green) and Line 2 (orange) have their last nighttime departures at 12:35 am weekdays, 1 am Saturday, and 12:30 am Sunday; Line 4 (yellow) runs until 1:00 am weekdays, 1:30 am Saturday, and 1 am Sunday; Line 5 (blue) takes it's last run at 12:15 am daily.

The best way to get around the city after hours is by taxi. Taxis are generally easy to hail on the street, cost roughly C$8 to C$12 to most nightlife spots, and are available if the white or orange light is on. Another option is to use a car service; before you leave you can get recommendations from your hotel concierge for the closest and most reliable company, which will minimize your wait time. Montréal Dorval Limousine Service (⊕ *www.montreallimo.ca*) is one good option.

TICKETS

For tickets to major pop and rock concerts, you can go to the individual box offices or contact **Admission** (☎ *514/790–1245 or 800/361–4595* ⊕ *www.admission.com*), **Ticketpro** (☎ *514/790–1111 or 866/908–9090* ⊕ *www.ticketpro.ca*), or **Evenko** (☎ *514/790–2525 or 877/668–8269* ⊕ *www.evenko.ca*).

NIGHTLIFE REVIEWS

OLD MONTRÉAL (VIEUX-MONTRÉAL)

BARS AND LOUNGES

Philémon Bar. Serving up more than the usual pub fare (oysters, anyone?), grab a glass of one of Philémon's well-priced private import Cavas, Proseccos, or Champagnes to wash it down. This sleek bar is packed with locals Thursday through Saturday—in fact, it's become quite a singles hangout. Don't worry, bouncers keep the ratio of guys to gals at a comfortable level. ⊠ *111 rue St-Paul Ouest, Old Montréal, Montréal* ☎ *514/289–3777* ⊕ *www.philemonbar.com* Ⓜ *Place-d'Armes.*

Montréal
Nightlife

0 — 1/2 mile
0 — 500 meters

rue Jarry

blvd. De l'Acadie

rue Duvocher

rue Duvocher

Parc Jarry

r. St-Denis

av. Henri-Julien

r. Beaubien

BEAUBIEN Ⓜ

Parc Pere-Marquette

av. Van Horne

Ⓜ **OUTREMONT**

av. Lajoie

r. Bernard

ch. de la Côte-Ste-Catherine

r. St-Viateur

Hartland

av. Stuart

av. McEachran

r. St-Hubert

r. de Bellechasse

r. des Carriéres

r. de Lorimier

av. Parthenais

r. Parthenais

r. Fullum

r. Fullum

OUTREMONT
Tame thirty-somethings relax over cocktails

ROSEMONT Ⓜ

av. Fairmount

av. de Gaspé

av. du Parc

av. Papineau

av. de Bordeax

Ⓜ **ÉDOUARD-MONTPETIT**

Cimetière Mont-Royal

av. Bloomfield

av. du Parc

av. Clark

av. de l'Esplanade

av. Durocher

Parc Sir-Wilfred Laurier

av. Laurier

blvd. St-Joseph

r. Gifford

r. de Lanaudiere

r. Garnier

r. de Brébeuf

av. de Bordeax

av. Christophe-Colomb

MILE END
Hipster spots with decent prices

Ⓜ **LAURIER**

MONT-ROYAL Ⓜ

r. Marie-Anne

r. Rachel

av. de Lorimier

r. de Champlain

r. de Champlain

Chemin Remembrance

Voie C. Houde

av. Duluth

r. St-Urbain

blvd. St-Laurent

av. des Pins

r. Roy

LE PLATEAU-MONT-ROYAL
Rock & Roll and house dancing clubs abound

av. du Mont-Royal

r. de Mentana

r. du Parc-Lafontaine

Parc Lafontaine

r. Sherbrooke

r. de Bordeax

av. de Papineau

r. Ontario

Parc du Mont-Royal

av. Cedar

av. Docteur-Penfield

r. Sherbrooke

blvd. de Maisonneuve

Ⓜ **GUY-CONCORDIA**

McTavish

r. Peel

r. University

r. de Bleury

r. Prince-Arthur

r. Milton

av. de l'Esplanade

r. Jeanne-Mance

r. Ste-famille

SHERBROOKE Ⓜ

r. Ontario

LATIN QUARTER
Students plus resto-lounges for young professionals

r. de la Visitation

r. Panet

r. Plessis

PAPINEAU Ⓜ

blvd. de Maisonneuve

PLACE-DES-ARTS Ⓜ

ST-LAURENT Ⓜ

PEEL Ⓜ

McGILL Ⓜ

DOWNTOWN
Densely packed with bars, clubs, and theaters

r. Ste-Catherine

BERRI-UQAM Ⓜ

r. St-Denis

r. St-Hubert

BEAUDRY Ⓜ

THE VILLAGE
Gay bars and partying till dawn

blvd. René-Lévesque

r. de la Gauchetière

autoroute Ville-Marie

Ⓜ **GEORGES-VANIER**

rue Guy

des Seigneurs

LUCIEN-L'ALLIER Ⓜ

BONAVENTURE

av. Viger

PL.-D'ARMES Ⓜ

SQ.-VICTORIA Ⓜ

CHAMP-DE-MARS Ⓜ

r. Notre-Dame

Pont Jacques-Cartier

r. Notre-Dame

r. St. Paul

Lachine Canal

r. St-Patrick

r. Augustin-Cantin

r. Grand Trunk

r. Charon

OLD PORT
Thriving 5 à 7 scene

av. Pierre-Dupuy

Pont de la Concorde

Île Ste-Hélène

JEAN-DRAPEAU Ⓜ

Parc Jean-Drapeau

Parc Leber

av. Pierre-Dupuy

St. Lawrence River

Île Notre-Dame

Parc Floral

autoroute Bonaventure

Pont Victoria

CASINO DE MONTRÉAL
Gaming and live musical shows around the clock

MONTRÉAL NIGHTLIFE BEST BETS

Best for music: Club Soda

Best kitsch: A Go Go Lounge

Best water view: Terrasse sur l'Auberge

Best martini: Jello Martini Lounge

Best comfort food: Baldwin Barmacie

Best off-the-beaten path: Le Sainte-Elisabeth

Best for a date: BU

Best patio: Reservoir

Best for expense accounts: Suite 701

Best wine bar: Pullman

Suite 701. Inside the chic Place-d'Armes Hotel, this is *the* place for drinks in Old Montréal—try the Moon Light martini, plump with fresh raspberries. If your 5 à 7 draws out, linger over a plate of the crispy gnocchi. Upstairs, a rooftop patio (Terrasse Place d'Armes) overlooks Notre-Dame Cathedral and serves finger food with a whole other selection of cocktails. ⊠ *701 Côte de la Place-d'Armes, Old Montréal, Montréal* ☎ *514/904–1201* ⊕ *www.suite701.com* Ⓜ *Place-d'Armes.*

★ **Terrasse sur l'Auberge.** For an unbeatable view of the Old Port and numerous Montréal landmarks, head to this unpretentious rooftop patio atop the Auberge du Vieux-Port Hotel. Open from the end of May through mid-October (5–11 weekdays, 2–11 on weekends), it's a great place to watch the International Fireworks Festival—if you're early enough to snag a table—and enjoy cocktails and a light tapas menu. The cod croquettes are a must-try, and pair nicely with the clear sangria (made with sparkling wine). ⊠ *97 rue de la Commune Est, Old Montréal, Montréal* ☎ *514/876–0081* ⊕ *www.terrassesurlauberge.com* Ⓜ *Place-d'Armes or Champs-de-Mars.*

DOWNTOWN

BARS AND LOUNGES

Burgundy Lion. This British pub offers grub that's a notch above the typical fare. Scotch eggs and the ploughman's lunch are paired with the English take on Québec's beloved poutine (though it's the fish & chips that really shine). Be sure to wash it down with a pint of the Burgundy Lion Ale, or any other of their myriad draft beers. It's very loud on weekends. ⊠ *2496 rue Notre-Dame Ouest, Downtown, Montréal* ☎ *514/934–0888* ⊕ *www.burgundylion.com* Ⓜ *Lionel-Groulx.*

Dominion Square Tavern. This gourmet pub feels like you've walked into a Hemingway novel, with its comfortable atmosphere, interesting cuisine, and prices that will leave you with some cash to continue the party elsewhere. From the post-work crowd to the pre-hockey game set (Centre Bell is nearby), to hipsters seeking a classic Scotch, the bar attracts characters of every stripe. ⊠ *1243 rue Metcalfe, Downtown, Montréal* ☎ *514/561–5056* ⊕ *www.tavernedominion.com.*

When the sun goes down in Montréal, the city's energy gets kicked up a notch, especially in the Old City and the Old Port.

Hurley's Irish Pub. For years this pub has been serving up a bounty of brews (19 different beers), with a healthy dose of Irish atmosphere on the side. Despite it's cavernous size, the arrangement of seating areas, flanked by bars, makes it feel cozy, and there's a stage for live entertainment. Incredibly, it still fills up quickly, so unless you don't mind standing while you sip your Guinness, arrive in time to snag a seat. ⊠ *1225 rue Crescent, Downtown, Montréal* ☎ *514/861–4111* ⊕ *www. hurleysirishpub.com* Ⓜ *Guy-Concordia.*

Le Sainte-Elisabeth. Situated in the *Quartier des Spectacles*, this European pub retains one of the city's most beautiful backyard terraces. The service is friendly, and there's a good selection of domestic and imported beers, as well as whiskey and Cognac. This is a great place to enjoy the fall color. ⊠ *1412 rue Ste-Elisabeth, Downtown, Montréal* ☎ *514/286–4302* ⊕ *www.ste-elisabeth.com* Ⓜ *Berri.*

Stogie's Lounge. If the surprisingly swish interior and views of rue Crescent aren't a big enough draw, then check out the conspicuous glass humidor housing a seemingly infinite supply of imported cigars. Thanks to the grandfather clause in Québec's tough no-smoking law, you can still puff a Cuban on-site. ⊠ *2015 rue Crescent, Downtown, Montréal* ☎ *514/848–0069* ⊕ *www.stogiescigars.com* Ⓜ *Guy-Concordia.*

DANCE CLUBS

Altitude 737. Go for the view, stay for the sunset. Summer is the time to visit this lounge, with the rooftop terrasse as the huge selling point. Take in the Montréal skyline from 37 floors up while sipping on a somewhat pricey cocktail (try the cosmopolitan) during the 5 à 7. On weekends it becomes a dance club frequented by a young professional crowd.

Dress code is in effect. ✉ *1 place Ville-Marie, Suite 4340, Downtown, Montréal* ☏ *514/397–0737* ⊕ *www.altitude737.com* ☾ *Closed Sun. and Mon.* Ⓜ *Bonaventure or McGill.*

Club Electric Avenue. The DJs here are unapologetically nostalgic for the 1980s and the clientele bops amid pulsing postmodern cubes. There's an excellent sound system and interior design. It's open Thursday to Saturday from 10 pm until last call. ✉ *1469 rue Crescent, Downtown, Montréal* ☏ *514/285–8885* ⊕ *www.clubsmontreal.com* Ⓜ *Guy-Concordia.*

Fodor'sChoice ★ **Pullman.** At this sophisticated yet relaxed wine bar, let yourself be guided by the expertise of the sommeliers. The tapas-style cuisine is top notch, and the green beans with truffle oil and roasted almonds are not to be missed. During cooler months things get going at 5 pm, but in summer don't arrive until the sun starts to set. ✉ *3424 ave. du Parc, Downtown, Montréal* ☏ *514/288–7779* ⊕ *www.pullman-mtl.com* Ⓜ *Place-des-Arts.*

Salsathèque. Though neon lights and disco balls abound, this flashy club is all about the Latin lover—dance lover, that is. Merengue, bachata, and salsa (of course) are the specialties, but themed evenings keep things interesting with R&B, Reggae, and Top 40 hits. Check the website to learn the week's schedule, and sign up for the guest list while you're at it; earn free entrance for yourself and your crew. ✉ *1220 rue Peel, Downtown, Montréal* ☏ *514/875–0016* ⊕ *www.clubsalsatheque.com* ☾ *Closed Mon. and Tues.* Ⓜ *Peel.*

LIVE MUSIC

Club Soda. The granddaddy of the city's rock clubs has evolved into one of the dominant venues for jazz, reggae, techno, and R&B. Club Soda is a tall, narrow concert hall with high-tech design and 500 seats—all of them with great sight lines. ✉ *1225 blvd. St-Laurent, Downtown, Montréal* ☏ *514/286–1010* ⊕ *www.clubsoda.ca* Ⓜ *St-Laurent.*

House of Jazz. The food is good but the music is outstanding. For more than 30 years, this institution has been plying the city with the best in jazz, with a little blues and soul thrown in for good measure. Mirrored walls and flashy interior design (read: over the top) add to the experience. Dress up and be prepared to pay a cover charge. ✉ *2060 rue Aylmer, Downtown, Montréal* ☏ *514/842–8656* ⊕ *www.houseofjazz. ca* Ⓜ *McGill or Place-des-Arts.*

McKibbin's Irish Pub. This beautiful old sandstone mansion includes three floors of food, drink, and good Irish *craic*, a hard-to-define Gaelic term that in this context means having fun with amiable companions—not hard to do with more than 20 different stouts, lagers, and ales on tap. There's live entertainment nearly every night of the week, so head to the basement if you're looking for a bit of quiet (or a good chin-wag). The house fries are excellent for noshing, but beware of the Rim Reaper— chicken wings made with the world's hottest pepper. ✉ *1426 rue Bishop, Downtown, Montréal* ☏ *514/288–1580* ⊕ *www.mckibbinsirishpub. com* Ⓜ *Guy-Concordia.*

Fodor'sChoice ★ **Upstairs Jazz Bar & Grill.** Local and imported jazz musicians headline here seven nights a week, and McGill university musicians frequently take over the intimate space for jam sessions. Wonderful, inexpensive

cuisine rounds out the club's appeal. Cover charges start at $5 and range from $10 to $25 for name performers. It's sometimes free after 11 pm. ✉ *1254 rue Mackay, Downtown, Montréal* ☎ *514/931–6808* ⊕ *www. upstairsjazz.com* Ⓜ *Guy-Concordia.*

SUPPERCLUBS

Newtown. Once owned by Grand Prix driver Jacques Villenueve (Newtown is his name in English), this restaurant, lounge, and nightclub is still trendy with the local folk. The lounge is *the* best spot on Crescent for martinis and people-watching—call to reserve a table on the street. But it's the lesser known rooftop terrasse that really shines on a hot summer day. ✉ *1476 rue Crescent, Downtown, Montréal* ☎ *514/284–6555* ⊕ *www.lenewtown.com* Ⓜ *Guy-Concordia.*

Rosalie. Posh, pricey, and a wee bit pretentious, this downtown supper club is usually bustling with beautiful people thanks to its central location, large outdoor terrace, and pulsating music. The pizza, cooked in a wood-fired oven, is alone worth a visit (the best in the city), but service can be slow, so plan your evening accordingly. ✉ *1232 rue de la Montagne, Downtown, Montréal* ☎ *514/392–1970* ⊕ *www. rosalierestaurant.com* Ⓜ *Guy-Concordia or Peel.*

Six Resto Lounge. With a prime view of the Quartier des Spectacles, Montréal's performing arts district, this huge terrace overlooking Place des Arts is the perfect place for pre-show drinks—try the 6 Hyattini, made with vodka, raspberry purée, and white cranberry juice. In cooler weather relax in the purple-and-slate-grey lounge, where the bar takes center stage. Check the website for special events. ✉ *Hyatt Regency Hotel, 1255 rue Jeanne-Mance, Downtown, Montréal* ☎ *514/841–2038* ⊕ *www.sixrestolounge.com* Ⓜ *Place des Arts.*

★ **Time Supper Club.** Perfect for partying with friends (or making new ones), this institution is known for its bottle service, but don't miss the marvelous martinis. The bartenders mix one of the city's best cosmopolitans. Hot DJs and great acoustics get the party started around 9:30 pm. On Saturday the place plays host to an older crowd. ✉ *997 St-Jacques ouest, Downtown, Montréal* ☎ *514/392–9292* ⊕ *www.timesupperclub. com* ⊗ *Open Thurs., Fri., and Sat.* Ⓜ *Bonaventure.*

THE LATIN QUARTER AND THE VILLAGE

BARS AND LOUNGES

Jello Martini Lounge. If you're looking for a post-dinner hot spot, Jello Martini Lounge offers the perfect mix of excellent live music, affordable alcohol, and nostalgic '70s vibe. The martinis pack a deceptive punch, as does the "Power Pat," a delicious shot created by über-friendly manager Patricia. ✉ *151 rue Ontario Est, Latin Quarter, Montréal* ☎ *514/285–2009* ⊕ *www.jellomartinilounge.com* Ⓜ *Saint-Laurent.*

GAY AND LESBIAN NIGHTLIFE

★ **Cabaret Mado.** Madame Simone leads the raucous team of female impersonators that performs nightly. Patrons are encouraged to get involved in the weekly karaoke and improv nights, but every night is filled with amazing costumes and energizing music. ✉ *1115 rue Ste-Catherine Est, Village, Montréal* ☎ *514/525–7566* ⊕ *www.mado.qc.ca* Ⓜ *Beaudry.*

Fodor'sChoice   **Club Unity.** Unity is actually the club's third incarnation on this spot (note
★   the flamelike lettering in the signage paying homage to Unity 2, which was tragically incinerated). Small, semiprivate lounges are scattered throughout the two-story complex, and the beautiful rooftop terrace is one of the finest in the Village. ✉ *1171 rue Ste-Catherine Est, Village, Montréal* ☎ *514/523–2777* ⊕ *www.clubunitymontreal.com* Ⓜ *Beaudry.*

Fodor'sChoice   **Le Drugstore.** This mammoth warehouse, featuring numerous dance
★   floors, lounges, and billiards rooms, is a mainstay of the city's lesbian scene and a veritable treasure trove of random urban artifacts like vintage subway signs and stoplights. The factory-like complex, part of the Hotel Bourbon, teems with gays of all types and has a revolving menu of karaoke, drag shows, and live bands. ✉ *1366 rue Ste-Catherine Est, Village, Montréal* ☎ *514/524–1960* ⊕ *www.le-drugstore.com* Ⓜ *Beaudry.*

Sky. This is one of the most popular destinations for gay twentysomethings, especially the dance floor on the second level. The pièce de résistance is the beachlike roof deck with city views and a hot tub. Other features include a street-level bar and a small dance floor on the third story. ✉ *1474 rue Ste-Catherine Est, Village, Montréal* ☎ *514/529–6969* ⊕ *www.complexesky.com* Ⓜ *Beaudry.*

THE PLATEAU AND MILE END

BARS AND LOUNGES

A Go Go Lounge. Firmly entrenched in the '60s disco vibe in its interior design, this intimate lounge and nightclub spans the decades when it comes to music. Go early to score one of the kitschy hand chairs, then order a martini off the vinyl menu—the Mr. Freeze is a classic. ✉ *3682 boul. St-Laurent, Plateau Mont-Royal, Montréal* ☎ *514/286–0882* Ⓜ *Sherbrooke.*

★   **Baldwin Barmacie.** Co-owner Alexandre Baldwin named the bar after his beloved grandmother and the tiny pharmacy where she worked (look for her portrait on the creamy white wall). This upscale yet unpretentious bar serves up drinks in old-fashioned syrup bottles and milk jugs. Relax in a refurbished scotch barrel chair and sip on a refreshing bourbon punch. ✉ *115 ave. Laurier Ouest, Mile End, Montréal* ☎ *514/276–4282* ⊕ *www.baldwinbarmacie.com* Ⓜ *Laurier.*

Bar Waverly. Named for the street that epitomizes the Mile End, this friendly neighborhood bar has a warm staff, lively ambience, and a great selection of Scotch. Owners Richard Holder and Olivier Farley have been in the business for years, and it shows. Nightly DJs provide an edgier vibe, while huge floor-to-ceiling windows make it the perfect corner for people-watching. ✉ *5550 boulevard St-Laurent, Mile-End, Montréal* ☎ *514/903–1121* ⊕ *www.barwaverly.com* Ⓜ *Laurier.*

Big in Japan Bar. Keep your eyes peeled for the red door: there's no sign above this inconspicuous speakeasy. Once past the faux suede curtains, the contemporary design and intricate seating plan will win you over—as will the sake and whiskey selection. The miso edamame hummus

3

with fresh veggies is delicious, and pairs nicely with sake (both filtered and unfiltered). Lines form on weekends, but weeknights aren't too bad. ⊠ *4175 blvd. St-Laurent, Plateau Mont-Royal, Montréal* ☎ *438/380–5658* Ⓜ *Sherbrooke or St-Laurent.*

Bily Kun. A hipster fave within the Plateau, Bily Kun serves up a mix of DJ sets and live jazz beats amid darkwood paneling and taxidermic emus. The menu includes fabulous sausage platters and the now-legal absinthe. ⊠ *354 av. du Mont-Royal Est, Plateau Mont-Royal, Montréal* ☎ *514/845–5392* ⊕ *www.bilykun.com* Ⓜ *Mont-Royal.*

Cabaret Playhouse. This former strip club is now a popular music venue with no cover charge, giving Montrealers a chance to discover new bands without breaking the bank. The "Faggity Ass Fridays" are very popular with the gay community. ⊠ *5656 ave. du Parc, Mile End, Montréal* ☎ *514/276–0594* Ⓜ *Rosemont or Laurier.*

Casa del Popolo. One of the city's treasured venues for indie rock, jazz, reggae, blues, folk, and hip-hop, this neighborhood bar is ideal for discovering up-and-coming local acts or forgotten international giants still touring. While you enjoy the music, take a look at the original art and sample some of the tasty vegetarian food. ⊠ *4873 blvd. St-Laurent, Plateau Mont-Royal, Montréal* ☎ *514/284–3804* ⊕ *www.casadelpopolo. com* Ⓜ *Mont-Royal.*

La Buvette chez Simone. Arrive early (it opens at 4 pm) at this easygoing wine bar—it's always busy and they don't take reservations. Lots of wines are available by the glass, in 2- and 4-ounce pours, with a heavy accent on French varietals. Dress is casual, though the after-work crowd ups the glam factor. Lively but not obnoxious, it's a great place to catch up with friends. ⊠ *4869 av. du Parc, MileEnd, Montréal* ☎ *514/750–6577* ⊕ *www.buvettechezsimone.com* Ⓜ *Laurier or Mont-Royal.*

Fodor's Choice ★ **Le Lab.** Fabien Maillard is Montréal's mixologist extraordinaire, and the name of his unpretentious bar is entirely apt. Creating cocktails is his passion, shared by the friendly, skilled staff, and with potent potions—including a C$28 Zombie loaded with liquor—inspired by everything from old, classic recipes to the fruits of the season (the C$13 Threesome with fresh raspberry, blackberry, and strawberry purées, for example), there's something for every palate. The entire menu changes twice a year and specials change monthly. Call to reserve on weekends; its packed despite being off the beaten track. ⊠ *1351 rue Rachel Est, Plateau Mont-Royal, Montréal* ☎ *514/544–1333* ⊕ *www.lab.mixoart. com* ⊙ *Closed Sun.* Ⓜ *Papineau.*

★ **Reservoir.** It's all about the beer at this friendly restaurant and bar, and it's brewed right on the premises. With everything from India pale ales to German-inspired wheat beers, they've got you covered. Packed almost every night of the week, the upstairs patio is the ideal spot for watching locals stroll along the cobblestone avenue. ⊠ *9 ave. Duluth Est, Plateau Mont-Royal, Montréal* ☎ *514/849–7779* ⊕ *www.brasseriereservoir.ca* Ⓜ *Sherbrooke.*

Royal Phoenix. The only gay bar outside of the Village, this hotspot serves the ever-growing hipster crowd, but is also a friendly neighborhood destination. Whether chowing down on the Poutine Royale or dancing to Fat Boy Slim, you'll feel right at home. Try the basil mojito. ⊠ *5788 blvd. St-Laurent, Mile End, Montréal* ☎ *514/658–1622* ⊕ *www.royalphoenixbar.com* Ⓜ *Rosemont.*

DANCE CLUBS

Cactus. Thursday through Saturday, the double-decker dance floor of this three-level restaurant and club is packed with patrons enjoying the rigorously authentic Latin music. Mexican food is served daily, and the terrace is friendly. ⊠ *4461 rue St-Denis, Plateau Mont-Royal, Montréal* ☎ *514/849–0349* ⊕ *www.lecactus.ca* Ⓜ *Mont-Royal.*

Tokyo Bar. One of Montréal's most popular discotheques, Tokyo Bar is located in the heart of the Plateau. The DJs spin house, hip-hop, or disco, depending on the night. For a breather, head up to the heated rooftop terrace, open rain or shine. ⊠ *3709 blvd. St-Laurent, Plateau Mont-Royal, Montréal* ☎ *514/842–6838* ⊕ *www.tokyobar.com* Ⓜ *St-Laurent.*

LIVE MUSIC

Divan Orange. Grab a seat on the "orange sofa" and catch emerging musical talent (both Francophone and Anglophone) at this popular Plateau bar, from Tuesday through Sunday. Credit cards aren't accepted. ⊠ *4234 blvd. St-Laurent, Plateau Mont-Royal, Montréal* ☎ *514/840–9090* ⊕ *www.divanorange.org* Ⓜ *Mont-Royal.*

SUPPER CLUBS

Buonanotte. In business for more than two decades, this restaurant, lounge, and weekend supper club continues to pull out all the stops. There's top-notch Italian cuisine, a comprehensive wine list, well-known DJs, and even a concierge. Celebrities are known to drop by when in town. ⊠ *3518 blvd. St-Laurent, Plateau Mont-Royal, Montréal* ☎ *514/848–0644* ⊕ *www.buonanotte.com* Ⓜ *St-Laurent.*

Koko. With one of the largest covered terrasses in downtown, this restaurant and bar at the Opus Hotel dominates the 5-à-7 lounge scene. On Friday and Saturday nights the supper club vibe takes over as people arrive for a late nibble and tableside dancing. ⊠ *8 Sherbrooke St. Ouest, Plateau Mont-Royal, Montréal* ☎ *514/657–5656* ⊕ *www.kokomontreal.com* Ⓜ *Saint-Laurent.*

THE ISLANDS

CASINOS

Casino de Montréal. One of the world's largest gaming rooms, the casino has more than 3,000 slot machines and 120 tables for baccarat, craps, blackjack, and roulette. Winners may want to spend some of their gains at Nuances or one of the casino's three other restaurants. The Cabaret de Casino also stages some great musical revues. Located on Île Notre-Dame, it's always open and easily accessible by car, bicycle, or bus. ⊠ *1 ave. du Casino, Île Notre-Dame, Montréal* ☎ *514/392–2746, 800/665–2274* ⊕ *www.casinosduquebec.com/montreal* Ⓜ *Jean-Drapeau.*

The Performing Arts

WORD OF MOUTH

"One of the joys of Montreal is the unexpected—a festival in a park, street entertainers, a fun outdoor cafe, etc."

—zootsi

Updated by
Vanessa Muri There's something uniquely Québecois about the kind of entertainment referred to as a *spectacle*. It's more than just a performance, usually involving some kind of multimedia projection, light show, and, if outdoors, fireworks. It's no wonder, then, that the ultimate *spectacle*, Cirque du Soleil, was founded in Montréal in the '80s. And it's also hardly surprising that North America's largest French-speaking metropolis should be the continent's capital of French theater.

Montréal is the home of nearly a dozen professional companies and several important theater schools. But there's also a lively English-language theater scene and one of the few Yiddish theaters in North America.

In 2012, the city completed a new theater district downtown called (again, not surprisingly) the Quartier des Spectacles, a 70-acre park with stages for outdoor performances and nearly 80 venues for dance, music, theater, and art.

For a city its size, Montréal offers a remarkable number of opportunities for fans of classical music to get their fill, from operas and symphonies to string quartets.

As for dance, there are several modern dance companies of note, including Montréal Danse, and Québec's premier ballet company, Les Grands Ballets Canadiens.

MONTRÉAL PERFORMING ARTS PLANNER

DRESS CODE

People tend to get a bit more dressed up for the symphony, the opera, and even theater performances in Montréal, perhaps more so than in several large U.S. cities. Men will wear sleek black pants, a button-down, and even a tie. Some women wear dark jeans, but it's not uncommon to see ladies decked out in skirts and dresses with strappy shoes (even in the dead of winter) and carrying clutches.

EVENTS INFORMATION

The bilingual *Nightlife* (⊕ *www. nightlife.ca*) and French-language *Le Voir* (⊕ *www.voir.ca*) list events and reviews, and are free and widely distributed.

Check out the *Gazette*'s "Friday Preview" section (⊕ *www. montrealgazette.com*) for events listings in English.

TICKETS

Tickets for most performances are available at the box offices of the various venues.

Ticketmaster. Tickets for theatrical and musical performances, plus a host of other cultural events, can be purchased online or by phone through Ticketmaster. ☎ *514/790– 1111, 855/985–5000* ⊕ *www. ticketmaster.ca.*

BEST FREE PERFORMANCES

Several of the outdoor concerts at the **Montréal International Jazz Festival** in July are free, as are summertime performances at the **Théâtre de Verdure** inside Lafontaine Park.

Two of the greatest places to catch free classical music indoors are at **Montréal Christ Church Cathedral,** where organ recitals are given throughout the year, and at the **Basilique Notre-Dame de Montréal,** where there are year-round concerts by chamber and choral groups (regular church entry fee required).

4

La Vitrine Culturelle. In its new location next to the Quartier des Spectacles, la Vitrine Culturelle (literally: Cultural Window) is the perfect place to get information and buy tickets for just about every type of show in town. Great last-minute deals can often be procured. ⊠ *2 rue Ste-Catherine Est, Downtown* ☎ *514/285–4545, 866/924–5538* ⊕ *www.lavitrine.com* Ⓜ *St-Laurent.*

MONTRÉAL PERFORMING ARTS REVIEWS

CIRCUS

Forget Barnum and Bailey: Montréal has reinvented the ancient art of circus for the 21st century. The revolution began in the 1980s when two street performers, Guy Laliberté and Daniel Gauthier, founded the now world-famous Cirque du Soleil. But it didn't stop there. The city is also home to a huge complex, out beyond Mont-Royal in the St-Michel district, housing Canada's National Circus School, En Piste (Circus Arts National Network), and Cirque du Soleil's head office. The school attracts budding acrobats and clowns from all over the world, as well as several other smaller schools, and puts on several performances throughout the year at the complex's performance venue, TOHU Cité des Arts du Cirque; check Web for details (⊕ www.tohu.ca).

Fodor's Choice **Cirque du Soleil.** This amazing circus is one of Montréal's great success
★ stories. The company—founded in 1984 by a pair of street performers—has revolutionized the ancient art of circus.

Its shows, now an international phenomenon, use no lions, tigers, or animals of any kind. Instead, colorful acrobatics flirt with the absurd

Cirque du Soleil is Montréal's hometown circus, founded here in 1984. Today there are several troupes across several countries that perform hundreds of shows per year.

through the use of music, humor, dance, and glorious (and often risqué) costumes.

The Cirque has four resident companies in Las Vegas, one in Orlando, one in Los Angeles, and even one in Macau, China—but none in Montréal. However, every couple of years one of its international touring companies returns to where it all began, the Old Port, and sets up the familiar blue-and-yellow tent for a summer of sold-out shows. ✉ *Montréal* ☎ *514/790–1245, 800/361–4595* ⊕ *www.cirquedusoleil.com.*

Cirque Éloize. This award-winning troupe has been touring the globe since 1993, and with 4,000 performances under its belt, shows no signs of slowing down. Constantly evolving, Cirque Éloize uses artistic mediums like video and music to bring the circus arts to the masses. ✉ *Montréal* ☎ *514/596–3838* ⊕ *www.cirque-eloize.com.*

Les 7 doigts de la main. Literally translated as "the seven fingers of the hand," the name is a play on a French expression about working collectively toward a common goal, and these seven fingers—the seven founding partners of the circus—have done just that, building up a world-renowned circus troupe over the past decade or so. Combining acrobatics, theater, and dance, they've performed at special events across the globe, from The Royal Variety Performance for Queen Elizabeth II to the Olympics in Turin and Vancouver. They even made an appearance on "America's Got Talent." ✉ *Montréal* ☎ *514/521–4477* ⊕ *www.7doigts.com.*

COMEDY

The Montréal Just For Laughs comedy festival, which takes place every July, has been the largest such festival in the world since its inception back in 1983.

But Montrealers don't have to wait until summer to get their comedy fix, as there are several downtown clubs catering exclusively to all things funny.

Comedy Nest. For decades, the Comedy Nest has been showering Montrealers with humor from some of the biggest names out there: Jim Carrey, Tim Allen, and Russell Peters included. For a mere C$5, Open Mic Wednesdays are always good for a laugh. Get there early to secure a decent spot near the stage (or perhaps away from it) and chow down on some Buffalo Bills chicken wings. ⊠ *Pepsi Forum, 2313 rue Ste-Catherine Ouest, 3rd fl., Downtown* ☎ *514/932–6378* ⊕ *www. thecomedynest.com* Ⓜ *Atwater.*

Comedyworks. Comedyworks hosts popular shows in a room on the second floor of a local watering hole, Jimbo's Pub. The program books both amateur and established comics and has a reputation for offering fairly risqué fare on occasion. ⊠ *1238 rue Bishop, 2nd fl., Downtown* ☎ *514/398–9661* ⊕ *www.comedyworksmontreal.com* Ⓜ *Guy-Concordia.*

Montreal Improv. The heart of the city's improv comedy scene offers shows in both English and French. Their Friday night Smackdowns, where the audience determines the winner, are definitely good for a laugh and usually sell out quickly. ⊠ *3713 boul St-Laurent, #202, Downtown* ☎ *514/507–3535* ⊕ *www.montrealimprov.com* Ⓜ *Sherbrooke.*

CLASSICAL MUSIC

Two symphony orchestras, an opera company of some renown, one of the best chamber orchestras in Canada, and several first-rate choirs make Montréal an ideal destination for music lovers. The music faculties of both McGill University and the Université de Montréal have international reputations and their campuses' concert halls feature performances by the schools' best talents throughout the academic year. The city's main performance halls are at Place des Arts.

★ **I Musici de Montréal Chamber Orchestra.** Arguably the best chamber orchestra in Canada, I Musici, under the direction of Jean-Marie Zeitouni, performs at several venues including Salle Bourgie at the Musée des Beaux-Arts and in Place des Arts' Nouvelle Salle, but its music is best suited to the wood-panelled **Tudor Hall** atop the Ogilvy department store where, about a dozen times a year (check the orchestra's website for schedule), you can enjoy a coffee or aperitif while you listen to a late-morning or early-evening concert. ⊠ *Montréal* ☎ *514/982–6038 tickets* ⊕ *www.imusici.com.*

Opéra de Montréal. Thanks to the expansion of Place des Arts, the renowned Opéra de Montréal can now maintain permanent exhibits in Salle Wilfred Laurier, allowing for a varied schedule and earlier start times for its performances. The "préOpéra" program gives attendees a look at the history, music, and artists in French (with a

Montréal is the province's hub for the arts, with dozens of local theaters and dance troupes, as well as its own opera and top-notch symphony orchestra, the Orchestre Symphonique de Montréal.

summary in English) 75 minutes before each show. ✉ *260 De Maisonneuve Boulevard 0 Montréal* ☎ *514/985–2222, 877/385–2222* ⊕ *www.operademontreal.com* Ⓜ *Place des Arts.*

Orchestre Métropolitain du Grand Montréal. The Met may lie in the shadow of the Orchestre Symphonique de Montréal, but its famous, talented young conductor Yannick Nézet-Séguin continues to draw the spotlight. He's in high demand, and conducts for other opera houses around the world, including the prestigious Philadelphia Orchestra. His charismatic approach has brought in the crowds since 2000 and produced highly acclaimed performances. Most shows take place at Place des Arts or Maison Symphonique de Montréal. ✉ *486 rue Ste-Catherine Ouest, Downtown* ☎ *514/598–0870* ⊕ *www.orchestremetropolitain.com* Ⓜ *Places-des-Arts.*

Fodor's Choice ★ **Orchestre Symphonique de Montréal.** Montréal's beloved orchestra is now at home in La Maison Symphonique (formerly L'Adresse Symphonique), the newest hall at Places des Arts. Under the direction of influential and renowned conductor Kent Nagano, the OSM continues to master the classics, with contemporary works thrown into the mix. The 2013 season promises Beethoven, Brahms, and Mahler, plus a repertoire of essential French composers including Debussy and Ravel. ✉ *1600 rue St-Urbain, Downtown* ☎ *514/842–9951, 888/842–9931* ⊕ *www.osm.ca* Ⓜ *Place des Arts.*

Place des Arts. Hosting everything from musicals to the symphony to the ballet for almost 50 years, Place des Arts has undergone a major facelift and makeover, to stunning effect. The glass-walled Maison Symphonique (formerly L'Adresse Symphonique) concert hall is now

LATE-NIGHT BITES

Da Emma: Hover over a plate of pasta or roasted lamb at this darkly lighted, romantic eatery.

Leméac: One of the best deals in town, their *"fin de soirée"* menu (after 10 pm) is just C$27 with a choice of 9 starters and 11 mains.

m:brgr: Sometimes nothing but a burger after hours will do, and those at this gourmet downtown destination hit the spot. The fries are a must.

Rotisserie Panama: For satisfyingly filling inexpensive fare, this Greek restaurant serves up some of Montréal's best grilled meat.

Schwartz's Delicatessen: Thanks to the take-out window, you can grab a hot smoked meat sandwich to enjoy back at your hotel room.

⇨ *For full reviews and locations of these restaurants, see Chapter 7, Where to Eat.*

the permanent home of the Montréal Symphony Orchestra. Boasting state-of-the-art acoustics and a more intimate setting (there are only 75 feet between the end of the stage and the last row), the sixth concert hall frees up the Salle Wilfred Laurier performance space for the Opéra de Montréal. The venue's four other performance spaces host dance, theater, and festival events. ⊠ *175 rue Ste-Catherine Ouest, Downtown* ☎ *514/842–2112, 866/842–2112* ⊕ *www.laplacedesarts. com* Ⓜ *Place-des-Arts.*

Pollack Concert Hall. McGill University's concert hall showcases the best talents from its formidable music faculty—the McGill Symphony, Opera McGill, the **McGill Baroque Orchestra**, and the **Montréal Chamber Orchestra**. ⊠ *555 rue Sherbrooke Ouest, Downtown* ☎ *514/398–4547* ⊕ *www.mcgill.ca/music* Ⓜ *McGill.*

Salle Claude-Champagne. Dedicated exclusively to music, this beautiful concert hall hosts more than 150 symphonic and operatic performances every year by the music faculty of the Université de Montréal. The repertoire includes both classic and contemporary fare. ⊠ *220 av. Vincent-d'Indy, Outremont* ☎ *514/343–6427* ⊕ *www.musique.umontreal. ca* Ⓜ *Édouard Monpetit.*

DANCE

Traditional and contemporary dance companies thrive in Montréal, although many take to the road or are on hiatus in summer. Place des Arts, Montréal's main concert hall, is a popular venue for visiting large-scale productions.

Agora de la Danse. More than just a performance space for contemporary dance, this center actively works in the dance community to encourage creativity and experimentation. Hosting acclaimed artists and companies from around the world, the company is also affiliated with the Université du Québec à Montréal dance faculty. ⊠ *840 rue Cherrier, Downtown* ☎ *514/525–1500* ⊕ *www.agoradanse.com* Ⓜ *Sherbrooke.*

La Fondation de Danse Margie Gillis. Margie Gillis, one of Canada's most exciting and innovative soloists, works with her own company and guest artists to stage performances at Place des Arts, Agora de la Danse, and other area venues. ✉ *Montréal* ☎ *514/845–3115* ⊕ *www.margiegillis.org.*

LaLaLa Human Steps. Casablanca-born choreographer Édouard Lock founded LaLaLa to explore the boundaries of modern dance. The popular troupe has a heavy international schedule, but also performs at Place des Arts and at Montréal festivals. ✉ *Montréal* ☎ *514/277–9090* ⊕ *www.lalalahumansteps.com.*

★ **BJM Danse Montréal.** Formerly known as Les Ballets Jazz de Montréal, the company changed its name to BJM Danse to reflect the shifting scope of their repertoire over the last decade. Under Artistic Director Luc Robitaille, the troupe is now more contemporary than jazz, fusing music and visual arts with extraordinary technique. Performances are held at Place des Arts and Agora de la Danse, and there are free shows at Théâtre de Verdure in Parc Lafontaine during the summer months. ✉ *Montréal* ☎ *514/982–6771* ⊕ *www.bjmdanse.ca.*

Fodor'sChoice **Les Grands Ballets Canadiens de Montréal.** One of Canada's premier ballet
★ companies, Les Grands has been moving audiences since 1957. Under the artistic direction of Gradimir Pankov, the company has continued to evolve a rich body of both classic and contemporary work. Their annual presentation of *The Nutcracker* has become a sell-out Christmas tradition. ✉ *Montréal* ☎ *514/842–2112, 866/842–2112 Tickets* ⊕ *www.grandsballets.qc.ca.*

Montréal Danse. Lavish sets and dazzlingly sensual choreography have helped make Montréal Danse one of Canada's most popular contemporary repertory companies. They have a busy touring schedule, but also regularly perform at Place des Arts, Agora de la Danse, Théâtre de Verdure, and elsewhere. ✉ *Montréal* ☎ *514/871–4005* ⊕ *www. montrealdanse.com.*

Tangente. For more than 30 years, Tangente has hosted weekly performances of contemporary and experimental dance between September and May. They also act as an archive for contemporary dance and experimental performance art, with more than 2,000 files focusing on major international dance schools and festivals, companies and choreographers. Tangente encourages national and international exchanges between dance companies and artists. ✉ *840 rue Cherrier, Plateau Mont-Royal* ☎ *514/525–5584* ⊕ *www.tangente.qc.ca* Ⓜ *Sherbrooke.*

FILM

Although many of the cinemas that once lined rue Ste-Catherine have closed down in recent years to make way for new, stadium-seating megaplexes like the Cineplex Odeon Forum Cinema, Montrealers remain uniquely privileged in the variety of cinema-going experiences available.

Ranging from the ultramodern, überhip Excentris theater on the Main to the gorgeous art deco confines of the majestic Imperial theater on Bleury Street downtown, various venues offer locals the opportunity to enjoy the numerous domestic productions released each year by the province's thriving French-language film industry in addition to the standard Hollywood fare consistently shown at the megaplexes.

Cineplex Odeon Forum Cinemas. Bought by the Cineplex group in the summer of 2012, this massive theater used to be the home of Montréal's beloved Canadiens ice hockey team (look for the old seating and hockey memorabilia in the lobby). With 22 screens showing everything from Hollywood blockbusters to indie flicks, choice is the main draw. That, plus the bowling alley, poolroom, and arcade complex. ⊠ *2313 rue Ste-Catherine Ouest, Downtown* ☎ *514/904–1274* ⊕ *www. cinemamontreal.com* Ⓜ *Atwater.*

Cinéma Banque Scotia. This four-level theater complex is right in the heart of downtown Montréal. The major attraction is movie-watching in either of the IMAX or the UltraAVX-3D theaters. The food hall offers more than just popcorn—sushi, poutine, and doughnuts are also up for grabs. The lines can be long, so go early or buy tickets online. ⊠ *977 rue Ste-Catherine Ouest, Downtown* ☎ *514/842–0549* ⊕ *www. cineplex.com* Ⓜ *Peel.*

Cinéma du Parc. A favorite of Montréal moviegoers for years, this theater has gone through several incarnations, now focusing on first-run movies from around the world. Retrospectives based on interesting themes and prominent directors are also screened. Located inside La Cité mall in the heart of the McGill ghetto, it caters to an Anglophone audience. ⊠ *3575 av. du Parc, Downtown* ☎ *514/281–1900* ⊕ *www. cinemaduparc.com* Ⓜ *Place des Arts.*

Cinéma Impérial. Recognized by the Québec government as a historical monument in 2001, then renovated in 2002, this beautiful, old-fashioned movie theater still screens independent films, though on a somewhat less regular basis. It plays host to many cultural activities, including the Montréal World Film Festival. ⊠ *1432 rue Bleury, Downtown* ☎ *514/884–7187* ⊕ *www.cinemaimperial.com* Ⓜ *Place des Arts.*

Cinémathèque Québécoise. With over 35,000 films in its collection, and a ticket price of just C$8, Montréal's Museum of the Moving Image is the best place in the city to catch a foreign flick in its original language (with subtitles), in addition to Québecois and other Canadian productions. The museum also stocks scripts, television shows, and various new media, with a permanent display of old-fashioned cinema equipment. ⊠ *335 boul. de Maisonneuve Est, Latin Quarter* ☎ *514/842–9763* ⊕ *www.cinematheque.qc.ca* Ⓜ *Berri-UQAM.*

Excentris. Although two of its three former screening rooms now host live performances by singers, musicians, and dancers, the remaining Cinéma Parallèle is a champion of independant cinema, running avant-garde Canadian and international movies. With a new candy bar and organic popcorn on tap, audiences can indulge in total comfort. Excentris plays host to lots of great festivals, including the Festival of New Cinema in October. ⊠ *3536 blvd. St-Laurent, Plateau Mont-Royal* ☎ *514/847–2206* ⊕ *www.cinemaexcentris.com* Ⓜ *Sherbrooke or St-Laurent.*

Montréal's world-renowned jazz festival lasts 11 days and features about 500 concerts and shows, more than half of which are free.

THEATER

There are at least 10 major French-language theater companies in town, some of which enjoy an international reputation. The choices for Anglophones are more limited.

Black Theatre Workshop. Promoting black Canadian theater in Montréal for more than 40 years, the only black English company in Québec (and the longest-running in Canada) continues to support and nourish the careers of many prominent artists on the national scene. Expect innovative new productions performed alongside classic plays, such as the timeless *A Raisin in the Sun*. Shows take place at the Centaur Theatre and other venues around the city. ⊠ *Downtown* ☎ *514/932–1104* ⊕ *www.blacktheatreworkshop.ca.*

★ **Centaur Theatre.** Montréal's best-known English-language theater company stages everything from frothy musical revues to serious works, and prominently features works by local playwrights. Its home is in the former stock-exchange building in Old Montréal. ⊠ *453 rue St-François-Xavier, Old Montréal* ☎ *514/288–3161, 514/288–1229* ⊕ *www.centaurtheatre.com* Ⓜ *Place-d'Armes.*

Centre Phi. Packed with intimate screening rooms, recording facilities, exhibition spaces, and a performance space, this sleek new addition to the Montréal arts scene is extensive, stretching out over four floors. Devoted to the arts, its mission is to promote artist-driven work—in film, design, and music—from locals as well as international artists. Films are in English and French. ⊠ *407 rue St-Pierre,*

Old Montréal ☎ *514/225–0525, 855/526–8888* ⊕ *www.phi-centre.com* Ⓜ *Place-d'Armes or Square-Victoria.*

Geordie Productions. Promoting itself as a theater for all audiences, this accomplished English company has been delighting people of all ages since 1982. The 2013 season includes the adventures of *Robin Hood* and *Jabber*, an interesting look at cultural stereotyping and relationships. Most productions are performed at the Centaur Theatre. ✉ *Downtown* ☎ *514/845–9810* ⊕ *www.geordie.ca.*

Mainline Theatre. Operated by the same people who present the Montréal Fringe Festival every summer, the Mainline opened in 2006 to serve the city's burgeoning Anglo theater community and has been going strong ever since. ✉ *3997 blvd. St-Laurent, Plateau Mont-Royal* ☎ *514/849–3378* ⊕ *www.mainlinetheatre.ca* Ⓜ *St-Laurent or Mont-Royal.*

Monument-National. The highly regarded National Theatre School of Canada—or the École Nationale de Théâtre du Canada—supplies world stages with a steady stream of well-trained actors and directors. It works and performs in the historic and glorious old theater that has played host to such luminaries as Edith Piaf and Emma Albani. (Québec's first feminist rallies in the early 1900s also took place here.) Graduating classes perform professional-level plays in both French and English. The theater also plays host to an assortment of touring plays, musicals, and concerts. ✉ *1182 boul. St-Laurent, Downtown* ☎ *514/871–2224, 866/844–2172* ⊕ *www.monument-national.qc.ca* Ⓜ *St-Laurent.*

Segal Centre for the Performing Arts. English-language favorites like *Harvey* and *Inherit the Wind* get frequent billing at this Côte-des-Neiges venue, along with locally written works. The center is best-known, however, as the home to the **Dora Wasserman Yiddish Theatre,** which presents such musical works as *The Jazz Singer* and *The Pirates of Penzance* in Yiddish. ✉ *5170 chemin de la Côte-Ste-Catherine, Côte-des-Neiges* ☎ *514/739–2301, 514/739–7944* ⊕ *www.segalcentre.org* Ⓜ *Côte-Ste-Catherine.*

Fodor's Choice ★ **Théâtre du Nouveau Monde.** In this North American temple of French and stage classics, a season's offerings can include works by locals Michel Tremblay and Robert Lepage as well as works by Shakespeare, Molière, Camus, Ibsen, Chekhov, and Arthur Miller. ✉ *84 rue Ste-Catherine Ouest, Downtown* ☎ *514/866–8668* ⊕ *www.tnm.qc.ca* Ⓜ *St-Laurent.*

Théâtre St-Denis. This is one of several theaters hosting events that are part of the Just For Laughs Festival, and touring Broadway productions, concerts, musicals and dance performances can often be seen here. ✉ *1594 rue St-Denis, Latin Quarter* ☎ *514/849–4211* ⊕ *www.theatrestdenis.com* Ⓜ *Berri-UQAM.*

Shopping

WORD OF MOUTH

"Are the stores in the Underground City mainly chain stores? Would I be better off finding boutiques in the Plateau area instead?"
—globtrotterxyz

"Your suspicions are correct."

—Daniel_Williams

Updated by
Vanessa Muri

Montrealers *magasinent* (shop) with a vengeance, whether they're scurrying down busy Ste-Catherine downtown checking out department store bargains, or strolling up St-Laurent browsing in boutiques that stock wares from local designers, or buying gourmet food or native crafts at one of the city's markets.

And if you're in the market for a new fur, you've come to the right city. Montréal has a long history of being one of the fur capitals of the world. If you think you might be buying fur, check with your country's customs officials to find out which animals are considered endangered and can't be imported.

If shopping for native Inuit art, the same caveat applies to ivory carvings, which can't be imported into the United States or some other countries. If you do buy Inuit art, make sure to look for the government of Canada's igloo symbol, which attests to the piece's authenticity.

MONTRÉAL SHOPPING PLANNER

HOURS

Most shops open by 10 am Monday through Saturday and close at 6 pm Monday through Wednesday. Stores stay open until 9 pm on Thursday and Friday, but on Saturday they usually close at 5 pm. On Sunday, most downtown shops open noon to 5 pm. There are, however, exceptions. Large chain stores downtown often stay open weeknights until 9, and boutiques in areas that draw a drinks-and-dinner crowd, such as in the Plateau and in Old Montréal, can stay open even later in summer.

SALES TAX

When the Canadian dollar drops in value against the greenback, U.S. visitors to Canada are in bargain heaven, despite hefty tax rates. You must pay 5% in federal tax, called the GST (or TPS in Québec), and an additional 9.5% in Québec tax on most goods and services. Still, even when the Canuck buck trades at par, there are deals on certain

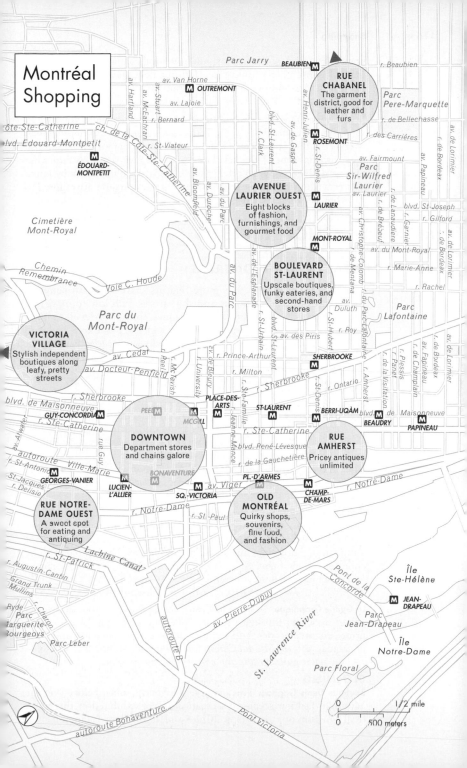

Montréal Shopping

Parc Jarry

RUE CHABANEL
The garment district, good for leather and furs

AVENUE LAURIER OUEST
Eight blocks of fashion, furnishings, and gourmet food

BOULEVARD ST-LAURENT
Upscale boutiques, funky eateries, and second-hand stores

VICTORIA VILLAGE
Stylish independent boutiques along leafy, pretty streets

DOWNTOWN
Department stores and chains galore

RUE AMHERST
Pricey antiques unlimited

RUE NOTRE-DAME OUEST
A sweet spot for eating and antiquing

OLD MONTRÉAL
Quirky shops, souvenirs, fine food, and fashion

Parc Pere-Marquette

Parc Sir-Wilfred Laurier

Cimetière Mont-Royal

Parc du Mont-Royal

Parc Lafontaine

Chemin Remembrance

Voie C. Houde

St. Lawrence River

Île Ste-Hélène

Parc Jean-Drapeau

Île Notre-Dame

Parc Floral

Parc Leber

Parc Marguerite-Bourgeoys

Lachine Canal

Pont de la Concorde

Pont Victoria

autoroute Bonaventure

METRO STATIONS: OUTREMONT, ÉDOUARD-MONTPETIT, ROSEMONT, LAURIER, MONT-ROYAL, SHERBROOKE, PLACE-DES-ARTS, ST-LAURENT, BERRI-UQÀM, BEAUDRY, PAPINEAU, GUY-CONCORDIA, PEEL, McGILL, GEORGES-VANIER, LUCIEN-L'ALLIER, BONAVENTURE, SQ.-VICTORIA, PL.-D'ARMES, CHAMP-DE-MARS, JEAN-DRAPEAU, BEAUBIEN

| 0 | 1/2 mile |
| 0 | 500 meters |

homegrown items: furs, fast fashion from local chains, and crafty goods that reflect Montréal's funky side. Unfortunately, Québec did away with the tax-back-for-non-Canadians program in 2007.

TOURS

If you want to take a less traditional tour of the city—and you love to shop—then Montreal Shopping Tours (⊕ *www.montrealshoppingtours. com*) is right up your alley. Half- and full-day excursions will take you on a sartorial tour of the best boutiques and give you a taste of what Québec designers have to offer (plus exclusive discounts). Run by Janna Zittrer, a Montréal native and fashion writer, excursions are tailored to suit your personal style needs.

MONTRÉAL SHOP REVIEWS

OLD MONTRÉAL (VIEUX-MONTRÉAL)

The old part of the city has more than its share of garish souvenir shops, but fashion boutiques and shoe stores with low to moderate prices line rues Notre-Dame and St-Jacques, from rue McGill to Place Jacques-Cartier. With gentrification in the west end of the area, high-end fashion boutiques and spas abound, especially along rue St-Paul Ouest. The area is also rich in art galleries and crafts shops along rue St-Paul and tucked inside the narrow rue des Artistes. Use the Place-d'Armes, Champ-de-Mars, or Square-Victoria métro stations.

ART

DHC/ART. Almost more a museum than a gallery, this large space showcases contemporary art with flair via exhibitions, screenings, and workshops. A free iPhone app takes visitors through the gallery and exhibits, and podcasts provide a fascinating look at the artists themselves. ⊠ *451 & 465 rue St-Jean, Old Montréal, Montréal* ☎ *514/849–3742, 888/934–2278* ⊕ *www.dhc-art.org* ☉ *Closed Mon. and Tues.* Ⓜ *Square-Victoria or Place-d'Armes*.

Galerie Le Chariot. If the friendly and knowledgeable staff don't win you over, the vast collection of Inuit and Iroquois art will. With more than 2,000 pieces of sculpture in soapstone and serpentine, government authenticated drawings and beautiful jewelry, the hardest part will be choosing among them. At least the guaranteed shipping service means you won't have to limit yourself by size. ⊠ *446 pl. Jacques-Cartier, Old Montréal, Montréal* ☎ *514/875–6134* Ⓜ *Champ-de-Mars*.

★ **La Guilde Graphique.** Get lost for hours inside this airy stone and wood gallery scouring through the vast collection of graphic art: original prints, engravings, oils, and etchings. It closes by 6 pm daily, and 5 pm on Sunday. ⊠ *9 rue St-Paul Ouest, Old Montréal, Montréal* ☎ *514/844–3438* ⊕ *www.guildegraphique.com* Ⓜ *Champ-de-Mars*.

CLOTHING

Boutique Denis Gagnon. This creative designer is much beloved on the Montréal fashion scene—his creations were exhibited at the Montréal Museum of Fine Arts in 2011—and at long last, Gagnon has his

Montréal's Shopping Districts

Most visitors to Montréal will have Downtown and Old Montréal on the itinerary, but for an authentic experience à la Montréalaise you should also venture into some of the other neighborhoods.

Avenue Laurier Ouest. Shops and boutiques along the eight blocks between boulevard St-Laurent and chemin de la Côte-Ste-Catherine sell medium- to high-end fashions, home furnishings, decorative items, artwork, books, kitchenware, toys and children's items, and gourmet food. There are plenty of restaurants, bars, and cafés in which to rest your feet and check out your purchases. The street is about a 10-minute walk from the Laurier métro station.

Boulevard St-Laurent. Affectionately known as The Main, St-Laurent has restaurants, boutiques, and nightclubs that cater mostly to an upscale clientele. Still, the area has managed to retain its working-class immigrant roots and vitality to some degree: high-fashion shops are interspersed with ethnic-food stores, secondhand clothing and decor boutiques, and hardware stores. Indeed, a trip up this street takes you from Chinatown to Little Italy.

Rue Amherst. Antiques shops began springing up in the Gay Village in the early 1990s, most of them on rue Amherst between rues Ste-Catherine and Ontario. Copious cafés and brunch spots nearby will fuel your quest. The area used to be less expensive than rue Notre-Dame, but it's not always the case these days. Use the Beaudry métro station.

Rue Bernard. Only a few blocks away from the Outremont métro station, this chic villagey street is well worth a detour. The street boasts many sidewalk cafés—called *terrasses* in local parlance—for fine or casual dining, as well as specialty food stores, decor shops, and some of the best ice cream in Montréal at Le Glacier Bilboquet.

Rue Chabanel. The eight-block stretch of Chabanel just west of boulevard St-Laurent is the heart of the city's garment district. The goods seem to get more stylish and more expensive the farther west you go. If you're lucky, you might come across signs for designer sample sales. Many of the city's furriers have also moved into the area. A few places on Chabanel accept credit cards, but bring cash anyway. If you pay in cash, the price will often include the tax. From the Crémazie métro station, take Bus 53 north.

Rue Notre-Dame Ouest. The fashionable place for antiquing is a formerly run-down five-block strip of Notre-Dame between rue Guy and avenue Atwater. Most of the action is at the western end of the strip, as are many of the restaurants and cafés that have sprung up to cater to shoppers. Walk east from Lionel-Groulx métro station.

Victoria Village. The carriage-trade area for wealthy Westmount citizens, who reside on the leafy slopes of Mont-Royal, has morphed into a shopping destination for all Montrealers with an eye for style. Independent boutiques offer distinctive home decor, shoes, gifts, stationery, and fashion along rues Victoria and Sherbrooke, with the epicenter between Victoria and Claremont. Cafés and fine specialty food shops also abound. Vendôme is the closest métro station.

5

TOP MONTRÉAL SHOPPING EXPERIENCES

Some of the best deals can be found at **La Maison Simons** department store, where there's something cheap and chic for everyone, from teenyboppers to mesdames and monsieurs on a budget. Along rue Ste-Catherine and in the underground malls, check out trendy Québecois fashion emporiums, including **Le Château, BEDO,** and **Jacob.** Also on the path of the penny pincher are **H&M, Zara, Forever 21,** and **Mango.**

Montréal's luxury lane runs from **Ogilvy** up to **Holt Renfrew** along rue de la Montagne, with designer fashion from **Marie Saint Pierre** and custom pearl jewelry from **Boutique Laura Aline** lining the route.

The path of luxury continues west along rue Sherbrooke, where you'll find the crème de la crème of international fashion and a plethora of art houses, with shops like **Les Créateurs** and **Galerie Walter Kinkhoff.**

Funky fashionistas will want to hit Mile End and the Plateau. In Mile End, hipster territory includes **Boutique Manhood** and **Unicorn,** for men and women, respectively, and **General 54** and **Maskarad** for crafty or recycled fashions. Moving down Montréal's beloved Main—boulevard St-Laurent—check out vintage, decor, and design shops.

Closer to downtown, **Lola & Emily, U&I,** and **M0851** are worth the walk. One-of-a-kind independent shops line avenue Mont-Royal and rue St-Denis.

own sleek subterranean boutique. His couture designs stand alongside his new prêt-à-porter collection, making his avant-garde clothing more accessible. He also designs shoes in collaboration with footwear giant ALDO. ⊠ *170B rue St-Paul Ouest, Old Montréal, Montréal* ☎ *514/935–6360* ⊕ *www.denisgagnon.ca* Ⓜ *Place-d'Armes.*

★ **Espace Pepin.** Talented painter and boutique owner Lysanne Pepin can now add "furniture designer" to her résumé, as she recently introduced her own line in collaboration with another Québecois artist. Her space is a delight to the senses, with a decidedly feminine mood. Funky shoes, romantic hats, and lots of international and local fashion labels make this shopping destination a must. ⊠ *350 rue St-Paul Ouest, Old Montréal, Montréal* ☎ *514/844–0114* ⊕ *www.pepinart. com* Ⓜ *Square Victoria.*

Reborn. If you love black, and the ultra–cutting edge of fashion, don't miss this long, narrow shop. Designs by Preen, Gareth Pugh, Rick Owens, and Montréal's Rad Hourani are on offer, for men or women. ⊠ *100, 231 rue St-Paul Ouest, Old Montréal, Montréal* ☎ *514/499–8549* ⊕ *www.reborn.ws* Ⓜ *Place-Victoria.*

QUÉBEC DESIGNERS

Boutique Anne de Shalla. Formerly known as Diffusion Griff 3000, Boutique Anne de Shalla has undergone a complete makeover. With a reduced square footage and a streamlined selection of Québecois fashion designers, the loft-like space sells haute de gamme lines, including Christian Chenail, the fanciful creations of Ophelie Hats, and the shop-owner's own exotic kimonos. ✉ *350 rue St-Paul Est, Old Montréal, Montréal* ☎ *514/398–0761* ⊕ *www.annedeshalla.com* Ⓜ *Champ-de-Mars.*

HOUSEWARES

★ **À Table Tout Le Monde.** Should you require the most refined disposable biodegradable plates for a picnic on the mountain, or in your hotel room, you can stop in at this shop and pick up a few Wasara pieces designed in Japan. The shop features fine designs from around the world, including Québec's own Jean-Claude Poitras for organic cotton table runners and Bousquet for playful porcelain designs. Of course, it's not all disposable. Quite the contrary. ✉ *361 rue St-Paul Ouest, Old Montréal, Montréal* ☎ *514/750–0311* ⊕ *www.atabletoutlemonde.com* Ⓜ *Place-Victoria.*

MALLS AND SHOPPING CENTERS

Marché Bonsecours. What was once the city's main public market in the 1800s, the silver-domed Marché Bonsecours has been restored and renovated with a modern edge. Fifteen boutique shops house everything from First Nations artwork to Québecois fashion designers, and jewelry to kitchenware. The paintings of Michel Sylvain on display at Art et Antiquités Médius capture eloquent Montréal street scenes. ✉ *350 rue St-Paul Est, Old Montréal, Montréal* ☎ *514/872–7730* ⊕ *www. marchebonsecours.qc.ca* Ⓜ *Champ-de-Mars.*

TOYS AND GAMES

☪ **Mortimer Snodgrass.** Since 2001, this gadget emporium has been supplying Montrealers (and tourists) with unique, quirky gifts. Kids and adults alike can spend hours pouring over the original plush toys, temporary tatoos, and funky kitchen gadgets. Don't miss the hilarious card selection tucked in the back, underneath the staircase. It stays open late (until 9 pm) daily. ✉ *56 rue Notre-Dame Ouest, Old Montréal, Montréal* ☎ *514/499–2851* ⊕ *www.mortimersnodgrass.com* Ⓜ *Place-d'Armes.*

DOWNTOWN

Montréal's largest retail district takes in rues Sherbrooke and Ste-Catherine, boulevard de Maisonneuve, and the side streets between them. Because of the proximity and diversity of the stores, it's the best shopping bet if you're in town overnight or for a weekend. The area bounded by rues Sherbrooke, Ste-Catherine, de la Montagne, and Crescent has antiques and art galleries in addition to designer salons. Fashion boutiques and art and antiques galleries line rue Sherbrooke. Rue Crescent holds a tempting blend of antiques, fashions, and jewelry displayed beneath colorful awnings. Rue de la Montagne is the corridor of chic, between the high-end Holt Renfrew and Ogilvy department stores, with designer boutiques—including top Québec labels—en route. Rue Ste-Catherine is the main shopping thoroughfare, with most of the chain stores and department stores. To get here, take the métro to the Peel, McGill, or Guy-Concordia stations.

ANTIQUES

Antiquités Pour La Table. As the name suggests, this store specializes in making your table look perfect. There's an extensive selection of antique porcelain, crystal, and linens—all impeccably preserved and beautifully displayed. There are also dining room tables and sideboards, cupboards, chairs, chandeliers, lamps, and much more. ⊠ *762 av. Atwater, Downtown, Montréal* ☎ *514/989–8945* ⊕ *www.antiquesforthetable. com* ☉ *Closed Sun. and Mon.* Ⓜ *St-Henri.*

Grand Central. Grand is the right word to describe this antiques emporium. It's filled to the brim with elegant chandeliers and candelabras, armchairs and secretaries, and other decorative elements from the 18th and 19th centuries that would add a touch of refinement to almost any home. It closes at 5:30 on weekdays, and is open 11 to 5 on Saturday. ⊠ *2448 rue Notre-Dame Ouest, St-Henri, Downtown, Montréal* ☎ *514/935–1467* ⊕ *www.grandcentralinc.ca* ☉ *Closed Sun.* Ⓜ *Lionel-Groulx.*

Viva Gallery. Unique along the Notre-Dame antique stretch is this shop proffering exquisite Asian furniture—armoires, chests, chairs, and screens with fine wood carvings—complemented by paintings from Xiaoyang Yu that depict life in Beijing. ⊠ *1970 rue Notre-Dame Ouest, Downtown, Montréal* ☎ *514/932–3200* ⊕ *www.vivagalerie.com* Ⓜ *Lucien-L'Allier.*

ART

★ **Edifice Belgo.** Celebrating 100 years of existence in 2012, Edifice Belgo (literally Belgo Building) is in essence a mall of approximately 30 art galleries and ateliers showing both established and emerging artists. Galerie Roger Bellemare is one of the best galleries in which to look for contemporary art, as is Galerie SAS. Galerie Trois Points showcases the work of Montréal and Québec artists. For wearable art, visit designer Véronique Miljkovitch's atelier on the second floor. ⊠ *372 rue Ste-Catherine Ouest, Downtown, Montréal* ☎ *514/861–2953* ☉ *Closed Sun.* Ⓜ *Place-des-Arts.*

★ **Galerie Walter Klinkhoff.** The Klinkhoffs know art. Since 1950, this family-run gallery boasts several floors of Canadian art, from both contemporary and historical artists. Check the website for hours as they vary depending on the season. ⊠ *1200 rue Sherbrooke Ouest, Downtown, Montréal* ☎ *514/288–7306* ⊕ *www.klinkhoff.com* Ⓜ *Peel.*

BOOKSTORES AND PAPERIES

Indigo. Indigo bought out main rival Chapters years ago and is now the largest Canadian bookstore chain. It's a downtown refuge, where you can peruse the vast collection of classic literature, novels, music, and magazines in both English and French. This location often plays host to booksignings and other events and has a lovely café to boot. ⊠ *1500 av. McGill College (corner of rue Ste-Catherine), Downtown, Montréal* ☎ *514/281–5549* ⊕ *www.chapters.indigo.ca* Ⓜ *McGill.*

★ **Paragraphe.** Stubbornly independent until 2003, when it was bought out by Archambault, a Montréal chain of music stores, Paragraphe carries the usual selection of best sellers and thrillers, but also stocks Canadian works and histories. It's a favorite with visiting authors, who stop by to read from their latest releases. Sip on a coffee from the adjacent Second Cup coffee shop while you peruse the stacks. ✉ *2220 av. McGill College, Downtown, Montréal* ☎ *514/845–5811* ⊕ *www.paragraphbooks. com* ⊙ *Weekdays 8–8, weekends 9–9* Ⓜ *McGill.*

Renaud-Bray. With almost 30 branches in Québec—nearly half of them in Montréal—Renaud-Bray is the largest French-language book chain in Canada. Its shops stock best sellers and thrillers in French and English as well as original works from Europe and Canada. There are also substantial gift, music, and magazine offerings. ✉ *150 Ste-Catherine Ouest, Downtown, Montréal* ☎ *514/288–4844* ⊕ *www.renaud-bray. com* Ⓜ *Place-des-Arts.*

Fodor's Choice **The Word.** Deep in the McGill University neighborhood, the Word is
★ a small shop bursting with used books—including first editions—and specializing in philosophy, poetry, and literature. The award-winning Montréal landmark shuns modern technology (including a cash register) in favor of timeless appeal. There's no sign, so keep your eyes peeled as you walk along Milton, though the bargain books lining the window are a good clue. It doesn't open until 11 on Saturday. ✉ *469 rue Milton, Downtown, Montréal* ☎ *514/845–5640* ⊕ *www.wordbookstore. ca* Ⓜ *McGill.*

CLOTHING

BCBG Max Azria. The gleaming downtown flagship store on rue Ste-Catherine Ouest near Mansfield is the largest in Max Azria's empire of more than 550 boutiques around the world. This is the place for dresses, from little sunny frocks to sundown gowns. Another branch is located in Outremont. ✉ *960 rue Ste-Catherine Ouest, Downtown, Montréal* ☎ *514/868–9561* ⊕ *www.bcbgmaxazriagroup.com* Ⓜ *Peel.*

Cuir Danier. Leather fashions for men and women are the specialty of this Toronto-based chain, which designs and manufactures its own lines of jackets, skirts, pants, hats, and purses. It has a downtown branch in Place Ville-Marie and a warehouse outlet at Marché Central. ✉ *1 Place Ville-Marie, 11098, Downtown, Montréal* ☎ *514/874–0472* ⊕ *www. danier.com* Ⓜ *McGill.*

Les Créateurs. The long, narrow but bright shop will feel like home to the avant-garde fashionista. For more than 25 years, owner Maria Balla has been offering clothes by the most innovative designers from around the world, Ann Demeulemeester and Julia Watanabe among them. ✉ *1444 rue Sherbrooke Ouest, Suite 100, Downtown, Montréal* ☎ *514/284–2102* ⊕ *www.lescreateurs.ca* ⊙ *Closed Sun.* Ⓜ *Guy-Concordia.*

Ursula B. Though cutting Giorgio Femme from the boutique's name—as well as the "boutique" part—Ursula B. still carries fashion-forward labels like The Row and Mary Katrantzou, with sexier designers like Carven and Cushnie et Ochs in the mix (among plenty of others). Be sure to head upstairs and visit the sale section. ✉ *Les Cours Mont-Royal, 1455 rue Peel, Suite 328, Downtown, Montréal* ☎ *514/282–0294* ⊕ *www.ursulab.com* ⊙ *Closed Sun.* Ⓜ *Peel.*

Winners. Tucked away on the lowest level of Place Montréal Trust lies a huge discount shopping mecca. Clothing, shoes, housewares; you name it. Just allot yourself enough time to scour the racks. ■ **TIP→** Head straight to the runway collections and sales racks for the best bargains. ⊠ *1500 av. McGill College, Downtown, Montréal* ☎ *514/788–4949* ⊕ *www.winners.ca* Ⓜ *McGill.*

MEN'S ONLY

Henri Henri. Simply the best men's hat store in Canada, Henri Henri has a huge stock of Homburgs, Borsalinos, fedoras, top hats, and derbies, as well as cloth caps and other accessories. Hat prices range from about C$155 to C$1,000, the top price fetching you a top-of-the-line Homburg or Panama. It closes early on Thursday (6 pm), but opens at 10 am on Sunday. ⊠ *189 rue Ste-Catherine Est, Downtown, Montréal* ☎ *514/288–0109, 888/388–0109* ⊕ *www.henrihenri.ca* Ⓜ *St-Laurent or Berri-UQAM.*

L'Uomo Montréal. You'll come to this store for the European selection of menswear and accessories, but you'll stay for the impeccable service and attention to detail. Expect suits from Kiton and Borrelli, bags from Prada, and ties from Massimo Bizzocchi. ⊠ *1452 rue Peel, Downtown, Montréal* ☎ *514/844–1008, 877/844–1008* ⊕ *www.luomo-montreal. com* Ⓜ *Peel.*

QUÉBEC DESIGNERS

★ **Harricana.** Yesterday's old fur coats and stoles are transformed into everything from car coats and ski jackets to baby wraps and cushions. For summer, vintage scarves become flirty little tops. The recycled furs are sold at dozens of shops, but the best place to see what's available is this combination atelier and boutique. ⊠ *3000 rue St-Antoine Ouest, Downtown, Montréal* ☎ *514/287–6517, 877/894–9919* ⊕ *www.harricana.qc.ca* ⊙ *Weekdays 10–6, Sat.10–5, Sun. 11–5* Ⓜ *Lionel-Groulx.*

★ **Marie Saint Pierre.** The doyenne of the Montréal design scene, Marie Saint Pierre interprets her signature pleats and ruffles in silks, jerseys, and mesh to suit the mood of each season. Consider this wearable art— and a must-see for serious fashion fans. ⊠ *2081 rue de la Montagne, Downtown, Montréal* ☎ *514/281–5547* ⊕ *www.mariesaintpierre.com* ⊙ *Mon.–Wed. 10–6, Thurs.–Fri. 10–8, Sat. 10–6, Sun. noon–6* Ⓜ *Peel or Guy-Concordia.*

VINTAGE AND RECYCLED

Boutique Encore. For years this quaint shop has been supplying Montrealers with gently used designer goods at reduced prices. Expect to find Hermès, Chanel, and Gucci for the ladies, while men can hunt for the likes of Armani and Hugo Boss. ⊠ *2145 rue Crescent, Downtown, Montréal* ☎ *514/849–0092* Ⓜ *Peel or Guy-Concordia.*

Eva B. If you fantasize about being a flapper—or if you want to revive the pillbox hat—then turn back the clock and perk up your wardrobe with an item from the vast collection sold here. And should your stomach start a-grumbling or your throat feel particularly parched, there's a café on the premises with a selection of teas, coffees, sandwiches, and salads. ⊠ *2015 boul. St-Laurent, Downtown, Montréal* ☎ *514/849–8246* ⊕ *www.eva-b.ca* ⊙ *Mon.–Sat. 10–9, Sun. noon–8* Ⓜ *St-Laurent.*

DEPARTMENT STORES

Fodor'sChoice **Holt Renfrew.** This upscale department store is Canada's answer to Berg-
★ dorf Goodman. Here's where you get your Prada, Chanel, and Gucci
fix, as well as contemporary labels like Theory, Diane Von Furstenberg, and Judith & Charles. A world design lab showcases avant-garde
fashion, including rising Canadian stars. The food at the downstairs
café is just as stylish, with bread flown in from the Poilâne bakery
in Paris several times weekly. ⊠ *1300 rue Sherbrooke Ouest, Downtown, Montréal* ☎ *514/842–5111* ⊕ *www.holtrenfrew.com* Ⓜ *Peel or
Guy-Concordia.*

La Baie. The Bay is a descendant of the Hudson's Bay Company, the great
17th-century fur-trading company that played a pivotal role in Canada's
development. La Baie has been a department store since 1891. In addition to selling typical department-store goods, it's known for its duffel
coats and signature red, green, and white striped blankets. ⊠ *585 rue
Ste-Catherine Ouest, Downtown, Montréal* ☎ *514/281–4422* ⊕ *www.
thebay.com* ⊙ *Mon.–Wed. 10–7, Thurs.–Fri. 10–9, Sat. 9–7, Sun. 10–7*
Ⓜ *McGill.*

★ **La Maison Simons.** Find the *trends du jour* at a great price from the youth-
oriented labels on the ground floor of this bustling department store.
Upstairs, the fare is more mature, ranging from respectable and affordable twinsets to luxe offerings from the likes of Chloé and Missoni. The
store is also known for its fashion-forward selection of menswear and
its excellent sales. ⊠ *977 rue Ste-Catherine Ouest, Downtown, Montréal* ☎ *514/282–1840* ⊕ *www.simons.ca* Ⓜ *Peel.*

Fodor'sChoice **Ogilvy.** Founded in 1865, Ogilvy was bought in 2011 by the Selfridge's
★ Group, and so far, the change has invigorated the department store. Still
boasting top brands and a vast selection of clothing and accessories for
men and women, it hasn't broken with tradition; a kilted piper marches
throughout the store between noon and 1 pm daily. The Louis Vuit-
ton boutique was redesigned to include more than 3,000 square feet
and a bag bar (also a good place to rest weary feet). ⊠ *1307 rue Ste-
Catherine Ouest, Downtown, Montréal* ☎ *514/842–7711, 855/842–
7711* ⊕ *www.ogilvycanada.com* Ⓜ *Peel.*

FOOD

Marché Atwater. Heading down Atwater Avenue toward the Lachine
Canal, you can't miss the art deco tower of the Atwater Market.
Expanded in 2011 to include 14 new seasonal stalls, this is the perfect
spot to pick up local produce, fresh flowers, and gourmet meats and
cheeses. ⊠ *138 av. Atwater, Downtown, Montréal* ☎ *514/937–7754*
⊕ *www.marche-atwater.com* ⊙ *Mon.–Wed. and Sat. 7–6, Thur.–Fri.
7–8, Sun. 7–5* Ⓜ *Lionel-Groulx.*

FURS

FURB Atelier. Onyx sheared beaver pillows, recycled chapkas and hand-
bags, and fur throws are among the offerings at this tiny shop run by
the folks at Natural Furs International, one of Canada's finest furriers.
The shop is tucked away in Montréal's historic fur district. ⊠ *401 rue
Mayor, Downtown, Montréal* ☎ *514/845–3182* ⊕ *www.furbatelier.com*
Ⓜ *Place des Arts.*

Salon Élégance, Ogilvy. On the third level of the cavernous department store you'll find the highest quality furs and shearlings, including extravagant, colorful sheared beavers from Montréal's Zuki. ✉ *1307 rue Ste-Catherine Ouest, Downtown, Montréal* ☎ *514/842–7711* ⊕ *www. ogilvycanada.com* Ⓜ *Peel or Guy-Concordia.*

JEWELRY

Birks. The Canadian equivalent of Tiffany's, Birks has been selling diamond engagement rings, exquisite jewelry, and fine crystal since 1879. To make the experience even more lavish, this downtown location recently opened Birks Café, where you can savor sandwiches, scones, and macaroons during the afternoon tea service. ✉ *1240 Phillips Sq., Downtown, Montréal* ☎ *514/397–2511* ⊕ *www.birks.com* Ⓜ *McGill.*

★ **Bleu Comme Le Ciel.** In France they call costume jewelry *bijoux de fantaisie,* and that's what you find here: fantasy in a sparkling array of colorful crystal baubles from France. Clean elegant lines from ginette_ny contrast with the bold bangles of Alex Bittar. The glass-walled boutique is easy to miss, as it blends into the surrounding building. ✉ *2000 rue Peel, Downtown, Montréal* ☎ *514/847–1128* ⊕ *www.bleucommeleciel.com* Ⓜ *Peel.*

Boutique Laura Aline. Third-generation jewelry designer Aline Papazian and daughter Laura Zakem are enamored with pearls, and devoted to changing the perception that they're too stuffy. Sourcing materials from around the world, they also use semiprecious stones, crystals, and diamonds to create unique, contemporary designs. Don't let the buzzer at the door deter you; their jewelry starts as low as C$80. ✉ *2017 rue de la Montagne, Downtown, Montréal* ☎ *514/507–6118* ⊕ *www.lauraaline. com* ⊘ *Closed Sun.* Ⓜ *Peel.*

Château d'Ivoire. All that glitters is not gold; at Château d'Ivoire, one of Canada's leading jewelers, eye-catching watches from Piaget and Rolex fight for attention with diamond jewelry from Bulgari and Chopard. ✉ *2020 rue de la Montagne, Downtown, Montréal* ☎ *514/845–4651* ⊕ *www.chateaudivoire.com* ⊘ *Closed Sun.* Ⓜ *Peel or Guy-Concordia.*

LINGERIE

La Senza. This international Québec chain, now allied with Victoria's Secret, is the place to get that fuchsia push-up bra and matching rhinestone-trimmed panty. The basics are here, too, and at low prices. ✉ *1133 rue Ste-Catherine Ouest, Downtown, Montréal* ☎ *514/281–0101* ⊕ *www.lasenza.com* Ⓜ *Peel.*

MALLS AND SHOPPING CENTERS

Centre Eaton de Montréal. Eaton Center has a youthful edge, with a huge Levi's outlet and some trendy sporting-goods stores. The five-story mall, the largest in the downtown core, has 175 boutiques and shops and is linked to the McGill métro station. ✉ *705 rue Ste-Catherine Ouest, Downtown, Montréal* ☎ *514/288–3708* ⊕ *www.centreeatondemontreal. com* ⊘ *Weekdays 10–9, Sat. 10–6, Sun. 11–5* Ⓜ *McGill.*

★ **Les Cours Mont-Royal.** This elegant mall caters to expensive and chic tastes, but there are options for budget-minded shoppers, too. The more than 80 shops include Club Monaco, DKNY, and Harry Rosen. The crème de la crème of avant-garde fashion is sold at Ursula B. For

MONTRÉAL'S BEST CHAIN STORES

BEDO. Nailing the trends season after season, BEDO is an affordable way to replenish your wardrobe without breaking the bank. Well regarded by fashionistas male and female, the company recently collaborated with star designer Denis Gagnon to put out an affordable collection of his avant-garde creations. ✉ *1256 rue Ste-Catherine Ouest, Downtown, Montréal* ☎ *514/866–4962* ⊕ *www.bedo.ca* Ⓜ *Peel.*

Buffalo David Bitton. Fans adore the fit and reasonable prices of Montrealer David Bitton's jeans. Aside from denim for men and women, there's a full line of trendy clothes and accessories. ✉ *1223 rue Ste-Catherine Ouest, Downtown, Montréal* ☎ *514/845–1816* ⊕ *www.buffalojeans.com* ⊗ *Weekdays 10–9, weekends 10–8* Ⓜ *Peel.*

Harry Rosen. It's hard to imagine that Harry Rosen and his brother Lou opened their first store in 1954 with only C$500. Now a nationwide high-end menswear destination, the collections continue to evolve with the trends. Their latest addition? A Tom Ford boutique inside this 22,000-square-foot downtown flagship. ✉ *Cours Mont-Royal, 1455 rue Peel, Suite 227, Downtown, Montréal* ☎ *514/284–3315* ⊕ *www.harryrosen.com* Ⓜ *Peel.*

Le Château. This Québec chain designs its own line of reasonably priced trendy fashions for men and women. You'll find chic suits, dresses, and eveningwear, plus shoes, handbags, and jewelry galore. The flagship store is on rue Ste-Catherine, but there's also a factory outlet at the Marché Central. ✉ *1310 rue Ste-Catherine Ouest, Downtown,* Montréal ☎ *514/866–2481* ⊕ *www.lechateau.com* Ⓜ *Peel.*

M0851. Sleek, supple leather wear and bags from local Québec designer Frédéric Mamarbachi have a cult following from Tokyo to Antwerp, and in Montréal, of course. ✉ *3526 boul. St-Laurent, Plateau Mont-Royal, Montréal* ☎ *514/849–9759* ⊕ *www.M0851.com* Ⓜ *St-Laurent or Sherbrooke.*

Parasuco. Montrealer Salvatore Parasuco—inventor of stretch jeans—has been making history in denim ever since he opened his first store in 1975 at the age of 19. He's since spread across the country, but his flagship shop is in Montréal. ✉ *1414 rue Crescent, Downtown, Montréal* ☎ *514/284–2288* ⊕ *www.parasuco.com* ⊗ *Weekdays 9:30–9, Sat. 9:30–6, Sun. noon–8* Ⓜ *Guy-Concordia or Peel.*

Roots. Quality materials and an approachable, sometimes retro look have made Canada's Roots chain a fashion favorite for the casual, outdoorsy look, as well as for good leatherwear and bags. ✉ *1025 rue Ste-Catherine Ouest, Downtown, Montréal* ☎ *514/845–7995* ⊕ *www.roots.com* ⊗ *Weekdays 10–9, Sat. 9–8, Sun. 10–6* Ⓜ *Peel.*

Rudsak. Sleek, minimalist leather jackets and coats for men and women are the *raison d'être* of this downtown store, though it's recently introduced more clothing and accessories to the line. ✉ *1400 rue Ste-Catherine Ouest, Downtown, Montréal* ☎ *514/399–9925* ⊕ *www.rudsak.com* Ⓜ *Guy-Concordia.*

5

trendy and affordable designer duds, check out ENRG.X.Change. Feet hurting from all the shopping? Terra Firma, in the basement, stocks stylish yet comfortable shoes. ✉ *1455 rue Peel, Downtown, Montréal* ☏ *514/842–7777* ⊕ *www.lcmr.ca* Ⓜ *Peel.*

Place Ville Marie. Place Ville-Marie is where weatherproof indoor shopping first came to Montréal in 1962. It was also the start of the underground shopping network that Montréal now enjoys. Stylish shoppers head to the 80-plus retail outlets for lunchtime sprees. ✉ *boul. René-Lévesque and rue University, Downtown, Montréal* ☏ *514/861–9393* ⊕ *www.placevillemarie.com* Ⓜ *McGill or Bonaventure.*

SHOES
Browns. This local institution stocks fashion footwear and accessories for men and women. It carries the store's own label as well as DKNY, Chie Mihara, House of Harlow, Pajar, and Stuart Weitzman. ✉ *1191 rue Ste-Catherine Ouest, Downtown, Montréal* ☏ *514/987–1206* ⊕ *www.brownsshoes.com* ☉ *Weekdays 10–9, Sat. 10–8, Sun. noon–6* Ⓜ *Peel.*

THE VILLAGE

It's interesting that the Gay Village is known for its excellent furniture stores as much as for its vibrant nightlife. Rue Amherst is nearly overflowing with antique shops; plenty of unique treasures are just waiting to be discovered, most being mid-century modern. Beaudry métro station is your best bet.

ANTIQUES
Antiquités Curiosités. A sea of chairs, lamps, and other furniture awaits at Antiquités Curiosités, but it's the Victorian-era goodies that draw many consumers through its doors. Fun retro accessories like rotary phones also tickle the fancy. ✉ *1769 rue Amherst, Village, Montréal* ☏ *514/525–8772* Ⓜ *Beaudry.*

Cité Déco. This store is filled with funky furniture and decor from the '20s to the '70s, with some '80s pieces thrown in for good measure. Art deco furnishings, teak armchairs, and beautiful rococo mirrors are for sale here. The owners also run Re Design a few doors down at 1699 Amherst. ✉ *1761 rue Amherst, Village, Montréal* ☏ *514/528–0659* ⊕ *www.citedecomeubles.com* Ⓜ *Beaudry.*

THE PLATEAU, MILE END, LITTLE ITALY, AND OUTREMONT

The Plateau has long been recognized as one of North America's hippest neighborhoods, and though trends typically come and go, its cachet endures. Rue St-Denis is home to both independent boutiques and chain stores selling local and international fashion, as well as numerous jewelry stores, all at prices for every budget. Boulevard St-Laurent and avenue Mont-Royal both offer opportunities for vintage shopping, with St-Laurent also known for contemporary furniture and decor stores. Just north of the Plateau, the Mile End offers an eclectic mix of artsy boutiques and shops stocked with up-and-coming Montréal designers. Avenue Laurier in Outremont is where those in pursuit of a little

MONTRÉAL'S MARKETS

If food is your first love, head to Montréal's markets, especially in the bountiful days of the autumn harvest.

Marché Jean-Talon in the north end of the city has an Italian flavor; the surrounding streets are home to some of the finest pizza and café lattes anywhere. **Marché Atwater** has a glorious indoor hall, packed with eateries, butchers, bakeries, and fine food emporiums.

The markets are a great place to pick up locally made nonperishables to bring home, such as jam from farms on Île d'Orléans near Québec City, plentiful in summer; or cranberries harvested late-September to mid-October; or maple syrup, taffy, and butter year-round.

luxury should tread, while Little Italy is a gourmet shopper's paradise. Use Sherbrooke, Mont-Royal, Laurier, or Jean Talon métro stations.

BOOKSTORES AND PAPERIES

L'Essence du Papier. With a wide variety of pens and writing instruments and a selection of imported and handmade papers, L'Essence du Papier (translated literally, "the essence of paper") is a reminder that letter writing can be an art form. The store also carries several lines of beautifully designed journals, agendas, and other fun items for stationery aficionados. Two other branches are located Downtown. ⊠ *4160 rue St-Denis, Plateau Mont-Royal, Montréal* ☎ *514/288–9691* ⊕ *www. essencedupapier.com* Ⓜ *Mont-Royal or Sherbrooke.*

CLOTHING

Billie. One of Montréal's favorite boutiques, Billie moved farther west on avenue Laurier in search of square footage. The increased space means new stock, including chic dresses and blouses from Alice + Olivia and eclectic shoes from Cynthia Vincent and Jean-Michel Cazabat lining the walls. ⊠ *1012 av. Laurier Ouest, Outremont, Montréal* ☎ *514/270– 5415* ⊕ *www.billiegirls.ca* Ⓜ *Laurier.*

Boutique 1861. Though named for the 1861 rue Ste-Catherine location, the store's St-Laurent branch is larger. Both are stocked with romantic, lacy, and affordable finds from local and international designers, including Arti Gogna and Champagne & Strawberry. With everything white— hardwood floors, walls, couches, and armoires—the boudoir vibe is irresistible. Just look for the pink and black cameo signage. ⊠ *3670 boul. St-Laurent, Plateau Mont-Royal, Montréal* ☎ *514/670–6110* .

Boutique Manhood. A woman, Julie Parenteau, is the friendly, stylish owner of this hip menswear boutique in the Mile End. Labels like J.C. Rags, Hip and Bone, and Zanerobe attract the contemporary dresser with accessible prices. Fun touches including crate-like dressing rooms and soccer balls make this a relaxed shopping experience. ⊠ *5226 boul. St-Laurent, Mile End, Montréal* ☎ *514/273–4626* ⊕ *www. boutiquemanhood.com* ☉ *Tue. Wed. 11–6, Thur.–Fri. 11–8, weekends noon–5* ☉ *Closed Mon.* Ⓜ *Laurier.*

5

One of the best things about Montréal's countless boutiques (such as Holt Renfrew, shown here) is the availability of European labels that are hard to find in the United States.

Citizen Vintage. If you're a fashion slave to all things vintage, then this Mile End boutique has your name on it. Bright, spacious, and carefully curated by the owners (who scour Canada and the United States for their finds), this store makes shopping easy, as everything is arranged by color. Stock changes almost daily, so do squeeze in a return visit if you can. ✉ *5330 boul. St-Laurent, Mile End, Montréal* ☎ *514/439–2774* ⊕ *www.citizenvintage.com* ⏱ *Mon.–Wed. 11–6, Thur.–Fri. 11–7, weekends 11–5* Ⓜ *Laurier.*

Kanuk. This company's owl trademark has become something of a status symbol among the shivering urban masses. These coats and parkas are built to keep an Arctic explorer warm and dry. ✉ *485 rue Rachel Est, Plateau Mont-Royal, Montréal* ☎ *514/284–4494, 877/284–4494* ⊕ *www.kanuk.com* Ⓜ *Mont-Royal.*

Lola & Emily. Take a look through your best-dressed friend's closet. Grab a piece here and there, throw on some pretty accessories, and slip into a pair of TOMS. That's the relaxed, welcoming vibe that permeates this apartment-style boutique. A staple shopping destination for Montrealers since 2001, the girls sell fun, flirty, one-of-a-kind fashion. ✉ *3475 boul. St-Laurent, Plateau Mont-Royal, Montréal* ☎ *514/288–7598* ⊕ *www.lolaandemily.com* Ⓜ *St-Laurent.*

Fodor's Choice ★ **Lyla.** Some of the finest lingerie in the city—including brands like Eres and La Perla—and the staff to find what fits and flatters you are augmented by recherché fashion from Europe and the United States. One of the city's best selections of swimsuits—and darling cover-ups—is another reason to stop and shop here. ✉ *400 av. Laurier Ouest, Outremont, Montréal* ☎ *514/271–0763* ⊕ *www.lyla.ca* Ⓜ *Laurier.*

Mousseline. With sizes running the gamut from 2 to 22, this place makes finding the perfect fit a snap. Choosing among the casual wear from designer labels James Perse, Nobis, and No-l-ita, on the other hand, might be a bit more difficult. Be sure to pick up a comforting sweater from Autumn Cashmere. ✉ *220 av. Laurier Ouest, Mile End, Montréal* ☎ *514/878–0661* ⊕ *www.boutiquemousseline.com* Ⓜ *Laurier.*

Tilley Endurables. The famous Canadian-designed Tilley hat is sold here, along with other easy-care travel wear. ✉ *1050 av. Laurier Ouest, Outremont, Montréal* ☎ *514/272–7791* ⊕ *www.tilley.com* Ⓜ *Laurier.*

Très Chic Styling. Hervé Léger dresses at two for C$500? Style-savvy cofounders Maryam Rafa and Angelica Koinis believe that women should look good and dress well without having to spend a fortune. Designer denim and fabulous cocktail dresses for 50% off (or more) have built the cofounders' reputations as *bargainistas.* If their opening hours don't suit your schedule, they'll open for private appointments too. ✉ *1069 av. Laurier Ouest, #2, Outremont, Montréal* ☎ *514/274–3078* ⊕ *www.tcstyling.com* ⊗ *Wed. 10–6, Thurs.–Fri. 10–8, Sat. 10–5, Sun. 12–5* ⊗ *Closed Mon. and Tues.* Ⓜ *Laurier.*

U&I. Hipsters flock to this shop on the Main for retailer Eric Toledano's latest finds from Europe. Men and women are equally well served in the double shop with avant-garde lines like Vivienne Westwood, Engineered Garments, and Phillip Lim. Look for special pieces from Montréal design darlings Mackage, Yso, and Denis Gagnon bags. ✉ *3650 boul. St-Laurent, Plateau Mont-Royal, Montréal* ☎ *514/844–8788* ⊕ *www.boutiqueuandi.com* Ⓜ *St-Laurent or Sherbrooke.*

Yoga-à-Porter. A clever blend of yoga and prêt-à-porter, this bright boutique sells yoga wear from OmGirl and a wide range of leisure and lifestyle clothing (great for traveling). Be sure to try on the Yoga Jeans, stretch cotton denim with 3% spandex, which offer a comfortable fit in a variety of washes. If you have time, pop into the studio upstairs for a yoga class. ✉ *100 av. Laurier Ouest, Mile End, Montréal* ☎ *438/380–6814, 877/904–9642 (YOGA)* ⊕ *www.yoga-a-porter.com* Ⓜ *Laurier.*

CLOTHING: MEN'S ONLY

Duo. This one-stop shop for the style-conscious male might be in an odd location—Prince Arthur is known for food, not fashion—but that just adds to the cachet. Ultra-hip labels like DSquared2 hang alongside slick suits and limited-edition Nikes. Visiting celebs have been known to pop in from time to time. ✉ *30 rue Prince-Arthur Ouest, Plateau Mont-Royal, Montréal* ☎ *514/848–0880* ⊕ *www.boutiqueduo.com* Ⓜ *St-Laurent or Sherbrooke.*

★ **Michel Brisson.** This is the go-to place for art directors, architects, and other dudes with an eye for European design from Etro, Jil Sander, or Dries Van Noten. The Laurier store is sleek, with clean lines and lots of grey. Another location in Old Montréal injects a bit of warmth with its rich wood paneling. ✉ *1074 av. Laurier Ouest, Outremont, Montréal* ☎ *514/270–1012* ⊕ *www.michelbrisson.com* Ⓜ *Laurier.*

QUÉBEC DESIGNERS

Aime Com Moi. Celebrating 12 years and counting, Aime Com Moi continues to promote young, hip Québecois designers. Gearing the selection toward trendy women 30 years and older, the shop includes feminine designs from Annie 50, flirty skirts from Dinh Bá, and colorful recycled creations from Créations Encore. ⊠ *150 av. Mont-Royal Est, Plateau Mont-Royal, Montréal* ☎ *514/982–0088* ☾ *Mon.–Wed. 11–6, Thur.–Fri. 11–7, Sat. 11–5, Sun. noon–5* Ⓜ *Mont-Royal.*

> ### SHOPPING ON THE MAIN
>
> Bargain-hunter alert: Twice a year—in mid-June and at the end of August—the Main Madness street sale transforms boulevard St-Laurent into an open-air bazaar.

Bodybag by Jude. When Nicole Kidman appeared on David Letterman in a zip denim dress from this line, the designer Judith Desjardins's star was set. The designer has a penchant for all things British, so look for cheeky checks and plaids. ⊠ *17 rue Bernard Ouest, Mile End, Montréal* ☎ *514/274–5242* ⊕ *www.bodybagbyjude.com* ☾ *Mon.–Wed. 11–6, Thurs.–Fri. 11–8, Sat. 11–5, Sun. noon–5* Ⓜ *Rosemont.*

General 54. Stores like this are what give Mile End its rep for cutting edge. The clothes—many by local designers—are very feminine and whimsical. Good vintage wear is on offer, as well. ⊠ *54 rue St-Viateur Ouest, Mile End, Montréal* ☎ *514/271–2129* ⊕ *www.general54.com* ☾ *Mon.–Wed. noon–6 , Thurs.–Fri. noon–7, weekends noon–6* Ⓜ *Laurier.*

Unicorn. Young Québebois designers like Barilà, Valérie Dumaine, and Eve Gravel are the stars of this beautiful Mile End boutique, which is also stocked with unique Canadian and international labels. Lots of black and white in the window displays speaks to the minimalist vibe within. ⊠ *5135 boul. St-Laurent, Mile End, Montréal* ☎ *514/544–2828* ⊕ *www.boutiqueunicorn.com* ☾ *Mon.–Wed. 1–6, Thurs.–Fri. 11–8, weekends 11–5* Ⓜ *Laurier.*

FOOD

La Vieille Europe. For a taste of the old Main, where generations of immigrants have come to shop, look no farther than this deli packed with sausages, cold cuts, jams, cheeses, coffee, and atmosphere. ⊠ *3855 boul. St-Laurent, Plateau Mont-Royal, Montréal* ☎ *514/842–5773* ☾ *Mon.–Wed. 7:30–6, Thurs.–Fri. 7:30 am–9 pm, Sat. 7:30–6, Sun. 9–5* Ⓜ *St-Laurent or Sherbrooke.*

Fodor's Choice ★ **Marché Jean-Talon.** This is the biggest and liveliest of the city's public markets. On weekends in summer and fall, crowds swarm the half acre or so of outdoor produce stalls, looking for the fattest tomatoes, sweetest melons, and juiciest strawberries. Its shops also sell meat, fish, cheese, sausage, bread, pastries, and other delicacies. The market is in the northern end of the city but is easy to get to by métro. ⊠ *7070 av. Henri-Julien, Little Italy, Montréal* ☎ *514/937–7754* ⊕ *www.marchespublics-mtl.com* Ⓜ *Jean-Talon.*

Marché Milano. One of the largest cheese selections in the city as well as fresh pastas of all kinds are the highlights of this market. An entire wall is devoted to olive oils and vinegars; there's also a butcher and a

It's well worth the métro ride up to the lively Marché Jean-Talon in Little Italy to experience seeing French Canadian farmers sell their local produce and prepared food.

sizable produce section. ⊠ *6862 boul. St-Laurent, Little Italy, Montréal* ☎ *514/273–8558* ⊗ *Mon.–Wed. 8–6, Thurs.–Fri. 8 am–9 pm, weekends 8–5* Ⓜ *Jean-Talon.*

Yannick Fromagerie. With an aroma to announce its vocation, this cheese shop is the go-to destination for the city's top chefs and cheese aficionados. Yannick Achim carries 400 varieties, buying from local dairies and stocking an astonishing international selection. Witness the look of surprise on shoppers' faces when they find Pykauba cheese from Québec beside Pecorino raw sheep's milk black truffles. Expect to be engaged in conversation by other cheese lovers, who eagerly trade advice on building the perfect after-dinner cheese plate. ⊠ *1218 rue Bernard O., Outremont, Montréal* ☎ *514/279 9376* ⊕ *www.yannickfromagerie.ca* Ⓜ *Outremont.*

JEWELRY

Charlotte Hosten. The celebrated jewelry designer opened her eponymous boutique in 2011. Watch the creativity happen in the atelier at the back of her charming shop while you peruse the vintage-look collections of necklaces and bracelets made with luxurious fabric. Gorgeous bridal couture includes headbands, belts, and clutches. ⊠ *122 rue Bernard Ouest, Mile End, Montréal* ☎ *514/274–8511* ⊕ *www.charlottehosten.com.*

HOUSEWARES

Arthur Quentin. Check out this elegant shop for fine French tableware from Gien and Maintenon, linens, gourmet kitchen gear, and a gift room with designer messenger bags, maps, pens, and notions. ⊠ *3960 rue St-Denis, Plateau Mont-Royal, Montréal* ☎ *514/843–7513* ⊕ *www. arthurquentin.com* Ⓜ *Sherbrooke.*

Zone. Fine and funky designs for kitchen, bath, and living, plus afford-able gifts galore, make this growing chain a must-stop for Montrealers on their Sunday strolls. It opens every day at 10, even Sunday. ✉ *4246 rue St-Denis, Plateau Mont-Royal, Montréal* ☎ *514/845–3530* ⊕ *www.zonemaison.com* Ⓜ *Sherbrooke or Mont-Royal.*

LINGERIE

Deuxième Peau. A tiny shop tucked away in a basement, Second Skin sells a fine assortment of French lingerie. While you're feeling brave and beautiful, kill two birds with one stone and try on a bathing suit. ✉ *4457 rue St-Denis, Plateau Mont-Royal, Montréal* ☎ *514/842–0811* ⊕ *www.deuxiemepeau.com* Ⓜ *Mont-Royal.*

SHOES

John Fluevog. Unusually curved lines, from the heels and vamps of his shoes to the interior design of his funky boutique, have cultivated a devout following for the Canadian shoe designer. Check the soles for curious and inspiring messages. ✉ *3857 rue St-Denis, Plateau Mont-Royal, Montréal* ☎ *514/509–1627* ⊕ *www.fluevog.com* Ⓜ *Sherbrooke.*

WESTMOUNT

The stylish locals, quaint architecture, and upscale boutiques work together to make Westmount a chic shopping destination. Rue Sher-brooke Ouest is a pleasant mix of hip boutiques, florists, home decor stores, and shops for mom and baby. Avenue Victoria is a smaller ver-sion of the same, with a few grocery stores and vintage shops thrown in for good measure. There are plenty of cafés and bistros scattered along the way where you can refuel after breaking out the plastic. The clos-est métro is Vendôme, or you can take Bus 24 west from downtown.

ANTIQUES

Ruth Stalker Antiques. She made her reputation finding and salvaging fine pieces of early Canadian pine furniture, but Ruth Stalker has also developed a good instinct for such folk art as exquisitely carved hunting decoys, weather vanes, and pottery. ✉ *4447 rue Ste-Catherine Ouest, Westmount, Montréal* ☎ *514/931–0822* ⊙ *Tues.–Sat. 11–5* ⊙ *Closed Sun. and Mon.* Ⓜ *Atwater.*

ART

Galerie de Bellefeuille. This Westmount gallery has a knack for discov-ering important new talents. It represents many of Canada's top con-temporary artists as well as some international ones. Its 5,000 square feet hold a good selection of sculptures, paintings, and limited-edition prints. ✉ *1367 av. Greene, Westmount, Montréal* ☎ *514/933–4406* ⊕ *www.debellefeuille.com* ⊙ *Mon.–Sat. 10–6, Sun. noon–5:30* ⊙ *Closed Sun. in July and Aug.* Ⓜ *Atwater.*

CLOTHING

James. Here you'll find shopping for the glamorous hippie. Shelves stocked with a great mix of designer jeans complement the well-edited collections of flirty dresses, romantic blouses, and soft knits. It closes on Thursday and Friday at 7. ✉ *4910 rue Sherbrooke Ouest, Westmount, Montréal* ☎ *514/369–0700* ⊕ *www.jamesboutique.com* Ⓜ *Vendôme.*

JoshuaDAVID. One of Victoria Village's best boutiques may be small, but it's packed with a great selection of contemporary labels, including Diane von Furstenberg, McQ Alexander McQueen, and plenty of Rich & Skinny denim. Rings by Kara Ross add bling to any outfit. ✉ *4926 rue Sherbrooke Ouest, Westmount, Montréal* ☎ *514/788–4436* ⊕ *www. joshuadavid.ca* Ⓜ *Vendôme.*

Mimi & Coco. Check out this local collection of basic and lace-trimmed T-shirts designed in Montréal and made in Italy of super-fine cotton. More branches around town include one downtown in Les Cours Mont-Royal, in Little Italy, and on avenue Laurier Ouest. Mandy's salads in the Westmount and Laurier shops are to die for. ✉ *4927 rue Sherbrooke Ouest, Westmount, Montréal* ☎ *514/482–6362* ⊕ *www. mimicoco.com* Ⓜ *Vendôme*

Pretty Ballerinas. Open since 2009, this charming shop was the first in North America to stock these exclusive ballerina flats from Spain. Handmade on the island of Menorca, they come in a wide variety of colors and accents, including bows, bold graphics, and Swarovski crystals. Starting at C$180 per pair, you'll want to keep the pink ballerina shoe box to protect them—and because it's well, pretty. ✉ *392 av. Victoria, Westmount, Montréal* ☎ *514/489–3030* ⊕ *www.prettyballerinas. ca* Ⓜ *Vendôme.*

★   **TNT.** Budget enough time for this stop—6,000 square feet of designer shopping pleasure awaits you. Upstairs, find a mix of international and homegrown labels for women; downstairs men can take part in the action. Sales of 50–70% off are a frequent occurrence, bringing luxe goods to the masses. Plot your plan of attack as you sip one of Montréal's best café au lait from the in-store Java U. ✉ *4100 rue Ste-Catherine Ouest, Westmount, Montréal* ☎ *514/935–1588* ⊕ *www. tntfashion.ca* Ⓜ *Atwater.*

Sports and Outdoor Activities

WORD OF MOUTH

"Montreal is probably the best bicycling city in North America. The free Montreal city maps show all the bike lanes."

—zootsi

Updated by Vanessa Muri

Most Montrealers would probably claim they hate winter, but the city is full of cold-weather sports venues—skating rinks, cross-country ski trails, and toboggan runs—that see plenty of action. During warm-weather months, residents head for the tennis courts, bicycle trails, golf courses, and two lakes for boating and swimming.

You don't have to travel far from Montréal to find good downhill skiing or snowboarding. There's a wealth of ski centers in both the Laurentians and Eastern Townships, which are within an hour's drive from the city *(see the Side Trips from Montréal chapter for directions)*. As for cross-country, excellent trails can be found right in Parc du Mont-Royal, or on the Islands (Île Sainte-Hélène and Île Notre-Dame).

Despite the bitter winters (or perhaps because of them), Montréal has fallen in love with the bicycle, with enthusiasts cycling year-round. More than 560 kilometers (348 miles) of bike paths crisscross the metropolitan area, and bikes are welcome on the first car of métro trains during off-peak hours.

The city is truly passionate about Canada's national sport, hockey. If you're here during the hockey season, try to catch a Montréal Canadiens game at Centre Bell, or at the very least find yourself a good sports bar.

BIKING

Weather permitting, one of the best ways to discover Montréal is on a bicycle. This is an incredibly bike-friendly metropolis, and there are thousands of designated bike paths connecting diverse neighborhoods across the island, running along the river and through parks and forests. If you like to bike but would rather not do it on city streets, ferries at the Old Port can take you to Île Ste-Hélène and the south shore of the St. Lawrence River, where riders can connect to hundreds of miles of trails in the Montérégie region.

DID YOU KNOW?

Not far from downtown Montréal is one of the area's best
white-water rafting spots, the
Lachine rapids.

SAUTE MOUTON
JET BOATING sur les rapids

Bixi. Available 24 hours a day, seven days per week, April through November, these bikes are a convenient way to explore the city. Public bicycle rental stations are located as far west as NDG (Notre-Dame-de-Grace, a western Montréal neighborhood) and east to the Parc Olympique (home of the Olympic Stadium from the 1976 Olympics), and as far south as Parc Jean-Drapeau and even Longueuil (a south shore neighborhood). Rental costs C$7 for a 24-hour period and C$15 for 72 hours, and is easily done with the swipe of a credit card. Designed for quick (but unlimited) trips between Bixi stations, anything over a 30-minute ride incurs an extra charge, so always keep your next Bixi station in mind. Monthly and yearly subscriptions are also available for longer stays. ⊠ *Montréal* ☎ *514/789–2494, 877/820– 2453* ⊕ *montreal.bixi.com.*

> **TOP FIVE SPORTS EXPERIENCES**
>
> ■ Catch a Montréal Canadiens game.
>
> ■ Bike around the Old Port, then take the ferry across to Parc Jean-Drapeau to finish your ride.
>
> ■ Go white-water rafting on the Lachine rapids.
>
> ■ Ice-skate for free on Île Ste-Hélène's huge rink.
>
> ■ Hike up to the top of Mont-Royal for a fantastic view of the city.

Fodor's Choice ★ **Féria de Vélo de Montréal** (*Montréal Bike Festival*). Montrealers enjoy a love affair with the bicycle, and thus it's no surprise that the Montréal Bike Festival has evolved into a week-long event. The biggest such celebration in North America includes the **Tour la Nui**t, a 22-kilometer (14-mile) ride through the city at night. It all culminates with as many as 50,000 cyclists taking over the streets for the **Tour de l'Île,** a 50-kilometer (31-mile) ride along a route encircling Montréal. ⊠ *Montréal* ☎ *514/521–8356, 800/567–8356* ⊕ *www.velo.qc.ca.*

Fitz & Follwell Co. There is no better way to explore Montréal than by bike—except with a friendly, knowledgeable guide pointing out the sights and taking you safely through the city, perhaps. Fitz & Follwell Co. offer a variety of tours, including the popular 'Montreal Highlights,' but go deeper and try 'Hoods & Hidden Gems' to really learn what makes this city tick. They also offer bike rentals, walking tours, and snow tours in winter. ⊠ *115 av. du Mont-Royal West, Plateau Mont-Royal* ☎ *514/840-0739* ⊕ *www.fitzandfollwell.co.*

★ **Lachine Canal.** The most popular cycling trail on the island begins at the Old Port and winds its way to the shores of Lac St-Louis in Lachine. Pack a picnic lunch; there are plenty of green spaces where you can stop and refuel along the way. ⊠ *Montréal.*

Vélo Montréal. For longer cycling excursions, renting a bike from Vélo Montréal is your best bet. Each rental includes a bicycle helmet, bottle cage, lock, and rear carrier rack. Packages start at C$15 for two hours and go all the way to C$120 for a full week. They even lease tandem bikes, a fun alternative for couples. ⊠ *3880 rue Rachel Est, Hochelaga-Maisonneuve* ☎ *514/259–7272* ⊕ *www.velomontreal.com* Ⓜ *Pie-IX.*

The Route Verte

Stretches of what's called the most extensive route of biking trails in North America pass right through the very heart of downtown Montréal.

The Route Verte (Green Route) is a free 4,000-kilometer (2,485-mile) network of paths, shared roadways, and paved shoulders that traverse the province of Québec.

The cycling group Vélo Québec began first talking about the possibility of a province-wide bike network back in the 1980s, but it wasn't until 1995 that the government announced it would fund the C$88.5 million project to be built over the next 12 years.

More than 200 miles of the Route Verte cover the streets of the city. It passes through downtown, stretches up Mont-Royal, hugs the coast near the Lachine Canal, and extends out to Parc Jean-Drapeau, just to name a few of the major areas covered.

For more information, including maps, suggested routes, and other trip-planning tools, check out the website at ⊕ www.routeverte.com.

6

BOATING

In Montréal you can climb aboard a boat at a downtown wharf and be crashing through Class V white water minutes later.

Lachine Rapids Tours. Discover the Lachine Rapids on a large jet boat— and bring a change of clothes. Lachine Rapids Tours offers daily departures (every two hours) from May through October. The price is C$67 per adult, with all gear included, and the trip lasts an hour. Another option is a 20-minute jaunt around the Islands in a 12-passenger boat that reaches speeds up to 80 kph (50 mph). Boats leave every half hour between 11 am and 6 pm from mid-May to Labor Day and cost C$26 for adults. Trips are narrated in French and English. ⊠ *47 de la Commune Ouest, Clock Tower Pier (for jet-boating) and Jacques Cartier Pier (for speedboating), at Old Port, Old Montréal* ☎ *514/284–9607* ⊕ *www.jetboatingmontreal.com* Ⓜ *Champ-de-Mars.*

FOOTBALL

When Montrealers think football, they think of their cherished Alouettes, who play their home games at the foot of Mont-Royal Park in the wonderfully intimate Molson Stadium.

Montréal Alouettes. From July to October, cheers from the Percival Molson Stadium can be heard around the city. Canadian Football League national champions in 2009 and 2010, the Montréal Alouettes keeps expanding their devoted fan base. The rules are slightly different than American football, with a bigger field (110 yards), 12 players on the field, and only three downs. End zone seats start at C$22, with Red Zone tickets reaching C$92. The STM offers a free shuttle to the game to ticket holders. ⊠ *475 av. des Pins Ouest, Downtown* ☎ *514/787– 2500 information, 514/787–2525 tickets* ⊕ *www.montrealalouettes. com* Ⓜ *McGill.*

GOLF

Montréal golf enthusiasts have several excellent golf courses available to them, many less than a half-hour drive from downtown. If you're willing to trek a bit farther (about 45 minutes), you'll find some of the best golfing in the province.

Club de Golf Métropolitain Anjou (*Anjou Metropolitan Golf Club*). A clubhouse featuring a steak-house restaurant, several banquet halls, a bistro, a pro shop with an indoor practice range (winter only), and an outdoor driving range all serve to make this a top-notch facility—not to mention, of course, the par-72, 18-hole championship golf course. The club is only a 20-minute drive from downtown Montréal. Dress code in effect. ⊠ *9555 boul. du Golf, Anjou* ☎ *514/353–5353* ⊕ *www. golfmetropolitainanjou.com* ⚐ *Championship golf course: 18 holes. Par 72. 7005 yards. Greens Fee: C$25–45. Executive course: 11 holes. Par 33. 2751 yards. Greens Fee: C$15–17* ☉ *Daily 6 am–9 pm* Ⓜ *Honoré-Beaugrand* ⚑ *Facilities: Driving range, golf carts, restaurant.*

The Falcon. A relative newcomer on the Greater Montréal golf scene—inaugurated in 2002—it rapidly became one of the best courses in Québec. Situated just 25 minutes west of downtown in the picturesque and largely Anglophone village of Hudson (which is worth a visit in itself). Recent improvements include a two million dollar clubhouse. Early bird specials profit those who don't mind a 7 am tee off. ⊠ *59 Cambridge, Hudson* ☎ *450/458–1997* ⊕ *www.falcongolf.ca* ⚐ *Championship golf course: 18 holes. Par 72. 7096 yards. Slope: 136 Greens Fee: C$50–60.* ⚑ *Facilities: Driving range, putting green, golf carts, rental clubs, lessons, restaurant, clubhouse, practice facilities.*

Golf Ste-Rose. Just a short hop over the bridge to the island of Laval, this course is perhaps the most beautiful in Québec, with lovely views of the Rivière des Mille-Îles, hardwood forests, and myriad number of ponds. The course features four sets of tees to accommodate different skill levels. ⊠ *1400 boul. Mattawa, Ste-Rose, Laval* ☎ *450/628–6072, 450/628–3573* ⊕ *www.golfsterose.groupebeaudet.com* ⚐ *Golf course: 18 holes. Par 70. 6134 yards. Slope: 125. Greens Fee: C$25–56.* ⚑ *Facilities: Driving range, golf carts, rental clubs, restaurant, bar.*

Tourisme Québec. For a complete listing of the many golf courses in the area, this is the best place to start. ⊠ *Montréal* ☎ *514/873–2015, 800/363–7777* ⊕ *www.bonjourquebec.com.*

HOCKEY

Ice hockey is nothing short of an institution in Montréal, the city that arguably gave birth to the sport back in the late 19th century. Although variations of the game are said to have been played in other U.S. and Canadian cities as early as 1800, the first organized game of modern hockey was played in Montréal in 1875, and the first official team, the McGill University Hockey Club, was founded in Montréal in 1880. The city's beloved Montréal Canadiens is the oldest club in the National Hockey League and, as Montrealers will be keen to tell you, one of the most successful teams in North American sports history. The

Hockey is Canada's national sport, so if you're here during the season, don't miss the chance to see the Montréal Canadiens take to the ice.

Habs, taken from Habitants, or early settlers, as they are affectionately referred to locally, have won 24 Stanley Cups, although they've been struggling in the standings for several years now and haven't won a cup since the 1992–93 season. Nevertheless, Les Canadiens are a great source of pride to the city's sports fans, and tickets for their local games continue to be a hot commodity.

Montréal Canadiens. The Habs meet National Hockey League rivals at the Centre Bell from October through April (and even later if they make the play-offs). Buy tickets in advance to guarantee a seat. ⊠ *1909 av. des Canadiens-de-Montréal, Downtown* ☎ *877/668–8269, 514/790–2525* ⊕ *canadiens.nhl.com* Ⓜ *Lucien-L'Allier or Peel.*

ICE-SKATING

Come the winter months, you don't have to look very far to find an ice-skating rink in Montréal. There are municipally run outdoor—and some indoor—rinks in virtually every corner of the city.

Accès Montréal. For information on the numerous ice-skating rinks (at least 195 outdoor and 21 indoor) in the city, it's best to call or check the website listed. Outdoor rinks are open from December until mid-March, and admission is free. The rinks on Île Ste-Hélène and at the Old Port are especially large, but there is a C$6 admission charge to skate at the latter. ⊠ *Montréal* ☎ *514/872–1111* ⊕ *www.ville.montreal.qc.ca.*

Atrium le 1000 de la Gauchetière. Inside the tallest building in Montréal, this skating rink lies under a glass atrium, allowing sunlight to shine down on the rink year-round. Adult admission is C$7, with skate rental at C$6.50 per day; they often offer 2-for-1 admission and specials for tourists on Wednesdays. After working up an appetite, hit any one of the 13 restaurants in the surrounding food court. ⊠ *1000 rue de la Gauchetière, Downtown* ☎ *514/395–0555* ⊕ *www.le1000.com* Ⓜ *Bonaventure.*

JOGGING

Parc du Mont-Royal. The gravel Olmsted Road in Parc du Mont-Royal is a superb place for a tranquil jog surrounded by nature. For a panoramic view of downtown, head to the Kondiaronk lookout. ⊠ *Montréal* ☎ *514/843–8240* ⊕ *www.lemontroyal.qc.ca* ⊙ *Daily 6 am–midnight* Ⓜ *Mont-Royal.*

RACING

Grand Prix. Every year in early June (except for a brief interruption in 2009), the Gilles Villeneuve Circuit plays host to the pinnacle of all racing events. The Formula One race attracts over 100,000 aficionados to the race track, where tickets start at C$45.25 for general admission (one day) and C$267.50 for grandstand tickets (three days). Be sure to book your accommodation early for that entire week, as hotels operate at maximum capacity (and maximum cost too). ⊠ *Parc Jean Drapeau, 222 Circuit Gilles Villeneuve, Île Notre-Dame* ☎ *514/350-0000* ⊕ *www. circuitgillesvilleneuve.ca.*

ROCK CLIMBING

If you're planning on scaling any of the considerable mountains in the nearby Laurentians or Eastern Townships, you might first want to practice your technique at an indoor climbing center in Montréal.

☺ **Escalade Horizon Roc.** Located deep in the heart of the city's east end, close to the Olympic Stadium, Escalade Horizon Roc has expanded to feature more than 27,000 square feet of climbing surfaces for all levels, making it the largest climbing center in the world. It's also the only one to offer an indoor course of high ropes with an 80-foot zip line. Because group visits take priority over individual visits, it's best to phone ahead. ⊠ *2350 rue Dickson, Hochelaga-Maisonneuve* ☎ *514/899-5000* ⊕ *www.horizonroc.com* ⊙ *Weekdays 10–11, Sat. 9–6, Sun. 9–5* Ⓜ *l'Assomption.*

SKIING AND SNOWBOARDING

There are pros and cons to skiing in the Eastern Townships and the Laurentians. The slopes in the Townships are generally steeper and slightly more challenging, but it requires more time to get out to them. Also, the Townships' centers tend to be quieter and more family-oriented, so if it's après-ski action you're looking for, you might prefer heading out to a Laurentian hill like Mont St-Sauveur where, for many, partying is as much the experience as is conquering the slopes.

As for cross-country skiing, you needn't even leave the city to find choice locations to pursue the sport. There's a network of winding trails stretching throughout Parc du Mont-Royal, and the Lachine Canal offers a 12-kilometer (7-mile) stretch of relatively flat terrain, making for both a scenic and relatively simple cross-country excursion.

Tourisme Québec. The "Ski-Québec" brochure available from the tourism office has a wealth of information about skiing in and around the city, while the website has a complete lists of all the hills and trails in the province. ✉ *Montréal* ☎ *514/873–2015, 877/266-5687* ⊕ *www. bonjourquebec.com.*

⇨ *For more information on skiing in the Eastern Townships and the Laurentians, see Chapter 9, Side Trips from Montréal.*

CROSS-COUNTRY

Cap-St-Jacques Regional Park. The best cross-country skiing on the island is found along the 32 km (20 miles) of trails in the 900-acre Cap-St-Jacques park in the city's west end, about a half-hour drive from downtown. To get to the park via public transportation, take the métro to the Henri-Bourassa station and then Bus 68 west. ✉ *20099 boul. Gouin Ouest, Pierrefonds* ☎ *514/280–6871, 514/280–7272* ⊕ *www. ville.montreal.qc.ca (French only)* Ⓜ *Henri-Bourassa to Bus 68 west.*

Parc du Mont-Royal. Within Montréal, "the mountain," as it's familiarly called, is essentially a toboggan run, but its modest slope makes it ideal for beginners and little ones learning to ski, and a good place to get in a quick cross-country workout. ✉ *Montréal* ☎ *514/843–8240* ⊕ *www. lemontroyal.qc.ca.*

DOWNHILL

Mont Sutton. A quaint village, beautiful mountain—lots of glades—and plentiful snow make this the best skiing in the Eastern Townships (and possibly the province). It gets busy, but multiple chairlifts can handle nearly 12,000 people per hour. ✉ *Sutton* ☎ *450/538-2545, 866/538-2545* ⊕ *www.montsutton.com.*

Mont Tremblant. This huge resort is the best in the Laurentians for skiing, though it can be pricey. Sleep, ski, and eat in total comfort—there are plenty of high-end hotels on site, some offering luxury spa services. The pedestrian village is like something out of a Disney fairytale, with charming storefronts and colorful rooftops. Four slopes, 95 runs, and 14 lifts await, all a two hours' drive north of Montréal. ✉ *1000 Chemin des Voyageurs, Mont-Tremblant* ☎ *866/356–2233* ⊕ *www.tremblant.ca.*

SOCCER

Although soccer isn't quite the phenomenon in Montréal that it is elsewhere around the globe, the city has been supporting one professional team, the Montréal Impact, since 1993. A stadium built expressly for the Impact that opened in May 2008 is a strong indication of the sport's increasing popularity.

Montréal Impact FC. The Impact have moved up a notch on the playing field. Now a Major League Soccer member, which represents the highest level in the United States and Canada, fans can expect the likes of

David Beckham to make the occasional appearance in Montréal. Still at Saputo Stadium, which underwent expansion to hold 20,341 seats (7,000 of which will be covered), teams play from March until December. ⊠ *4750 Sherbrooke Est, Rosemont* ☎ *514/328–3668, 866/955–4672* ⊕ *www.impactmontreal.com* Ⓜ *Viau.*

SWIMMING

Most of the city's municipal outdoor pools are open from mid-June through August. Admission is free on weekdays. On weekends and holidays there's a small fee of no more than C$4 at some pools, depending on the borough.

Parc-Plage l'Île Notre-Dame. Île Notre-Dame is home to the city's man-made beach. It's probably the cleanest water in Montréal, which makes the C$8 entrance fee totally worth it. The beach is open from 10 am to 7 pm daily, from mid-June to mid-August. To get there by public transit, take Bus 167 from the métro station. ⊠ *West side of Île Notre-Dame, Île Notre-Dame* ☎ *514/872–6120* ⊕ *www.parcjeandrapeau.com* Ⓜ *Jean-Drapeau.*

TENNIS

The City of Montréal maintains public tennis courts in several neighborhood parks. Fees vary from court to court but are generally quite reasonable. If you prefer to watch, the Rogers Cup in August is the perfect opportunity to catch international tennis stars hit center court.

Accès Montréal. The Jeanne-Mance, Kent, Lafontaine, and Somerled parks all have public courts. For details, contact Accès Montréal. ⊠ *Montréal* ☎ *514/872–1111* ⊕ *www.ville.montreal.qc.ca.*

The Rogers Cup. Tennis fans will definitely enjoy this international tournament, which draws some of the biggest names in tennis to the metropolis every year. In existence since 1881, only Wimbledon and the U.S. Open have been around longer. Women play in Montréal the even years, while men play odd (with the opposite taking place simultaneously in Toronto). Tickets start as low as C$10 for single sessions. Lots of shops and restaurants are also on site. ⊠ *285 Faillon St. Ouest, Villeray* ☎ *855/836-6470* ⊕ *www.rogerscup.com.*

TRAPEZE

If you've ever longed to run away and join the circus, then the Trapezium can help you fulfill that fantasy.

↺ **Trapezium.** Instructors assess your skill level and then teach you how to fly through the air with the greatest of ease. Even the faint of heart have been known to take the plunge on the trapeze in the center's safe and friendly environment. ⊠ *2350 rue Dickson, Montréal Est* ☎ *514/251–0615* ⊕ *www.trapezium.qc.ca* ✑ *C$40 for 1 class* Ⓜ *l'Assomption.*

WINDSURFING AND SAILING

Although people have been sailing it for centuries, and windsurfing it for at least a couple of decades, who would ever have thought in a city where winters can last six months there would be opportunities to actually surf the St. Lawrence River? In 1999, South African champion kayaker and river surfer Corran Addison discovered a heretofore unknown yet ever-present 6-foot-tall standing wave that never breaks, thus allowing for an epic ride.

École de Voile de Lachine. The Lachine Sailing School offers windsurfing and sailing courses for groups or individuals. Windsurfing boards and small sailboats are available to rent upon completion of the required courses. ⊠ *3045 boul. St-Joseph, Lachine* ☎ *514/634-4326* ⊕ *www. voilelachine.com* Ⓜ *Angrignon.*

6

Where to Eat

WORD OF MOUTH

"Poutine is best bought from a chip wagon late at night (that is unless you go for Normand Laprise's version with fois gras at Toqué in Montreal)."

—laverendrye

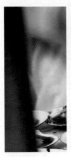

Updated by
Marcella De
Vincenzo

Montréal's restaurant scene is one of Canada's most cosmopolitan, with trendy eateries popping up regularly, their menus heavily influenced by flavors from around the globe, often with an added touch of French flair.

The thing to know is that many can be found in the most unlikely locations. Toqué!, for example, long touted as one of the city's best, is on the ground floor of an office tower in the financial district. Still, there are those certain areas—such as rue St-Denis and boulevard St-Laurent between rues Sherbrooke and Mont-Royal—that have long been the city's hottest dining strips, with everything from sandwich shops to high-price gourmet shrines. The bring-your-own-wine craze started on rue Prince-Arthur and avenue Duluth, two lively pedestrian streets in the Plateau that still specialize in good, relatively low-cost meals. Most downtown restaurants are clustered between rues Guy and Peel on the side streets that run between boulevard René-Lévesque and rue Sherbrooke. Some interesting little cafés and restaurants have begun to spring up in the heart of the antiques district along rue Notre-Dame Ouest near avenue Atwater. Old Montréal, too, has a sizable collection of well-regarded restaurants, most of them clustered on rue St-Paul and place Jacques-Cartier.

You can usually order à la carte, but make sure to look for the table d'hôte, a two- to four-course package deal. It's often more economical, offers interesting specials, and may also take less time to prepare. For a splurge, consider a *menu dégustation,* a five- to seven-course tasting menu executed by the chef. It generally includes soup, salad, fish, sherbet (to cleanse the palate), a meat dish, dessert, and coffee or tea. At the city's finest restaurants, such a meal for two, along with a good bottle of wine, can cost more than C$200 and last four hours.

Menus in many restaurants are bilingual, but some are only in French. If you don't understand what a dish is, don't be shy about asking; a good server will be happy to explain. If you feel brave enough to order in French, remember that in French an *entrée* is an appetizer, and what Americans call an entrée is a *plat principal,* or main dish.

Dinner reservations are highly recommended for weekend dining.

MONTREAL'S TOP POUTINE SPOTS

Poutine (fries with gravy and cheese curds) is one of Montréal's favorite snacks. Try the dish at one of these top spots.

Go to **La Banquise** (✉ *994 rue Rachel Est* ☎ *514/525–2415* ✛ *G3*) any time of day or night and join the crowd for a classic poutine. Or pick from their generous menu consisting of many varieties, such as poutine with guacamole, sour cream, and tomatoes, or poutine with turkey and peas. Newcomer **PoutineVille** (✉ *1348 Beaubien St. Est, corner Lanaudière* ☎ *514/544–8800* ✛ *G1*) allows you to express your creative side with their design-your-own poutine concept. With a base of three different types of potatoes and many high quality toppings, the combinations are endless. **Patati Patata Friterie De Luxe** (✉ *4177 St-Laurent* ☎ *514/844–0216* ✛ *F2*) may be small but it packs a big punch on the poutine circuit. This quaint location is always filled with locals but is well worth the wait.

MONTRÉAL DINING PLANNER

RESERVATIONS

Reservations are key. Call at least three nights ahead for busy bistros. Because Montrealers eat quite late, it's possible to arrive unannounced before 7 pm and get a table—if you're lucky.

HOURS

Montréal restaurants keep unpredictable schedules. Some close Sunday, some close Monday, some are open every day. Call ahead. Kitchens generally stop taking orders at 10 or 11 pm, but eateries in the Old Port can remain open later in summer, as do hot spots in the Plateau and Mile End. Downtown locations tend to focus on lunch, so they close earlier. Brunch is over by 3 pm.

DINING WITH KIDS

Since smoking was banned in restaurants, it's more common to see kids in bistros, brasseries, and even upscale dining rooms. *Eateries that welcome families are marked with a ducky symbol.*

WHAT TO WEAR

Dress up! Women in Montréal take pride in their appearance, which features heels, pretty scarves, dresses, and jewelry. What about men? The standard uniform for hipsters is a fashionable shirt with dark jeans or dress pants. No running shoes, please. Men should also wear a jacket for restaurants in the $$$ range and above.

PRICES

Long live the table d'hôte. This cost-cutting special is a regular feature at many Montréal restaurants. Chefs enjoy changing the three-course special on a daily or weekly basis, so it never gets boring. ■**TIP→** Upscale restaurants serve elaborate lunch tables d'hôte at cut-rate prices, while some eateries have early-bird prix-fixe deals. When it comes time to pay, it's not a "given" that you can use your debit card. Many eateries only accept cash or credit.

OLD MONTRÉAL

In the early 1990s, the food scene in Old Mon-tréal was dismal—limited to a few steak houses and kitschy cafés. It was easy to find a sandwich shop, but not much else.

Old Montréal buzzes at lunch: (above) Artists gather for light fare at Cluny Art Bar; (below, left) Office workers grab grub from Café Titanic; (above, right) Muvbox draws lines of hungry lobster fans.

An influx of chef-owned restaurants changed the dining scene of the neighborhood, so now office workers and tourists alike can find a plethora of culinary options. The decor in most restaurants tend to be uniform, with exposed stone and brick walls, old beams, and refinished wooden floors, but the cuisine is quite diverse, from regional game (especially deer) and seafood to fine dining and French cafés. It's common to see daily changing menus written on chalkboards, since market-fresh food is the current trend. Boutique hotels in the area, like the Nelligan and the Hôtel Place d'Armes, are proud of their on-site restaurants, where you find some of the city's top dining options.

GOURMET TO-GO

Follow the office workers at noon, and head to **Café Titanic** (✉ *445 rue St-Pierre, near St. Paul* ☎ *514/849–0894* ✛ *E6*) for specialty sandwiches and gourmet salads. Just below street level, it's hard to find, but worth the hunt. You'll see customers outside, nibbling Brie and pesto baguette sandwiches and homemade chunky chocolate cookies. There are a handful of tables inside, but the trade is mostly takeout.

COUTURE CAFETERIAS

Old Montréal is home to many cafeteria-style eateries for lunch with long communal tables and lively chat. They all seem to have a common aesthetic: chalkboard menus, hardwood floors, and an "industrial chic" ethos. Here are our favorites:

Beniaminos (✉ *455 rue Viger Ouest, near rue McGill* ☎ *514/861-7770* ✛ *D6*). This colorful Italian eatery is more than just a humble take-out restaurant, serving delectable homemade panini, flavorful meat loaf, pasta, and meatballs. The orzo, fennel, and chicken salad, adorned with walnuts, pistachios, and peaches is the perfect light lunch on a hot summer day. If possible, order the olive bread (it runs out quickly!) and accompany it with an imported Italian soft drink or a bracing coffee.

Cluny Art Bar (✉ *257 rue Prince, near rue William* ☎ *514/866-1213* ☉ *Closed weekends* ✛ *D6*). Tucked into the Darling Foundry, this is a hip artist hangout serving yummy breakfast, good coffee, and light lunches. Sandwiches come on olive, onion, and ciabatta bread. On a cold day, there's nothing better than a bowl of the hearty beef and new potato stew paired with a glass of red wine.

Le Cartet (✉ *106 rue McGill, near rue St. Paul* ☎ *514/871-8887* ✛ *D6*). It feels like Paris here, where an international crowd reads newspapers and orders hot gourmet lunches at a decent price. Duck confit and fillet of dory are popular items, and the weekend brunch is always a hit. Chocolates, nuts, olives, and oils sold in the shop up front make for great gifts.

Soupe Soup (✉ *649 rue Wellington, near rue McGill* ☎ *514/759-1159* ✛ *D6*). Come to this airy, high-ceilinged loft for the exceptional lunch (think goat cheese and fig sandwiches; red chili soup with papaya; and bread pudding). A dozen types of soup are made fresh each day, and the grilled cheese sandwich—the perfect accompaniment—is sublime. For just C$3.50, you can order a small glass of wine and admire the street views through thick casement windows.

LOBSTER LUNCH

Finally, some street food in Old Montréal! **Muvbox** (⊕ *www.muvboxconcept. com* ✛ *D6*) isn't the typical lunch truck or hot-dog cart; it's a lobster shack parked permanently by the water, at the bottom of rue McGill. It opens its doors in May, with the good weather, and packs up shop when it gets cold again (usually in October). Made from a refurbished shipping container, Muvbox is a fine example of eco-design, with bright red signage, recycled bits, and fold-out walls. Regulars are torn between the juicy lobster rolls (grab plenty of napkins)—and the tasty lobster pizza, baked in a wood-burning oven. The bike path runs right in front of Muvbox, so nearby tables and chairs are full of helmeted diners wearing spandex. To avoid outdoor lineups under the midday sun, arrive before noon or after 1:30 pm. The box shuts at 9 pm (depending on weather) and is open daily. ✛ *E6*

7

THE PLATEAU AND ENVIRONS

Once a residential area, the Plateau is now the bohemian stomping ground for students, actors, and artists. Jewelry makers and drummers mix with web designers and playwrights, and sidewalks are alive with conversation.

(above) Act like a local and browse the stalls at Marché Jean-Talon; (above, right) Sip on a coffee at Au Deux Marie; (below, right) Or nibble on pastries at Brioche Lyonnaise.

The food scene on the Plateau ranges from trendy "dinner clubs"—restaurants that turn into riotous dance bars at midnight—to oyster bars, noodle joints, and esteemed steak houses. Café culture is vibrant, as is the famous bagel trade. The Plateau is where you'll find the perfect French bistro, where fresh bread is a point of pride, as is the new interest in sustainable fish. When sous chefs finish their training at a kitchen in the Old Port, they often open their own place here, hoping to make their mark—and their own designer poutine. Yet, the Plateau isn't limited to bistro fare. There's plenty of Thai food, sushi, *pho* (Vietnamese noodles), and luncheonettes for a simple wrap and salad. The ritzy dinner clubs are found on lower boulevard St-Laurent near Sherbrooke Street, but more homey bistros are tucked into the side streets.

MARKET TO MARKET

Rub elbows with the city's top chefs at the **Jean-Talon Market** (⊠ *7075 av. Casgrain, near Jean-Talon Est* ☎ *514/277–1379* ✛ *F1*). Marché Jean-Talon is a fun destination for browsing and is ringed with separate stores for cheese, fish, gourmet groceries, and fruit. The Marché des Saveurs du Québec, a store inside the market, delights visitors with local delicacies.

CAFÉ CULTURE

Montrealers get defensive about "the best café" on the Plateau, but a few stand out beyond argument:

Au Deux Marie (✉ *4329 rue St-Denis, near rue Marie-Anne Est* ☎ *514/844-7246* ✥ ✥ *F2*) intoxicates patrons with the aroma of coffee and pastries. Light streams in; chat is lively.

Brioche Lyonnaise (✉ *1593 rue St-Denis, near rue Ontario* ☎ *514/842-7017* ✥ *F4*) is where to get a sinfully buttery brioche and a steaming bowl of café au lait.

Café Olympico (✉ *24 rue St-Viateur Ouest, near rue Clark* ☎ *514/495-0746* ✥ *C2*), also known as "Open Da Night," has been serving up excellent espresso and café au lait to actors, hippies, and poets for 30 years.

Caffé in Gamba (✉ *5263 av. du Parc, near rue Fairmount Ouest* ☎ *514/656-6852* ✥ *C2*) is revered for buying their beans from top micro-roasters in North America.

THE BAKERY BIBLE

Baked goods are taken seriously in Montréal. Locals swear by the cakes and cupcakes at **Cocoa Locale** (✉ *4807 av. du Parc, near Mt. Royal* ☎ *514/271-7162* ✥ *E2*). Ditto goes for the Australian pie shop, **Ta** (✉ *4520 av. du Parc, near Mt. Royal* ☎ *514/277-7437* ✥ *E2*). Bagels should be purchased at **St-Viateur Bagel & Café** (✉ *263 St. Viateur Ouest* ☎ *514/276-8044* ✥ *C2*) and **Fairmount Bagel** (✉ *74 Fairmount Ouest* ☎ *514/272-0667* ✥ *C2*). Those in the know go to bakery **Kouign Amann** for the city's best croissants (✉ *322 av. du Mont-Royal Est* ☎ *514/845-8813* ✥ *F2*). For exceptional bread, there are multiple locations of **Première Moisson** (⊕ *www.premieremoisson.com*), but foodies opt for the imported French Retrodor flour used to make baguettes at **Mamie Clafoutis** (✉ *1291 rue Van Horne, near av. Outremont* ☎ *514/750-7245* ✥ *B1*). And **La Cornetteria** never disappoints with their fabulous *cornetti* (crescent-shaped pastry) (✉ *6528 boul. St-Laurent* ☎ *514/277-8030* ✥ *C1*).

BRUNCH DATE

Students and families head to **Chez Cora** (✉ *1396 rue Mont Royal, near rue Garnier* ☎ *514/525-9495* ✥ *H2*) to get their fix of breakfast favorites. **Beauty's Restaurant** (✉ *93 av. du Mont-Royal, near rue St-Urbain* ☎ *514/849-8883* ✥ *E2*), a landmark spot for bagels and smoked salmon, is another crowd-pleaser. Locals love the artsy ambiance of **L'Avenue** (✉ *922 av. du Mont-Royal* ☎ *514/523-8780* ✥ *G2*). **Leméac** (✉ *1045 av. Laurier Ouest* ☎ *514/270-0999* ✥ *B3*) packs its terrace each weekend with fans of the potato and leek *tartelette* and the chocolate French toast. **Le Petit Italien** (✉ *1265 av. Bernard* ☎ *514/278-0888* ✥ *B1*) offers a "dim sum"-style brunch, with a cart of pastries, fruit dishes, and small bites. New-ish to the brunch scene, **Lawrence** (✉ *5201 boul. St-Laurent* ☎ *514/503-1070* ✥ *C2*) guarantees a packed house with its homemade chocolate doughnuts.

7

MONTRÉAL RESTAURANT REVIEWS

Listed alphabetically within neighborhood.

OLD MONTRÉAL

$$$
MODERN
CANADIAN
✕ **Aix Cuisine du Terroir.** Planters of fresh flowers and semicircular banquettes provide a little privacy for couples sharing the seven-hour braised lamb with hashed fingerling potatoes, or the elk tartar. The crowd is made up of foodies pursuing dishes made with local products, and a great lunchtime menu starting at C$16 also attracts office workers in the area. In the summertime, the magnetic pull of raspberry mojitos and lychee martinis give guests the fortitude to trek up to the rooftop terrace. Brunch is available weekends from 11 to 3. ⑤ *Average main: C$25* ✉ *711 Côte de la Place-d'Armes, Old Montréal, Montréal* ☎ *514/904–1201* ⊕ *www.aixcuisine.com* ⚲ *Reservations essential* Ⓜ *Place-d'Armes* ⚓ *E6.*

$$$
FRENCH
✕ **Bonaparte.** Book a table in one of the front window alcoves and watch the carriages jostle by over the cobblestones as you dine. You can order à la carte—try the tuna steak or the venison—but the restaurant's best deal is the seven-course tasting menu, which includes such classics as lobster bisque flavored with anise, and breast of duck cooked with maple syrup and berries. Don't be intimidated by the number of courses, because portions are generally smaller than main-menu versions. Their delivery is gently paced by one of the city's most professional staffs. Regulars and guests from afar, including Sharon Stone, Angelina Jolie, Madonna, and tennis star Roger Federer, are no doubt charmed by host Michael Banks, a leading tastemaker and bon vivant in the Old Port. Guests that never want to leave might be heartened to discover there's a small inn upstairs. ⑤ *Average main: C$30* ✉ *443 rue St-François-Xavier, Old Montréal, Montréal* ☎ *514/844–4368* ⊕ *www. restaurantbonaparte.ca* ⚲ *Reservations essential* ⊗ *No lunch weekends and Mon. and Tues.y* Ⓜ *Place-d'Armes* ⚓ *E6.*

$$
EASTERN
EUROPEAN
✕ **Café Stash.** On chilly nights many Montrealers come here for sustenance—for borscht, pierogi, or cabbage and sausage—in short, for all the hearty specialties of a Polish kitchen. Live piano music is the perfect accompaniment for roasted wild boar or Wiener schnitzel served atop tables salvaged from an old convent. Seating is appropriately on pews from a chapel. Owner Anita Karski brings her know-how from 10 years waitressing at Stash, and service reflects that. ⑤ *Average main: C$15* ✉ *200 rue St-Paul Ouest, Old Montréal, Montréal* ☎ *514/845–6611* ⊕ *www.stashcafe.com* ⊗ *Mon.–Thurs. 11:30–10, Fri. 11:30–11, Sat. noon–11, Sun. noon–10* Ⓜ *Place-d'Armes* ⚓ *E6.*

$$$$
FRENCH
Fodor's Choice
★
✕ **Chez l'Épicier.** The menus at this classic French fusion restaurant are printed on brown paper, but the tables have crisp white linens and there's nothing down-market about the seasonal creative dishes: white asparagus soup with truffle oil, slow poached salmon, and a chocolate "club sandwich" with pineapple "fries." When you get here, take a moment to browse through the small section of shelves that showcase some fine ingredients, from top olive oils to tasty spreads. This is the kind of quiet place you go to canoodle with an old flame or new

BEST BETS FOR MONTRÉAL DINING

With hundreds of restaurants to choose from, how will you decide where to eat? Here are our favorite restaurants by price, cuisine, and experience. In the first column, Fodor's Choice properties represent the "best of the best" in every price category.

Fodor'sChoice★

Chez l'Épicier, p. 156
Joe Beef, p. 166
La Chronique, p. 173
La Croissanterie Flgaro, p. 176
L'Orignal, p. 162
Olive + Gourmando, p. 163
Osteria Venti, p. 163
Schwartz's Delicatessen, p. 172
St-Viateur Bagel & Café, p. 172
Toqué!, p. 163
Verses, p. 164

Best By Price

$

Café Souvenir, p. 176
Chalet Bar-B-Q, p. 178
Le Gourmet Burger, p. 167
Melina Phyllo Bar, p. 173
Olive + Gourmando, p. 163
Qing Hua Dumplings, p. 168
Schwartz's Delicatessen, p. 172

St-Viateur Bagel & Café, p. 172
Toi Moi et Café, p. 177

$$

Bottega Pizzeria, p. 174
Chez Doval, p. 169
Kazu, p. 167
La Croissanterie Figaro, p. 176
L'Express, p. 170
m:brgr, p. 168
Osteria Venti, p. 163
Rotisserie Panama, p. 174

$$$

Bonaparte, p. 156
Garde Manger, p. 161
Leméac, p. 177
Le Taj, p. 167
Pintxo, p. 171
Rosalie, p. 168
Tavern on the Square, p. 178
Toqué!, p. 163

$$$$

Chez l'Épicier, p. 156
Club Chasse et Pêche, p. 160
Joe Beef, p. 166

La Chronique, p. 173
L'Orignal, p. 162
Moishe's, p. 171
Verses, p. 164

Best By Cuisine

CAFÉS

Café Myriade, p. 164
Olive + Gourmando, p. 163
Toi Moi et Café, p. 177

FRENCH

Bonaparte, p. 156
Chez l'Épicier, p. 156
Le Mas des Oliviers, p. 167
L'Express, p. 170

ITALIAN

Bottega Pizzeria, p. 174
Da Emma, p. 160
Le Petit Italien, p. 177
Macaroni Bar, p. 171
Osteria Venti, p. 163
Ristorante Lucca, p. 175
Vinizza, p. 176

STEAK

Moishe's, p. 171
Gibbys, p. 161
Mister Steer, p. 168

VEGETARIAN

Chu Chai, p. 169

Best By Experience

BRUNCH

Brasserie Les Enfants Terribles, p. 176
Café Souvenir, p. 176
Leméac, p. 177
Toi Moi et Café, p. 177

HOT SPOTS

Garde Manger, p. 161
Joe Beef, p. 166
L'Express, p. 170
Les 400 Coups, p. 162
Hambar, p. 161

MOST ROMANTIC

Aix Cuisine du Terroir, p. 156
Chez l'Épicier, p. 156
Club Chasse et Pêche, p. 160

7

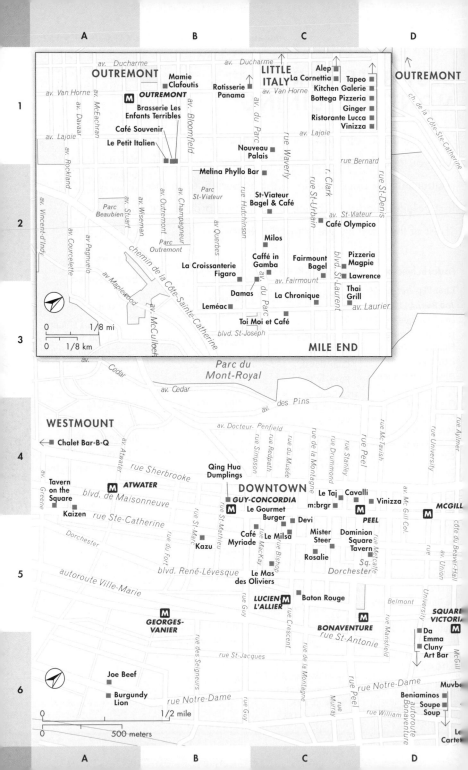

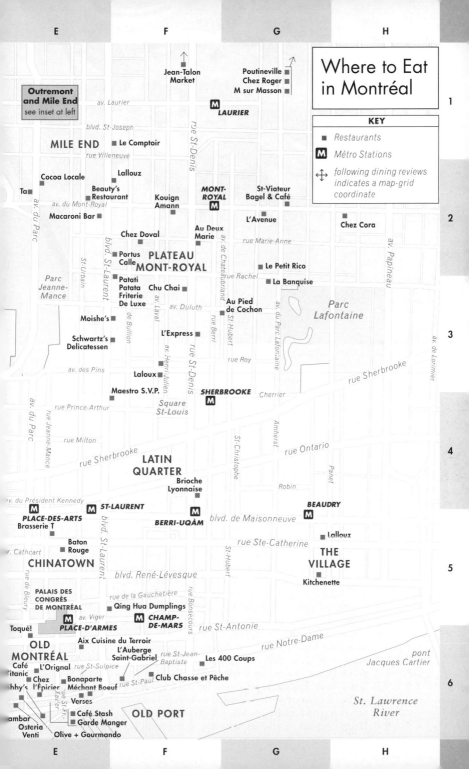

Where to Eat in Montréal

Outremont and Mile End
see inset at left

KEY
- ■ Restaurants
- Ⓜ Métro Stations
- ⟷ following dining reviews indicates a map-grid coordinate

Jean-Talon Market

Poutineville
Chez Roger
M sur Masson

Ⓜ **LAURIER**

av. Laurier

blvd. St-Joseph

MILE END

■ Le Comptoir

rue Villeneuve

Cocoa Locale ■

Lallouz ■

St-Viateur Bagel & Café ■

Ⓜ **MONT-ROYAL**

Ta ■

Beauty's ■ Restaurant

Kouign Amann ■

L'Avenue ■

Chez Cora ■

av. du Mont-Royal

Macaroni Bar ■

Au Deux Marie ■

rue Marie-Anne

Chez Doval ■

PLATEAU MONT-ROYAL

Le Petit Rico ■

Portus Calle ■

rue Rachel

La Banquise ■

Patati Patata Friterie De Luxe ■

Chu Chai ■

av. Duluth

Parc Lafontaine

Moishe's ■

L'Express ■

Au Pied de Cochon ■

Schwartz's Delicatessen ■

rue Roy

av. des Pins

Laloux ■

Maestro S.V.P. ■

Square St-Louis

Ⓜ **SHERBROOKE**

Cherrier

rue Sherbrooke

rue Prince-Arthur

rue Milton

rue Sherbrooke

LATIN QUARTER

rue Ontario

Brioche Lyonnaise

Robin

PLACE-DES-ARTS Ⓜ
Brasserie T ■

Ⓜ **ST-LAURENT**

Ⓜ **BERRI-UQÀM**

blvd. de Maisonneuve

Ⓜ **BEAUDRY**

Lallouz ■

Baton Rouge ■

rue Ste-Catherine

CHINATOWN

blvd. René-Lévesque

THE VILLAGE

Kitchenette ■

PALAIS DES CONGRÈS DE MONTRÉAL

rue de la Gauchetière

Qing Hua Dumplings ■

Ⓜ **CHAMP-DE-MARS**

av. Viger

Ⓜ **PLACE-D'ARMES**

rue St-Antoine

Toqué! ■

OLD MONTRÉAL

Aix Cuisine du Terroir ■
L'Auberge Saint-Gabriel ■

Les 400 Coups ■

pont Jacques Cartier

Café Titanic ■ L'Orignal ■

rue St-Jean-Baptiste

Chez l'Épicier ■

Bonaparte ■ Méchant Boeuf ■

Club Chasse et Pêche ■

Verses ■

OLD PORT

St. Lawrence River

Café Stash ■
Garde Manger ■

ambar Osteria Venti

Olive + Gourmando ■

Aix Cuisine du Terroir in Old Montréal has great seafood as well as a rooftop terrace.

date, sipping glasses of vino from the new wine cellar. $ *Average main: C\$35* ✉ *311 rue St-Paul Est, Old Montréal, Montréal* ☎ *514/878–2232* ⊕ *www.chezlepicier.com* ⌂ *Reservations essential* ◷ *No lunch Mon.– Wed. and weekends* Ⓜ *Place-d'Armes* ✛ *E6.*

\$\$\$\$
MODERN
CANADIAN

✕ **Club Chasse et Pêche.** Don't fret—this isn't a hangout for the local gun-and-rod set. The name—which means Hunting and Fishing Club—is an ironic reference to the wood-and-leather decor Chef Claude Pelletier and co-owner Hubert Marsolais inherited from the previous owners. Marsolais has jazzed it up, though, to reflect his innovative style, but the entrance is still one of the most discrete in town. Impeccable service has made this a favorite with the city's serious foodies. They gather to sip glasses of German and Austrian Riesling on the covered terrace, set in a garden across the street at the Château Ramezay. Try Pelletier's seared scallops, the seared foie gras, or suckling piglet with risotto. In the summer only (May to September) you can book lunch on their terrace; truly worth it. $ *Average main: C\$35* ✉ *423 rue St-Claude, Old Montréal, Montréal* ☎ *514/861–1112* ⊕ *www.leclubchasseetpeche.com* ⌂ *Reservations essential* ◷ *Closed Sun. and Mon.* Ⓜ *Champ-de-Mars* ✛ *F6.*

\$\$\$
ITALIAN

✕ **Da Emma.** The cellar of what used to be Montréal's first women's prison hardly sounds like the ideal setting for an Italian restaurant, but Grandma Emma's cooking is satisfying enough to drive out any bad vibes from those days. The place's stone walls and heavy beams make an ideal, catacomb-like setting for such Roman specialties as roasted lamb with grilled vegetables, fettuccini with porcini mushrooms, stuffed breast of veal, and tripe in tomato sauce. The local staff also serves harried celebrities like Jake Gyllenhaal, Frida Pinto, and Johnny Depp—repeat customers who enjoy the semi-privacy of the covered terrace and private garden. Note: no debit cards are accepted. $ *Average main: C$30 ⊠ 777 rue de la Commune Ouest, Old Montréal, Montréal* ☎ 514/392–1568 ⊙ *Closed Sun. No lunch Sat.* Ⓜ *Square-Victoria* ✛ *D6.*

$$$
MODERN
CANADIAN
✕ **Garde Manger.** It's no wonder that chef Chuck Hughes has his own television show, *Chuck's Day Off,* considering how much charm and skill he possesses, attracting pretty young patrons to his trendy dinner club. And this boy can cook. Diners gorge themselves on bountiful platters of seafood and lobster poutine. Vegetarians should go elsewhere, since bacon and meat feature prominently on the menu. Everyone, however, enjoys the recycled antiques and rustic ambience. Singles eat at the bar, where flirting is in high gear. After 11 pm, the music gets cranked and the party rages until 3 am. $ *Average main: C$28 ⊠ 408 rue St-Francois-Xavier, Old Montréal, Montréal* ☎ 514/678–5044 ⊕ *www. crownsalts.com/gardemanger* ⌲ *Reservations essential* ⊙ *Tues. Sat. 6 pm–closing* ⊙ *Closed Mon.* Ⓜ *Square-Victoria* ✛ *E6.*

$$$$
STEAKHOUSE
✕ **Gibbys.** Open 365 days per year, Gibbys is one of Montréal's most famous steak houses. Everything about it is old school: the historic building, the wooden beams, big fireplaces, and quality service. The restaurant is quite large, so it can accommodate large groups. Oysters Rockefeller, two-pound lobsters, and the rib steak are some of the most popular dishes here. Be sure to take an after-dinner stroll around the cobblestone streets as you view Old Montréal at night. $ *Average main: C$35 ⊠ 298 Place d'Youville, Old Montréal, Montréal* ☎ 514/282–1837 ⊕ *www.gibbys.com* ⌲ *Reservations essential* Ⓜ *Square-Victoria* ✛ *E6.*

$$$
MODERN
CANADIAN
✕ **Hambar.** Hambar is the type of place that satisfies at all hours. Head there for lunch, and make a beeline to the back counter to pick up a sandwich filled with charcuterie imported from Italy and Spain, along with some marinated vegetables made on-site. Or swing by for dinner and you might hobnob with the corporate world dressed to the nines, sitting next to locals sharing a *salumi* platter in their flip-flops. The menu changes with the seasons, but obviously ham plays a starring role. The dining room is beautifully decorated with huge windows, and the long communal tables are great for large groups. If you're coming on a date, side tables are perfect for a romantic tête-à-tête. In summer, enjoy the terrace with a glass of Tuscan Chianti. $ *Average main: C$30 ⊠ 355 rue McGill, Old Montréal, Montréal* ☎ 514/879–1234 ⊕ *www. hambar.ca* ⌲ *Reservations essential* ⊙ *No lunch on weekends* ✛ *E6.*

$$$$
MODERN FRENCH
✕ **L'Auberge Saint-Gabriel.** The wow factor is dialed up at this historic inn and restaurant: stone walls and wood-beamed ceilings give it an appropriate dash of drama. Thankfully, the food matches the ambience— dishes created by chef Eric Gonzalez are simply extraordinary. The best approach to dinner is to give Chef Gonzales carte blanche to create an eight-course menu for you and your guests (C$95; everyone at the table must take part). But if you prefer to orchestrate your own meal from the menu, their stunning paella is a great choice; the charcuterie platter is also winning. End the meal with a theatrical dessert: "The Abracadabra" begins as a chocolate sphere filled with apricots and chocolate, but once the waiter pours hot fudge all over it, everything magically

7

In Old Montréal, there are tons of restaurants with *terrasses* like this one, where you can enjoy the cobblestone streets and stone buildings while eating outside.

(and deliciously) melts. $ *Average main: C$35* ✉ *426 rue St-Gabriel, Old Montréal, Montréal* ☎ *514/878–3561* ⊕ *www.lesaint-gabriel.com* ⊘ *Closed Sun. and Mon. No lunch Sat.* Ⓜ *Place-d'Armes* ✛ *F6* .

$$$
MODERN
CANADIAN
✕ **Les 400 Coups.** Situated in Old Montréal, but away from the main tourist hubs, this gorgeous food and wine destination is perfect for both an intimate dinner for two or for a large group. The market fresh menu changes frequently but there's always a variation of the signature scallops dish or the beef tartare served with mustard ice cream. Popular among local foodies is the "green" dessert (apples, pistachios, olive oil, cilantro, in white chocolate yogurt). Lunch is served only on Friday, but dinner is available from Tuesday to Saturday evenings. A food and wine tasting is offered, starting at C$65 per person. $ *Average main: C$30* ✉ *400 Notre-Dame Est, Old Montréal, Montréal* ☎ *514/985–0400* ⊕ *www.les400coups.ca* ⌖ *Reservations essential* ⊘ *Closed Sun. and Mon.* ✛ *F6*

$$$$
MODERN
CANADIAN
Fodor's Choice
★
✕ **L'Orignal.** It's hard to know what to rave about first—the hunting lodge decor or the Québecoise cuisine. L'Orignal is the French word for moose, if you're wondering, and the restaurant's outdoorsy profile is reinforced in "chalet chic" details like maple tables, antlers, wooden paneling, and birch tree trunks. The menu is equally rustic, featuring boar shank, lamb burgers, deer, and grass-fed veal. All the game comes from specialty farmers in the region. If you get the chance, be sure to speak with resident oysterologist Daniel Notkin, who will happily explain his trade. $ *Average main: C$35* ✉ *479 rue St-Alexis, Old Montréal, Montréal* ☎ *514/303–0479* ⊕ *www.*

restaurantlorignal.com ⚷ *Reservations essential* ☺ *Open every day from 6 pm* Ⓜ *Place-d'Armes* ✛ *E6.*

$$$ ✕ **Méchant Boeuf.** If burgers are your thing, Hôtel Nelligan's casual din-
BRASSERIE ing room amplifies the comfort-food experience. The mighty Méchant hamburger is a winner, or try their beer-can chicken, crab cakes, hanger steak, or designer poutine. For dessert, the cheesecake is a splendid treat for two to share. The food may be humble, but the atmosphere is cheeky and chic, with an interior waterfall, brick walls, and an illuminated bar. A DJ spins music Thursday to Sunday, and different rock bands perform Tuesday and Wednesday nights. If you're hungry after a show, they have a C$23 late night menu starting at 11 pm. Ⓢ *Average main: C$25* ✉ *124 rue St-Paul Ouest, Old Montréal, Montréal* ☎ *514/788–4020* ⊕ *www. mechantboeuf.com* Ⓜ *Place-d'Armes* ✛ *E6.*

$ ✕ **Olive + Gourmando.** Successful hipsters arrive at lunchtime en masse
CAFÉ to wait for a table at this bustling bakery and sandwich shop. Owners
Fodor'sChoice Dyan Solomon and Éric Girard have a romantic backstory straight out
★ of a movie: they fell in love while working the bread ovens at upscale Toqué! before going out on their own. Fittingly, movie stars like Jake Gyllenhaal, Kirsten Dunst, and musician Bono have been spotted here nibbling panini, sour cherry ginger scones, chocolate brioches, and focaccia bread. Fresh crab is flown in for salads, while organic farmers supply heirloom tomatoes. Wait for a seat, then order your sandwiches at the back; and get your pastries at the side counter. Ⓢ *Average main: C$10* ✉ *351 rue St-Paul Ouest, Old Montréal, Montréal* ☎ *514/350– 1083* ⊕ *www.oliveetgourmando.com* ▭ *No credit cards* ☺ *Open Tues.– Sat. 8–6* ☺ *Closed Sun. and Mon.* Ⓜ *Square-Victoria* ✛ *E6.*

$$ ✕ **Osteria Venti.** Authentic regional Italian cuisine comes to life at this
ITALIAN restaurant, housed in a rustic 200-year-old building. You can enjoy
Fodor'sChoice delicious dishes from the comfort of your table or take a seat at the
★ bar facing the open kitchen and watch the action. The menu, which features homemade options like ricotta gnocchi, a delicious lasagna, or a juicy porchetta, will not disappoint. Be sure to leave room for dessert; the true winner is the tiramisu. Ⓢ *Average main: C$17* ✉ *372 St-Paul Ouest, Old Montréal, Montréal* ☎ *514/284–0445* ⊕ *www. osteriaventi.com* ⚷ *Reservations essential* ☺ *Closed Sun. and Mon.* Ⓜ *Square Victoria* ✛ *E6.*

$$$ ✕ **Toqué!.** Toqué is slang for "just a little stubborn," as in Chef Nor-
FRENCH mand Laprise's insistence on using fresh, local ingredients from the best
Fodor'sChoice providers. Located on the ground floor of a glass tower, this celebrated
★ bastion of fine dining attracts government rainmakers and the expense-account crowd. The menu changes daily, depending on what Laprise finds at the market, but foie gras, duck, and wild venison are staples. Some clients wouldn't consider ordering anything but the seven-course tasting menu. Chitchat at the tables revolves around Laprise's latest award and how lucky everyone is to have gotten a reservation. You can also eat at the quartz bar, sitting on the comfy bar stools. Ⓢ *Aver-age main: C$25* ✉ *900 pl. Jean-Paul-Riopelle, Old Montréal, Montréal* ☎ *514/499–2084* ⊕ *www.restaurant-toque.com* ⚷ *Reservations essen-tial* ☺ *Closed Sun. and Mon. and 2 wks at Christmas* Ⓜ *Square-Victoria or Place-d'Armes* ✛ *E6.*

7

$$$$ ✗ **Verses.** The setting—a stone-walled room overlooking the hubbub
MODERN of rue St-Paul—is the most romantic in the Old City; and the food is
CANADIAN poetic—especially the pan seared elk; but the reason for this restau-
Fodor's Choice rant's name is that it's housed on the ground floor of Hôtel Nelligan,
★ named after the Romantic Québecois poet Émile Nelligan. Start with
the princess scallops served with celeriac puree, Granny Smith apple,
and kohlrabi salad with maple smoked ham emulsion. For a main
course, sample the truffle crusted beef tenderloin with Anna potatoes
and seasonal baby vegetables. Wash it all down on the rooftop terrace with a pitcher of Verses' signature drink, clear sangria. Weekend
brunch is elegant, with à la carte options galore. $ *Average main:*
C$35 ✉ *100 rue St-Paul Ouest, Old Montréal, Montréal* ☎ *514/788–*
4000 ⊕ *www.versesrestaurant.com* ⚓ *Reservations essential* Ⓜ *Place-*
d'Armes ✛ *E6.*

DOWNTOWN

$$$ ✗ **Baton Rouge.** Louisiana-style pork ribs, burgers, and chicken fingers
STEAKHOUSE are all on the menu of this popular Montréal restaurant. Portions are
big and satisfying. Dark mahogany wood and booths add to the cozi-
ness and good vibes. Head over before or after a show—the staff is
used to this type of crowd and hustle when they know you've got
somewhere to be. There's another location downtown at 180 rue St-
Catherine Ouest; both can usually accommodate quite a number of peo-
ple but it's best to make a reservation. $ *Average main: C$30* ✉ *1050*
rue de la Montagne, Downtown, Montréal ☎ *514/931–9969* ⊕ *www.*
batonrougerestaurants.com Ⓜ *Lucien-l'Allier* ✛ *E5, C5.*

$$ ✗ **Brasserie T.** The team behind Montréal's famous Toqué! restaurant
MODERN introduced this see-and-be-seen brasserie in the heart of the Quartier
CANADIAN des Spectacles. A wall of windows keeps things bright, and the uniquely
styled restaurant is an excellent spot to eat before or after a show at
Place des Arts. This is also a fantastic perch to look out on the many
festivals that take place in this neighborhood. Share the seafood platters or keep the salmon tartare (a must) all to yourself. The cured meats
plate is another favorite. During the warm season try to snag a seat out
on the terrace for great people watching. $ *Average main: C$20* ✉ *1425*
rue Jeanne-Mance, Downtown, Montréal ☎ *514/282–0808* ⊕ *www.*
brasserie-t.com ⚓ *Reservations essential* Ⓜ *Place-des-Arts* ✛ *E5.*

$$ ✗ **Burgundy Lion.** Authentically British and filled with young profes-
BRITISH sionals, this two-floor restaurant is the perfect place for someone
needing an English fix. Lunch is served seven days a week, but it's the
modern take on the classic British breakfast that has the place busy
every weekend. Crumpets are aplenty, as are smoked herring and the
signature fish-and-chips (a favorite amongst the locals). With over
200 varieties of whisky on the menu, it's also a great place if you
like Scotch. $ *Average main: C$20* ✉ *2496 rue Notre-Dame Ouest,*
Downtown, Montréal ☎ *514/934–0888* ⊕ *www.burgundylion.com*
Ⓜ *Lionel-Groulx* ✛ *A6.*

$ ✗ **Café Myriade.** Café Myriade aficionados are willing to wait for a
CAFÉ seat, where the foam on your café au lait is artfully arranged in waves,
hearts, or curlicues, by award-winning barista Anthony Benda. Benda's

Toqué!, in Old Montréal, has been a fixture on the local scene for ages, known for its market meat- and game-based menu.

delicious coffee—imported from Ethiopia, Guatemala, Brazil, Bolivia, and elsewhere via the famed 49th Parallel Coffee Roasters in Vancouver—is brewed in a siphon pot. Don't drink coffee? Try the molten hot chocolate or the homemade iced teas. If you're peckish, you can sample baked goods sourced from six different local bakeries, all of which are delicious. ⑤ *Average main: C$7* ⊠ *1432 rue Mackay, Downtown, Montréal* ☎ *514/939–1717* ⊕ *www.cafemyriade.com* ⊙ *Weekdays 8–7, weekends 9–7* Ⓜ *Guy-Concordia* ✛ *C5.*

$$$$ ✕ **Cavalli.** Pretty young things like to sip cocktails by Cavalli's big front
ITALIAN window, which in summer is open to the passing scene on busy rue Peel. The interior—a black illuminated bar, green and pink velvet chairs, and blond-wood paneling—makes an enticing backdrop. The food is Italian, mostly, with Asian influences. Chef Frank Gioffre marinates Chilean sea bass in miso and serves his mac 'n' cheese with truffles and brioche breadcrumbs. Models order the endive salad, but heartier eaters love the scallops wrapped in bacon or the rack of fresh Australian lamb. ⑤ *Average main: C$35* ⊠ *2040 rue Peel, Downtown, Montréal* ☎ *514/843–5100* ⊕ *www.ristorantecavalli.com* ⚱ *Reservations essential* ⊙ *No lunch weekends* Ⓜ *Peel* ✛ *C4.*

$$ ✕ **Devi.** The lavish Bollywood decor is a mood enhancer here, while
INDIAN the food appeals to true aficionados and initiates alike. Don't worry, chefs know there's more to food of the Asian subcontinent than hot, hotter, and scalding—although some of their less subtly spiced dishes (the lamb vindaloo, for example) can still take your breath away. For dishes of middling intensity, try the new baby lamb from south India, the whole red snapper, the *achari paneer tikka* (tangy salted cheese), the *kararee bhindi* (deep-fried okra), and the Manchurian cauliflower.

Joe Beef, known for its excellent organic rib steak, is located in downtown Montréal.

Cool your palate with a pint of Indian beer, such as Cobra or Taj Mahal. $ *Average main: C$20* ✉ *1450 rue Crescent, Downtown, Montréal* ☎ *514/286–0303* ⊕ *www.devimontreal.com* ⊙ *Daily 11–11* Ⓜ *Guy-Concordia or Peel* ⊕ *C5*.

$$
ECLECTIC ✕ **Dominion Square Tavern.** New owners rescued this bistro, throwing out video gambling terminals and big-screen televisions; now, the original floors, lamps, and walls from 1927 set the tone, together with antique chairs and a 40-foot brass bar. Chef Eric Depuis makes everything from scratch, including the ketchup, tonic, and ginger ale. His menu is a bit of everything, ranging from beet salad, corn fritters, and deviled eggs to pulled pork sandwiches and the ploughman's lunch. End your evening with the well-chosen cheese plate, featuring raw milk cheddar and Guinness cheddar. Night owls take note: it's open until midnight. $ *Average main: C$20* ✉ *1243 rue Metcalfe, Downtown, Montréal* ☎ *514/564–5056* ⊕ *www.tavernedominion.com* ⊙ *Weekdays 11:30–midnight; weekends 4:30–midnight* Ⓜ *Peel* ⊕ *D5*.

$$$$
BISTRO
Fodor'sChoice ★ ✕ **Joe Beef.** Dining at Joe Beef is a little like being invited to a dinner party by a couple of friends who just happen to be top-notch chefs. David MacMillan and Frédéric Morin were pioneers in Montréal's modern dining scene until they got tired of living on the edge and opened this little restaurant to rediscover the joy of cooking. Everything written on the chalkboard menu is simple and good, from the oysters to organic rib steak. Diners leaf through their copies of Joe Beef's new cookbook, while savoring dishes like lobster spaghetti. Take time to wander out back, where there's a vegetable garden, a greenhouse, a smoker, and 25 more seats. $ *Average main: C$40* ✉ *2491 rue Notre-Dame Ouest, Downtown, Montréal* ☎ *514/935–6504* ⊕ *www.*

joebeef.ca ⌛ *Reservations essential* ☉ *Closed Sun. and Mon. No lunch* Ⓜ *Lionel-Groulx* ✛ *A6.*

$$ ✕ **Kazu.** You could almost walk right by this tiny establishment, but the
JAPANESE big giveaway is the line of people waiting to get in. Kazu has created a
foodie mania with its fabulous Japanese dishes. Popular plates include
the tuna and salmon bowls, or get messy and try the pork necks—you'll
be licking the BBQ sauce off your hands, but you won't be sorry. So,
how do you beat the line? Arrive at the restaurant 15 minutes before
opening time (noon for lunch or 5:30 for dinner) or visit later in the
evening, after 8 pm. $ *Average main: C$15* ✉ *1862 rue St-Catherine
Ouest, Downtown, Montréal* ☎ *514/937–2333* ▭ *No credit cards*
☉ *Closed Tues. No lunch Sat.* Ⓜ *Guy-Concordia* ✛ *B5.*

$ ✕ **Le Gourmet Burger.** A university hang-out joint with a charcoal grill and
MODERN fancy brioche buns. The 'create it yourself' beef burgers (C$6) are juicy
CANADIAN and tasty, even before adding decadent toppings like guacamole, grilled
☾ beets, caramelized onions, and basil pesto. Kids and small eaters love
the C$3 mini burgers, as well as big glasses of homemade iced tea and
lemonade. Late-night diners (the kitchen is open until 1 am) appreciate
the soft ambience, which is devoid of neon and plastic. Instead, exposed
brick walls and lime green tiles make you forget it's the cheapest destina-
tion in town. $ *Average main: C$10* ✉ *1433B rue Bishop, Downtown,
Montréal* ☎ *514/435–3535* ⊕ *www.legourmetburger.com* ▭ *No credit
cards* ☉ *Open daily 11 am–1 am* Ⓜ *Guy-Concordia or Peel* ✛ *C5.*

$$$ ✕ **Le Mas des Oliviers.** The textbook definition of "classic French Bis-
BISTRO tro," Le Mas des Oliviers has been around since 1966 and they pride
themselves on their dishes, some of which have been on the menu
40-plus years. The dining room looks the part with white tablecloths,
dark wooden beams, exposed brick walls, and rustic decor like wagon
wheels. The staff ups the elegance with vests and ties. Try the fish soup,
one of the dishes around since the begining, truly a house specialty.
Another choice locals adore is the lamb shanks. $ *Average main: C$30*
✉ *1216 rue Bishop, Downtown, Montréal* ☎ *514/861–6733* ⊕ *www.
lemasdesoliviers.ca* ⌛ *Reservations essential* ☉ *No lunch weekends*
Ⓜ *Lucien-L'Allier* ✛ *C5.*

$$$$ ✕ **Le Milsa.** Carnivores take note—this Brazilian restaurant could be
BRAZILIAN your favorite meal in Montréal. There's a bit of pageantry to the service: Staff circle the tables with grilled meats on a sword and you signal
if you want more by showing the green side of a token (or if you're
ready to fold, flip the red side up). The room gets louder as the evening
progresses and if you're lucky, the resident dancers will come around
and show you how to move those hips. Don't wait too long to flip your
token or you'll be too full for the grilled pineapple with cinnamon, a
perfect sweet ending to the evening. $ *Average main: C$35* ✉ *1445 rue
Bishop, Downtown, Montréal* ☎ *514/985–0777* ⊕ *www.lemilsa.com*
⌛ *Reservations essential* Ⓜ *Guy-Concordia* ✛ *C5.*

$$$ ✕ **Le Taj.** The focus here is on northern Indian cuisine, which is less
INDIAN spicy and more delicate than that of the south. Tandoor clay ovens
seal in the flavor, enhancing the grilled meat, like lamb and fish. It's
noteworthy that a new vegetarian tandoor platter was added to the
menu. Veggies can also try the Taj Vegetable Thali—one vegetable

7

entrée, lentils, and basmati rice—and *saag paneer* (rich white cheese with spinach). The lunch buffet costs C$15.95, and the nightly "Indian feast" is C$38. $ *Average main: C$25* ✉ *2077 rue Stanley, Downtown, Montréal* ☎ *514/845–9015* ⊕ *www.restaurantletaj.com* ☾ *No lunch Sat.* Ⓜ *Peel* ✛ *C4.*

$$
AMERICAN
✕ **m:brgr.** Build your own specialty burger here with toppings like applewood bacon, grilled pineapple, and goat cheese. Even highfalutin foodies admit that m:brgr is a cut above, with designer mac 'n' cheese (served with truffle carpaccio, if you want), Angus beef hot dogs, and pulled pork sandwiches. Surrounded by panoramic murals of Montréal, students, families, and young couples come here to share dipping sauces, sweet potato fries, and deep dish cookies and ice cream for dessert. There are a few tables on the front sidewalk, but the real action is inside. $ *Average main: C$20* ✉ *2025 rue Drummond, Downtown, Montréal* ☎ *514/906–2747* ⊕ *www.mbrgr.com* Ⓜ *Peel* ✛ *C4.*

$$
STEAKHOUSE
☾
✕ **Mister Steer.** Why mess with a winning formula? Brisk service, vinyl booths, and juicy, almost spherical hamburgers served slightly *saignant* (rare) with heaps of curled "Suzie Q" french fries. Since 1958, locals have been chowing down on steer burgers at this unpretentious spot in the downtown shopping district, near the major cinemas. Steak, too, is available at reasonable prices. $ *Average main: C$15* ✉ *1198 rue Ste-Catherine Ouest, Downtown, Montréal* ☎ *514/866–3233* ⊕ *www. mistersteer.com* ☾ *Sun.–Wed. 8 am–10 pm; Thurs. 8 am–11 pm; Fri.– Sat. 8 am–12 am* Ⓜ *Peel* ✛ *C5.*

$
CHINESE
✕ **Qing Hua Dumplings.** Groups of students and young lovers crowd around tables ordering soup dumplings—just like they make 'em in North East China. And the price is right: 15 steamed or boiled dumplings for C$8.99. Demand is high for the lamb coriander, as well as the coleslaw with carrot and egg. Service can be a bit slow, but it's worth the wait. There are six varieties of frozen dumplings for takeout. And there's another Qing Hua in Chinatown at 1019 boulevard St-Laurent. $ *Average main: C$10* ✉ *1676 av. Lincoln, Downtown, Montréal* ☎ *438/288–5366* ▭ *No credit cards* Ⓜ *Guy-Concordia* ✛ *F5, B4.*

$$$
ITALIAN
✕ **Rosalie.** The dining room may be trendy here, but the menu is pure Italian classics, such as pastas and rustic pizzas baked in wood-burning ovens. Rosalie has modern wooden tables and a private wine cellar upstairs, but it's the big terrasse out front that draws the crowds on late summer afternoons. And the lychee martinis should get some credit. Thirtysomething professionals pour in after work and often stay for an early supper before heading out on the town. $ *Average main: C$30* ✉ *1232 rue de la Montagne, Downtown, Montréal* ☎ *514/392–1970* ⊕ *www. rosalierestaurant.com* ☾ *No lunch weekends* Ⓜ *Guy-Concordia* ✛ *C5.*

THE VILLAGE

$$$
AMERICAN
✕ **Kitchenette.** A welcome alternative to all the French bistros, this new family-run eatery tips its hat to Southern cuisine. Hailing from Texas, chef Nick Hodge specializes in fancy comfort food like Maryland-style crab cakes, fried chicken po'boys, sloppy joes with pulled beef, barbequed short ribs, and lots of sustainable fish. You can watch Hodge braising lamb in the open kitchen or sit back and admire the stunning

floors made from 200-year old barn boards. The napkins are white, but the atmosphere is casual, with a brisk turnover and friendly service. Try Grandma Hodge's bread pudding with Jack Daniels, her maple pecan pie, or the sticky sundae pudding with popcorn. $ *Average main: C$25 ✉ 1353 boul. René-Lévesque Ouest, Village, Montréal* ☎ *514/527–1016* ⊕ *www.kitchenetterestaurant.ca* ⌣ *Reservations essential* ☉ *Closed Sun. and Mon. No lunch Sat.* Ⓜ *Beaudry* ✛ *G5.*

THE PLATEAU, MILE END, LITTLE ITALY, AND OUTREMONT

THE PLATEAU

$$$ ✕ **Au Pied de Cochon.** Not for the timid, the menu at this famous bistro
MODERN   is an ode to whole-animal cooking . . . and fat. Chef Martin Picard—
CANADIAN from the Food Network's show *The Wild Chef*—doesn't hesitate to
serve pigs' feet stuffed with foie gras, pickled tongue, bison tongue, guinea hen liver mousse, pig's head for two, pork hocks braised in maple syrup, or *oreilles-de-crisse* (literally, Christ's ears)—crispy, deep-fried crescents of pork skin. But it's the foie gras that Picard really loves. He lavishes the stuff on everything, including hamburgers and his own version of poutine. Oddly enough, the trendy crowd that packs his noisy brasserie every night seems to stay trim despite this avalanche of meat. All eyes are on the open kitchen, where Picard entertains, concentrates, smirks, and educates like a pro. $ *Average main: C$30* ✉ *536 av. Duluth, Plateau Mont-Royal, Montréal* ☎ *514/281–1114* ⊕ *www.restaurantaupieddecochon.ca* ⌣ *Reservations essential* ☉ *Closed Mon. No lunch* Ⓜ *Sherbrooke or Mont-Royal* ✛ *G3.*

$$ ✕ **Chez Doval.** Chez Doval is a neighborhood restaurant with a split
PORTUGUESE personality. If you're looking for a little intimacy, book a table in the softly lighted dining room by the main entrance; if you're looking for something a little more raucous—guitar music, maybe a friendly argument about sports or politics—try the tavern on the far side. Foodwise, it doesn't really matter where you sit. The chicken, sardines, grouper, and squid—all broiled à-la-Portugaise on an open charcoal grill behind the bar—are succulent, simple, and good. Good prices attract artists and university kids with visiting parents. $ *Average main: C$15* ✉ *150 rue Marie-Anne Est, Plateau Mont-Royal, Montréal* ☎ *514/843–3390* ⊕ *www.chezdoval.com* Ⓜ *Mont-Royal* ✛ *F2.*

$$ ✕ **Chu Chai.** Vegetarians dine well in this Thai restaurant, as vegetable
VEGETARIAN dishes abound, but chefs also prepare meatless versions of such classics as calamari with basil, crispy duck with spinach, chicken with green beans, fish with three hot sauces, and beef with yellow curry and coconut milk, substituting soy and *seitan* (a chewy mock-meat made from wheat gluten) for the real thing. Don't leave without trying the prizewinning *miam kram* (coconut, ginger, nuts, and lime) appetizer or duck with soy sauce. $ *Average main: C$20* ✉ *4088 rue St-Denis, Plateau Mont-Royal, Montréal* ☎ *514/843–4194* ⊕ *www.chuchai.com* ⌣ *Reservations essential* ☉ *Mon.–Wed. and Sun. 5 pm–10 pm; Thur.–Sat. 5pm–11 pm. No lunch* Ⓜ *Sherbrooke or Mont-Royal* ✛ *F3.*

$$ ✕ **Lallouz.** Grilled meats and delicious salads are served at this Mediter-
NORTH AFRICAN ranean–North African café and kebab shop. This is a great option for lunch: the $12 "Kit" lunchtime menu gives plenty of interesting options

beyond the usual sandwich. Dishes are tasty and seasoned perfectly, and even the sides are getting praise—french fries aficionados argue Lallouz has some of the best fries in the city. There are a few locations around Montréal, including one in the Village at 1327 rue St-Catherine Est. $ *Average main: C$15* ✉ *4461 boul. St-Laurent, Plateau Mont-Royal, Montréal* ☎ *514/439–3967* ⊕ *www.lallouz.ca* ⊙ *Closed Sun.* Ⓜ *Mont-Royal.*

$$$
BISTRO
✕ **Laloux.** Serious foodies keep Laloux on their must-eat list, and it's not hard to see why: the prices are good and the food is delicious. New Chef Jonathan Lapierre-Réhayem has taken over the kitchen, and he keeps the dishes creative and entertaining. A real hit is the homemade tagliatelle with summer vegetables, lemon butter, and egg yolks. The grilled beef tartare is another specialty. For wine lovers, leave time for a pre-dinner drink at the adjoining wine bar, Pop! $ *Average main: C$25* ✉ *250 av. des Pins Est, Plateau Mont-Royal, Montréal* ☎ *514/287–9127* ⊕ *www.laloux.com* ⚲ *Reservations essential* ⊙ *No lunch weekends* Ⓜ *Sherbrooke* ✛ *F3.*

$$
MODERN
CANADIAN
✕ **Le Comptoir.** The team at Le Comptoir know their stuff, and they proudly display their knowledge on the plate. Technically, the full title of the restaurant is "Le Comptoir Charcuteries and Wine" and in both aspects, they excel—the housemade charcuterie is so good, it has a local following. The dining room is modern and paired down, with blond-wood counters and exposed brick; on one wall is the chalkboard menu, a lineup that changes nightly. The salumi platters are perfect as appetizers, or you can pick the larger size and gorge on it as a main meal. Don't forget the second half of that title—the wine. Pair up your dish with a glass from their selection of private imports. $ *Average main: C$20* ✉ *4807 boul. St-Laurent, Plateau Mont-Royal, Montréal* ☎ *514/844–8467* ⊕ *www.comptoircharcuterieetvins.ca* ⚲ *Reservations essential* Ⓜ *Laurier* ✛ *F1.*

$$
FRENCH
☺
✕ **L'Express.** Mirrored walls and noise levels that are close to painful make L'Express the closest thing Montréal (and maybe even Canada) has to a Parisian bistro. Maybe that's why the city's celebrity chefs congregate here for dinner after hours. Service is fast—most waiters have been there for 20 and 30 years—prices are reasonable, and the food is good, even if the tiny, crowded tables barely have room to accommodate it. The steak tartare with french fries, salmon with sorrel, and calves' liver with tarragon are marvelous. Don't expect the menu to change—diners would have a conniption. Jars of gherkins, fresh baguettes, and aged cheeses make the pleasure last longer, as do the reasonably priced bottles of imported French wine. Kids are warmly welcome. $ *Average main: C$18* ✉ *3927 rue St-Denis, Plateau Mont-Royal, Montréal* ☎ *514/845–5333* ⊕ *www.restaurantlexpress.ca* ⚲ *Reservations essential* ⊙ *Weekdays 8 am–2 am; Sat. 10 am–2 am; Sun. 10 am –1 am* Ⓜ *Sherbrooke* ✛ *F3.*

$
FRENCH
✕ **Le Petit Rico.** Students, artists, and locals fill the communal tables and counters at this homey luncheonette. It's a one-woman operation, as Chef Asma Mezni uses local and organic products to cook up French cuisine inspired by her Tunisian homeland. Wafts of thyme make diners hungry as they peruse the chalkboard menu. Mezni's quiche, soups,

salads, and tartelettes are popular, along with the delectable fondant au chocolat. $ *Average main: C$10* ⊠ *4210 rue Boyer, Plateau Mont-Royal, Montréal* ☎ *514/529–1321* ⊕ *www.caferico.qc.ca* ▬ *No credit cards* ☉ *Mon.–Wed. 10 am–6 pm; Thurs.–Fri. 10 am–7 pm; Sat. 9 am–6 pm* Ⓜ *Mont-Royal* ✛ *G2.*

$$ ✕ **Macaroni Bar.** *Top Chef Canada* contender chef Sergio Mattoscio has
ITALIAN built up a fan following, and his restaurant Macaroni Bar draws fans and foodies alike. The menu changes nightly but a staple, and the restaurant's claim to fame, is the gnocchi poutine, an absolute must-try. Also on that must-try list, the nutella pizza—rich chocolate spread over warm pizza dough—arguably, the best way to end an evening. During warmer weather, sit outside on the huge terrace and listen to the sounds of the city. $ *Average main: C$20* ⊠ *4448 boul. St-Laurent, Plateau Mont-Royal, Montréal* ☎ *514/287–0287* ⊕ *www.macaronibar. ca* ⌂ *Reservations essential* ☉ *Closed Mon.* Ⓜ *Mont-Royal* ✛ *E2.*

$$$ ✕ **Maestro S.V.P.** Regulars belly up to the glass oyster bar and stay put.
SEAFOOD Owner Ilene Polansky imports oysters from all over the world, so you can compare the subtle differences between, say, a delicate little bivalve from Kumamoto, Japan, and a big meaty Kawakawa from New Zealand. A free lesson in shucking techniques comes with the order. Famous guests, from Leonard Cohen and William Hurt to Laura Linney and Bo Derek, sign their oyster shells and Polansky displays them in a frame. If oysters aren't your thing, don't despair: Polansky also serves grilled salmon, king crab, calamari, and the inevitable *moules et frites* (mussels and french fries). Tuesday through Thursday, the menu features smaller, tapas-style portions to accommodate big groups of people who want to share. $ *Average main: C$25* ⊠ *3615 boul. St-Laurent, Plateau Mont-Royal, Montréal* ☎ *514/842–6447* ⊕ *www.maestrosvp.com* ⌂ *Reservations essential* ☉ *No lunch weekends* Ⓜ *Sherbrooke* ✛ *F4.*

$$$$ ✕ **Moishe's.** The motto says it all: "There is absolutely nothing trendy
STEAKHOUSE about Moishe's." Yet, this is a place to be seen, enjoying your largess and ordering a bone-in fillet. If you want a thick, marbled steak, perfectly grilled—preceded perhaps by a slug of premium single-malt Scotch—you've found the right clubhouse. All grilled meat comes with the famous, buttery Monte Carlo potato. Members of the Lighter family, who have been operating Moishe's since 1938, offer other dishes, such as lamb and fish, but people come for the beef, which the family ages in its own lockers. There's also a C$25 "Three Hours to Midnight" special (after 9 pm) Thursday through Saturday. $ *Average main: C$35* ⊠ *3961 boul. St-Laurent, Plateau Mont-Royal, Montréal* ☎ *514/845–3509* ⊕ *www.moishes.ca* Ⓜ *St-Laurent* ✛ *F3.*

$$$ ✕ **Pintxo.** You don't dine at Pintxo—you graze. And what a lovely pas-
SPANISH ture it is, too, with bare brick walls, white tablecloths, and a welcoming new wine display near the door. Pintxos (pronounced "pinchos") are the Basque version of tapas, tiny two-bite solutions to the hunger problem, best enjoyed with a good beer or a glass of Spanish wine. There are about 15 pinxtos on the menu every night, ranging from tiny stacks of grilled vegetables to more substantial dishes, such as duck tartare, foie gras, shrimp, octopus, and the crowd-pleasing strawberry gazpacho. It takes about six pintxos to make a meal. If creating your dinner one

7

bite at a time doesn't appeal, there are more normal-size dishes on the menu, such as black cod and beef cheeks braised in wine. The best way to end the night is with the C$15 cheese plate, stocked with 10 types of Spanish imports. $ *Average main: C$23* ✉ *256 rue Roy Est, Plateau Mont-Royal, Montréal* ☎ *514/844–0222* ⊕ *www.pintxo.ca* ⌘ *Reservations essential* ◷ *No lunch Sat.–Tues.* Ⓜ *Sherbrooke* ✢ *F3.*

$$$$
PORTUGUESE

✕ **Portus Calle.** Sunny yellow and cobalt-blue decor greets you at this fabulous Portuguese restaurant run by celebrated chef Helena Loureiro. Seafood is served as tapas style or as main meals. Try one of their many specialties such as *caldo verde* soup (traditional potatoes and chorizo soup), *chouriço* (pork) sausage, or the grilled seafood platter for two. But it's hard to go wrong when the ingredients are top-drawer: fresh fish arrives daily and vegetables are local and market-fresh. $ *Average main: C$38* ✉ *4281 boul. St-Laurent, Plateau Mont-Royal, Montréal* ☎ *514/849–2070* ⊕ *www.portuscalle.ca* ⌘ *Reservations essential* ◷ *No lunch weekends* Ⓜ *Mont-Royal* ✢ *F2.*

$
AMERICAN
Fodor's Choice
★

✕ **Schwartz's Delicatessen.** Schwartz's has no frills. The furniture's shabby, the noise level high, and the waiters are—well, trying harder to be pleasant these days. The cooks do such a good job of curing, smoking, and slicing beef brisket that even when it's 20 below zero locals line up outside to get a seat at the city's most famous deli and order a sandwich thick enough to dislocate jaws. Fodorites agree, it's worth the wait for the famous smoked meat. Both Angelina Jolie and Halle Berry couldn't resist the medium-fat sandwich on rye. Avoid lunch and dinner hours, and when you do get in, don't ask for a menu; there isn't one. Just order a smoked meat on rye with fries and a side order of pickles. If you're in a rush, use the take-out counter next door. $ *Average main: C$10* ✉ *3895 boul. St-Laurent, Plateau Mont-Royal, Montréal* ☎ *514/842–4813* ⊕ *www.schwartzsdeli.com* ⌘ *Reservations not accepted* ▭ *No credit cards* ◷ *Sun.–Thurs. 8 am–12:30 am; Fri. 8 am–1:30 am; Sat. 8 am–2:30 am* Ⓜ *Sherbrooke* ✢ *F3.*

$
CAFÉ
Fodor's Choice
★

✕ **St-Viateur Bagel & Café.** Even expatriate New Yorkers have been known to prefer Montréal's light, crispy, and slightly sweet bagel to its heavier Manhattan cousin. (The secret? The dough is boiled in honey-sweetened water before baking.) St-Viateur's wood-fired brick ovens have been operating since 1957. With coffee and smoked salmon, these bagels make a great breakfast. There's another St-Viateur in Mile End at 263 rue St-Viateur Ouest. $ *Average main: $4* ✉ *1127 av. Mont-Royal Est, Plateau Mont-Royal, Montréal* ☎ *514/528–6361* ⊕ *www. stviateurbagel.com* ▭ *No credit cards* Ⓜ *Laurier* ✢ *C2, G2.*

$$$
THAI

✕ **Thai Grill.** Behold, an 18-foot gold statue of Buddha! He's right in the middle of the room, presiding over the scrumptious pad thai dishes, mussaman curry with beef; sautéed chicken with cashews, onions, and dried red peppers; plus the ever popular big shrimp and crab cakes. All the cooks are Thai, so this is the real deal. $ *Average main: C$30* ✉ *5101 boul. St-Laurent, Plateau Mont-Royal, Montréal* ☎ *514/270–5566* ◷ *No lunch Sat.–Wed.; Mon.–Sun. 5:30 pm–11 pm* Ⓜ *Laurier* ✢ *C3.*

MILE END

$$$
MIDDLE EASTERN

✗**Damas.** New to the Mile End, Damas has been getting rave reviews from Montréalers. The ambiance is colorful and cozy, and suits the food—authentic Syrian cuisine—which is difficult to find in North America. Dishes like *fatta* (yogurt, tahini, pita, pistachios, pine nuts, and herbs) combined with a variety of meats or vegetables are quickly gaining popularity. Add a glass of wine from their vast list of Mediterranean imports to make the meal complete. $ *Average main: C$25* ⊠ *5210 av. du Parc, Mile End, Montréal* ☎ *514/439–5435* ⊕ *www. restaurant-damas.com* Ⓜ *Laurier* ✢ *C2.*

$$$$
MODERN
CANADIAN
Fodor's Choice
★

✗**La Chronique.** It's a pretty place with scarlet walls and black-and-white pictures, but people don't come to Chef Marc De Canck's little 36-seat restaurant for the ambience or for the crowd; they come, quite simply, for the food. Without fuss or fanfare, De Canck has been cranking out the city's most adventurous dishes ever since he opened in 1995. The man doesn't seem capable of compromise or playing safe. His work seamlessly blends lightened French fare with Japanese, Italian, Chinese, and Creole touches. Starters like red tuna tartare might precede milk-fed pig or duck dishes. Lately, he has been using more lobster, foie gras, and veal. To spend hours savoring the food, order the *prix-fixe* meals—five courses are C$89. $ *Average main: C$42* ⊠ *99 rue Laurier Ouest, Mile End, Montréal* ☎ *514/271–3095* ⊕ *www.lachronique.qc.ca* ⚞ *Reservations essential* ☾ *No lunch weekends* Ⓜ *Laurier* ✢ *C3.*

$
GREEK

✗**Melina Phyllo Bar.** It may be in the heart of Mile End, but this newly opened phyllo bar looks like it was transported directly from Athens, with food arriving on checkered cobalt-blue wax paper. Focusing on take-out, this charming spot turns out delicious spanakopita, with a perfect crunchy exterior, that's an excellent lunch on-the-go. The menu is brief, but every item is well made, including the Melina sandwich, with its spicy feta spread, kalamata hummus, cucumbers, tomatoes, and *graviera* (Swiss-like cheese). Another must-try, the *bougatsa*, is a warm custard-filled phyllo pastry with cinnamon. $ *Average main: C$10* ⊠ *5573 av. du Parc, Mile End, Montréal* ☎ *514/270–1675* ▬ *No credit cards* Ⓜ *Rosemont or Beaubien* ✢ *C2.*

$$$$
GREEK

✗**Milos.** Don't let the nets and floats hanging from the ceiling fool you: Milos is no simple taverna (a fact reflected in the prices, which some argue are exorbitant). The main dish is usually the catch of the day grilled over charcoal and seasoned with parsley, capers, and lemon juice. Fish are priced by the pound and often displayed, along with the vegetables, in the restaurant's colorful, open-market interior. ▪**TIP→** If **you're on a budget, consider the affordable fixed-price late-night menu from Thursday to Saturday between 10 and midnight for C$20.** $ *Average main: C$40* ⊠ *5357 av. du Parc, Mile End, Montréal* ☎ *514/272– 3522* ⊕ *www.milos.ca* ⚞ *Reservations essential* ☾ *No lunch weekends* Ⓜ *Laurier* ✢ *C2.*

$$
DINER

✗**Nouveau Palais.** Hipsters head to Nouveau Palais both for the '70s diner decor (wood paneling and vinyl seats) and the simple, delicious dishes. The Palace Burger is gaining a reputation among Montrealers as the best the city has to offer, and their sweet potato pie also has fans. Another reason hipsters love it here: in addition to weekend brunch, daily lunch and dinner, you can stop in for a late-night meal. (Nouveau Palais stays open until 3 am.) When you're outside Mile End, keep an eye out for the Winneburger, their new food truck. $ *Average main: C$15* ⊠ *281 rue Bernard Ouest, Mile End, Montréal* ☎ *514/273–1180* ⊕ *www.nouveaupalais.com* ⊙ *Closed Mon.* Ⓜ *Rosemont or Beaubien* ⊹ *C1.*

> **THE BAGEL DEBATE**
>
> Visitors may not know that within the city, there has always been a great bagel debate. You're either on Team St. Viateur (⊠ *263 St. Viateur West)* or Team Fairmount (⊠ *74 Fairmount West)*. But some split the vote, saying if you want a basic, consistent bagel such as sesame or poppy seed, go to St. Viateur and for something a little more creative, head to Fairmount. Why not do a taste test? Be scientific about it: Grab a sesame seed bagel from St. Viateur and do the five-minute walk over to Fairmount bagels to pick up the same type. Whatever the result, it'll be delicious.

$$ ✕ **Pizzeria Magpie.** It's all about the
PIZZA   pizza and oysters at this spot. Tucked away on a small side street in Mile End, this classic pizzeria with white-washed walls and pressed tin ceilings turns out some of the best pizza the city offers. The Magpie Margherita and three-cheese meatball pizza are favorites, and the homemade cookies are a hit with the young and old. But don't forget to start with fresh oysters; they have a fantastic selection. $ *Average main: C$15* ⊠ *16 rue Maguire, Mile End, Montréal* ☎ *514/507–2900* ⊕ *www.pizzeriamagpie. com* ⊙ *Closed Mon. No lunch on Tues.* Ⓜ *Laurier* ⊹ *C2.*

$$ ✕ **Rotisserie Panama.** Some of the best grilled meat in Montréal is what
GREEK   attracts big, noisy crowds to the Rotisserie Panama. The dining room is simple, with beige walls and black checkered table clothes, but chicken and crispy lamb chops are excellent, as is the grilled red snapper and sea bass. Extended families come on the weekend for the roasted baby lamb. Prices won't empty your wallet. $ *Average main: C$16* ⊠ *789 rue Jean-Talon Ouest, Mile End, Montréal* ☎ *514/276–5223* ⊕ *www. rotisseriepanama.com* Ⓜ *Parc or Acadie* ⊹ *B1.*

LITTLE ITALY

$$ ✕ **Alep.** Bring your entire clan to Alep, where the music, plants, ivy, and
MIDDLE EASTERN   exposed-stone walls encourage relaxation. Graze and share the *mouhamara* (pomegranate and walnuts), *sabanegh* (spinach and onions), *fattouche* (salad with pita and mint), and *yalandji* (vine leaves stuffed with rice, chickpeas, walnuts, and tomatoes). For an Armenian flavor, try the salad with cumin and *flefle*. Kebabs dominate the main courses. Appetizers are very vegetarian friendly. $ *Average main: C$20* ⊠ *199 rue Jean-Talon Est, Little Italy, Montréal* ☎ *514/270–6396* ⊙ *Closed Sun. and Mon.* Ⓜ *Jean-Talon or de Castelnau* ⊹ *C1.*

$$ ✕ **Bottega Pizzeria.** Nobody questions the authenticity of the Neapolitan
PIZZA   pizza here, seeing as there's a 3,500-kilogram Vesuvian rock wood-
Fodor's Choice   burning pizza oven in the kitchen. It cooks pizza in 90 seconds flat, at
★   500 degrees Celsius (932 °F). But the pizza isn't the only reason to go to Bottega; there's a delightful array of tapas-style appetizers, called "sfizi," to share. Plates of meatballs, eggplant, grilled peppers, and Buffalo mozzarella crowd onto tables, where young diners chat and text

their friends. This is a hot date place, too, so dress to impress. There's free parking behind the restaurant, which is as miraculous as the pizza. Bottega's open for dinner only—no lunch—but the kitchen is open until midnight, so the city's top chefs often come by for their dinner after work. ⑤ *Average main: C$20* ✉ *65 rue St-Zotique Est, Little Italy, Montréal* ☎ *514/277–8104* ⊕ *www.bottega.ca* ⚑ *Reservations essential* ⏱ *Tues.–Sat. 5 pm–midnight. No lunch* Ⓜ *Beaubien* ✛ *D1.*

$$$ ✕**Ginger.** Nothing says tranquil like Ginger. This sushi restaurant in the
SUSHI   Villeray area next to the Jean-Talon Market captures the ambiance and the flavor matches: the decor is minimalist but there's beauty in the way the restaurant is arranged to provide privacy at every table and bring focus back to the sushi on the plate. Options on the menu seem endless and everything tastes divine, but top choices are the Spicy Scallop Roll and the Hanzo. ⑤ *Average main: C$25* ✉ *345 rue Villeray, Little Italy, Montréal* ☎ *514/277–5552* ⏱ *Sun.–Wed. 5–11, Thurs.–Sat. 5–midnight* Ⓜ *De Castelneau* ✛ *D1.*

$$$ ✕**Kitchen Galerie.** Keeping the menu small and structured, this homey
MEDITERRANEAN   bistro is an example of excellence through simplicity. The two chefs do everything—the shopping, the chopping, the cooking, the greeting, and the serving. They focus on six main courses, six appetizers, and three desserts, all inspired by what's fresh at the nearby Jean-Talon market. From the open kitchen, they serve classic Mediterranean dishes, including foie gras and rib-eye steak for two. That intimacy trickles down to the guests, who like to discuss the wine with fellow diners sitting at the 20-foot banquet table. The menu may change, but you can expect a pasta or risotto, plus two kinds of meat and two kinds of fish. ⑤ *Average main: C$30* ✉ *60 rue Jean-Talon Est, Little Italy, Montréal* ☎ *514/315–8994* ⊕ *www.kitchengalerie.com* ⏱ *No lunch. Closed Sun. and Mon.* Ⓜ *Jean-Talon* ✛ *D1.*

$$$ ✕**Ristorante Lucca.** Small and cozy, Ristorante Lucca is one of the go-to
ITALIAN   places in Little Italy for the definitive Italian meal. And it doesn't disappoint: food is always top-notch with great ingredients and solid traditional dishes. Some of the most popular choices are the veal chops served with spinach and polenta, and the seafood linguini. The decor is simple: wooden table are clusters around deep terra-cotta-colored walls. It's ideal for a date night, but they're usually quite busy, so don't forget to make reservations. ⑤ *Average main: C$30* ✉ *12 rue Dante, Little Italy, Montréal* ☎ *514/278–6502* ⊕ *www.restaurantlucca.ca* ⚑ *Reservations essential* ⏱ *No lunch Sun.* Ⓜ *Jean-Talon* ✛ *D1.*

$ ✕**Tapeo.** Bringing tapas uptown, this Spanish-inspired eatery is a chic
SPANISH   yet casual place to gulp down imported wine and share plates of seared scallops wrapped in bacon. Recently renovated for maximum impact, Tapeo has a "must do" experience: book the chef's table in the open kitchen, where 18 people can watch the action and get special attention. Out of nowhere, a plate of confit cherry tomatoes with goat cheese will arrive, followed by other treats. Dessert, of course, is the house churros. ⑤ *Average main: C$10* ✉ *511 rue Villeray, Little Italy, Montréal* ☎ *514/495–1999* ⊕ *www.restotapeo.com* ⚑ *Reservations essential* ⏱ *Open Tues.–Fri. noon–3 and 5:30–11; Sat. 5–11; Sun. 5–10* ⏱ *Closed Mon.* Ⓜ *Jarry or Jean-Talon* ✛ *D1.*

7

$$
ITALIAN
✕**Vinizza.** The name, a portmanteau of *vino* (wine) and pizza, will clue you into what the focus is at Vinizza. And you can't go wrong with the pizza, made to perfection in a wood-burning oven, or fresh pasta made on-site. The ingredients are market-fresh and superb. One more reason to visit this restaurant: with every main dish sold, a donation is made to l'Accueil Bonneau to help feed the homeless in the city. There's another location of Vinizza downtown at 2044 rue Metcalfe. $ *Average main: C$20* ⊠ *150 rue Jean-Talon Est, Little Italy, Montréal* ☎ *514/904–2250* ⊕ *www.vinizza.com* ⌂ *Reservations essential* ⊗ *No lunch weekends* Ⓜ *Jean-Talon* ✛ *D1, D4.*

OUTREMONT

$$$
FRENCH
✕**Brasserie Les Enfants Terribles.** With its cavernous corner spot on Outremont's trendy avenue Bernard, sophisticated yet playful decor, and artfully prepared comfort food, Les Enfant Terribles packs 'em in at all hours. The menu at this brasserie-with-a-twist, owned and run by native-born Montrealer Francine Brûlé, is a mix of high-class cuisine and comfort food favorites: shepherd's pie; beef tartare with truffle oil; fish-and-chips; roasted salmon with tomato, mango, and basil salsa; and mac 'n' cheese. While the food is the main attraction, take notice of the interior decor: a lane from an old bowling alley was transformed into the bar, the metal chairs are from an area school, and a demolished barn's faded wood lines the walls. As for the photos on the menu and clear thumbprints infused on the glasses? Those are from Brûlé's very own enfants terribles. $ *Average main: C$25* ⊠ *1257 Bernard Ouest, Outremont, Montréal* ☎ *514/759–9918* ⊕ *www.lesenfantsterriblesbrasserie. ca* ⊗ *Open weekdays 11 am–midnight; weekends 9:30 am–midnight* Ⓜ *Outremont* ✛ *B1.*

$
CAFÉ
✕**Café Souvenir.** From media moguls to Olympic medalists, a wide range of clientele can be found here, nibbling crêpes with Chantilly cream or hauling on double espressos. Weekend brunch is the signature meal at this Parisian-style eatery, where omelets and *croque matins* (melted cheese sandwiches) come with generous mounds of fresh fruit. Diners exchange sections of the *New York Times* and check their iPhones, happy to chat at the breakfast bar or at the bistro tables. For a casual evening meal, regulars rave about the hamburgers, the quesadillas, and the Caesar salad with chicken. $ *Average main: C$12* ⊠ *1261 rue Bernard Ouest, Outremont, Montréal* ☎ *514/948–5259* ⊕ *www. cafesouvenir.com* ⊗ *Open Mon., Tues., and Sun. 7 am–10 pm, Wed.– Sat. 7 am–11 pm* Ⓜ *Outremont or Parc* ✛ *B1.*

$$
BISTRO
Fodor's Choice
★
✕**La Croissanterie Figaro.** Famous for its wraparound patio and Parisian vibe, La Croissanterie is comfortable inside its 100-year old corner building. It's hard to know which architectural detail to admire first—the art deco chandelier, the art nouveau bar imported from Argentina, the "gilded" tables, the copper vats, the stained glass, or the woodwork. It's fun to sit and stare at the antique decor, while local television stars nibble the homemade croissants and nurse big bowls of café au lait. Although this is a full bistro, serving three meals every day of the week, it shines brightest in the morning, serving the Special Bonjour croissant with ham-and-cheese and hearty sandwiches. Lunch diners munch on AAA-beef burgers, and the new farm

sandwiches served with bread made of organic flour. Evenings boast an ever-evolving wine selection and feature unique daily cocktails. ⑤ *Average main: C$15* ⊠ *5200 rue Hutchison, Outremont, Montréal* ☎ *514/278–6567* ⊕ *www.lacroissanteriefigaro.com* ⊗ *Daily 7 am– 1 am* Ⓜ *Outremont* ⊹ *E6.*

$$ ✕ **Le Petit Italien.** Three key factors conspire to make this a great date
ITALIAN spot: flattering lighting over intimate two-top tables; late-night hours seven days a week; and savory comfort food at reasonable prices. The longest wall of this modern bistro is lined, to dramatic effect, with glass mason jars of the house tomato sauce, reminding diners that everything served at Le Petit Italien is lovingly prepared from scratch. One bite of the *buongustaio* pasta dish, enriched with chicken, raisins, and white wine sauce and you're a believer. For a memento, take home a jar of the house tomato sauce for C$10, or spend another C$2 and get the exceptionally tasty Bolognese sauce. ⑤ *Average main: C$20* ⊠ *1265 rue Bernard Ouest, Outremont, Montréal* ☎ *514/278–0888* ⊕ *www.lepetititalien.com* ⚥ *Reservations essential* ⊗ *Mon.–Wed. 11:30–10, Thurs.–Fri. 11:30–11, Sat. 5–11, Sun. 5–10* Ⓜ *Parc or Outremont* ⊹ *B1.*

$$$ ✕ **Leméac.** Enlivening a popular street corner in Outremont, this French
BISTRO bistro creates good karma by heating its outdoor terrace for eight months of the year. The other winning move is its late-night special: between 10 pm and midnight, get the table d'hôte (host's table) for only C$27. Regulars gravitate toward the calf liver, the beef tartare, grilled Cornish hen, roasted cod, and the hanger steak—all served with ceremonial aplomb on white linen table cloths. Plus the fries at Leméac are world-class, as is the weekend brunch. ⑤ *Average main: C$30* ⊠ *1045 rue Laurier Ouest, Outremont, Montréal* ☎ *514/270–0999* ⊕ *www. restaurantlemeac.com* ⚥ *Reservations essential* Ⓜ *Outremont* ⊹ *B3.*

$ ✕ **Toi Moi et Café.** Film producers and poets congregate at this cor-
BISTRO ner café-bistro, sitting on the terrace to sip award-winning espresso. Although there's a hearty lunch and dinner menu of salads, tofu salads, and grilled meat, brunch is the big draw. It features soft-boiled eggs with strips of toast for dipping, fruit, and cheese. Regular breakfast is served seven days a week, so you can get a morning meal throughout the week. Try the Baklava Coffee topped with toasted almonds and honey. ⑤ *Average main: C$12* ⊠ *244 rue Laurier Ouest, Outremont, Montréal* ☎ *514/279–9599* ⊕ *www.toimoicafe.com* Ⓜ *Laurier* ⊹ *C3.*

MONTRÉAL EST

$$$ ✕ **Chez Roger.** A French bistro with a modern feel, Chez Roger is great
BISTRO for everyone from large groups to couples on a date. The ribs dish for two is a favorite with the locals as is the huge fish-and-chips. For a little theater with your meal, the beef and salmon tartares are prepared at your table. If you get there a little early, head next door to Bar Roger while you wait. On a warm summer evening you can sip your drink outside while perched on a stool just in front of the restaurant—a delightful start to the evening. ⑤ *Average main: C$25* ⊠ *2316 rue Beaubien Est, Montréal Est, Montréal* ☎ *514/593–4200* ⊕ *www.barroger.com* ⚥ *Reservations essential* ⊗ *No lunch* Ⓜ *Fabre* ⊹ *G1.*

$$$ ✕ **M sur Masson.** Chef Alexandre Fortier has a faithful following at M sur
BISTRO   Masson, and it's easy to see why—his dishes are satisfyingly traditional
with creative twists. His onion soup is some of the best around, and if
veal liver is your thing, this is the place to have it. Or try the heavenly
grilled cheese with duck confit and Gruyère cheese. The dining room,
lined with wooden benches and globe-shaped light fixtures, is appro-
priately bistro-esque. If you're coming for brunch, be sure to reserve a
table as the place can get mobbed with locals. ⑤ *Average main: C$30*
✉ *2876 rue Masson, Montréal Est, Montréal* ☎ *514/678–2999* ⊕ *www.
msurmasson.com* ⏦ *Reservations essential* Ⓜ *Laurier* ✛ *G1.*

WESTMOUNT

$ ✕ **Chalet Bar-B-Q.** Fast-food restaurants across Canada sell what they call
CANADIAN   "Montréal-style barbecued chicken." The claims are laughable. For the
real thing, head to Chalet Bar-B-Q and line up with the cabbies, truck
drivers, and local families for crispy, spit-barbecued chicken served with
a slightly spicy, gravylike sauce and mountains of french fries. You can
eat in—surrounded by rustic vinyl—or order your chicken to go. ⑤ *Av-
erage main: C$10* ✉ *5456 rue Sherbrooke Ouest, Westmount, Montréal*
☎ *514/489–7235* ⊕ *www.chaletbbq.com* ☉ *Sun.–Wed. 11–10; Thurs.
11–11; Fri.–Sat. 11 am–midnight* Ⓜ *Vendôme* ✛ *A4.*

$$$ ✕ **Kaizen.** If you like a little drama with your sushi, Kaizen's black-
JAPANESE   clad waitresses, floor-to-ceiling blue curtains, and glassed-in wine cel-
lar certainly add a dash of theater to dinner. It's a buzz-filled place
that attracts the kind of well-dressed patrons who can't bear to leave
their cell phone and Blackberry at home. After 10 pm, there's a new
late-night menu for C$22, while the Omakase (chef's choice) menus
(C$75 and up) attract the adventurous. ⑤ *Average main: C$25* ✉ *4075
rue Ste-Catherine Ouest, Westmount, Montréal* ☎ *514/932–5654*
⊕ *www.70sushi.com* ⏦ *Reservations essential* ☉ *No lunch weekends*
Ⓜ *Atwater* ✛ *A4.*

$$$ ✕ **Tavern on the Square.** Happy chatting and goodwill fills this easygoing
MODERN   bistro, where owner-chef Steven Leslie pleases everyone from business
AMERICAN   moguls and media personalities to visiting grandparents. The corporate
crowd sips martinis at the bar, while well-dressed young families enter-
tain their toddlers on the terrace. The daytime clientele is devoted to
the tangy salads, spicy tuna burgers, and fresh pastas, while the evening
crowd comes for updated Italian classics like mac 'n' cheese with three
cheeses, bacon, bread crumbs, and truffle paste (oh my!), rigatoni with
meatballs, or the daily fish special. There are plenty of private-import
wines available by the glass. ⑤ *Average main: C$25* ✉ *1 Westmount Sq.,
Suite C-310, Westmount, Montréal* ☎ *514/989–9779* ⊕ *www.taverne.
ca* ☉ *Closed Sun. No lunch Sat.* Ⓜ *Atwater* ✛ *A4.*

Where to Stay

WORD OF MOUTH

"In Montreal, there are dozens of good hotels in the center of 'city life,' like the Delta, Sheraton, Queen Elizabeth, etc. However, I find the Plateau area with its outdoor cafés, bars, and shops more interesting and European feeling."

—zootsi

Updated by
Joanne Latimer

Montréal is a city of neighborhoods with distinct personalities, which creates a broad spectrum of options when it comes to deciding on a place to stay. The downtown core provides more of a universal lodging experience with all the big chain hotels you'd find in any city, while Old Montréal, the Plateau, and other surrounding areas have unique *auberges* (French inns) and boutique hotels.

Most of the major hotels downtown—the ones with big meeting rooms, swimming pools, and several bars and restaurants—are ideal for those who want all the facilities along with easy access to the big department stores and malls on rue Ste-Catherine, the museums of the Golden Square Mile, and nightlife on rues Crescent and de la Montagne. If you want something a little more historic, consider renting a room in one of the dozen or so boutique hotels that occupy the centuries-old buildings lining the cobbled streets of Old Montréal. Most of them offer all the conveniences along with the added charm of stone walls, casement windows, and period-style furnishings.

If your plans include shopping expeditions to avenue Mont-Royal and rue Laurier with maybe a few late nights at the jazz bars and dance clubs of Main Street and rue St-Denis, then the place to bed down is in one of Plateau Mont-Royal's small but comfortable hotels. Room rates in the area tend to be quite reasonable, but be careful: the hotels right in the middle of the action—on rue St-Denis for example—can be noisy, especially if you get a room fronting the street.

WHERE SHOULD I STAY

	NEIGHBORHOOD VIBE	PROS	CONS
Old Montréal	Horse-drawn carriages, boutique hotels, designer clothes, and historic architecture; very touristy although it quiets down at night.	Quaint; easy access to bike paths; nice to walk along the waterfront; several hip restaurants have recently opened at the Old Port.	Can be desolate in the late evening outside hotel lobbies; parking is scarce; depending on the exact location, métro and bus access can be limited.
Downtown	Montréal's epicenter for all the hustle and bustle, centering around always-crowded rue Ste-Catherine and boulevard René Lévesque.	Extremely convenient; big-name hotel chains; central location; garage parking; perfect for families as well as business travelers.	Traffic congestion can be unpleasant; not as many dining options as other neighborhoods, and what is there tends to be at either extreme—fast food or very pricey (and not always worth it).
The Latin Quarter	Hopping with university kids and cinema-goers, this area boasts a crazy mix of cafés, handmade chocolate shops, and folks carrying library books.	Quick stroll to main festival artery; easy métro access; right between the Plateau and Downtown; local characters abound.	Uneven gentrification means dodgy pockets; litter; bad roads.
The Plateau and Environs	Scattered auberges and B&Bs host the artsy crowd and academics, with streets filled with local boutiques and hip restaurants; perfect for strolling.	Stumbling distance to the best bistros and pubs; unique shopping that focuses on local designers and craftspeople.	Limited métro and bus access; limited hotel selections; can be noisy at night; panhandlers galore.
Mont-Royal and Environs	There are only a few hotels in this quiet section of the city, located in the shadow of the immense Parc du Mont-Royal.	Unhurried pace; lots of green space; lower rates.	Limited métro access; few dining options.

8

MONTRÉAL LODGING PLANNER

RESERVATIONS

Montréal is always hosting a festival or an international convention, so the hotels are consistently booked. This takes tourists by surprise. Many of the quaint auberges have a small number of rooms, so they fill up fast. It's necessary to book months ahead for the Grand Prix, the Jazz Festival, the World Film Festival, and all holiday weekends.

■ **TIP→** From mid-November to early April rates often drop, and throughout the year many hotels have two-night, three-day, double-occupancy packages at substantial discounts.

FACILITIES

When pricing accommodations, ask what's included. You can assume that all rooms have private baths, phones, and TVs unless otherwise noted. If no meals are included in the room rate, "No meals" is stated toward the end of the review. Breakfast is noted when it's included in the rate.

Most hotels are wired, with a business center in the lobby. Smaller auberges may not have televisions and air-conditioning, but often have Wi-Fi.

Bathtubs, plush bathrobes, and fluffy white duvets are popular here for winter comfort. Bigger hotels have day spas and health clubs, as well as some of the city's finest restaurants.

WITH KIDS

Most of the chain hotels—Hilton, for example—have great pools. Avoid smaller auberges, however, because noise travels and the charming ambience doesn't translate to the little ones. Hotels in the Old Port are popular with families because they're near the Centre des Sciences de Montréal and the Lachine Canal bike path.

For a major city, the hotel rooms in Montréal are generous. Budget rooms and auberges are the exception, with rooms measuring less than 300 square feet. Otherwise, expect standard sizes of about 400–700 square feet.

PARKING

Parking is a sore point in Old Montréal. Your car will feel like a tank on the narrow streets, and you can expect to pay heftily for valet service in this part of town. Elsewhere, there's often parking available under the large-scale hotels. This is a blessing in winter, when you don't want to shovel snow and de-ice your car. If possible, avoid taking your car.

PRICES

Aside from during the Grand Prix, the World Film Festival, and the Jazz Festival, it's possible to get a decent hotel room in high season for C$200 to C$300. Take advantage of web-only deals and ask about promotions.

MONTRÉAL HOTEL REVIEWS

Listed alphabetically within neighborhoods. The following reviews have been condensed for this book. Please go to Fodors.com for full reviews of each property.

OLD MONTRÉAL

Let's start with the name. Nobody says "Old Town." That's an American phrase. You may call it Old Montréal, but street signs say "Vieux-Montréal," in French. Either way, it's full of charm—from narrow, cobblestone streets to horse-drawn carriages. You can find boutique hotels, auberges, and cozy bed-and-breakfasts nestled inside heritage buildings. Most properties have exposed beams, stone walls, wooden floors and thick, casement windows. History buffs find this area pleasing, as do people who want to wander around boutiques and art galleries. But remember, this is no place for stilettos. Bring your walking shoes.

BEST BETS FOR MONTRÉAL LODGING

Fodor's offers a selective listing of quality lodging experiences in every price range, from the city's best budget beds to its most sophisticated luxury hotels. Here, we've compiled our top recommendations by price and experience. The very best properties—in other words, those that provide a particularly remarkable experience in their price range—are designated in the listings with the Fodor's Choice logo.

Fodor'sChoice★

Auberge du Vieux-Port, p. 186
Auberge les Passants du Sans Soucy, p. 186
Hôtel Gault, p. 186
Hôtel Le St-James, p. 186
Hôtel Nelligan, p. 186
Le Petit Hôtel, p. 187
Le Place d'Armes Hôtel & Suites, p. 187
Loews Hôtel Vogue, p. 193
Ritz-Carlton Montréal, p. 193
Sofitel Montréal, p. 194
W Montréal, p. 188

Best by Price

$

Hôtel Terrasse Royale, p. 195

$$

Auberge les Passants du Sans Soucy, p. 186
Delta Montréal, p. 188
Hôtel Chez Swann, p. 192
Hôtel St. Paul, p. 186
Sofitel Montréal, p. 194

$$$

Hilton Montréal Bonaventure, p. 192
Hôtel Gault, p. 186
Hôtel Nelligan, p. 186
Le Petit Hôtel, p. 187
Le Place d'Armes Hôtel & Suites, p. 187
Le Saint-Sulpice, p. 187
Loews Hôtel Vogue, p. 193

$$$$

Hôtel Le St-James, p. 186
Ritz-Carlton Montréal, p. 193
W Montréal, p. 188

Best by Experience

BEST CELEBRITY RETREAT

Le Saint-Sulpice, p. 187
Loews Hôtel Vogue, p. 193
Ritz-Carlton Montréal, p. 193
Sofitel Montréal, p. 194

BEST HOTEL BAR

Hôtel Nelligan, p. 186
InterContinental Montréal, p. 187
Le Place d'Armes Hôtel & Suites, p. 187
Ritz-Carlton Montréal, p. 193

BEST FOR ROMANCE

Auberge du Vieux-Port, p. 186
Auberge les Passants du Sans Soucy, p. 186
Hôtel Nelligan, p. 186
Le Petit Hôtel, p. 187

BEST BOUTIQUE HOTELS

Hôtel Le St-James, p. 186
LHOTEL, p. 187

BEST HIPSTER HOTELS

Hôtel Chez Swann, p. 192
Hôtel St. Paul, p. 186
W Montréal, p. 188

BEST INTERIOR DESIGN

Hôtel Chez Swann, p. 192
Hôtel Gault, p. 186
W Montréal, p. 188

BEST POOLS

Delta Montréal, p. 188
Hilton Montréal Bonaventure, p. 192

BEST BUILDING ARCHITECTURE

Hôtel Gault, p. 186
Hôtel Le St-James, p. 186
Hôtel St. Paul, p. 186
Le Loft Hôtel, p. 194
Le Place d'Armes Hôtel & Suites, p. 187
Ritz-Carlton Montréal, p. 193
W Montréal, p. 188

BEST NEW HOTELS

Hôtel Chez Swann, p. 192
Le Loft Hôtel, p. 194
Le Petit Hôtel, p. 187
Le St-Martin Hôtel Particulier, p. 193

8

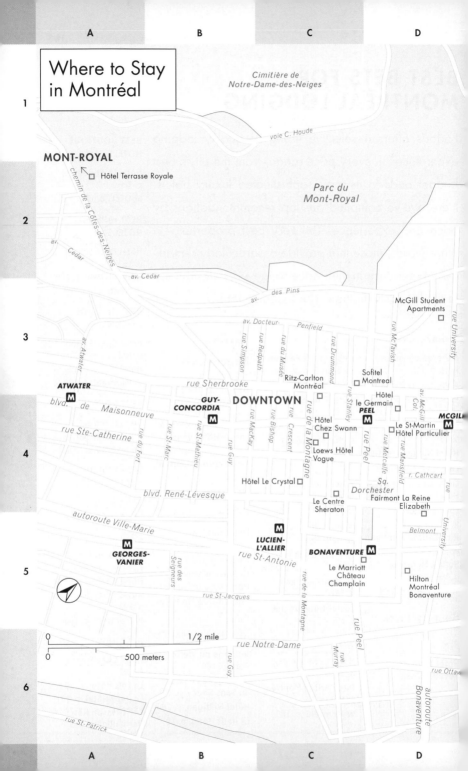

Where to Stay in Montréal

Cimitière de Notre-Dame-des-Neiges

MONT-ROYAL

Hôtel Terrasse Royale

Parc du Mont-Royal

chemin de la Côtes-des-Neiges

av. Cedar

av. Cedar

av. des Pins

McGill Student Apartments

av. Docteur-Penfield

rue McTavish

rue University

rue Simpson

rue Redpath

rue du Musée

rue Drummond

Ritz-Carlton Montréal

Sofitel Montreal

rue Stanley

Hôtel le Germain

av. McGill Col.

ATWATER Ⓜ

rue Sherbrooke

GUY-CONCORDIA Ⓜ

DOWNTOWN

PEEL Ⓜ

Le St-Martin Hôtel Particulier

MCGILL Ⓜ

blvd. de Maisonneuve

rue MacKay

rue Bishop

rue Crescent

rue de la Montagne

Hôtel Chez Swann

rue Metcalfe

rue Mansfield

rue Ste-Catherine

rue du Fort

rue St-Marc

rue St-Mathieu

rue Guy

Loews Hôtel Vogue

rue Peel

r. Cathcart

rue

Hôtel Le Crystal

blvd. René-Lévesque

Sq. Dorchester

Fairmont La Reine Elizabeth

autoroute Ville-Marie

Le Centre Sheraton

University

Belmont

GEORGES-VANIER Ⓜ

rue des Seigneurs

LUCIEN-L'ALLIER Ⓜ

rue St-Antonie

rue de la Montagne

BONAVENTURE Ⓜ

Le Marriott Château Champlain

Hilton Montréal Bonaventure

rue St-Jacques

rue St-Jacques

0 _____ 1/2 mile

0 _____ 500 meters

rue Notre-Dame

rue Guy

rue Murray

rue Peel

rue Ottaw

autoroute Bonaventure

rue St-Patrick

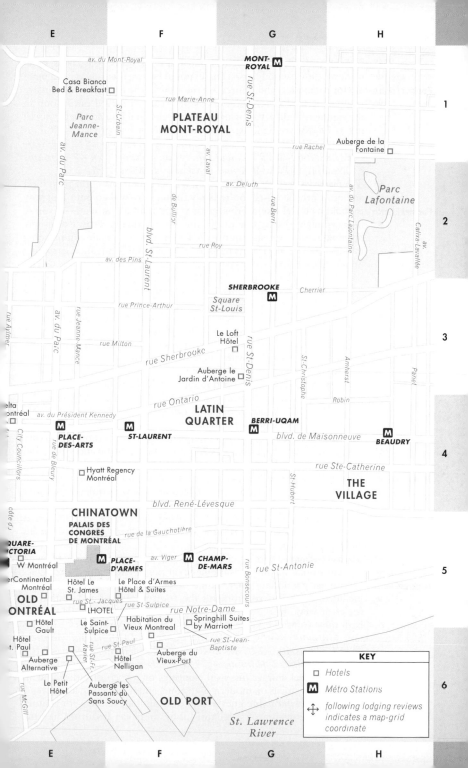

$$$
B&B/INN
Fodor's Choice
★

🛏 **Auberge du Vieux-Port.** With stone and brick walls, brass beds, case-ment windows, wood floors, and exposed beams, this auberge is a mag-net for romantics who appreciate the view of the river. **Pros:** expansive rooftop deck with retractable cover; breakfast served until noon in the summer; multi-jet showers. **Cons:** occasional bouts of street noise; not as fun for young kids; glass showers afford no privacy. ⑤ *Rooms from: C$229* ✉ *97 rue de la Commune Est, Old Montréal* ☎ *514/876–0081, 888/660–7678* ⊕ *www.aubergeduvieuxport.com* ⟿ *45 rooms* ⊚⊙ *Breakfast* Ⓜ *Place-d'Armes or Champ-de-Mars* ✛ *F6.*

$$
B&B/INN
Fodor's Choice
★

🛏 **Auberge les Passants du Sans Soucy.** Daniel Soucy, one of the friendliest and most urbane hosts you're likely to run into, will go out of his way to make you feel like a houseguest rather than a customer—if you're lucky enough to snag one of his nine rooms, that is. **Pros:** exquisitely personal service; guests can use the fridge downstairs; air-conditioning in each room. **Cons:** rooms need to be booked far in advance; carpeting up the stairs is well-worn; parking is a hassle. ⑤ *Rooms from: C$165* ✉ *171 rue St-Paul Ouest, Old Montréal* ☎ *514/842–2634* ⊕ *www. lesanssoucy.com* ⟿ *8 rooms, 1 suite* ⊚⊙ *Breakfast* Ⓜ *Square-Victoria or Place-d'Armes* ✛ *E6.*

$$$
HOTEL
Fodor's Choice
★

🛏 **Hôtel Gault.** A heritage boutique hotel with serious design chops, the Gault attracts movie stars—hello, Charlotte Rampling!—and style mavens, none of whom would ever guess it used to be a cotton factory in the 1800s. **Pros:** Fodorites love the intimate vibe; iPads available to borrow at front desk; 24/7 room service; heated bathroom floors; DVDs to rent. **Cons:** a bit hard to find; C$32 valet; no pool. ⑤ *Rooms from: C$239* ✉ *449 rue Ste-Hélène, Old Montréal* ☎ *514/904–1616, 866/904–1616* ⊕ *www.hotelgault.com* ⟿ *22 rooms, 8 suites* ⊚⊙ *No meals* Ⓜ *Square-Victoria* ✛ *E5.*

$$$$
HOTEL
☾
Fodor's Choice
★

🛏 **Hôtel Le St-James.** Rock royalty frequents this lavishly furnished luxury hotel, which quietly pampers European nobility, the business elite, and Hollywood moguls who appreciate the splendor. **Pros:** civility reigns; Fodorites like the lush experience and stately lobby; kids get milk and cookies at check in. **Cons:** rue St-Jacques is a very quiet street after 6 pm; dog rate starts at C$40 per day. ⑤ *Rooms from: C$400* ✉ *355 rue St-Jacques, Old Montréal* ☎ *514/841–3111, 866/841–3111* ⊕ *www. hotellestjames.com* ⟿ *23 rooms, 38 suites, 1 apartment* ⊚⊙ *No meals* Ⓜ *Square-Victoria* ✛ *E5.*

$$$
HOTEL
Fodor's Choice
★

🛏 **Hôtel Nelligan.** There's a cultivated air of refinement echoing through this ultraromantic hotel, a landmark on rue St-Paul named after Qué-bec's most passionate poet, Émile Nelligan. **Pros:** welcome cocktail included; Fodorites recommend the rooftop terrace and restaurant for great views of the Old City; lively bar right on rue St-Paul; huge bath tubs. **Cons:** weekend wedding traffic; valet parking is C$28 plus tax. ⑤ *Rooms from: C$229* ✉ *106 rue St-Paul Ouest, Old Montréal* ☎ *514/788–2040, 877/788–2040* ⊕ *www.hotelnelligan.com* ⟿ *105 rooms, 28 suites, 2 penthouses* ⊚⊙ *No meals* Ⓜ *Place-d'Armes* ✛ *F6.*

$$
HOTEL

🛏 **Hôtel St. Paul.** Forget fussy oil paintings or rococo furniture, the St. Paul keeps the focus on modern silk, stone, and raw-metal decor accents admired by fashionable guests who also appreciate the 19th-century facade. **Pros:** decorator's delight; lobby fireplace; Fodorites like the location. **Cons:** under-lit hallways and elevators can be spooky; fur throws and off-white sofas in lobby need refreshing; Wi-Fi is C$15 for 24 hours in rooms, but free in lobby and business center. ⑤ *Rooms from: C$199* ⊠ *355 rue McGill, Old Montréal* ☎ *514/380–2222, 866/380–2202* ⊕ *www.hotelstpaul.com* 🖙 *96 rooms, 24 suites* ¶◎¶ *No meals* Ⓜ *Square-Victoria* ✛ *E6.*

$$ 🏨 **InterContinental Montréal.** On the edge of Old Montréal, this award-
HOTEL winning luxury hotel across from Toqué! restaurant is part of the Montréal World Trade Center, drawing international business travelers and design-savvy tourists who appreciate decor accents like leather and suede bed headboards. **Pros:** iPod alarm clocks; easy underground access to shopping and nightlife; new Java U café in lobby. **Cons:** business-oriented (the convention center is across the street); a bit posh for families with youngsters. ⑤ *Rooms from: C$199* ⊠ *360 rue St-Antoine Ouest, Old Montréal* ☎ *514/987–9900, 800/361–3600* ⊕ *www.montreal.intercontinental.com* 🖙 *357 rooms, 23 suites* ¶◎¶ *No meals* Ⓜ *Square-Victoria or Place-d'Armes* ✛ *E5.*

$$$ 🏨 **Le Petit Hôtel.** Couples seeking romance have a new hideaway in this
HOTEL quiet boutique hotel that marries modern design with old stone walls
♺ and exposed beams. **Pros:** fun design; Aveda bath products; close to
Fodor's Choice the best restaurants; cribs, playpens, and babysitters available. **Cons:**
★ smallish bathrooms have no tubs; C$28 valet is steep, but it's the going rate. ⑤ *Rooms from: C$219* ⊠ *168 rue St-Paul Ouest, Old Montréal* ☎ *514/940–0360, 877/530–0360* ⊕ *www.petithotelmontreal.com* 🖙 *24 rooms* ¶◎¶ *Breakfast* Ⓜ *Square-Victoria* ✛ *E6.*

$$$ 🏨 **Le Place d'Armes Hôtel & Suites.** Three splendidly ornate commercial
HOTEL buildings dating from the Victorian era were merged to create Old
♺ Montréal's largest boutique hotel, pleasing jetsetters and business execs
Fodor's Choice alike. **Pros:** free arrival cocktail; houses the best spa in town; easy access
★ to the sights of Old Montréal; kids get milk and cookies when families check in. **Cons:** late sleepers may be disturbed by the noontime Angelus bells at the Basilique Notre-Dame de Montréal; a steep approach from métro is slippery in winter; no pool. ⑤ *Rooms from: C$239* ⊠ *55 rue St-Jacques, Old Montréal* ☎ *514/842–1887, 888/450–1887* ⊕ *www.hotelplacedarmes.com* 🖙 *81 rooms, 52 suites* ¶◎¶ *No meals* Ⓜ *Place-d'Armes* ✛ *F5.*

$$$ 🏨 **Le Saint-Sulpice.** Celebrities emerging from limousines outside,
HOTEL the Basilique Notre-Dame de Montréal next door, and a chic lobby lounge opening onto a courtyard garden that's one of the rare green spots in Old Montréal's stony landscape—all of it adds to the winning appeal of this hotel. **Pros:** in-room massage service; excellent celebrity-spotting; easy access to the Basilique Notre-Dame de Montréal. **Cons:** church bells on Sunday morning may disturb late sleepers; dark hallways a bit gloomy; too fancy for kids to relax. ⑤ *Rooms from: C$239* ⊠ *414 rue St-Sulpice, Old Montréal* ☎ *514/288–1000, 877/785–7423* ⊕ *www.lesaintsulpice.com* 🖙 *108 suites* ¶◎¶ *Breakfast* Ⓜ *Place-d'Armes* ✛ *F6.*

$$$ 🏨 **LHOTEL.** George Marciano, the fashion mogul behind Guess? jeans,
HOTEL bought this opulent hotel—formerly Hôtel XIXe Siècle—to double as a personal art gallery and guest house for his well-heeled friends. (Note

8

the Ferraris parked outside.) **Pros:** pop art galore; big high-ceilinged rooms; lively bar in lobby. **Cons:** purists won't like the pop art that belies a Grande Dame exterior; street parking is scarce; rue St-Jacques is deadly dull after 6 pm. ⑤ *Rooms from: C$205* ✉ *262 rue St-Jacques Ouest, Old Montréal* ☎ *514/985–0019, 877/553–0019* ⊕ *www. lhotelmontreal.com* ↘ *45 rooms, 14 suites* ⦿ *No meals* Ⓜ *Square-Victoria* ✛ *E5.*

$$ ⛾ **Springhill Suites by Marriott.** Clean and basic, this all-suites hotel fits
HOTEL   seamlessly into one of the narrowest and oldest streets of Old Mon-
☽   tréal. **Pros:** Fodorites love the free, bountiful breakfast; large rooms and underground parking—both rarities in Old Montréal; salt water pool; Häagen-Dazs for sale in the lobby. **Cons:** not much style for the money; difficult access on a narrow street; poor views. ⑤ *Rooms from: C$200* ✉ *445 rue St-Jean-Baptiste, Old Montréal* ☎ *514/875–4333, 888/287–9400* ⊕ *www.springhillsuites.com* ↘ *124 suites* ⦿ *Breakfast* Ⓜ *Champ-de-Mars* ✛ *F5.*

$$$$ ⛾ **W Montréal.** This ultraluxurious chain opened its first Canadian
HOTEL   hotel here in 2004, inside the old Bank of Canada building, but you'd
Fodor's Choice   never know it once you walk through those whooshing sliding doors:
★   upon entry, guests see a cubic water fountain and glowing red walls throughout the lobby. **Pros:** guests feel like rock stars; good people-watching; sexy bathrooms; fastest room service in town; pet pro-gram. **Cons:** C$15 per night fee for in-room Wi-Fi, but it's free in the lobby; lobby noisy at night; glass showers afford no privacy. ⑤ *Rooms from: C$299* ✉ *901 Square-Victoria, Old Montréal* ☎ *514/395–3100* ⊕ *www.whotels.com/montreal* ↘ *152 rooms, 28 suites* ⦿ *No meals* Ⓜ *Square-Victoria* ✛ *E5.*

DOWNTOWN

The hub for countless festivals, Downtown is a convenient place to unpack your bags. This is where you'll find the major chain hotels, with underground parking, pools, and all the amenities that families enjoy. A few new boutique hotels have appeared this year, providing more options for couples without kids. From Downtown, it's just a short trip to the city's other neighborhoods of interest, so this is a good central point from which to see the city.

$$ ⛾ **Delta Montréal.** Government employees and jazz festival performers
HOTEL   cycle through the Delta regularly, ignoring the airport-like lobby to exhale
☽   in plush new rooms that overlook the mountain or downtown. **Pros:** gym has a play area for kids; excellent soundproofing; kids have their own "check in" procedure. **Cons:** the lobby screams for a makeover; no safes in room; Restaurant Aroma is serviceable but no place for a date. ⑤ *Rooms from: C$199* ✉ *475 av. du Président-Kennedy, Downtown* ☎ *514/286–1986, 877/286–1986* ⊕ *www.deltamontreal.com* ↘ *447 rooms, 9 suites* ⦿ *No meals* Ⓜ *McGill or Place des Arts* ✛ *E4.*

$$$ ⛾ **Fairmont Le Reine Elizabeth.** Built to impress international guests dur-
HOTEL   ing Expo 67, The Queen E is the iconic setting for John Lennon and Yoko Ono's "bed-in for peace" protest of 1969, but it's hardly stuck in the past—answering the contemporary call for locavore food with a roof-top garden for heirloom vegetables, beehives, and a honey house.

Hôtel Gault

Auberge les Passants du Sans Soucy

Hôtel Nelligan

CLOSE UP

Lodging Alternatives

There are many reasons for travelers to consider apartment rentals or other lodging alternatives, but we tend to recommend hotel suites instead. Why? Unfortunately, apartment rental scams in Montréal are prevalent—especially when booked online. In some published reports, potential guests have arrived to find that the apartment they rented doesn't exist, or that they're paying for an illegal sublet. (Note: Never wire money to an individual's account.)

There are, however, reputable providers of short- and long-term rentals; our favorites are below.

LOFT AND APARTMENT RENTALS
Fully furnished lofts—some with closed bedrooms—and apartments are available through these esteemed companies:

Habitation du Vieux Montreal.
Habitation du Vieux Montreal rents out five apartments in one building in the Old Port on St. Laurent Boulevard at the corner of St. Paul. Completely independent, each unit is fully equipped—from kitchen to bathroom to bedding. Expect street noise at night in the summer. Prices range from C$130 to C$275 a night. ☎ 514/892-1238 ⊕ www.habitationvieuxmontreal.ca ✛ F6.

Lofts du Vieux-Port.
Lofts du Vieux-Port has 24 apartment-style lofts scattered throughout the Old Port. The lofts are chic and sexy, with a mix of antiques and modern design. No elevators, but valets carry your luggage. Short- and long-term rentals. ☎ 514/876-0081 ⊕ www.loftsduvieuxport.com.

HOSTEL
⊡ Auberge Alternative.
Exposed stone walls and wild colors make for cheery dorms, while live musical performances keep the hostel's common room hopping. $ Rooms from: C$27 ⊠ 358 rue St-Pierre, Old Montréal ☎ 514/282-8069 ⊕ www.auberge-alternative.qc.ca ☜ 7 dorms, 2 rooms ⊟ No credit cards M Square-Victoria ✛ E6.

STUDENT HOUSING
McGill Student Apartments.
Summer backpackers and families stay in this fancy new residence, once a hotel, off McGill campus from mid-May to mid-August. Smug budget travelers congratulate themselves for finding this gem. Use of the school's swimming pool and gym facilities costs a small fee. The university cafeteria is open during the week, serving breakfast and lunch. Rates start at C$110 for a private room with a double bed. Rates reach C$149 for a suite. ☎ 514/398-5200 ⊕ www.mcgill.ca/residences ✛ D3.

B&BS
Some B&Bs are off the grid. They prefer to remain private and hush-hush. To find them, simply walk the streets of the Village, specifically rues St-Andre, St-Christophe, and St-Timothée, below rue Sherbrooke. Or, ask any of the friendly locals, who'll be more than glad to point you in the direction of their friend's B&B. ⇨ For more information on B&Bs, see Travel Smart Montréal and Québec City.

—Joanne Latimer

Le Place d'Armes Hôtel & Suites

W Montréal

Loews Hôtel Vogue

Hôtel Le St-James

Le Petit Hôtel

Sofitel Montréal

Pros: chic gym open 24 hours; easy access to trains, métro, and the Underground City; baronial restaurant with pastries and chocolates made on-site. **Cons:** lobby is expansive but drab and busy as a train station; conventioneers abound. $ *Rooms from: C$239* ⊠ *900 boul. René-Lévesque Ouest, Downtown* ☎ *514/861–3511, 800/441–1414* ⊕ *www.fairmont.com* ⇱ *937 rooms, 100 suites* ⦿| *No meals* Ⓜ *Bonaventure* ⊹ *D5.*

$$$ 🏨 **Hilton Montréal Bonaventure.** Two and a half acres of rooftop gar-
HOTEL dens and an open-air swimming pool set the Hilton apart from the
🜃 usual corporate hotels, and make it a great place to take the family.
Pros: almost every room has a view of the rooftop garden; the four-season pool is heated by the kitchen's steam; in-room spa services. **Cons:** full of conventioneers; ground-floor entrance—with elevator ride to reception—isn't so welcoming. $ *Rooms from: C$229* ⊠ *900 rue de la Gauchetière, Downtown* ☎ *514/878–2332, 800/267–2575* ⊕ *www. hilton.com* ⇱ *395 rooms, 15 suites* ⦿| *No meals* Ⓜ *Bonaventure* ⊹ *D5.*

$$ 🏨 **Hôtel Chez Swann.** Young culture vultures are tripping over themselves
HOTEL to get a room at Chez Swann—the name's a reference to Proust—to bask in the drama of this new boutique hotel's quirky decor. **Pros:** hip design; in-room spa treatments; downtown location; spin room; free phone calls within North America. **Cons:** no bath tubs; no pets; not suitable for kids. $ *Rooms from: C$200* ⊠ *1444 rue Drummond, Downtown* ☎ *514/842–7070* ⊕ *www.hotelchezswann.com* ⇱ *7 rooms, 16 suites* ⦿| *Breakfast* Ⓜ *Peel* ⊹ *C4.*

$$$ 🏨 **Hôtel Le Crystal.** It's no wonder A-list performers stay here, considering
HOTEL Le Crystal's dramatic style and luxury suites, which pamper travelers with spa-style bathrooms and separate soaking tubs. **Pros:** best city view from the treadmills; saltwater pool; outdoor year-round whirlpool hot tub. **Cons:** lofty rates; rather formal; right on the sidewalk of a busy intersection. $ *Rooms from: C$249* ⊠ *1100 de la Montagne, Downtown* ☎ *514/861–5550* ⊕ *www.hotellecrystal.com* ⇱ *131 suites* ⦿| *No meals* Ⓜ *Lucien-L'Aller* ⊹ *C4.*

$$$$ 🏨 **Hôtel le Germain.** The lobby in this sleek boutique hotel is a who's who
HOTEL of models, record producers, and all varieties of international hipsters who delight in the details like bedding designed by Québec fashion icon Marie Saint Pierre. **Pros:** top chef Daniel Vézina in the restaurant; deluxe Continental breakfast included; quiet location in the heart of Downtown; connectivity panels project your laptop onto 42-inch screen. **Cons:** on a charmless urban street; parking is scarce and valet is C$25; the scene-y lobby is starting to bore regulars. $ *Rooms from: C$250* ⊠ *2050 rue Mansfield, Downtown* ☎ *514/849–2050, 877/333–2050* ⊕ *www.hotelgermain.com* ⇱ *99 rooms, 2 suites* ⦿| *Multiple meal plans* Ⓜ *Peel or McGill* ⊹ *D4.*

$$$ 🏨 **Hyatt Regency Montréal.** The Hyatt is *the* place to stay during the
HOTEL Just For Laughs Festival and the International Jazz Festival in July—if you're a jazz fan or comedy buff, that is—or if you appreciate easy access to Musée d'Art Contemporain across the street and Chinatown, one block south. **Pros:** great location for shoppers and concert lovers; easy access to the Underground City; indoor pool and lounge. **Cons:** strange approach to lobby via elevator; you have to pay C$12.95 per

day for Wi-Fi in the rooms; networking and careerism rules the bar and reception areas. $ *Rooms from: C$219* ✉ *1255 rue Jeanne-Mance, Downtown* ☎ *514/982–1234, 800/361–8234* ⊕ *www.montreal.hyatt. com/property* ⤳ *605 rooms, 30 suites* ⦿| *No meals* Ⓜ *Place des Arts or Place-d'Armes* ✛ *E4.*

$ ⊞ **Le Centre Sheraton.** A magnet for conventioneers, hockey fans and
HOTEL   businesspeople—this hotel draws boisterous hotel guests who gravitate
☼   to the lobby bar for drinks and networking. **Pros:** "Sheraton Link" digital hub in lobby has big-screen televisions, cameras, and computer stations; huge new gym on 6th floor with views; free breakfast for kids under four years old and half off breakfast for kids 5–12 years old; close to the Centre Bell for hockey and concerts. **Cons:** lobby marred by convention signs; no in-hotel access to the métro; executive rooms on the 37th club lounge floor cost C$50 more. $ *Rooms from: C$159* ✉ *1201 boul. René-Lévesque Ouest, Downtown* ☎ *514/878–2000, 800/325–3535* ⊕ *www.sheraton.com/lecentre* ⤳ *785 rooms, 40 suites* ⦿| *No meals* Ⓜ *Bonaventure or Peel* ✛ *C4.*

$$$$ ⊞ **Le Marriott Château Champlain.** An icon from the 1967 Olympics with
HOTEL   it's distinctive half-moon windows, this 36-floor skyscraper has unofficial landmark status in Montréal, where it's a magnet for business guests and families alike. **Pros:** expansive views; park-side location; top three floors have private lounges. **Cons:** a favorite for parties and receptions—especially with the high-school-prom crowd in spring; off-putting reception desk. $ *Rooms from: C$279* ✉ *1050 rue de la Gauchetière Ouest, Downtown* ☎ *514/878–9000, 800/200–5909* ⊕ *www.marriott.com* ⤳ *578 rooms, 33 suites* ⦿| *No meals* Ⓜ *Bonaventure* ✛ *C5.*

$$ ⊞ **Le St-Martin Hôtel Particulier.** Built on hallowed ground once occupied
HOTEL   by a beloved diner, this tasteful new hotel with abstract art and deep-
☼   soak tubs doesn't reflect the Formica decor of the former down-market eatery. **Pros:** windows have excellent soundproofing; kids under 12 stay for free; tartares in the French fusion restaurant are outstanding. **Cons:** reception is just steps from the sidewalk and gets crowded at checkout; no spa; not all rooms have tubs. $ *Rooms from: C$200* ✉ *980 boul. de Maisonneuve, Ouest, Downtown* ☎ *514/843–3000, 877/843–3003* ⊕ *www.lestmartinmontreal.com* ⤳ *71 rooms, 42 suites* ⦿| *No meals* Ⓜ *Peel* ✛ *D4.*

$$$ ⊞ **Loews Hôtel Vogue.** Serious shoppers like the location—a five-minute
HOTEL   walk from Holt Renfrew, Ogilvy, and other high-end boutiques—and
☼   the luxury of this downtown boutique hotel, which just overhauled the
Fodor's Choice   guest rooms. **Pros:** cocktails with a view in the new lobby bar; huge
★   bathrooms with flat-screen TVs and phones; kids under 12 eat free in high season. **Cons:** exterior facade is a ghastly steel-and-glass ode to the 1980s; valet parking costs C$35. $ *Rooms from: C$239* ✉ *1425 rue de la Montagne, Downtown* ☎ *514/285–5555, 800/465–6654* ⊕ *www. loewshotels.com* ⤳ *126 rooms, 16 suites* ⦿| *No meals* Ⓜ *Peel* ✛ *C4.*

$$$$ ⊞ **Ritz-Carlton Montréal.** Montréal's grandest hotel in the Golden Square
HOTEL   Mile reopened its doors triumphantly, after spending well over a hun-
Fodor's Choice   dred million dollars to secure its place as a preeminent hotel for the
★   world's elite. **Pros:** upscale all the way; a great conversation piece as the location of Liz Taylor's wedding to Richard Burton in 1964; high-end

8

shopping and galleries within a five-minute walk; celebrity chef in lobby restaurant. **Cons:** poor métro access; basement gym is a bit underwhelming; no pool yet. $ *Rooms from: C$425* ✉ *1228 rue Sherbrooke Ouest, Downtown* ☎ *514/842–4212, 800/363–0366* ⊕ *www.ritzmontreal.com* ⌁ *98 rooms, 31suites* ⃝ *No meals* Ⓜ *Peel or Guy-Concordia* ✛ *C4.*

$$
HOTEL
Fodor's Choice
★

Ⓣ **Sofitel Montréal.** The carpets in the lobby at this exquisite hotel were made by the same company that carpeted Versailles for King Louis XIV, yet the Sofitel remains modern and cheery, with sleek leather sofas and a stained-glass installation. **Pros:** excellent location; menswear boutique in the lobby; breakfast options galore. **Cons:** scarce street parking; valet is C$30 plus tax; views from east-facing rooms are obstructed. $ *Rooms from: C$172* ✉ *1155 rue Sherbrooke Ouest, Downtown* ☎ *514/285–9000* ⊕ *www.sofitel.com* ⌁ *241 rooms, 17 suites* ⃝ *No meals* Ⓜ *Peel* ✛ *C3.*

THE LATIN QUARTER

Bustling with cinema-goers and university kids rushing to cafés and libraries, The Quartier Latin is alive with expectation. No, it isn't as pristine as the Old Port, since gentrification has been slow and uneven, but it's full of local flavor—artisanal chocolate shops, gastro-pubs, and hippy boutiques. The panhandlers are funny, not dangerous, and beg in two languages.

$
B&B/INN

Ⓣ **Auberge le Jardin d'Antoine.** Antique-reproduction furniture and hardwood floors give this small hotel plenty of shabby-chic charm, but its best selling point is its location right on rue St-Denis, among the Latin Quarter's trendy restaurants, cinemas, and poutine joints. **Pros:** located on one of the liveliest stretches of rue St-Denis; secure luggage room in the lobby for late departures; new coffee machines in rooms. **Cons:** Victorian doll-house decor isn't very fashionable; the lively location means it can be noisy. $ *Rooms from: C$104* ✉ *2024 rue St-Denis, Latin Quarter* ☎ *514/843–4506, 800/361–4506* ⊕ *www. aubergelejardindantoine.com* ⌁ *25 rooms* ⃝ *Breakfast* Ⓜ *Berri-UQAM* ✛ *G3.*

$$$$
HOTEL

Ⓣ **Le Loft Hotel.** New on the scene, this chic hotel is bucking for design awards and Prada-wearing clients who will appreciate the architectural glory of this art deco landmark. **Pros:** 10-foot ceilings; great for entertaining; superior soundproofing. **Cons:** street parking is scarce; a bit hard to find. $ *Rooms from: C$345* ✉ *334 Terrace St-Denis, Latin Quarter* ☎ *888/414-5638* ⊕ *www.lofthotel.ca* ⌁ *35 lofts* ⃝ *Breakfast* Ⓜ *Berri-UQAM* ✛ *G3.*

THE PLATEAU

Full of artists and academics, the Plateau is a bustling neighborhood with a high density of bistros, brewpubs, martini bars, designer boutiques, and parks. This is no place for quiet contemplation. In the summer, join the crowds at outdoor markets and street fairs. Accommodations aren't plentiful, but there are lovely auberges and B&Bs.

$ ⊡ **Auberge de la Fontaine.** A winner of the city's Prix Ulysse for the best
B&B/INN three-star hotel, this turn-of-the-20th-century residence overlooks Parc
☺ Lafontaine and one of the city's major bicycle trails. **Pros:** joggers paradise; Fodorites like the park-side location on a bicycle trail, near restaurants; kids under 12 stay for free. **Cons:** out-dated lobby is a little sad;
some rooms are quite small and not well soundproofed; parking can be
difficult. ⑤ *Rooms from: C$159* ⊠ *1301 rue Rachel Est, Plateau Mont-
Royal* ☎ *514/597–0166, 800/597–0597* ⊕ *www.aubergedelafontaine.
com* ↝ *18 rooms, 3 suites* ❢◎❙ *Breakfast* Ⓜ *Mont-Royal* ✛ *H1.*

$ ⊡ **Casa Bianca Bed & Breakfast.** Popular with love-struck couples, this
B&B/INN renovated maison d'hôte is an ode to French Renaissance Revival architecture. **Pros:** squeaky clean; dripping with style; organic emphasis;
facing Mont-Royal and public tennis courts (fee). **Cons:** there are only
five rooms, so book early; creaky hardwood floors; no soundproofing in bedrooms; serious carnivores might miss bacon at breakfast.
⑤ *Rooms from: C$129* ⊠ *4351 av. de L'Esplanade, Plateau Mont-Royal*
☎ *514/312–3837, 866/775–4431* ⊕ *www.casabianca.ca* ↝ *3 rooms, 2
suites* ❢◎❙ *Breakfast* Ⓜ *Mont-Royal* ✛ *F1.*

MONT-ROYAL

If you rent a car or don't mind riding the métro, Mont-Royal is an
affordable place to stay. Away from boisterous nightlife, it's quiet and
less hurried than more central accommodations.

$ ⊡ **Hôtel Terrasse Royale.** Near the Oratoire St-Joseph in a busy local
HOTEL neighborhood called Côte-des-Neiges, this serviceable hotel attracts
tourists and families who enjoy ethnic markets and restaurants where
you can dine cheaply and well. **Pros:** practical kitchens; breakfast downstairs is only C$3.85; multilingual neighborhood; easy access to métro.
Cons: noisy; the glum exterior is disappointing; lobby needs a renovation. ⑤ *Rooms from: C$119* ⊠ *5225 chemin de la Côte-des-Neiges,
Mont-Royal* ☎ *514/739–6391, 800/567–0804* ⊕ *www.terrasse-royale.
com* ↝ *56 rooms* ❢◎❙ *No meals* Ⓜ *Côte-des-Neiges* ✛ *A2.*

8

Side Trips from Montréal

WORD OF MOUTH

"The colors [at Mont Orford] were so breathtaking and it seemed like I stopped every few feet just to take pictures of everything around me (and maybe to catch my breath from climbing uphill). . . . It was as if the hillsides were on fire because they were glowing bright orange and red."

—globetrotterxyz

SIDE TRIPS FROM MONTRÉAL

TOP REASONS TO GO

★ **Ski at Mont-Tremblant:** For some of the best skiing east of the Rockies, Mont-Tremblant, about 150 km (90 miles) north of Montréal, also has fine hotels and restaurants as well as a lively ski village and great golf courses.

★ **Take a Driving Tour of Eastern Township Wineries:** The vineyards here are often compared to those in the Niagara Region and Okanagan Valley.

★ **Visit Abbaye St-Benoit-du-Lac:** The Benedictine monks built this splendid church—with its fairy-tale castle bell tower—on the shores of Lake Memphrémagog.

★ **Spend a night among wolves in Parc Omega:** Go with an experienced guide to explore the lives of these great predators in their natural habitat—the magnificent Outaouais region.

★ **Go leaf-peeping . . . anywhere:** From mid-September through mid-October the entire Laurentians, Eastern Townships, and Outaouais are ablaze with spectacular fall foliage.

1 The Laurentians. With its ski hills and lakes, this is sheer paradise for those looking for a quick break from the hustle and bustle of urban life. Quaint villages, many steeped in colorful history, line the delightful countryside—all hardly a stone's throw away from the center of Montréal.

2 The Outaouais. Noted for its rugged beauty, the Outaouais is an excellent place to go wildlife spotting.

GETTING ORIENTED

The Laurentians resort area begins 60 km (37 miles) north of Montréal. The Eastern Townships start approximately 80 km (50 miles) east of the city in a southern corner of the province. The Outaouais lies about 110 km (68 miles) to the west, bordering Ontario. All three are an easy drive from Montréal.

9

3 **The Eastern Townships.** A favorite ski and sun destination for those looking to get away from it all, this is also an increasingly popular culinary tourism destination for its artisan food producers and wineries. Settled by British Loyalists fleeing the American Revolution, the region's redbrick villages, charming bed-and-breakfasts, and excellent regional dining offer a unique blend of New England and Nouvelle France.

Updated by
Chris Barry

In the minds of many who live here, one of Montréal's greatest attributes is its proximity to the sheer physical beauty of the surrounding countryside. From downtown Montréal you can head in pretty well any direction and within an hour or so you'll be, if not quite in the wilderness, then at least in the thick of cottage country.

The three most popular side-trip destinations from Montréal are the Laurentians, the Eastern Townships, and the Outaouais—each possessing its own distinct characteristics and flavor.

The Laurentians (les Laurentides) range, which begins roughly 45 minutes north of Montréal, is one of Eastern Canada's great year-round playgrounds, with everything from golf to white-water rafting in summer, and skiing, snowmobiling, and dogsledding in winter.

The Eastern Townships (also known as les Cantons de l'Est, and formerly as l'Estrie) refers to the southeast corner of the province of Québec—bordering Vermont, New Hampshire, and Maine. In winter, the Townships are the place to be for serious ski and snowboard enthusiasts, boasting many of the province's highest peaks and most challenging trails. In summer, boating, swimming, sailing, golfing, in-line skating, hiking, and bicycling take over. And every fall the inns are booked solid with visitors eager to take in the brilliant foliage. Fall is also a good time to visit the wineries (although most are open all year). Because of its mild microclimate, the Townships area has become one of the fastest-developing wine regions in Canada, with a dozen of Québec's 33 commerical wineries.

The Outaouais (pronounced: ewt–away) region encompasses an enormous body of land located in the southwest corner of the province. Bordered to the northwest by Abitibi-Témiscamingue, to the east by the Laurentians, and to the southwest by Ontario and the Ottawa River, it's home to the iconic Château Montebello, the largest log structure ever built. First settled in the mid-19th century, the primary industry here has traditionally been logging, but with its 20,000 lakes, countless rivers, 400 km (249 miles) of hiking trails, and 2,730 km (1,696 miles) of snowmobile trails, the Outaouais region can aptly be described as a nature lover's paradise.

MONTRÉAL SIDE TRIPS PLANNER

WHEN TO GO

The Laurentians are a big skiing destination in winter, but the other seasons all have their own charms: you can drive up from Montréal to enjoy the fall foliage; to hike, bike, or play golf; or to engage in spring skiing—and still get back to the city before dark. The only slow periods are early November (aka "mud season"), when there isn't much to do, and June, when the area has plenty to offer but is plagued by black flies. Control programs have improved the situation somewhat.

The Eastern Townships are best in fall, when the foliage is at its peak; the region borders Vermont and has the same dramatic colors. It's possible to visit wineries at this time, but you should call ahead, since harvest is a busy time.

The Outaouais is beautiful at any time of year, but unless you're looking to spend several days there it's best to go in summer and stay in the lower region around Montebello. Making your way up to the provincial parks in the north is a lengthy journey at best, but in winter, potentially hazardous road conditions could well add several more hours to your trip.

GETTING HERE AND AROUND

Autoroute 15 is the fastest and most direct route from Montréal to the beauty spots of the Laurentians. This limited access highway peters out at Ste-Agathe and morphs into Autoroute 117, which runs all the way to Rouyn-Noranda. Exit numbers on Autoroute 15 reflect the distance from Montréal. Autoroute 15 starts at the New York–Québec border where it connects to Interstate 87, so it's also the most direct route for most visitors from the United States. The highway crosses into Montréal on the Champlain Bridge and follows the Décarie and Metropolitan expressways across the island. Visitors arriving from Boston and points east on Interstate 91 can follow Autoroute 55 from the border north to Autoroute 10 (the Autoroute des Cantons de l'Est) and then drive west until it merges with Autoroute 15 at the Champlain Bridge.

Most people traveling to this region do so by car, making it easy to spend as much or as little time in any given area as desired. However, Québec has created the Route Verte, or the Green Route, a 4,000-km (2,485-mile) network of bike trails in the southern part of the province. Many of the trails are currently open for access.

For the Eastern Townships, take Autoroute 10 Est (the autoroute des Cantons de l'Est) from Montréal, or U.S. 91 from New England, which becomes Autoroute 55 as it crosses the border to the Eastern Townships.

To get to the Outaouais take Autoroute 15 North roughly 40 km (25 miles) until you get to Autoroute 50 West heading toward Lachute. Drive another 70 km (43 miles) past Lachute and you'll soon be in Montebello.

⇨ *For more information on getting here and around, see Travel Smart Montréal and Québec City.*

9

RESTAURANTS

The variety of dining options throughout the region provides for all budgets, and although you're not likely to find much in the way of quality ethnic dishes, the major towns in the region serve a range of cuisines, with French and regional specialties dominating the higher end of the price scale. The Eastern Townships are particularly strong on gourmet regional cuisine utilizing ingredients from local artisan producers.

HOTELS

Accommodations here range from resort hotels to cozy *auberges* (inns). Many inns—especially in high season—will include two meals, usually breakfast and dinner, in the cost of a night's stay. In addition, hotels and inns often require a minimum two-night stay on weekends in high season, so inquire in advance.

VISITOR INFORMATION

Tourisme Cantons-de-l'Est ⊠ *20 rue Don-Bosco Sud, Sherbrooke* ☎ *800/355-5755* ⊕ *www.easterntownships.org.*

Tourisme Laurentides (Porte des Nord) ⊠ *1000 Highway 15 North, St-Jérôme* ☎ *450/224-7007 from Montréal area, 800/561-6673 from rest of North America.*

THE LAURENTIANS

The Laurentians (les Laurentides) range is a delightful year-round destination less than an hour's drive from downtown Montréal, traffic allowing. The main tourist region, which actually encompasses only a small part of the Laurentian mountain range, is divided into two major regions: the Lower Laurentians (les Basses Laurentides) and the Upper Laurentians (les Hautes Laurentides). But don't be fooled by the designations; they don't signify great driving distances. The rocky hills here are relatively low, but many are eminently skiable, with a few peaks above 2,500 feet. Mont-Tremblant, at 3,150 feet, is the region's highest.

The P'tit Train du Nord—the former railroad line that's now a 200-km (124-mile) "linear park" used by cyclists, hikers, skiers, and snowmobilers—made it possible to transport settlers and cargo easily to the Upper Laurentians. It also opened up the area to skiing by the early 1900s. Before long, trainloads of skiers replaced settlers and cargo as the railway's major trade. At first a winter weekend getaway for Montrealers who stayed at boardinghouses and fledgling resorts, the Upper Laurentians soon began attracting international visitors.

Ski lodges and private family cottages for wealthy city dwellers were accessible only by train until the 1930s, when Route 117 was built. Today there's an uneasy peace between the longtime cottagers, who want to restrict development, and resort entrepreneurs, who want to expand. At the moment, commercial interests seem to be prevailing. A number of large hotels have added indoor pools and spa facilities, and efficient highways have brought the country even closer to the city—45 minutes to St-Sauveur, 1½–2 hours to Mont-Tremblant.

The resort area begins at St-Sauveur-des-Monts (Exit 60 on Autoroute 15) and extends north to Mont-Tremblant. Beyond, the region turns into a wilderness of lakes and forests best visited with an outfitter. Fishing guides are concentrated around Parc du Mont-Tremblant. To the first-time visitor, the hilly areas around St-Sauveur, Ste-Adèle, Morin Heights, Val-Morin, and Val-David up to Ste-Agathe-des-Monts form a pleasant hodgepodge of villages, hotels, and inns that seem to blend one into another. Tourisme Laurentides in Mirabel provides information and offers a daily lodging-booking service. Its main information center is at the Porte du Nord complex at Exit 51 on Autoroute 15.

OKA

40 km (25 miles) west of Montréal.

Urban sprawl has driven the Cistercian monks from their abbey in Oka, on the shores of Lac des Deux-Montagnes, to seek solace farther north in St-Jean-de-Matha in the Lanaudière region, but the cheese they made famous is still produced by a private firm here and is available in local shops. The rolling hills around the little town of Oka are famous for their apple orchards. If you love cider, follow the *Route des Vergers*, stopping at various properties along this "Orchard Route" to sample the local wares. There's also a winery on the route: La Roche des Brises, whose whites and reds include the portlike *L'été Indien* (Indian Summer).

EXPLORING

Auberge Roches des Brises. You can tour the vineyard (reservations are required), taste the wines for C$7, and dine in the adjacent four-star restaurant serving the best in regional cuisine. Across the road overlooking some of the grapevines is a charming five-room bed-and-breakfast with a spa. It's worth the trip if only to take in the splendor of the exceptionally lovely grounds. ✉ *2007 rue Principale, St-Joseph-du-Lac* ☎ *450/472–2722, 450/472–3477* ⊕ *www.rochedesbrises.com* ⊗ *Mid-Feb.–Dec.*

Parc d'Oka. Surrounded by low hills, this provincially operated park has a lake fringed by a sandy beach with picnic areas and hiking and biking trails. This is a good place for kayaking, canoeing, fishing, and, in winter, snowshoeing and cross-country skiing. There are nearly 900 campsites here, and the park's office rents equipment, including bicycles, cross-country skis, snowshoes, canoes, and kayaks. Be aware, as you walk down the beach: the strip at the far eastern end has, by popular consensus, been deemed "clothing optional," or in effect, "clothing nonexistent." ✉ *2020 chemin Oka* ☎ *450/479–8365, 800/665–6527* activities ⊕ *www.sepaq.com* 🎫 *C$6 plus C$11 per car* ⊗ *Daily 8–10.*

EN
ROUTE **Hudson.** A quick detour on the ferry (C$10 one-way) across Lac des Deux-Montagnes brings you to this small town with old homes housing art galleries, boutiques, and Christmas shops. In winter there's an ice bridge: basically a plowed path across a well-frozen lake. Taking a walk across the bridge is a singular experience. ✉ *Hudson.*

9

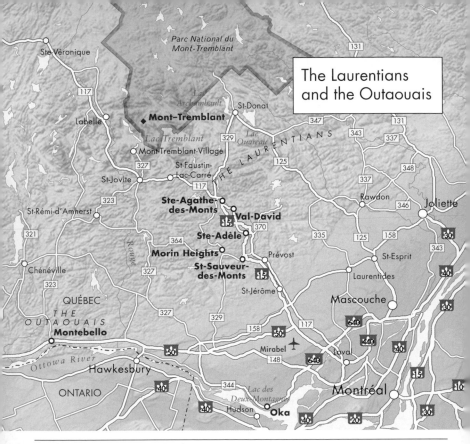

ST-SAUVEUR-DES-MONTS

85 km (53 miles) north of Oka, 63 km (39 miles) north of Montréal.

Just a 45-minute drive from Montréal (or 90 minutes when the traffic's heavy, as it frequently is), St-Sauveur is probably the busiest little town in Québec, especially on weekends. Its rue Principale bristles with bars and restaurants that serve everything from lamb brochettes and spicy Thai stir-fries to steaks and burgers. On summer weekends, the street is so jammed with cars and the sidewalks so packed with visitors it's sometimes called Crescent Street North after the action-filled street in Montréal. Despite the glitz and the sea of condos that surround it, however, the town has managed to retain a bit of rural charm in its fine old church and veranda-fronted clapboard homes.

St-Sauveur in winter is no less busy. The "mountains" surrounding the town hardly qualify as Alpine—none has a vertical drop of more than 700 feet—but they're close to Montréal and well serviced by lifts and night lights.

GETTING HERE AND AROUND

Take Highway 15 north from Montréal and get off at Exit 60. The best way to explore the main street is to find a parking lot and walk around. Driving through town is difficult in winter, impossible in summer.

ESSENTIALS

Tourist Welcome Bureau of Pays-d'en-Haut ⊠ *605 chemin des Frênes, Exit 60, Hwy. 15 N., Piedmont* ☏ *800/898–2127, 450/227–3417* ⊕ *www. lespaysdenhaut.com.*

EXPLORING

Mont-St-Sauveur Water Park. Mont-St-Sauveur Water Park keeps children occupied with slides, a giant wave pool, a wading pool, and snack bars. The river rafting attracts an older, braver crowd; the nine-minute ride follows the natural contours of steep hills. On the tandem slides, plumes of water flow through figure-eight tubes. But if you'd rather not get wet at all, you might want to consider taking a ride through the trees on their Acro-Nature zip-line. ⊠ *350 rue St-Denis* ☏ *450/227–4671* ⊕ *www.mssi.ca* ⊠ *C$33.92* ☉ *Early June–mid-June and late Aug.–early Sept., daily 10–5; mid-June–late Aug., daily 10–7.*

Musée du ski des Laurentides. The Laurentians are one of the oldest ski regions in North America and this little museum traces that long history with photos, artifacts, and some interesting models of early ski lifts. It also houses the Temple de la Renomée du ski (the Ski Hall of Fame). ⊠ *30 rue Filion* ☏ *450/227–2564* ⊕ *www.museeduskideslaurentides. com* ⊠ *Free* ☉ *Wed.–Sun. 11–6.*

WHERE TO EAT AND STAY

For expanded hotel reviews, visit fodors.com.

$

AMERICAN

✕ Le Café de la Gare. During the day, St-Sauveur's old train station serves breakfast and lunch, but on most Saturday nights it adopts an entirely different personality when it becomes the setting for cabaret evenings. A show featuring some of Québec's best singers, dancers, and comics plus a four-course dinner featuring local delicacies will set you back C$50 to C$60 a person. Not bad for one of the liveliest evenings in the Laurentians. $ *Average main: C$12* ⊠ *90 rue de la Gare* ☏ *450/227–2228 restaurant, 450/227–1368 for the show* ⊕ *www.lecafedelagare.com* ☉ *No dinner, except dinner-shows; call or check the website for schedule.*

$

B&B/INN

Relais St-Denis. A traditional sloping Québécois roof and dormer windows cap this inn, where every guest room has a fireplace and a whirlpool bath. **Pros:** walking distance to a variety of restaurants, outlet shopping, and activities in St-Sauveur. **Cons:** there are no activities offered for children. $ *Rooms from: C$139* ⊠ *61 rue St-Denis* ☏ *450/227–4766, 888/997–4766* ⊕ *www.relaisstdenis.com* ⊅ *18 rooms, 24 suites* ⦿ *No meals.*

SHOPPING

Fodor'sChoice

★

Factoreries St-Sauveur. Canadian, American, and European manufacturers sell goods—from designer clothing to household items—at reduced prices at this emporium. The factory-outlet mall has more than 35 stores and sells labels such as Bench, Guess, Parasuco, and Rockport. ⊠ *100 rue Guindon, Highway 15, Exit 60* ☏ *450/240–0880, 800/363–0332* ⊕ *www.factoreries.com.*

Rue Principale. Fashion boutiques and gift shops adorned with bright awnings and flowers line this popular shopping street.

9

One of the most popular times to visit the region is in fall, when the mountains are splashed with a spectrum of warm yellows, oranges, and reds.

SPORTS AND THE OUTDOORS

Mont St-Sauveur International (MSSI). It was the low hills that circle St-Sauveur that first drew leisure visitors to the city, and the area remains a vibrant ski resort to this day. What they lack in height, the hills make up in snowmaking, lift capacity, and total skiable area. Many of the trails are also lit at night, which makes it possible for energetic Montrealers to drive up after work for a couple hours of skiing before returning home. Most of the village's formerly independent ski operations now belong to MSSI, which also owns hills in other nearby towns. ⊠ *350 av. St-Denis, St-Sauveur* ☎ *450/227–4671, 514/871–0101* ⊕ *www.mssi.ca.*

In St-Sauveur, MSSI's **Mont-Avila** (⊠ *500 chemin Avila, Piedmont* ☎ *450/227–4671, 514/871–0101* ⊕ *www.montavila.com*) has 13 trails (2 beginner, 3 intermediate, 5 difficult, 3 extremely difficult), a snow park, and (for those who can't ski) a tubing park. **Mont-St-Sauveur** (⊠ *350 av. St-Denis, St-Sauveur*) is the largest of the MSSI properties with a 700-foot vertical drop and 142 acres of skiable terrain. Seventeen of its 38 trails are for beginners and intermediates, 16 are for experts, and 5 are rated extreme.

Station de Ski Mont-Habitant. The last of the independent ski operations in St-Sauveur still retains some of that rustic charm of yesteryear and remains a favorite among families, beginners, and intermediates. With a vertical drop of just 600 feet, it has three lifts and 11 trails, most of them relatively gentle. Mont-Habitant also boasts St-Sauveur's only beach, which makes it very popular in the summer. ⊠ *12 chemin des Skieurs* ☎ *450/227–2637, 866/887–2637* ⊕ *www.monthabitant.com.*

MORIN HEIGHTS

10 km (6 miles) west of St-Sauveur-des-Monts, 73 km (45 miles) north-west of Montréal.

The town's British architecture and population reflect its settlers' heritage; most residents here speak English. Although Morin Heights has escaped the overdevelopment of neighboring St-Sauveur, there are still many restaurants, bookstores, boutiques, and craft shops to explore.

In summer, windsurfing, swimming, and canoeing on the area's two lakes—Claude and Lafontaine—are popular. You can also head for the region's golf courses (including the 18 holes at Mont-Gabriel) and the campgrounds at Val-David and the two lakes, which have beaches. In fall and winter, come for the foliage and the alpine and Nordic skiing.

EXPLORING

★ **Amerispa Station Baltique.** Hidden in a Laurentian forest of maples, firs, and birches, this beautifully rustic pavilion houses a spa with hot tubs and cold pools. The Elixir Ice Cider Massage and companion body wrap infuse vitamins and minerals which hydrate, tone, and smooth the skin. ✉ *160 Watchorn St., Morin Heights* ☎ *450/226–7722, 866/263–7477* ⊕ *www.amerispa.ca.*

WHERE TO EAT AND STAY

For expanded hotel reviews, visit fodors.com.

$$$$
FRENCH
Fodor's Choice
★

✕ **Auberge Restaurant Clos Joli.** If you're looking for superior French cuisine and are prepared to pay top dollar for the privilege, this family-owned and -operated establishment offers an outstanding gastronomic experience. Award-winning chef Gemma Morin cooks up a wide variety of dishes, but locals will tell you that her legendary venison dishes are to die for. ⑤ *Average main: C$40* ✉ *19 chemin Clos Joli* ☎ *450/226–5401, 866/511–9999* ⊕ *www.aubergeclosjoli.net* ⊘ *No lunch.*

$$$
B&B/INN

⌂ **Refuge Morin Heights.** An all-weather outdoor water garden with waterfalls and cold-water pools and a traditional underground Finnish spa make Le Refuge one of the best-equipped spa destinations in the Laurentians. **Pros:** some rooms have beautiful views of the Rivière du Nord; spectacular spa; whirlpool baths and fireplaces in some units. **Cons:** isolated from village. ⑤ *Rooms from: C$224* ✉ *500 Rte. 364* ☎ *866/996–1796, 450/226–1796* ⊕ *www.spalerefuge.com* ⟿ *27 rooms* ⫟ *Breakfast.*

9

STE-ADÈLE

12 km (7 miles) north of Morin Heights, 85 km (53 miles) north of Montréal.

With a permanent population of more than 10,000, Ste-Adèle is the largest community in the lower part of the Laurentians. A number of government offices and facilities for residents are here: movie theaters, shopping malls, and summer theater (in French). Of interest to visitors are boutiques, restaurants, and family-oriented amusements.

ESSENTIALS

Tourist Welcome Bureau of Pays-d'en-Haut ✉ *1490 rue St-Joseph, Exit 67, Hwy, 15 North* ☎ *450/229–3729* ⊕ *www.lespaysdenhaut.com.*

EXPLORING

♻ **Au Pays des Merveilles.** Fairy-tale characters such as Snow White, Little Red Riding Hood, and Alice in Wonderland wander the grounds, playing games with children. Small fry may also enjoy the petting zoo, amusement rides, wading pool, and puppet show. A ride called Le Petit Train des Merveilles (the Little Train of Wonders) is a nod to the historic train that launched the tourism industry in the Laurentians. There are 45 activities, enough to occupy those aged two to nine for about half a day. Check the website for discount coupons. The theme park is completely accessible to wheelchairs. ⊠ *3795 rue de la Savane* ☎ *450/229–3141* ⊕ *www.paysmerveilles.com* ⊡ *C$18.25* ⊙ *Mid-June–late Aug., daily 10–6.*

WHERE TO EAT AND STAY

For expanded hotel reviews, visit fodors.com.

$$$$
FRENCH FUSION
✕ **La Clef des Champs.** The French-influenced cuisine served at this romantic restaurant tucked amid trees is quite good. With a heavy concentration on fresh fish and seafood, the table d'hôte includes dishes such as poached Arctic char and Chilean sea bass as well as classics like frogs' legs and escargots *provençales.* The dessert selection is small but adequate, featuring palate-cleansers like sorbet and fresh fruits and more indulgent treats like crème brûlée and profiteroles with Grand Marnier. ⑤ *Average main: C$40* ⊠ *875 chemin Pierre-Péladeau* ☎ *450/229–2857* ⊕ *www.restaurantlaclefdeschamps.com* ⊙ *Closed Mon. during low season. No lunch.*

$
HOTEL
Fodor's Choice
★
⊡ **Hôtel Spa H20.** Superb service, stunning rooms awash with color, a Nordic spa, and a terrace with a flower garden are highlights of this charming inn. **Pros:** outstanding restaurant; stunning outdoor Nordic spa. **Cons:** located uncomfortably close to busy highway. ⑤ *Rooms from: C$135* ⊠ *3003 blvd. Ste-Adèle* ☎ *450/229–2991* ⊕ *www.hotelspah2o.com* ⤴ *20 rooms, 1 suite* ⑩ *Some meals.*

$
HOTEL
⊡ **Le Chantecler.** This favorite of Montrealers is nestled alongside lovely Lac Ste-Adèle, and its rooms and chalets, furnished with Canadian pine, have a rustic appeal. **Pros:** friendly, helpful staff; lakeside rooms. **Cons:** due to its outstanding reputation, early bookings are highly recommended. ⑤ *Rooms from: C$109* ⊠ *1474 chemin Chantecler* ☎ *450/229–3555, 888/916–1616* ⊕ *www.lechantecler.com* ⤴ *150 rooms, 29 suites* ⑩ *No meals.*

SPORTS AND THE OUTDOORS

Club de Golf Chantecler. This mountain course is noted for its exceptional views of the surrounding countryside. ⊠ *2520 chemin du Club* ☎ *450/476–1339, 450/229–3742* ⊕ *www.golflechantecler.com* ⛳ *18 holes. 5885 yds. Par 72. Greens Fee: C$31.60–C$40.38* ⌖ *Facilities: Putting green, golf carts, pull carts, rental clubs, pro-shop, restaurant, bar.*

Ski Mont-Gabriel. About 19 km (12 miles) northeast of Ste-Adèle, Mont-Gabriel has 18 superb downhill trails, which are primarily for intermediate and advanced skiers, and five lifts. Part of the Mont St-Sauveur International chain of ski resorts, Mont Gabriel has a vertical drop of 656 feet. ⊠ *1501 chemin du Mont-Gabriel* ☎ *450/227–1100, 514/871–0101* ⊕ *www.skimontgabriel.com.*

VAL-DAVID

33 km (20 miles) west of Ste-Adèle, 82 km (51 miles) north of Montréal.

Val-David is a premier destination for mountain climbers, hikers, and campers. Offering several galleries and marvelous art shops, Val-David is home to many Québec artists and artisans.

GETTING HERE AND AROUND

The village is just a couple of kilometers east of Exit N6 on Autoroute 15, making it easy to get to by car, but it's also accessible by bicycle as Le P'tit Train du Nord cycling trail runs right through town.

ESSENTIALS

Tourist Bureau of Val-David ⊠ *2579 rue de l'Église, Exit 76, Hwy. 15 North* ☎ *888/322–7030, 819/324–5678* ⊕ *www.valdavid.com.*

EXPLORING

Village du Père Noël (*Santa Claus Village*). At Santa Claus's summer residence kids can sit on his knee and speak to him in French or English. The grounds contain bumper boats, a petting zoo (with goats, sheep, horses, and colorful birds), games, and a large outdoor pool. There is a snack bar, but visitors are encouraged to bring their own food (there are numerous picnic tables). ⊠ *987 rue Morin* ☎ *819/322–2146, 800/287–6635* ⊕ *www.noel.qc.ca* ⊠ *C$15* ⊙ *Early June–late Aug., daily 10–6; check website for winter schedule.*

SHOPPING

1001 Pots. One of the most interesting events in Val-David is this boutique, which showcases the Japanese-style pottery of Kinya Ishikawa—as well as pieces by up to 100 other ceramists. The exhibition takes place from mid-July through mid-August. Ishikawa's studio also displays work by his wife, Marie-Andrée Benoît, who makes fish-shaped bowls with a texture derived from pressing canvas on the clay. There are workshops for adults and children throughout the exhibition and there is a tea salon on the premises. ⊠ *2435 rue de l'Église* ☎ *819/322–6868* ⊕ *www.1001pots.com* ⊠ *C$2 for exhibition* ⊙ *July and Aug., daily 10–6; call for hrs in other seasons.*

Atelier Bernard Chaudron, Inc. Atelier Bernard Chaudron sells hand-forged, lead-free pewter objets d'art such as oil lamps, hammered-silver beer mugs, pitchers, candleholders, and animal-themed knife rests among an interesting variety of other useful and decorative items, as well as some crystal. ⊠ *2449 chemin de l'Île* ☎ *819/322–3944, 888/322–3944* ⊕ *www.chaudron.ca* ⊙ *Daily 10–4.*

SPORTS AND THE OUTDOORS

Centre de Ski Vallée-Bleue. Geared toward intermediate skiers, Vallée-Bleue has 17 trails, three lifts, and a vertical drop of 365 feet. ⊠ *1418 chemin Vallée-Bleue* ☎ *866/322–3427* ⊕ *www.vallee-bleue.com.*

Mont-Alta. This ski resort has 27 downhill trails—about 40% of them for advanced skiers, but none of them terribly difficult—and one lift. The vertical drop is 584 feet. ⊠ *2114 Rte. 117* ☎ *819/322–3206* ⊕ *www. mont-alta.com.*

9

STE-AGATHE-DES-MONTS

5 km (3 miles) north of Val-David, 96 km (60 miles) northwest of Montréal.

The wide, sandy beaches of Lac des Sables are the most surprising feature of Ste-Agathe-des-Monts, a tourist town best known for its ski hills. Water activities include canoeing, kayaking, swimming, and fishing. Ste-Agathe is also a stopover point on the Linear Park, the bike trail between St-Jérôme and Mont-Laurier.

ESSENTIALS
Tourist Bureau of Ste-Agathe-des-Monts ⊠ *24 rue St-Paul* ☎ *819/326–3731, 888/326–0457* ⊕ *www.sainte-agathe.org.*

WHERE TO STAY
For expanded hotel reviews, visit fodors.com.

$

HOTEL

⚞ **Auberge Watel.** A steep driveway leads up to this white-painted, distinguished hotel overlooking Lac des Sables. **Pros:** adjacent to three beaches; indoor and outdoor pools; close proximity to boutiques and cultural activities in Ste-Agathe. **Cons:** not all rooms have lake view. Ⓢ *Rooms from: C$120* ⊠ *250 rue St-Venant* ☎ *819/326–7016, 800/363–6478* ⊕ *www.hotelspawatel.com* ↵ *25 rooms* ⦿| *Some meals.*

SPORTS AND THE OUTDOORS
Alouette V and VI. These sightseeing boats offer guided 50-minute tours of Lac des Sables. They leave the dock at least seven times a day from mid-June to mid-August and five times a day from mid-August to mid-October. ⊠ *Municipal Dock, rue Principale* ☎ *819/326–3656, 866/326–3656* ⊕ *www.croisierealouette.com.*

MONT-TREMBLANT

25 km (16 miles) north of Ste-Agathe-des-Monts, 100 km (62 miles) north of Montréal.

Mont-Tremblant, at more than 3,000 feet, is one of the highest peaks in the Laurentians and a major draw for skiers. The resort area at the foot of the mountain (called simply Tremblant) is spread around 14-km-long (9-mile-long) Lac Tremblant and is consistently ranked among the top ski resorts in eastern North America.

The hub of the resort is a pedestrians-only village that gives an architectural nod to the style of New France, with dormer windows and steep roofs on buildings that house pubs, restaurants, boutiques, sports shops, a movie theater, self-catering condominiums, and hotels. A historical town this is not: built for the resort, it may strike you as a bit of Disney in the mountains.

GETTING HERE AND AROUND
The easiest way to get here is by car. Drive north on Autoroute 15 until it ends just beyond Ste-Agathe-des-Monts and then continue on Route 117 (a four-lane highway) for another 30 km (18 miles) to the Mont-Tremblant exit (Exit 119). The resort's parking lots are vast, but they fill up quickly. A shuttle bus links them to the main resort and ski area. Mont-Tremblant has two tourist offices, one in the village and one in the downtown area.

ESSENTIALS

Tourisme Mont-Tremblant ✉ *5080 Montée Ryan, Exit 119, Rte. 117* ☎ *877/425–2434, 819/425–2434* ⊕ *www.tourismemonttremblant. com* ✉ *48 chemin de Brebeuf, Exit 117, Rte. 117* ☎ *877/425–2434, 819/425–3300.*

EXPLORING

Fodor's Choice

★

Parc National du Mont-Tremblant. Created in 1894, the park was the home of the Algonquins, who called this area Manitonga Soutana, meaning "mountain of the spirits." Today it's a vast wildlife sanctuary of more than 400 lakes and rivers holding nearly 200 species of birds and animals. In winter its trails are used by cross-country skiers, snowshoers, and snowmobilers. Camping and canoeing are the main summer activities. 🎫 *C$6.*

The park entrance closest to Mont-Tremblant is at **La Diable Vistors' Centre** (✉ *3824 chemin du Lac Supérieur, Lac Supérieur* ☎ *819/688– 2281, 800/665–6527 for Sépaq, the government agency that administers the province's national parks* ⊕ *www.sepaq.com/pq/mot*) just beyond the village of Lac-Supérieur, about a half-hour drive from the resort.

WHERE TO EAT

$$$

ITALIAN

✕ **Auberge du Coq de Montagne.** This restaurant on Lac Moore (which opens onto a terrace during the summer months), five minutes from the ski slopes, has garnered much praise for its Italian cuisine. Menu offerings include tried-and-true favorites such as veal marsala and veal *fiorentina* (cooked with spinach and cheese). Hosts Nino and Kay are reputed to be some of the friendliest folks you'll ever meet—and they prepare good food, too! 💲 *Average main: C$25* ✉ *2151 chemin du Village* ☎ *819/425–3380* 🍴 *Reservations essential* 🕐 *No lunch.*

$$$

FRENCH

✕ **Restaurant Le Cheval de Jade.** "The Jade Horse" specializes in French haute cuisine. The elegant dining room has lace curtains, white linens, and ivory china. The food is the real thing—local ingredients and organic produce are used to create classic fare such as grilled beef filet mignon, bouillabaisse, and piña colada tiger prawns flambéed with rum, pineapple, and coconut sauce. Their Discovery menu (C$79.95) includes a half rack of lamb with cranberries, garlic, and thyme *jus* and seared duck foie gras with pear and port wine sauce while their gastronomic menu (C$89.95) features snow crab and Matane shrimp cake as well as Atlantic grouper fillet with clam and tarragon sauce. 💲 *Average main: C$40* ✉ *688 rue de St-Jovite* ☎ *819/425–5233* ⊕ *www. chevaldejade.com* 🍴 *Reservations essential* 🕐 *Closed Sun. Sept.–June, Mon. year-round. No lunch.*

WHERE TO STAY

For expanded hotel reviews, visit fodors.com.

$$$

HOTEL

🏨 **Fairmont Tremblant.** The sporty but classy centerpiece of the Tremblant resort area takes its cues from the historic railroad "castle hotels" scattered throughout Canada. **Pros:** poolside barbecue during the summer months; dogs (under 50 lbs.) allowed; easy access to ski hills. **Cons:** nature lovers may be disappointed to find that the hotel is in the center of a fairly busy village and not on more-scenic grounds. 💲 *Rooms from:*

9

C$229 ⊠ *3045 chemin de la Chapelle* ☎ *819/681–7000, 800/257–7544* ⊕ *www.fairmont.com/tremblant* ⟿ *252 rooms, 62 suites* ⦶ *Breakfast.*

$ **⊡ Hôtel du Lac.** Built as a family house in the early 1900s, this build-
HOTEL ing has been a rooming house, brothel, and private club—now it's a rustic but comfortable European-owned hotel with excellent facilities, just down the lakeside road from the ski station at Mont-Tremblant. **Pros:** excellent service; beautiful, tranquil grounds. **Cons:** not within walking distance of town. ⑤ *Rooms from:* C$120 ⊠ *121 rue Cuttle* ☎ *819/425–2731, 800/567–8341* ⊕ *www.clubtremblant.com* ⟿ *122 suites* ⦶ *Some meals.*

$$$ **⊡ Le Grand Lodge.** This Scandinavian-style log-cabin hotel is on 13½
HOTEL acres on Lac Ouimet. **Pros:** friendly staff; good food; peaceful environ-
ment; ice rink and ice path in winter; very family-friendly; beach on the lake. **Cons:** no facilities for people with disabilities. ⑤ *Rooms from:* C$179 ⊠ *2396 rue Labelle* ☎ *819/425–2734, 800/567–6763* ⊕ *www. legrandlodge.com* ⟿ *11 rooms, 101 suites* ⦶ *Breakfast.*

SPORTS AND THE OUTDOORS
GOLF

Mont-Tremblant. The same company that operates the ski resort also operates two of the most challenging golf courses in Québec—Le Géant (the Giant), designed by Thomas McBroom, and **Le Diable** (the Devil), designed by Michael Hurdzan and Dana Fry. ⊠ *1000 chemin des Voyageurs* ☎ *888/904–4653, 819/681–4653* ⊕ *www.tremblant. ca* ⑂ *Le Diable: 18 holes. 7056 yds. Par 71. Slope, 135 from black. Greens fee C$119 (weekdays); C$120 (weekends); Le Géant: 18 holes. 6836 yds. Par 72. Slope, 131 from double black. Greens fee C$99 (weekdays); C$109 (weekends)* ⌇ *Facilities: Le Diable: Driving range, putting green, golf carts, caddies (digital/GPS), rental clubs, pro-shop, golf academy/lessons, restaurant, bar; Le Géant: Driving range, put-ting green, golf carts, rental clubs, pro-shop, gold academy/lessons, restaurant, bar.*

SKIING

Mont-Tremblant. With a 2,116-foot vertical drop, 654 acres of skiable terrain, 94 trails, 18 acres of ramps and jumps for snowboarders, and enough state-of-the-art snowmaking equipment to blanket a small city, Mont-Tremblant is truly one of the great ski resorts of North America, arguably the best east of the Rockies. Its 14 lifts—including two heated gondolas and five high-speed, four-passenger chairlifts—can handle 27,230 skiers an hour. It has some of the toughest expert runs on the continent, but it also has long, gentle runs like the 5-km (3.5-mile) Nansen and dozens of exciting trails for intermediate skiers. Its altitude and location, as well as all that snowmaking equipment, gives it some of eastern Canada's most reliable ski conditions, especially now that winters are getting warmer. All this doesn't come cheap, mind you. A day lift ticket costs about C$75, but for serious skiers there is no better mountain in Québec. ⊠ *1000 chemin des Voyageurs* ☎ *866/356–2233, 819/681–3000* ⊕ *www.tremblant.ca.*

THE OUTAOUAIS

To fully experience the majesty of the Outaouais wilderness you should plan to spend close to a week here, as simply driving to any of the region's major provincial parks is a good one-day journey. But you can still get a taste of what the region has to offer by heading out to Montebello, a little country village on the banks of the Ottawa River that's only an hour-and-a-half drive from Montréal. From there you can find excursions to take you to the surrounding countryside or if you'd prefer, you can simply take in nearby Omega Park, a safari adventure where you'll bear witness to many of the region's creatures interacting within their natural environment.

MONTEBELLO

130 km (80 miles) west of Montréal.

On the banks of the Ottawa River, Montebello is a quaint little village best known for the spectacular hotel within its boundaries, the Fairmont Le Château Montebello, touted as the largest log cabin in the world. Given the town's relative proximity to Ottawa, the nation's capital, more than a few world leaders and dignitaries have graced Montebello with their presence over the years, here for the many international summits hosted by the Château since it was built in 1930. Now that Autoroute 50 has finally been extended to the Outaouais region it only takes about 90 minutes to get here from downtown Montréal, making it a very worthwhile side trip. The Outaouais in general is well-known for the rugged beauty of its wilderness, and even in this more populated southern section of the region there's still excellent fishing, hunting, canoeing, hiking, and wildlife-spotting, with a series of hiking paths known to be good for nature-watching starting right beside the Château Montebello. Even if an expedition into the bush isn't quite your thing, you can still get up close to the local wildlife in a more controlled environment at Parc Omega, home to a wide variety of indigenous species and domestic animals.

9

ESSENTIALS

Montebello Tourist Information Office ⊠ *Gare de Montebello, 502-A rue Notre-Dame, Montebello* ☎ *819/423–5602, 800/265–7822* ⊕ *www.tourismeoutaouais.com.*

Tourisme Outaouais ⊠ *103 rue Laurier, Gatineau* ☎ *819/778–2222, 800/265–7822* ⊕ *www.tourismeoutaouais.com.*

EXPLORING

Parc Omega. In the 1,800 acres of hills, valleys, rivers, and streams that make up the park, visitors drive along designated trails to view wild animals roaming free in their beautiful natural environment. These include bear, Alpine ibexes, buffalo, wolves, elk, and more. There are also walking trails among non-aggressive species like white-tailed deer, with golf-cart rental available in summer to save the legwork. Also in summer, you can visit farm animals in the restored 19th-century Léopold's Farm and see the birds of prey show. ⊠ *323 North Road, Montebello* ☎ *819/423–5487* ⊕ *www.parc-omega.com* ☑ *C$17–C$21,*

DID YOU KNOW?

Mont-Tremblant's alpine pedestrian village has a wide variety of shops and restaurants housed in buildings with classic Québecois mansard roofs.

RENTING A SKI CHALET IN MONT-TREMBLANT

If you think you'd like to spend more than a few days in the Laurentians you might want to consider renting a chalet from a private owner. There are generally plenty to choose from and for many people, not only is a private rental often less expensive than staying at a hotel, but it's a lot homier as well, especially if you are traveling with children. And even with the smorgasbord of dining options available in Mont-Tremblant, every once in a while it's nice to buy groceries and come home to cook your own dinner.

Options range from cozy little cottages for four to multi-bedroom properties where you could have a real house-party with family and friends, and if you fill to capacity the cost can be very competitive, particularly if you don't mind being outside the main hub of the resort or out of the peak season. Some places offer weekend rates as well as renting by the week. Very good sources for chalet rentals in this part of the province are the websites ⊕ *www.chalets-mont-tremblant.com* and ⊕ *www.cottagesquebec.com,* and the Montréal pages for ⊕ *Craigslist.com* and ⊕ *Kijiji.ca* are full of posts advertising private chalet rentals in the Laurentians. If you'd prefer to go through a third party, most area real estate agents broker short and long-term cottage and chalet rentals as well. Try Remax Laurentides at 286 Principal in St-Sauveur (☎ 450/227–8411) for starters.

depending on season ⊙ Daily, late June–early Sept. 9–7 (last admission 5); mid-May–late June and early Sept.–mid-Oct. 9:30–7 (last admission 5); mid-Oct.–mid-May 10–6 (last admission 4).

WHERE TO EAT AND STAY

For expanded hotel reviews, visit fodors.com.

$

CANADIAN

✕ **La Belle Bédaine Casse-Croûte.** If you're looking for fine dining keep on going, but if it's a bit of local color, a cold beer, and a good burger that you want, La Belle Bédaine (which translates as "the happy belly") is just the place. It offers a good basic menu of fast food and a terrace overlooking the river. ⑤ *Average main: C$7* ✉ *664 rue Notre-Dame, Montebello* ☎ *819/423–5053* ▭ *No credit cards.*

$$

ITALIAN

✕ **Le Napoleon.** In what is basically a one-street town, outstanding food at affordable prices is served by knowledgeable, personable wait staff in an exquisite environment—this is the kind of place you dream about stumbling across but rarely do. Though the cuisine is primarily Italian, some Mediterranean, French, and Québecois influences are also in evidence, backed up by a fairly extensive and reasonably priced wine list. In the warmer seasons you can dine out on the covered terrace, while the fireplace inside makes those colder, harsher evenings downright cozy. ⑤ *Average main: C$19* ✉ *489 rue Notre-Dame, Montebello* ☎ *819/423–5555* ⊕ *www.le-napoleon.com.*

$$$$ HOTEL Fodor's Choice ★ **Fairmont Le Château Montebello.** Half way between Montréal and Ottawa, the Fairmont Le Château Montebello is an annual family destination for many well-heeled Canadians who love the log cabin construction and local flavor. **Pros:** indoor tennis; magnificent six-sided fireplace in lobby; state-of-the-art conference facility. **Cons:** 75-minute drive from Montréal; no nearby restaurants of note; pricey without a meal package. *Rooms from: C$279 ✉ 392 rue Notre-Dame, Montebello ☎ 819/423–6341 ⊕ www.fairmont.com 211 rooms Some meals.*

$ HOTEL **Hotel Domaine Monté-Bello.** It may be considerably less grand than the nearby Château Montebello, but this budget-friendly alternative is stylish and comfortable, and most rooms have lovely views of the Ottawa River. **Pros:** standard of hospitality is first-rate; close to Parc Omega. **Cons:** guests in lower-priced rooms have to share a bathroom. *Rooms from: C$89 ✉ 696 rue Notre-Dame, Montebello ☎ 819/423–5096, 877/420–5096 ⊕ www.domainemontebello.com 5 rooms, 6 suites, 1 log cabin No meals.*

THE EASTERN TOWNSHIPS

Québec's Eastern Townships are unlike anything else the province has to offer. For starters, there remains a sizable, albeit dwindling, English population here, mostly the descendants of Empire Loyalists who fled first the Revolutionary War and later the newly created United States of America. The Loyalists were followed, around 1820, by the first wave of Irish immigrants. Some 20 years later the potato famine sent more Irish pioneers to the Townships. The area became more Francophone after 1850, as French Canadians moved in to work on the railroad and in the lumber industry, but the region still looks more like New England than New France, with its redbrick villages, tidy Protestant churches, and white clapboard farmhouses with big verandas. During the late 19th century, English families from Montréal and Americans from the border states began summering at cottages along the lakes.

9

BROMONT

78 km (48 miles) east of Montréal.

The boating, camping, golf, horseback riding, swimming, tennis, biking, canoeing, fishing, hiking, cross-country and downhill skiing, and snowshoeing available here make this a place for all seasons. Bromont has the only night skiing in the Eastern Townships—and there's even a slope-side disco, Le Bromontais. The town also has more than 100 km (62 miles) of maintained trails for mountain bikers.

GETTING HERE AND AROUND

Bromont is about one hour from Montréal on Autoroute 10. Get off at Exit 78.

ESSENTIALS

Bromont Tourism Office *✉ 15 blvd. de Bromont ☎ 877/276–6668, 450/534–2006 ⊕ www.tourismebromont.com.*

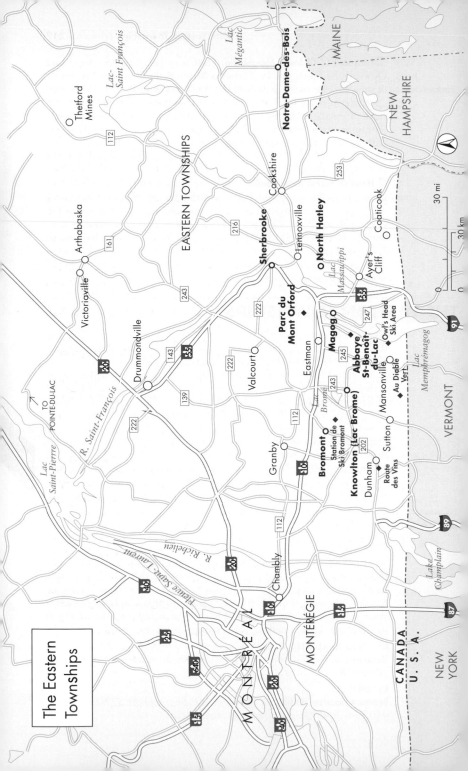

The Eastern Townships

MONTRÉAL

MONTÉRÉGIE

EASTERN TOWNSHIPS

CANADA
U. S. A.

NEW YORK

VERMONT

MAINE

NEW HAMPSHIRE

Notre-Dame-des-Bois

Thetford Mines

Arthabaska

Victoriaville

Drummondville

Valcourt

Granby

Chambly

Bromont
Station de Ski Bromont

Knowlton (Lac Brome)

Dunham
Route des Vins

Sutton

Mansonville

Au Diable Vert

Abbaye St-Benoît-du-Lac

Owl's Head Ski Area

Magog

Parc du Mont Orford

Eastman

Sherbrooke

Cookshire

Lennoxville

North Hatley

Ayer's Cliff

Coaticook

Lac Mégantic

Lac Saint-François

Lac Saint-Pierre

Fleuve Saint-Laurent

R. Richelieu

R. Saint-François

Lac Brome

Lac Massawippi

Lac Memphrémagog

Lake Champlain

TO POINTE-DU-LAC

112
161
112
243
216
253
222
222
143
139
222
112
112
202
243
245
247
55
55

30 mi
30 km

EXPLORING

Balnea Réserve Thermale. Tucked in a forest and overlooking a lake is this strikingly contemporary spa. In addition to steam rooms, saunas, and baths, Balnea offers 30 body treatments and special experiences like airbeds that float among lily pads, and tiers of sundecks with gorgeous views. You can bliss out with the Abenaki Native ritual, a chocolate massage, or yoga. Full and half-day spa packages run from C$115–C$175. ⊠ *319 chemin Lac Gale, Bromont* ☎ *866/734–2110* ⊕ *www. balnea.ca* ⊗ *Mon.–Wed. 10–8, Thurs.–Sun. 10:30–9; reduced hours Dec. 24–Jan. 8.*

Route des Vins (*Wine Route*). Almost a dozen wineries along the Route des Vins in and around the town of Dunham, about 20 km (12 miles) south of Bromont on Route 202, offer tastings and tours. Call for business hours, which can be erratic, especially in autumn, when harvesting is under way.

The **Vignoble Domaine Côtes d'Ardoise** winery (⊠ *879 rue Bruce, Rte. 202, Dunham* ☎ *450/295–2020* ⊕ *www.cotesdardoise.com*) opened in 1980; it was one of the first to set up shop in the area.

Before walking through the **Vignoble de l'Orpailleur** (⊠ *1086 Rte. 202, Dunham* ☎ *450/295–2763* ⊕ *www.orpailleur.ca*) vineyard, be sure to stop by the economuseum to learn about the history and production of wine, from the growing of the grapes right up to the bottling process. There's a gift shop, patio restaurant, and daily tastings.

The lovely **Vignoble Les Trois Clochers** (⊠ *341 chemin Bruce, Rte. 202, Dunham* ☎ *450/295–2034*) produces a dry, fruity white from Seyval grapes as well as several other white, red, and ice wines.

WHERE TO STAY

For expanded hotel reviews, visit fodors.com.

$
HOTEL
Château Bromont. Massages, "electropuncture," algae wraps, and aromatherapy are just a few of the services at this European-style resort, which also includes a large, Turkish-style *hammam* (steam room). **Pros:** outdoor hot tubs; friendly staff. **Cons:** some rooms are on the small side so specify which type of room you want when reserving; windows do not open in rooms that face the hotel interior, and thus can cause rooms to feel claustrophobic. $ *Rooms from: C$150* ⊠ *90 rue Stanstead* ☎ *450/534–3433, 888/276–6668* ⊕ *www.chateaubromont. com* ↪ *156 rooms, 8 suites* ¶◎¶ *Some meals.*

$
HOTEL
Hôtel Bromont. Among the rolling hills of the Townships and with great views of the local countryside from every room, this modern hotel is well priced, considering all the amenities available. **Pros:** outstanding views from each room; friendly staff; proximity to ski hill. **Cons:** lack of an elevator makes it difficult for guests on the upper floors, especially with ski equipment and luggage. $ *Rooms from: C$119* ⊠ *125 blvd. Bromont* ☎ *450/534–3790, 800/461–3790* ⊕ *www.hotelbromont.com* ↪ *42 rooms* ¶◎¶ *Breakfast.*

9

SHOPPING

Shopping for bargains at yard sales and flea markets is a popular weekend activity in the Townships.

Fodor's Choice
★ **Bromont Five-Star Flea Market.** The gigantic sign on Autoroute 10 is hard to miss. More than 1,000 vendors sell their wares here—everything from T-shirts to household gadgets—each Saturday and Sunday from May to the end of October, 10–6. Shoppers come from Montréal as well as Vermont, just over the border.

SPORTS AND THE OUTDOORS

International Bromont Equestrian Competition. Once an Olympic equestrian site, Bromont hosts this equestrian competition every July. ☎ *450/534–0787, 450/534–3255 ⊕ www.internationalbromont.org.*

Royal Bromont. Designed by Graham Cooke, one of the most respected golf course architects in North America, this is a superior bent-grass course. ⊠ *400 chemin Compton ☎ 450/534–4653, 888/281–0017 ⊕ www.royalbromont.com ⅄ 18 holes. 7036 yds. Slope 122. Par 72. Greens Fee: C$25–C$69. ☞ Facilities: Driving range, putting green, golf carts, pull carts, rental clubs, pro-shop, golf academy/lessons, restaurant, bar.*

⌕ **Station de Ski Bromont.** Not many metropolises in eastern North America can boast a 1,300-foot ski mountain within an hour's drive of downtown. That height and proximity has made Bromont very popular with Montréal day-trippers and weekenders. But Bromont's 145 trails (75 of them lighted at night) and nine lifts can handle the crowds quite comfortably. Like many ski hills, Bromont operates as a year-round resort. In summer and early fall, you can take a mountain bike to the summit aboard a chairlift and test your nerves on one of 15 downhill trails. If you're looking for something a little wetter, part of the ski hill is converted into the **Bromont Aquatic Park** from June until August, with a 24,000-square-foot wave pool and 25 rides and slides. ⊠ *150 rue Champlain ☎ 450/534–2200, 866/276–6668 ⊕ www.skibromont. com ☑ Skiing C$25.50–C$53 per day; Aquatic Park C$33.05 ☉ Daily. Aquatic Park: June 11–15, 10–4; June 16–22 and Aug. 13–26, 10–5; June 23–July 6, 10–6; July 7–Aug. 12, 10–6:30.*

KNOWLTON (LAC BROME)

49 km (29 miles) northeast of Bromont, 101 km (63 miles) southeast of Montréal.

Knowlton is the quintessential Eastern Townships resort town, with its Loyalist-era buildings, old inns, and its Volvo-driving, antique-hunting weekend visitors. Despite its absorption into the municipality of Lac Brome, it's managed to retain its particular identity and remains a mecca for shoppers with a main street full of stores selling antiques, art, clothes, and gifts. Interesting little restaurants have taken residence in renovated clapboard houses painted every color of the rainbow. A frequent feature on most menus here is Brome Lake duck served in every conceivable fashion. These internationally renowned birds are raised at a farm on the shores of Brome Lake just a few miles outside

town. The main regional tourist office is in Foster, one of the other old villages that constitute Lac Brome, but walking maps of Knowlton are available from many local businesses.

ESSENTIALS

Lac Brome Tourism Office ⊠ *696 rue Lakeside, Lac Brome* ☎ *450/243–6111* ⊕ *www.cclacbrome.com.*

EXPLORING

Musée Historique du Comté de Brome. Several buildings, including the former County Courthouse dating back to 1859, the old firehall and a former school, house an eclectic collection that ranges from 19th-century farm tools and Native Canadian arrowheads to military uniforms and a World War I Fokker aircraft. It offers visitors a wonderful opportunity to learn about the Loyalists who settled the area after fleeing the American Revolution. The museum also maintains the Tibbits Hill Pioneer School, a stone schoolhouse built in 1834 to serve rural families—it's a great place for the kids to find out what education was like in the mid–19th century. ⊠ *130 rue Lakeside* ☎ *450/243–6782* ⊕ *www.bromemuseum.com* ⊠ *C$5* ⊙ *Mid-May–mid-Oct., Mon.–Sat. 10–4:30, Sun. 11–4:30; Tibbits Hill School and the Old Court House: Sun. 1–4.*

WHERE TO STAY

For expanded hotel reviews, visit fodors.com.

$
B&B/INN
Fodor's Choice
★

Auberge Knowlton. This 12-room inn, at the main intersection in Knowlton, has been a local landmark since 1849, when it was a stagecoach stop. **Pros:** within walking distance of everything Knowlton has to offer, including the local beach and charming village with an assortment of antiques shops and clothing boutiques; dog-friendly; cyclist-friendly; fine restaurant. **Cons:** on the main road that runs through the town, so not the most scenic location. $ *Rooms from: C$125* ⊠ *286 chemin Knowlton, Lac Brome* ☎ *450/242–6886* ⊕ *www.aubergeknowlton.ca* ⟿ *12 rooms* ⊙ *No meals.*

NIGHTLIFE AND THE ARTS

Fodor's Choice
★

Théâtre Lac Brome. This local theater company stages plays, musicals, and productions of classic Broadway and West End hits. It hosts professional and amateur English-language productions, but has also dabbled in bilingual productions as well as contemporary works by Canadian playwrights. The 175-seat, air-conditioned theater is behind the Knowlton Pub. ⊠ *9 Mount Echo Rd.* ☎ *450/242–2270, 450/242–1395* ⊕ *www.theatrelacbrome.ca.*

SHOPPING

Camlen. Cameron and Helen Brown (get it? Cam + len) import gorgeous antiques from China and Eastern Europe and manufacture their own "antiques" using old wood. Their passion for and dedication to the art of furniture making is reflected in their—and their team's—workmanship. They claim to have reinvented the antiques business and, in their own way, they most certainly have. ⊠ *110 Lakeside Rd.* ☎ *450/243–5785* ⊕ *www.camlenfurniture.com* ⊙ *Daily 10–5:30.*

Rococo. This boutique is owned by U.S.-born Anita Laurent, a former model. Drawing on her many contacts in the fashion world, she buys samples directly from manufacturers and sells her stylish, elegant suits and pants at a fraction of the price charged by large retail stores. ⊠ *299 chemin Knowlton* ☎ *450/243–6948* ⊙ *Daily 10–5:30.*

ABBAYE ST-BENOÎT-DU-LAC

99 km (61 miles) south of Valcourt, 132 km (82 miles) southeast of Montréal.

GETTING HERE AND AROUND

To get to the abbey from Magog, take Route 112 and follow the signs for the side road (Rural Route 2, or rue des Pères) to the abbey.

EXPLORING

Fodor'sChoice ★ **Abbaye St-Benoît-du-Lac.** The abbey's bell tower juts above the trees like a fairy-tale castle. Built by the Benedictines in 1912 on a wooded peninsula on Lac Memphrémagog, the abbey is home to upwards of 50 monks who sell apples and sparkling apple wine from their orchards, as well as cheeses: Ermite (which means "hermit"), St-Benoît, and ricotta. Gregorian prayers are sung daily, and some masses are open to the public; call for the schedule. Dress modestly if you plan to attend vespers or other rituals, and avoid shorts. If you wish to experience a few days of retreat, there are guesthouses for both men and women. Reserve well in advance (a contribution of C$60 per night, which includes meals, is suggested). ⊠ *1 rue Main, St-Benoît-du-Lac* ☎ *819/843–4080, 819/843–2861 Boutique* ⊕ *www.st-benoit-du-lac.com* ⊙ *June–mid-Oct., Mon.–Sat. 9–6, Sun. 12:15–6; mid-Oct.–May, 9–5. Closed daily 10:45–11:45 am for mass.*

PARC DU MONT-ORFORD

19 km (12 miles) north of Abbaye St-Benoît-du-Lac, 115 km (72 miles) east of Montréal.

EXPLORING

Orford Arts Centre. Since 1951 thousands of students have come to the center to study and perform classical music year-round. The annual summertime celebration of music and art, Festival Orford, brings classical music, jazz, and chamber orchestra concerts to Parc du Mont-Orford. ⊠ *3165 chemin du Parc* ☎ *819/843–3981, 800/567–6155 in Canada* ⊕ *www.arts-orford.org.*

Parc du Mont-Orford. White-tailed deer and blue herons share Parc du Mont-Orford's 58.2 square km (22.5 square miles) with hikers, campers, and canoers. In winter, snowshoers and cross-country skiers take over. The park—part of Québec's network of "national" parks—also has a supervised beach and a golf course. ⊠ *3321 chemin du Parc, Canton d'Orford* ☎ *819/843–9855, 800/665–6527, 800/567–2772 Golf Mont-Orford, 819/642–6548 Golf Mont-Orford* ⊕ *www.sepaq. com/pq/mor/.*

9

WHERE TO STAY

For expanded hotel reviews, visit fodors.com.

$$ ⊡ **Estrimont Suites & Spa.** An attractive complex built of cedar, Estri-
HOTEL   mont has an outdoor Nordic waterfall and is close to ski hills, riding
stables, and golf courses. **Pros:** very reasonably priced spa packages;
excellent place for conferences or business retreats; two outdoor hot
tubs in scenic surroundings. **Cons:** only one suite is wheelchair acces-
sible. ⑤ *Rooms from: C$189* ⊠ *44 av. de l'Auberge (Rte. 141 Nord)*
☎ *800/567–7320, 819/843–1616* ⊕ *www.estrimont.ca* ↝ *95 suites*
⊺⊙⊦ *Breakfast.*

MAGOG

*11 km (6 miles) south of Parc du Mont-Orford, 118 km (74 miles)
east of Montréal.*

This bustling town is at the northern tip of Lac Memphrémagog, a large
body of water that reaches into northern Vermont. Its sandy beaches
are a draw, and it's also a good place for boating, bird-watching, sail-
boarding, horseback riding, dogsledding, in-line skating, golfing, and
snowmobiling. You might even see Memphré, the lake's sea dragon, on
one of the many lake cruises—there have been more than 100 sight-
ings since 1816.

In recent years this formerly depressed textile town has enjoyed some-
thing of an economic and cultural rebirth, partially due to the substan-
tial number of artists who have chosen to relocate to this welcoming,
and relatively inexpensive, region of the province. The streets down-
town are lined with century-old homes that have been converted into
boutiques, stores, and eateries.

ESSENTIALS

Memphrémagog Tourism Office ⊠ *55 rue Cabana* ☎ *819/843–2744, 800/
267–2744* ⊕ *www.tourisme-memphremagog.com* ⊙ *Late June–Labor
Day, daily 8:30–7; early Sept.–late June, daily 9–5.*

EXPLORING

Le Cep d'Argent. The sparkling white wine at this winery is particularly
good, and the dessert wine, which is similar to a port and flavored with
a little maple syrup, goes well with the local cheese. The guided visit and
tasting of five different wines for C$11—or C$18 for the VIP visit—is
available only from May to mid-October. Le Cep d'Argent plays a lead-
ing role in the annual wine festival that's held in Magog (late August
and early September). ⊠ *1257 chemin de la Rivière* ☎ *819/864–4441,
877/864–4441* ⊕ *www.cepdargent.com* ⊙ *Daily 10–5.*

WHERE TO STAY

For expanded hotel reviews, visit fodors.com.

$$ ⊡ **Auberge l'Étoile Sur-le-Lac.** The rooms at this popular inn on Magog's
B&B/INN   waterfront are modern and have fresh furnishings; the majority have
water views and some have fireplaces. **Pros:** right on Lac Memphrémagog; the popular cycling "Route Verte" is directly accessible from
the Auberge; boutiques, restaurants, bars, and theaters of Magog all
within comfortable walking distance. **Cons:** not recommended for

guests who are looking for isolated, peaceful surroundings. $ *Rooms from: C$175* ✉ *1200 rue Principale Ouest* ☎ *819/843–6521, 800/567–2727* ⊕ *www.etoile-sur-le-lac.com* ⇨ *51 rooms, 1 suite, 8 condos* ❐ *Some meals.*

$$
HOTEL
❐ **Spa Eastman.** The oldest spa in Québec has evolved from a simple health center into a bucolic haven for anyone seeking rest and therapeutic treatments, including lifestyle and weight-management counseling. **Pros:** dinner is included in the room rate; perfectly adapted for those seeking a totally relaxing and peaceful respite; with everything on-site, there is no need to leave the premises; wheelchair-accessible rooms. **Cons:** no phone or TV might prove too isolating for some. $ *Rooms from: C$175* ✉ *895 chemin des Diligences, Eastman* ☎ *450/297–3009, 800/665–5272* ⊕ *www.spa-eastman.com* ⇨ *46 rooms* ❐ *Some meals.*

NIGHTLIFE AND THE ARTS

Magog is lively after dark, with many bars, cafés, bistros, and restaurants catering not only to the local population, but to the numerous tourists and weekend escapees from nearby Montréal who flock here for the exceptional beauty of the surrounding region.

Auberge Orford. A patio bar overlooks the Magog River (you can moor your boat alongside it). Sometimes there's live entertainment, but when musicians aren't around to keep them at bay, flocks of ducks line up alongside the café to beg crumbs from patrons' plates—an entertaining sight in itself. ✉ *20 rue Merry Sud* ☎ *819/843–9361.*

Café St-Michel. In a century-old building, this chic pub, outfitted in shades of charcoal and ebony, serves Tex-Mex food, pasta, and local beers. Its patio bar, which is noisy because it's at Magog's main intersection, is a great spot to watch the world go by. *Chansonniers* (singers) belt out popular hits for a full house on weekends—and every night except Wednesday in summer. ✉ *503 rue Principale Ouest* ☎ *819/868–1062.*

Le Vieux Clocher de Magog. One of two former churches converted into theaters by local impresario Bernard Caza (the other is in Sherbrooke), Le Vieux headlines well-known comedians and singers. Most performances are in French. ✉ *64 rue Merry Nord* ☎ *819/847–0470* ⊕ *www. vieuxclocher.com.*

Microbrasserie La Memphré. A pub named after the monster said to lurk in Lake Memphrémagog, La Memphré dates back to the 1800s, when it belonged to Magog's first mayor. Now a microbrewery, it serves Swiss-cheese fondue, sausages with sauerkraut, and panini (pressed sandwiches)—good accompaniments for a cold one. ✉ *12 rue Merry Sud* ☎ *819/843–3405.*

SPORTS AND THE OUTDOORS

GOLF

Golf Owl's Head. This course, close to the Vermont border, has some spectacular views. Laid out with undulating fairways, bent-grass greens, and 64 sand bunkers, the course, designed by Graham Cooke, is surrounded by mountain scenery. The clubhouse, a stunning timber-and-fieldstone structure with five fireplaces and 45-foot-high ceilings, is a favorite

9

watering hole for locals and visitors alike. ⊠ *181 chemin du Mont-Owl's Head, Mansonville* ☎ *450/292–3666, 800/363–3342* ⊕ *www. owlshead.com* ⅃ *18 holes. 6701 yds. Par 72. Slope 127. Greens Fee C$50 (weekdays); C$60 (weekends)* ⊂ﾞ *Facilities: Driving range, putting green, pitching area, golf carts, pull carts, rental clubs, pro-shop, golf lessons, restaurant, bar.*

Manoir des Sables golf course. Tucked away between Mount Orford and Lake Memphrémagog, the golf course at this exclusive resort offers some of the best scenery in the Eastern Townships. ⊠ *90 av. des Jardins, Magog-Orford* ☎ *819/847–4299, 800/567–3514* ⊕ *www.hotelsvillegia. com* ⅃ *18 holes. 6400 yds. Par 71. Slope 118. Greens Fee: C$37.50–C$41.95.* ⊂ﾞ *Facilities: golf carts, equipment rental, pro-shop, golf lessons, (snack) bar.*

Mont-Orford Golf Club. This venerable course winds through forested land, with the peak of Mont-Orford visible from many of its greens. ⊠ *3074 chemin du Parc* ☎ *819/843–5688, 866/673–6731* ⊕ *www. mt-orford.com* ⅃ *18 holes. Par 72. 6095 yds. Slope: 126. Greens Fee: C$25 (weekdays); C$32 (weekends)* ⊂ﾞ *Facilities: Golf carts, rental clubs, pro-shop, lessons, restaurant.*

SKIING

Owl's Head Ski Area. On the Knowlton Landing side of Lake Memphrémagog, Owl's Head is great for skiers seeking sparser crowds. It has eight lifts, a 1,772-foot vertical drop, and 44 trails, including a 4-km (2½-mile) intermediate run, the longest such run in the Eastern Townships. It's also one of the least expensive hills in the Townships—and the views from its peak are truly exceptional. ⊠ *40 chemin du Mont-Owl's Head, Rte. 243 Sud; Highway 10, Exit 106* ☎ *450/292–3342, 800/363–3342* ⊕ *www.owlshead.com.*

NORTH HATLEY

9

10 km (6 miles) east of Magog, 133 km (83 miles) east of Montréal.

North Hatley, the small resort town on the tip of Lac Massawippi, has a theater and excellent inns and restaurants. Set among hills and farms, it was discovered by rich vacationers in the early 1900s, and has been drawing visitors ever since. It was particularly popular with magnates from the former Confederate States of America looking for a cool summer refuge that wasn't controlled by the Yankees. The result is that some of the village's most majestic buildings are more reminiscent of Georgia than Vermont.

WHERE TO EAT AND STAY

For expanded hotel reviews, visit fodors.com.

$$
AMERICAN

✕ **Pilsen Pub.** Québec's first microbrewery no longer brews beer on-site, but Massawippi pale and brown ales and a vast selection of microbrews and imports are on tap here. Good pub food—pasta, homemade soups, burgers, and the like—is served in the upstairs restaurant and in the tavern, both of which overlook the water. It can get busy at lunch, so try to get here by noon. ⑤ *Average main: C$15* ⊠ *55 rue Principale* ☎ *819/842–2971* ⊕ *www.pilsen.ca.*

$ 　🛏 **Manoir Hovey.** Overlooking Lac Massawippi, this retreat feels like a
HOTEL　private estate, with many of the activities included in room rates. **Pros:**
lakeside setting; secluded; historic buildings; wheelchair accessible.
Cons: restaurant overpriced; grounds often taken over by weddings on
weekends. *⑤ Rooms from: C$150 ⊠ 575 chemin Hovey ☎ 819/842–
2421, 800/661–2421 ⊕ www.manoirhovey.com ⛵ 38 rooms, 7 suites,
1 4-bedroom cottage ⑩ Some meals.*

NIGHTLIFE AND THE ARTS

Fodor's Choice　**Piggery.** Enriching the Townships' cultural landscape since 1965, this
★　theater that was once a pig barn is still thriving. The venue, which has
an on-site restaurant and is nestled in the mountains off a quiet road,
often presents new plays by Canadian writers and experiments with
bilingual productions. In addition to traditional theater, the venue hosts
concerts, musical revues, magic shows, and comedy acts. The season
runs mid-May through mid-September. *⊠ 215 chemin Simard, off Rte.
108 ☎ 819/842–2431 ⊕ www.piggery.com.*

SHERBROOKE

*21 km (12 miles) northeast of North Hatley, 130 km (81 miles) east
of Montréal.*

Sherbrooke bills itself as the *Reine des Cantons de l'Est* (Queen of the
Eastern Townships), and with a population of more than 150,000, it's
far and away the region's largest and most important city. The Loyalists who founded the city in the 1790s and named it for Sir John Coape
Sherbrooke, one of Canada's pre-Confederation governor-generals,
used the power of the Rivière St-François to build a strong industrial
base. Though the city's economic importance has waned, it still has
significant manufacturing and textile plants. On the corner of rues Dufferin and Frontenac is a realistic mural illustrating storefronts and businesses from Sherbrooke's past.

GETTING HERE AND AROUND

Sherbrooke is easy to get to by car via Autoroute 10. From the U.S.,
it's an easy stop on the way to Montréal if you cross the border via
Interstate 91 and take Autoroute 55. There are also frequent bus connections between Montréal and Sherbrooke. The city is large and quite
hilly, so getting around on foot can be difficult. However, there's a well-
developed bus system.

ESSENTIALS

Sherbrooke Tourism Office *⊠ 785 rue King Ouest ☎ 819/821–1919,
800/561–8331 ⊕ www.tourismesherbrooke.com.*

EXPLORING

Musée de la Nature et des Sciences. This museum is in what used to be
the Julius-Kayser & Co. factory, famous for the silk stockings it made.
The elegant building has granite floors and marble stairs, and makes
good use of its lofty space. State-of-the-art light and sound effects
(the buzzing of mosquitoes may be *too* lifelike) and hands-on displays enhance the exhibits of everything from fossilized lizards and
ancient arrowheads to dried butterflies and stuffed beavers. *⊠ 225 rue*

Frontenac ☎ *819/564–3200, 877/434–3200* ⊕ *www.naturesciences. qc.ca* ✉ *C$7.50* ⊙ *Late Sept.–mid-June, Wed.–Sun. 10–5 (late June–early Sept., daily 10–5).*

Musée des Beaux-Arts de Sherbrooke. This fine-arts museum has a permanent exhibit on the history of art in the region from 1800 to the present. ⊠ *241 rue Dufferin* ☎ *819/821–2115* ⊕ *www.mbas.qc.ca* ✉ *C$10* ⊙ *early Sept.–late June, Tues.–Sun. noon–5; late June–early Sept., daily 10–5.*

NIGHTLIFE AND THE ARTS

Centennial Theatre. The 600-seat Centennial Theatre is a part of Bishops University and presents a roster of jazz, classical, and rock concerts, as well as opera, dance, mime, and children's theater. ⊠ *Bishop's University, Lennoxville* ☎ *819/822–9600, 819/822–9692 box office* ⊕ *www. centennialtheatre.ca.*

NOTRE-DAME-DES-BOIS

72 km (43 miles) east of Sherbrooke, 204 km (127 miles) east of Montréal.

Notre-Dame-des-Bois is a sleepy little one-street village just north of the Maine border. It sits in the shadow of one of the region's tallest and steepest mountains—Mont Mégantic, which soars 576 meters (1,890 feet) above the surrounding plain, with a height of 3,601 feet above sea level. It also has some of the clearest night skies in Québec, a quality that has endeared it to stargazers, both professional and amateur.

GETTING HERE AND AROUND

Getting here is no simple day trip from Montréal. Count on a three-hour journey, some of it over paved but bumpy secondary roads. To get here, follow Autoroute 10 east past Sherbrooke to its end near Ascot Corner, then follow Route 112 to East Angus, then Route 253 to Cookshire, and finally Route 212 through L'Avenir to Notre-Dame-des-Bois. If you want to make the journey comfortably, plan to stay overnight somewhere.

EXPLORING

Astrolab du Mont-Mégantic (*Mont-Mégantic's Observatory*). Both amateur stargazers and serious astronomers head to his observatory, located in a beautifully wild and mountainous area. The observatory is at the summit of the Townships' second-highest mountain (3,601 feet above sea level and 1,890 feet above the surrounding landscape), whose northern face records annual snowfalls rivaling any in North America. A joint venture of the University of Montréal and Laval University, the observatory has a powerful telescope, the largest on the East Coast. In the Astrolab at the welcome center at the mountain's base, you can view an exhibition and a multimedia show to learn about the night sky. ⊠ *Parc Mégantic, 189 Rte. du Parc* ☎ *819/888–2941* ⊕ *www.astrolab-parc-national-mont-megantic.org* ✉ *Observatory: C$10.25 during day, C$21.25 at night; Astrolab: C$14.25 during day, C$18.25 at night; additional C$6 to enter Parc Mégantic.* ⚇ *Reservations essential* ⊙ *Mid-May–mid-June, weekends noon–5; mid-June–late Aug., daily* *noon–4:30 and 8–11 pm; late Aug.–early Oct., weekends noon–5 and 7:30–10:30 pm. Closed Mon. night.*

Parc du Mont-Mégantic. If you're short on time or don't feel like a hike you can take a shuttle bus to the top of Mont-Mégantic for spectacular views of Québec, Maine, New Hampshire, and on really clear days, Vermont. But if you want the full experience, walk up. The park has 75 km (65 miles) of hiking trails that are also open in winter to snowshoers and cross-country skiers. And if you want a real adventure, the park offers accommodations in rustic shelters. ⊠ *189 route du Parc* ☎ *819/888–2941, 800/665–6527* ✆ *C$6.*

WHERE TO STAY

For expanded hotel reviews, visit fodors.com.

$

B&B/INN

Fodor's Choice

★

🖼 **Aux Berges de l'Aurore.** This delightful century-old inn is perfectly located less than a minute's drive from the area's primary tourist attractions, Mont Mégantic Provincial Park and the Astrolab housed within it. **Pros:** stunning scenery; close proximity to area activities; delicious breakfasts made exclusively from local produce; lots of interesting wildlife in the area, including wolves, moose, and wild cats. **Cons:** compulsory C$2 gratuity at breakfast. ⑤ *Rooms from: C$120* ⊠ *139 Rte. du Parc* ☎ *819/888–2715* ⊕ *www.auberge-aurore.qc.ca* ⟐ *3 rooms, 2 suites* ⊠⊙⊠ *Some meals.*

Québec City

WORD OF MOUTH

"Most visitors focus the majority of their time strolling and exploring Vieux Québec—a 17th century walled (fortressed) city with many preserved historic buildings—most now used as inns, shops, and restaurants. . . . There is an "Upper" and "Lower" town (it's built into a cliffside overlooking the St. Lawrence River)."

—mat54

WELCOME TO QUÉBEC CITY

TOP REASONS TO GO

★ **See the Château Frontenac:** Even if you're not staying at Québec City's most famous landmark, make sure to pop into one of the world's legendary hotels.

★ **Dine at World-Class Restaurants:** From high-end bistros to hip, hole-in-the-wall cafés to amazing breweries, Québec City has it all.

★ **Explore La Citadelle:** Québec City's highest perch is the largest fortified base in North America, and site of the daily Changing of the Guard in summer.

★ **Play on the Plains of Abraham:** From cross-country skiing and sledding in winter to picnicking and in-line skating in summer, this huge park is a popular place for outdoor fun.

★ **Experience Carnaval de Québec:** Dance at the Ice Palace, catch the night parade, or sluice down a snow slide. For three weekends in January and February, the city hosts one of the biggest winter festivals in the world.

1 Upper Town. Crowning Cap Diamant and partially surrounded by the Fortifications, a 5-km-long (3-mile-long) wall, Upper Town hosts the city's main attractions, including the majestic Château Frontenac and La Citadelle, a star-shaped fortress. Sweeping views of the St. Lawrence River and the Laurentians enchant visitors at every turn.

2 Lower Town. A maze of cobblestone streets with tucked-away cafés, artisan shops, and crêperies characterizes Lower Town, but there's a modern flair thrown in, as converted warehouses have become hip boutiques and art galleries.

3 Beyond the Walls. There's an entire city to explore beyond the Old City that many visitors never see. Rue St-Jean, avenue Cartier, the Grande-Allée, and the St-Roch district have restaurants, shops, and nightlife well worth checking out.

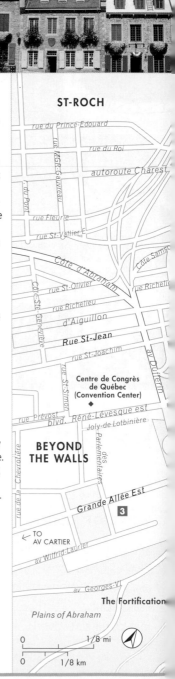

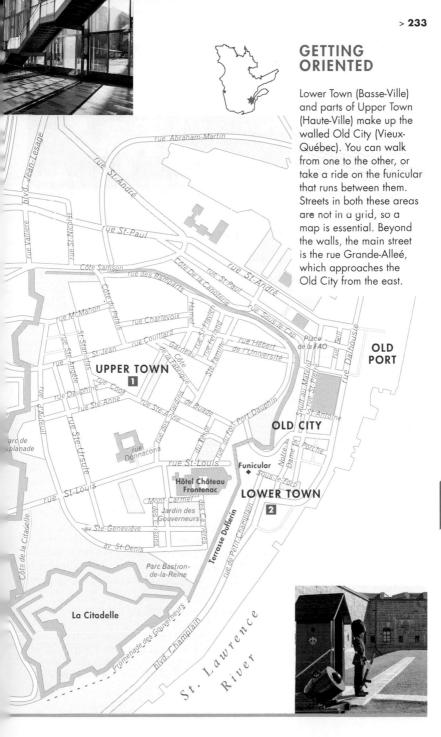

GETTING ORIENTED

Lower Town (Basse-Ville) and parts of Upper Town (Haute-Ville) make up the walled Old City (Vieux-Québec). You can walk from one to the other, or take a ride on the funicular that runs between them. Streets in both these areas are not in a grid, so a map is essential. Beyond the walls, the main street is the rue Grande-Alleé, which approaches the Old City from the east.

rue Abraham-Martin

blvd. Jean-Lesage

rue St-André

rue Vallière

rue St-Nicolas

rue St-Paul

Côte Samson

Côte De la Canoterie

rue des Remparts

rue St-Paul

rue St-André

Côte du Palais

rue McMahon

rue Charlevoix

Hamel

rue Sous-le-Cap

rue Couillard

St-Jean

St-Stanislas

St-Flavien

rue St-Frauen

Garneau

rue St-Angèle

rue Hébert

Place de la FAO

OLD PORT

Côte de la Fabrique

rue Ferland

Ste-Famille

rue de l'Université

rue Dalhousie

UPPER TOWN 1

rue Cook

rue Dauphine

de Buade

du Fort-Port-Dauphin

Sault-au-Matelot

rue St-Pierre

rue Ste-Anne

Parc de l'Esplanade

rue Ste-Ursule

rue Ste-Anne

rue du Trésor

des Jardins

OLD CITY

St-Antoine

rue Donnacona

rue St-Louis

Funicular ◆

Sous-le-Fort

Notre-Dame

du Porche

LOWER TOWN 2

Hôtel Château Frontenac

rue St-Louis

Mont-Carmel

10

Jardin des Gouverneurs

des Carrières

av. Ste-Geneviève

Côte de la Citadelle

av. St-Denis

Terrasse Dufferin

rue de Petit Champlain

Parc Bastion-de-la-Reine

La Citadelle

Promenade des Gouverneurs

blvd. Champlain

St. Lawrence River

Updated by
Amanda Halm
Québec City's alluring setting atop Cape Diamond (Cap Diamant) speaks to travelers of high adventure, military history, and exploration. This French-speaking capital city is the only walled city north of Mexico. Visitors come for the delicious and inventive cuisine, the remarkable historical continuity, and to share in the seasonal exuberance of the largest Francophone population outside of France.

The essence of this community is the Old City (Vieux-Québec), comprising the part of Upper Town (Haute-Ville) surrounded by walls and Lower Town (Basse-Ville), which spreads out at the base of the hill. Many sets of staircases and the popular funicular link the top of the hill with the bottom. Cobblestone streets, horse-drawn carriages, and elaborate cathedrals here are charming in all seasons. The Old City earned recognition as an official UNESCO World Heritage Site in 1985, thanks largely to city planners who managed to update and preserve the 400-year-old buildings and attractions without destroying the historic feel. The most familiar icon of the city, Fairmont Château Frontenac, set on the highest point in Upper Town, holds court over the entire city.

At the confluence of the St-Lawrence and St-Charles rivers, the city's famous military fortification, La Citadelle, was built of sandstone and remains the largest of its kind in North America. Visitors in summer should try to catch the Changing of the Guard, held every morning at 10 am; you can get much closer to the guards here than at Buckingham Palace in London.

Enchanting as it is, the Old City is just a small part of the true Québec City experience. Think outside the walls and explore St-Roch, Québec's new hot spot with artsy galleries and a bustling square. Cruise the Grand Allée and avenue Cartier to find a more lively part of town dotted with nightclubs and chic eateries. Or while away the hours in St-Jean-Baptiste, the bohemian quarter of the city with trendy shops and hipster hangouts.

QUÉBEC CITY PLANNER

WHEN TO GO

Winter is formidable, but the city stays lively—especially during the popular Winter Carnival. Spring is short and sweet with the *cabanes à sucre* bringing fresh maple goodies. In summer, the city's terraces and courtyards open and everyone comes out to enjoy the sunshine. During leaf peeping season, sometimes as early as September, the region blazes with color.

GETTING HERE AND AROUND

The Funiculaire du Vieux-Québec, a small elevator up the side of the steep embankment, travels between Upper and Lower towns. Another option, and a good workout, is to take one of the sets of stairs that start in Upper Town and end at the Quartier du Petit Champlain in Lower Town. Renting a car isn't recommended unless you're taking day trips outside the city.

AIR TRAVEL

If you're flying in, Jean Lesage International Airport is about 19 km (12 miles) northwest of downtown. Driving into town, take Route 540 (Autoroute Duplessis) to Route 175 (boulevard Laurier). The ride takes about 30 minutes. Taxis are available immediately outside the airport exit near the baggage-claim area. A ride into the city costs about C$34.

BUS TRAVEL

The electric Écolobus, which shuttles around Vieux-Québec, costs C$1 and runs every 10 minutes in both directions.

CAR TRAVEL

Montréal and Québec City are linked by Autoroute 20 on the south shore of the St. Lawrence River and by Autoroute 40 on the north shore. On both highways, the ride between the two cities is about 240 km (149 miles) and takes about three hours. U.S. I–87 in New York, U.S. I–89 in Vermont, and U.S. I–91 in New Hampshire connect with Autoroute 20, as does Highway 401 from Toronto. Driving northeast out of Montréal on Autoroute 20, follow signs for Pont Pierre-Laporte (Pierre Laporte Bridge) as you approach Québec City. After you've crossed the bridge, turn right onto boulevard Laurier (Route 175), which becomes the Grande Allée.

TRAIN TRAVEL

VIA Rail, Canada's passenger rail service, has service between Montréal and Québec City. The trip takes less than three hours and costs C$76.35 one-way. A taxi from the train station to the Fairmont Le Château Frontenac is only about C$6.

VISITOR INFORMATION

Québec City Tourist Information ⊠ *835 av. Wilfred-Laurier, Montcalm* ☎ *418/641–6290, 877/783–1608* ⊕ *www.quebecregion.com.*

UPPER TOWN

No other place in Canada has so much history squeezed into such a small spot. Upper Town was a barren, windswept cape when Samuel de Champlain decided to build a fort here just over 400 years ago. Now, of course, it's a major tourist destination surrounded by cannon-studded stone ramparts.

Home to many of the city's most famous sites, Upper Town's Old City offers a dramatic view of the St. Lawrence River and the countryside, especially from a ride on the funicular (C$2), or while walking along the Terrasse Dufferin, or standing in front of the Château Frontenac. Historic buildings that house bars, cafés, and shops, along with hotels and bed-and-breakfasts line the neighborhood's winding streets. A 5-km-long (3-mile-long) wall neatly splices off this section of the city with entrances on rues St-Jean and St-Louis. The wall itself is a national historic monument. It began as a series of earthworks and wooden palisades built by French military engineers to protect the Upper Town from an inland attack following the siege of the city by Admiral Phipps in 1690. Over the next century, the French expended much time, energy, and money to strengthen the city's fortifications. After the fall of New France, the British were equally concerned about strengthening the city's defenses and built an earth-and-wood citadel atop Cap Diamant. Slowly, the British replaced the wooden palisades that surrounded the city with the massive cut-stone wall that has become the city's trademark attraction. The crowning touch to the fortifications came after the War of 1812, with the construction of the cut-stone, star-shaped citadel, perched high on Cap Diamant.

Like La Citadelle, most of the many elegant homes that line the narrow streets in Upper Town are made of granite cut from nearby quarries in the 1800s. The stone walls, copper roofs, and heavy wooden doors on the government buildings and high-steepled churches in the area also reflect the Upper Town's place as the political, educational, and religious nerve center of both the province and the country during much of the past four centuries.

GETTING HERE AND AROUND
Many people begin their tours in Upper Town, taking in the Château Frontenac, perhaps Québec City's top site, and the spectacular views. The Fortifications border this section of the city. Walk down rues St-Louis or St-Jean to get a good sense of where the wall divides the Old City.

Québec City's Terrasse Dufferin offers unobstructed views of the St. Lawrence River with the peaks of the Laurentians visible in the distance.

If coming from Lower Town, take the funicular. Otherwise, consider braving one of the many staircases that connect the top of the hill to the bottom and bypass the line, which gets long in the summer. Shops and restaurants provide the opportunity for a quick rest along the way.

TIMING

Plan to spend a whole day visiting the many sights and shops clustered around the Château Frontenac. Rue St-Jean offers plenty of lunch options. Or do as the locals do, grab a sandwich and bench in one of the area's lovely parks.

Mark out at least a half-day for walking the walls of La Citadelle—set out early in the morning to catch the changing of the guard at 10 am in summer. Afterward, picnic on the Plains, or try one of the many terraces on the Grande Allée and avenue Cartier.

EXPLORING

TOP ATTRACTIONS

★ **Basilique Cathédrale Notre-Dame de Québec** (*Our Lady of Québec Basilica Cathedral*). François de Laval, the first bishop of New France, and his successors once ruled a diocese that stretched all the way to the Gulf of Mexico. Laval's original cathedral burned down and has been rebuilt several times, but the current basilica still has a chancel lamp that was a gift from Louis XIV, the Sun King himself.

The church's somber, ornate interior includes a canopy dais over the episcopal throne, a ceiling of painted clouds decorated with gold leaf, and richly colored stained-glass windows. The large crypt was Québec

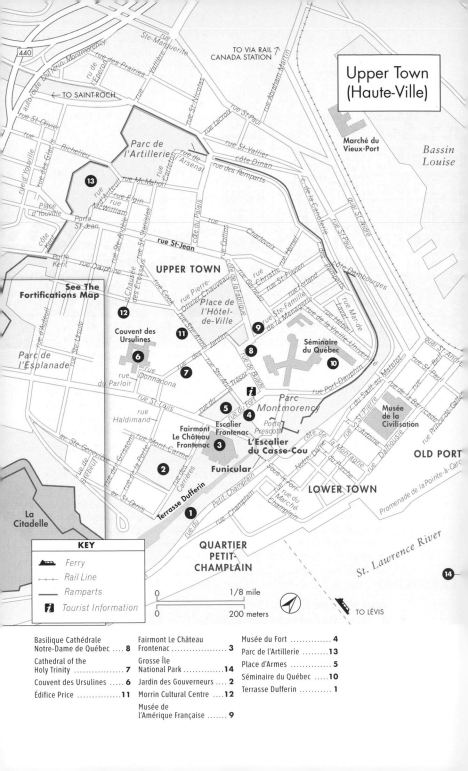

City's first cemetery; more than 900 bodies are interred here, including 20 bishops and four governors of New France. Samuel de Champlain may be buried near the basilica: archaeologists have been searching for his tomb since 1950. There are information panels that allow you to read about the history of this church. Or, if you prefer, guided tours of the cathedral and crypt (appointment only) are available. The Centre d'animation François-de-Laval uses videos and pictures to illustrate the life of Québec's first bishop and founder of Canada's Catholic Church. ⊠ *16 rue de Buade, Upper Town* ☎ *418/692–2533 church* ⊕ *www. patrimoine-religieux.com* 🖾 *Basilica free, guided tour C$3* ⊙ *Oct.– May, daily 7:30–4; June–Sept. 7:30–8:30; guided tours May–Oct., upon reservation Nov.–Apr.*

Couvent des Ursulines (*Ursuline Convent*). Founded in 1639, this is the oldest institution of learning for women in North America. Adolescent girls still study academics with the Ursulines, who are famous for their handmade lace. Today, there are two satellite schools, one in another part of Québec City for girls ages 5 to 12, and a co-ed campus in nearby Lorettville. The convent has many of its original walls intact and houses a little chapel and a museum.

The Chapelle des Ursulines (*Ursuline Chapel*) (⊠ *2 rue du Parloir, Upper Town* ☎ *418/694–0694* 🖾 *Free* ⊙ *Chapel May–Oct., Tues.– Sat. 10–11:30 and 1:30–4:30, Sun. 1:30–4:30*) is where French general Louis-Joseph Montcalm was buried after he died in the 1759 battle that decided the fate of New France. The chapel houses the finest examples of woodcarving anywhere in Québec, gilded by the nuns themselves. In September 2001 Montcalm's remains were transferred to rest with those of his soldiers at the Hôpital Général de Québec's cemetery, at 260 boulevard Langelier. The exterior of the Ursuline Chapel was rebuilt in 1902, but the interior contains the original chapel, which took sculptor Pierre-Noël Levasseur from 1726 to 1736 to complete.

Once the residence of Madame de la Peltrie, the laywoman who helped found the convent, the **Musée des Ursulines** (⊠ *12 rue Donnacona, Upper Town* ☎ *418/694–0694* 🖾 *C$8* ⊙ *May–Sept., Tues.–Sat. 10–5; Oct.– Apr., Tues.–Sun. 1–5*) provides an informative perspective on the Ursuline nuns, and includes an exhibition on their work in education during the 19th and 20th centuries. It took an Ursuline nun nine years of training to attain the level of a professional lace embroiderer, and the museum contains magnificent examples of their ornate work, such as altar frontals with gold and silver threads intertwined with semiprecious jewels.

10

Fodor'sChoice
★ **Fairmont Le Château Frontenac.** The most photographed landmark in Québec City, this imposing turreted castle with a copper roof owes its name to the Comte de Frontenac, Governor of the French colony between 1672 and 1698. The site itself is significant; it once held the St-Louis châteaux and forts, residence and seat of power for most governors. Samuel de Champlain was responsible for Château St-Louis, the first structure to appear on the site of the Frontenac; it was built between 1620 and 1624 as a residence for colonial governors. In 1784 Château Haldimand was constructed here, but it was demolished in 1892 to make way for Château Frontenac, built as a hotel a year later. The

THE HISTORY OF QUÉBEC CITY

Québec City was founded by French explorer Samuel de Champlain in 1608, and is the oldest municipality in the province. In the 17th century the first French explorers, fur trappers, and missionaries arrived to establish a colony.

French explorer Jacques Cartier arrived in 1535, but it was Champlain who founded "New France" some 70 years later, and built a fort on the banks of the St. Lawrence (called Place Royale today).

The British were persistent in their efforts to dislodge the French from North America, but the colonists of New France built forts and other military structures, such as a wooden palisade (defensive fence) that reinforced their position on top of the cliff. It was Britain's naval supremacy that ultimately led to New France's demise. After capturing all French forts east of Québec, General James Wolfe led his army to Québec City in the summer of 1759.

After a months-long siege, thousands of British soldiers scaled the heights along a narrow cow path on a moonless night. Surprised to see British soldiers massed on a farmer's field so near the city, French general Louis-Joseph Montcalm rushed out to meet them in what became known as the Battle of the Plains of Abraham. The French were routed in the 20-minute skirmish, which claimed the lives of both Wolfe and Montcalm. The battle marked the death of New France and the birth of British Canada.

British rule was a boon for Québec City. Thanks to more robust trade and large capital investments, the fishing, fur-trading, shipbuilding, and timber industries expanded rapidly. As the city developed and diversified, the quality of people's lives also greatly improved.

Wary of new invasions from its former American colonies, the British also expanded the city's fortifications. They replaced the wooden palisades with a massive stone wall and built a star-shaped fortress. Both structures still stand.

The constitution of 1791 established Québec City as the capital of Lower Canada, a position it held until 1840, when the Act of Union united Upper and Lower Canada and made Montréal the capital. When Canada was created in 1867 by the Act of Confederation, which united four colonial provinces (Québec, Ontario, New Brunswick, and Nova Scotia), Québec City was named the province's capital city, a role it continues to play. In Québec, however, the city is known officially as "*la capitale Nationale*," a reflection of the nationalist sentiments that have marked Québec society and politics for the past 40 years.

Frontenac was remarkably luxurious for the time: guest rooms contained fireplaces, bathrooms, and marble fixtures, and a special commissioner purchased antiques for the establishment. The hotel was designed by New York architect Bruce Price, who also worked on Québec City's Gare du Palais (train station). It's one in a series of château-style hotels built across Canada to attract wealthy railroad travelers and promote luxury tourism. The addition of a 20-story central tower in 1924 completed the hotel. It's accumulated a star-studded guest roster, including

Queen Elizabeth II, Princess Grace of Monaco, Alfred Hitchcock, and Ronald Reagan, as well as Franklin Roosevelt and Winston Churchill, who met here in 1943 and 1944 for two wartime conferences.

Santol, the hotel's appointed Canine Ambassador, a former guide dog in the Mira Foundation for the blind, can often be found in the lobby helping children and adults alike to feel more at home. ⊠ *1 rue des Carrières, Upper Town* ☎ *418/692–3861* ⊕ *www.fairmont.com/frontenac.*

Fortifications of Québec National Historic Site. In the early 19th century this was a clear space surrounded by a picket fence and poplar trees. The French began building ramparts along the city's cliffs as early as 1690 to protect themselves from British invaders. However, the colonists had trouble convincing the French government to take the threat of invasion seriously, and when the British invaded in 1759 the walls were still incomplete. The British, despite attacks by the Americans during the American Revolution and the War of 1812, took a century to finish them. From June 1 to early October, the park can also be the starting point for walking the city's 5 km (3 miles) of walls. There are two guided tours (C$9.80 each); one starts at the interpretation center and the other begins at Terrasse Dufferin.

What's here now is the **Poudrière de l'Esplanade** (⊠ *100 rue St-Louis, Upper Town* ☎ *418/648–7016* ⊕ *www.pc.gc.ca* ⌐ *C$3.90* ⊙ *May–early Oct., daily 10–6*), the powder magazine (used to store gunpowder) that the British constructed in 1820, and an interpretation center with a multimedia video and a model depicting the evolution of the wall surrounding Vieux-Québec.

Fodor'sChoice **Jardin des Gouverneurs** (*Governors' Park*). In this small park just south
★ of the Château Frontenac stands the **Wolfe-Montcalm Monument,** a 50-foot-tall obelisk that is unique because it pays tribute to both a winning (English) and a losing (French) general. The monument recalls the 1759 battle on the Plains of Abraham, which ended French rule here. British general James Wolfe lived only long enough to hear of his victory; French general Louis-Joseph Montcalm died shortly after Wolfe, with the knowledge that the city was lost. On the south side of the park is **avenue Ste-Geneviève,** lined with well-preserved Victorian houses dating from 1850 to 1900. Quite a few have been converted to inns, B&Bs, and hotels. ⊠ *Upper Town.*

Fodor'sChoice **La Citadelle.** Built at the city's highest point, on Cap Diamant, the Cita-
★ delle is the largest fortified base in North America still occupied by troops. The 25-building fortress was intended to protect the port, prevent the enemy from taking up a position on the Plains of Abraham, and provide a refuge in case of an attack. Having inherited incomplete fortifications, the British completed the Citadelle to protect themselves against French retaliations. By the time the Citadelle was finished in 1832, the attacks against Québec City had ended.

Since 1920 the Citadelle has served as a base for Canada's most storied French-speaking military formation, the Royal 22e Régiment (Royal 22nd Regiment), affectionately known across Canada as the Van Doos, from the French "vingt-deux" (twenty-two). Firearms, uniforms, and decorations from the 17th century are displayed in the **Musée Royal 22e Régiment**

10

(Royal 22nd Regiment Museum) in the former powder magazine, built in 1750. If weather permits, you can watch the changing of the guard, a ceremony in which troops parade before the Citadelle in red coats and black fur hats, and a band plays. The regiment's mascot, a well-behaved goat, also watches the activity. The queen's representative in Canada, the governor-general, has a residence in the Citadelle, which is sometimes open for tours in summer. Québec City's oldest military building, the Cape Diamond Redoubt, was constructed in 1693 under the supervision of the engineer Josué Boisberthelot de Beaucours and is now included in the guided tours. A guide must accompany visitors to the Citadelle, as it is a military base. ⊠ *Côte de la Citadelle, Upper Town* ☎ *418/694–2815* ⊕ *www.lacitadelle.qc.ca* ✉ *C$10* ⊙ *May–Sept., 9–5; Oct.–Apr., 10–4; Closed Dec. 25–Jan.1, bilingual tour daily, group reservations available daily. Changing of the Guard June 24–1st Mon. in Sept., daily at 10 am; Beating of the Retreat June 24–1st Mon. in Sept., Sat. at 6 pm.*

Montcalm Monument. France and Canada jointly erected this monument honoring Louis-Joseph Montcalm, the French general who gained his fame by winning four major battles in North America. His most famous battle, however, was the one he lost, when the British conquered New France on September 13, 1759. Montcalm was north of Québec City at Beauport when he learned that the British attack was imminent. He quickly assembled his troops to meet the enemy and was wounded in battle in the leg and stomach. Montcalm was carried into the walled city, where he died the next morning. The monument depicts the standing figure of Montcalm, with an angel over his shoulder. ⊠ *Cours du Général-De Montcalm, Upper Town.*

★ **Musée National des Beaux-Arts du Québec** (*National Museum of Fine Arts of Québec*). A neoclassical beaux arts showcase, the museum has more than 22,000 traditional and contemporary pieces of Québec art. The original building houses 5,635 objects, including portraits by Jean-Paul Riopelle (1923–2002), Jean-Paul Lemieux (1904–90), and Horatio Walker (1858–1938) that are particularly notable, as well as legions of other artifacts. The museum's dignified building in Parc des Champs-de-Bataille was designed by Wilfrid Lacroix and erected in 1933 to commemorate the 300th anniversary of the founding of Québec. Incorporated within is part of an abandoned prison dating from 1867. A hallway of cells, with the iron bars and courtyard, has been preserved as part of a permanent exhibition on the prison's history. ⊠ *Parc des Champs-de-Bataille, Upper Town* ☎ *418/643–2150* ⊕ *www.mnba.qc.ca* ✉ *Free, special exhibits C$15* ⊙ *Sept.–May, Tues. and Thurs.–Sun. 10–5, Wed. 10–9; June–Aug., Thurs.–Tues. 10–6, Wed. 10–9.*

★ **Parc de l'Artillerie** (*Artillery Park*). Nineteenth-century British officers certainly knew how to party in style, if the ornate china and regimental silver glittering in the beautifully restored officers' mess in this national historic site are anything to go by. They and their families didn't live too badly, either, as you'll see if you visit the gardens and rooms of the restored **Officers' Quarters,** all decorated in the style of the 1830s.

In July and August you can sample a taste (literally) of life in the lower ranks by trying a piece of chewy "soldier's bread" baked in an outdoor

Kids will love watching the Royal 22nd Regiment's Changing of the Guard every summer day at 10 am, from June 24 until the first Monday in September.

oven, share in a tea ceremony, or watch a costumed actor in a French uniform of the 18th century demonstrate shooting with a flintlock musket. Artillery Park's four buildings all have long histories. The Officers' Quarters, for example, were built 1817, and are housed in the Dauphin Redoubt, which, as the name suggests, were virtually impenetrable to enemy attacks. The British took it over in 1759, and from 1785 until 1871 it served as the mess for the officers of the Royal Artillery Regiment. The old iron foundry houses a magnificent scale model of Québec City built in 1808, allowing visitors to get a sense of the city as it looked then, as well as its geography, and history. ⊠ *2 rue d'Auteuil, Upper Town* ☎ *888/773–8888, 418/648–7016* ⊕ *www.pc.gc.ca/fra/lhn-nhs/qc/ fortifications/index.aspx* ⊠ *C\$3.90, C\$9.80 for guided tour* ☉ *Apr.–mid-May, by reservations only; mid-May–mid-June, daily 10–5; mid-June– Labor Day, daily 10–6; Day after Labor Day–early Oct., daily 10–5.*

Parc des Champs-de-Bataille (*Battlefields Park*). These 250 acres of gently rolling slopes have unparalleled views of the St. Lawrence River. Within the park and west of the Citadelle are the Plains of Abraham. ⊠ *835 Avenue Laurier, Upper Town.*

Fodor's Choice ★ Parc Jeanne d'Arc. An equestrian statue of Joan of Arc is the focus of this park, which is bright with colorful flowers in summer. A symbol of military courage and of France itself, the statue stands in tribute to the heroes of 1759 near the place where New France was lost to the British. The park also commemorates the Canadian national anthem, "O Canada"; it was played here for the first time on June 24, 1880. ⊠ *avs. Laurier and Taché, Upper Town.*

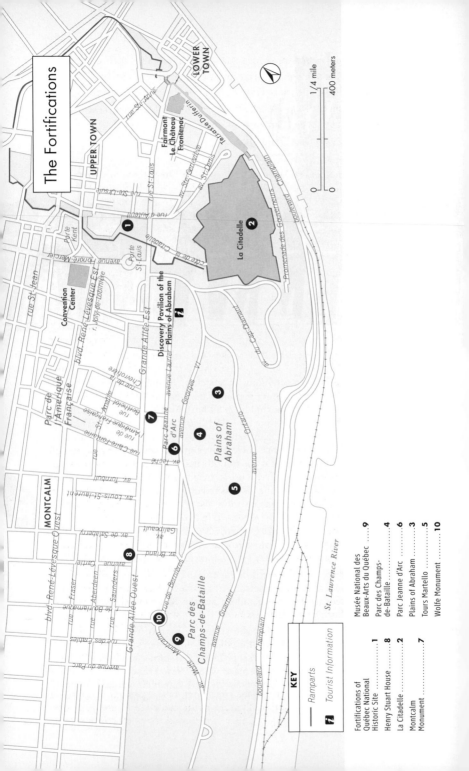

The Fortifications

UPPER TOWN

LOWER TOWN

Fairmont
Le Château
Frontenac

La Citadelle

Convention
Center

Parc de
l'Amérique
Française

Discovery Pavilion of the
Plains of Abraham

Plains of
Abraham

MONTCALM

Parc des
Champs-de-Bataille

St. Lawrence River

KEY

— Ramparts

🛈 Tourist Information

Fortifications of
Québec National
Historic Site **1**
Henry Stuart House **8**
La Citadelle **2**
Montcalm
Monument **7**

Musée National des
Beaux-Arts du Québec **9**
Parc des Champs-
de-Bataille **4**
Parc Jeanne d'Arc **6**
Plains of Abraham **3**
Tours Martello **5**
Wolfe Monument **10**

1/4 mile

400 meters

QUICK BITES

L'Inox. Beer has been brewed in Québec since the early 1600s, and L'Inox carries on the tradition with a combination brewpub and museum. A large, sunny terrace is open in summer. L'Inox serves many of its own beers, as well as other beverages, alcoholic and not. Tours of the brewery are available for groups of eight or more. ⊠ *655, Grande Allée Est, Upper Town* ☎ *418/692–2877* ⊕ *www.inox.qc.ca.*

Place d'Armes. For centuries, this square has been used for parades and military events. It's bordered by government buildings; at its west side stands the majestic **Ancien Palais de Justice** (Old Courthouse), a Renaissance-style building from 1887. The plaza is on land that was occupied by a church and convent of the Récollet missionaries (Franciscan monks), who in 1615 were the first order of priests to arrive in New France. The Gothic-style **fountain** at the center of Place d'Armes pays tribute to their arrival. ⊠ *rues St-Louis and du Fort, Upper Town.*

Ⓒ **Plains of Abraham.** This park, named after Abraham Martin, who used
Fodor's Choice the plains as a pasture for his cows, is the site of the famous 1759
★ battle that decided New France's fate. People cross-country ski here in winter and in-line skate in summer. At the **Discovery Pavilion of the Plains of Abraham,** check out the multimedia display, "Odyssey: A Journey Through History on the Plains of Abraham," which depicts 400 years of Canada's history. ⊠ *Discovery Pavilion of the Plains of Abraham, 835 av. Wilfrid-Laurier, Level 0 (next to Drill Hall), Upper Town* ☎ *418/649–6157 for Discovery Pavilion and bus-tour information* ⊕ *www.ccbn-nbc.gc.ca* ⊠ *Discovery Pavilion C$14 for 1-day pass (summer only), bus tour and Odyssey exhibition included* ⊗ *Discovery Pavilion July–Labor Day, daily 8:30–5:30; day after Labor Day–June, weekdays 8:30–5, Sat. 9–5, Sun. 10–5.*

Terrasse Dufferin. This wide boardwalk with an intricate wrought-iron guardrail has a panoramic view of the St. Lawrence River, the town of Lévis on the opposite shore, Île d'Orléans, and the Laurentian Mountains. It was named for Lord Dufferin, governor of Canada between 1872 and 1878, who had this walkway constructed in 1878. Château St-Louis was home to the governors from 1626 to 1834, when it was destroyed by fire. There are 90-minute tours of the fortifications that leave from here. The **Promenade des Gouverneurs** begins at the boardwalk's western end; the path skirts the cliff and leads up to Québec's highest point, Cap Diamant, and also to the Citadelle. ⊠ *Upper Town.*

Venture under the boardwalk to see archaeological treasures from the official residence and power base of the French and British governors, **St-Louis Forts and Châteaux National Historic Site** (⊠ *Upper Town* ☎ *418/648–7016* ⊕ *www.pc.gc.ca* ⊠ *C$3.90* ⊗ *Late May–mid-Oct., daily 10–6*). Two-year excavations, completed in 2007, unearthed objects from the first château, built under the direction of Governor Montmagny, to the time the Château St-Louis burned in 1834. Wine bottles, kitchenware—even remains of walls and doorframes—give clues to the luxurious life of the governors, who were among the most powerful men in the nation. Don't miss the guided tours and activities, such as chocolate tasting from a centuries-old recipe (details available

10

at the kiosk on the Terrasse Dufferin). History buffs might consider attending one of the in-depth archaeology conferences held here.

Wolfe Monument. This tall monument marks the place where the British general James Wolfe died in 1759. Wolfe landed his troops about 3 km (2 miles) from the city's walls; 4,500 English soldiers scaled the cliff and began fighting on the Plains of Abraham. Wolfe was mortally wounded in battle and was carried behind the lines to this spot. ⊠ *rue de Bernières and av. Wolfe-Montcalm, Upper Town.*

WORTH NOTING

Cathedral of the Holy Trinity. The first Anglican cathedral outside the British Isles was erected in the heart of Québec City Upper Town between 1800 and 1804. Its simple, dignified facade is reminiscent of London's St. Martin-in-the-Fields, and the pediment, archway, and Ionic pilasters introduced Palladian architecture to Canada. The land on which the cathedral was built was originally given to the Récollet fathers (Franciscan monks from France) in 1681 by the king of France for a church and monastery. When Québec came under British rule, the Récollets made the church available to the Anglicans for services. Later, King George III ordered construction of the present cathedral, with an area set aside for members of the royal family. A portion of the north balcony is still reserved exclusively for the use of the reigning sovereign or his or her representative. The church houses precious objects donated by George III. The cathedral's impressive rear organ has 3,058 pipes. Even more impressive is the smaller English Chamber Organ, built in 1790, which was donated to the cathedral for the Bicentennial Celebrations in 2004. ⊠ *31 rue des Jardins, Upper Town* ☎ *418/692–2193* ⊕ *www.cathedral.ca* ☞ *Free* ☉ *June 24–Labor Day, Mon.–Thurs. 9–5, Fri. and Sat. 9–8, Sun. noon–5; morning services year-round in English weekdays at 8:30 am, Sun. at 11 am, in French on Sun. at 9:30 am.*

Édifice Price. Styled after the Empire State Building, the 15-story, art deco structure was the city's first skyscraper. Today it's one of the Premier's official residences—he uses the top two floors. Built in 1929, it served as headquarters of the Price Brothers Company, a lumber firm founded by Sir William Price. Don't miss the interior: exquisite copper plaques depict scenes of the company's early pulp and paper activities, and the two maple-wood elevators are '30s classics. ⊠ *65 rue Ste-Anne, Upper Town.*

Grosse Île National Park. For thousands of immigrants from Europe in the 1800s, the first glimpse of North America was the hastily erected quarantine station at Grosse Île—Canada's equivalent of Ellis Island. During the time Grosse Île operated (1832–1937), 4.3 million immigrants passed through the port of Québec. For far too many passengers on plague-racked ships, particularly the Irish fleeing the potato famine, Grosse Île became a final resting place. Several buildings have been restored to tell the story of the tragic period of Irish immigration. It's necessary to take a boat tour or ferry to visit the park, and you should reserve in advance. ☎ *418/234–8841 Parks Canada, 888/773–8888* ⊕ *www.grosseile.ca* ☞ *C$49.50, including boat tour or ferry* ☉ *May 3–Oct. 12, daily 9–6.*

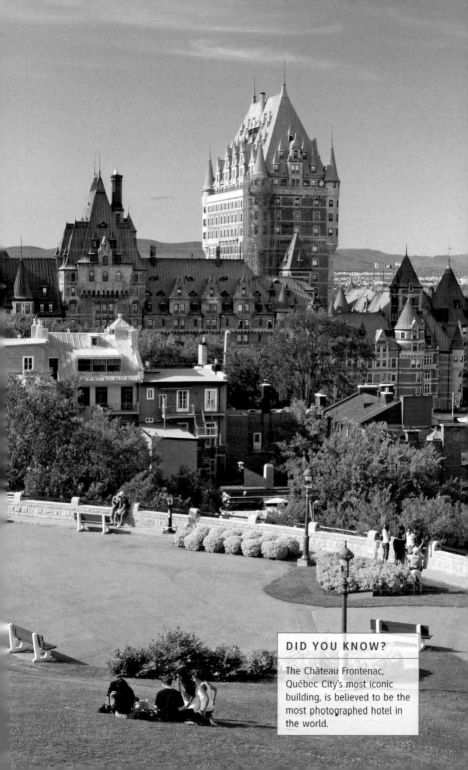

DID YOU KNOW?

The Château Frontenac, Québec City's most iconic building, is believed to be the most photographed hotel in the world.

OFF THE
BEATEN
PATH

Croisières Le Coudrier (☎ 888/600–5554 ⊕ *www.croisierescoudrier. qc.ca*) has tours that depart from Québec City's Old Port, Lévis, Île d'Orléans, and Ste-Anne-de-Beaupré for Grosse Île. Tours cost C$62.50, which includes admission to the island.

Croisières Lachance (☎ 888/476–7734 ⊕ *www.croisiereslachance. ca*) runs a ferry that departs from Berthier-sur-Mer to Grosse Île for C$49.50, which includes admission to the island. From Québec City, head south on the Pont Pierre-Laporte (Pierre Laporte Bridge) and follow Autoroute 20 east for about an hour to Berthier-sur-Mer. Follow the signs to the marina.

Henry Stuart House. If you want to get a firsthand look at how the well-to-do English residents of Québec City lived in a bygone era, this is the place. Built in 1849 by the wife of wealthy businessman William Henry, the Regency-style cottage was bought in 1918 by the sisters Adèle and Mary Stuart. Active in such philanthropic organizations as the Red Cross and the Historical and Literary Society, the sisters were pillars of Québec City's English-speaking community. They also maintained an English-style garden behind the house. Soon after Adèle's death in 1987 at the age of 98, the home was classified a historic site for its immaculate physical condition and the museum-like quality of its furnishings, almost all of them Victorian. Guided tours of the house and garden start on the hour and include a cup of tea and piece of lemon cake. ⊠ *82 Grande Allée Ouest, Upper Town* ☎ *418/647–4347* ⊕ *www. maisonhenrystuart.qc.ca* ⊠ *C$8* ⊗ *Mid-June–Labor Day, Wed.–Sun. 11–4; day after Labor Day–early June, available for groups of 6 or more with reservations.*

Morrin Cultural Centre. This stately gray-stone building has served many purposes, from imprisoning and executing criminals to storing the national archives. Built between 1808 and 1813, it was the first modern prison in Canada. Two blocks of half a dozen cells remain intact and are open to visitors. The scaffold, which was used to hang criminals, is long gone.

When the jail closed in 1868, the building was converted into Morrin College, one of the city's first private schools, and the **Literary and Historical Society of Québec** moved in. Founded in 1824, this forerunner of Canada's National Archives operates an active lending library and has a superb collection that includes some of the first books printed in North America. The college is no longer in operation, but historical and cultural talks are held in English, and tours of the building are available. Don't miss the Victorian-era library and College Hall. ⊠ *44 rue Chaussée des Ecossais, Upper Town* ☎ *418/694–9147* ⊕ *www.morrin. org* ⊠ *Library free; guided tours C$8* ⊗ *Library: Sun., Wed., Fri. 12 pm–4 pm; Tues., Thurs. 12 pm–8 pm; Sat. 10 am–4 pm. Closed Mon. Guided tours in English late May–early Sept., Mon.–Sat. 11 am and 3 pm, Sun. 1:30 pm. Tours for groups by arrangement.*

Musée de l'Amérique Française. A former student residence of the Séminaire de Québec à l'Université Laval (Québec Seminary at Laval University) houses this museum that focuses on the history of the French in North America. You can view about 20 of the museum's 400 landscape

QUÉBEC CITY'S BEST WALKING TOURS

Tours Voir Québec. This company offers English- and French-language (and Spanish from June through September) walking tours of the Old City, starting at C$22.95. They also have a popular food tour with tastings at various establishments for C$37.95. ✉ *12 rue St-Anne, Upper Town* ☎ *418/694-2001, 866/694-2001* ⊕ *www.toursvoirquebec.com.*

Ghost Tours of Québec. Costumed actors lead ghoulish 90-minute evening tours of Québec City murders, executions, and ghost sightings. The tours (C$20) are available in English or French, from May through October. After the walk, you can purchase a copy of *Ghost Stories of Québec,* featuring stories not told on the tours. ✉ *34 blvd. Champlain, Lower Town* ☎ *418/692-9770* ⊕ *www.ghosttoursofquebec.com.*

La Compagnie des Six-Associés. This company gives several historical theme-driven walking tours year-round for groups, and in the summer for individuals, starting at C$17. A tour-ending drink is included with some of the tours. The themes cover such timeless topics as "Doctors, Healers, and Gravediggers," "Crime and Punishment," "The Lily and the Lion," and "Lust and Drunkenness." ✉ *820 boul. Charest Est, Upper Town* ☎ *418/692-3033* ⊕ *www.sixassocies.com.*

and still-life paintings, some from as early as the 15th century, along with French colonial money and scientific instruments. The attached former chapel is used for exhibits, conferences, and cultural activities. There's a great exhibition called "On the Road: Francophones Odyssey," about the Francophones' journey across North America. ✉ *2 côte de la Fabrique, Upper Town* ☎ *418/692-2843* ⊕ *www.mcq.org* 🎟 *C$8* ⊘ *June 24–early Sept., daily 9:30–5; early Sept.–June 23, Tues.–Sun. 10–5.*

Musée du Fort. A 30-minute sound-and-light show reenacts the area's important battles, including the Battle of the Plains of Abraham and the 1775 attack by American generals Arnold and Montgomery. The museum's permanent expositions feature a history on soldiers' weaponry, uniforms, and military insignia; a glossary of lesser-known New France facts; and a diorama on the background of the show and building. A 400-square-foot replica of the city—complete with ships, cannons, and soldiers lined up for battle is the highlight of the museum and helps guests visualize the area's strategic importance. ✉ *10 rue Ste-Anne, Upper Town* ☎ *418/692-2175* ⊕ *www.museedufort.com* 🎟 *C$8* ⊘ *Feb., Mar., and Nov., Thurs.–Sun. 11–4; Apr.–Oct., daily 10–5; Dec. 26–Jan. 2, daily 11–4; Closed Nov. 28– Dec. 25 and Jan. 4–27.*

10

Séminaire du Québec. Behind these gates lies a tranquil courtyard surrounded by austere stone buildings with rising steeples; these structures have housed classrooms and student residences since 1663. François de Montmorency Laval, the first bishop of New France, founded Québec Seminary to train priests in the new colony. In 1852 the seminary became Université Laval, the first Catholic university in North America. In 1946 the university moved to a larger campus in suburban Ste-Foy.

Today priests live on the premises, and Laval's architecture school occupies part of the building. The on-site **Musée de l'Amérique Française** gives tours of the seminary grounds and the interior in summer. Tours start from the museum, at 2 côte de la Fabrique. The small Second Empire–style **Chapelle Extérieure,** at the west entrance of the seminary, was built in 1888 after fire destroyed the 1750 original. Joseph-Ferdinand Peachy designed the chapel; its interior is patterned after that of the Église de la Trinité in Paris. ⊠ *1 côte de la Fabrique, Upper Town* ☎ *418/692–2843, 866/710–8031* ✉ *C$7; free Tues., Nov.–Mar.* ⊙ *Tours late June–Labor Day, daily 9:30–5; Sept.–late June, daily 10–5.*

Tours Martello (*Martello Towers*). Of the 16 Martello towers in Canada, four were built in Québec City because the British government feared an invasion after the American Revolution. In summer, visitors can tour Martello Tower No. 1, and watch a presentation on the history of the four structures. A haunted maze is held for youngsters on Halloween at Martello Tower No. 2, at avenues Taché and Laurier, and a mystery dinner show is available by reservation. Martello Tower No. 3, which guarded the westward entry to the city, was demolished in 1904. Martello Tower No. 4, on rue Lavigueur overlooking the St. Charles River, isn't open to the public. ⊠ *Battlefields Park, Upper Town* ☎ *418/648–4071 for information on towers* ⊕ *www.ccbn-nbc.gc.ca* ✉ *C$14 for day pass to tower, Discovery Pavilion on Plains of Abraham, and a bus tour of park* ⊙ *Daily 10–5.*

LOWER TOWN

Lower Town is the new hot spot, its once-dilapidated warehouses are now boutique hotels, trendy shops, chic art galleries, and popular restaurants and bars, filled with locals and tourists alike. After exploring Place Royale and its cobblestone streets, you can walk along the edge of the St. Lawrence River and watch the sailboats and ships go by, shop at the market, or kick back on a *terrasse* with an ice cider. Rue Petit-Champlain also has charming places to stop and listen to street musicians, and the scene near the Old Port starts buzzing as soon as the sun goes down.

But looking back in time, if there's a cradle of French civilization in North America, you're standing in it when you visit Lower Town. In 1608 Champlain chose this narrow, U-shaped spit of land sandwiched between the frigid waters of the St. Lawrence River and the craggy heights of Cap Diamant as the site for his settlement. Champlain later abandoned the fortified *abitation* (residence) at the foot of Cap Diamant and relocated to the more easily defendable Upper Town.

However, the area continued to flourish as a bustling port and trading center for French merchants, fur traders, *coureurs de bois* (woodsmen), and France's Native American allies. It was also the base from which dozens of military campaigns and fact-finding missions were launched into the heart of an unknown continent. A bust of France's "Sun King," Louis XIV, was erected in the main square, Place du Marché, which was renamed Place Royale in 1686. Destroyed by British cannons that were set up on the opposite shore during the siege of 1759, the port and buildings were rebuilt by the British, and the area quickly regained its role as Canada's leading commercial and business center.

Lower Town went into an economic tailspin in the mid-1800s, becoming a slum whose narrow streets were lined with pawnshops, rough-and-tumble taverns, and smoky brothels that catered to sailors and lumberjacks. This lasted until the 1960s, when it received a multimillion-dollar face-lift that remade it into a sanitized version of its 1700s self. Today, once-dilapidated houses and warehouses contain stylish boutiques, popular restaurants, and chic art and antiques galleries. Bounded by the Dufferin-Montmorency Highway to the west, the St. Charles River to the north, the St. Lawrence River to the east, and Petit Champlain shopping area to the south, the Lower Town is also home to approximately 850 people.

10

GETTING HERE AND AROUND

Because Lower Town is the oldest part of the city, many prefer to see it first to get a sense of how the city developed chronologically. If coming from Upper Town, head down L'Escalier du Casse-Cou, a steep stairway nicknamed the "Breakneck Stairs." Have your camera ready, as the top of the staircase is where to snap that quintessential Petit-Champlain photo.

TIMING

You'll need one full day to see two of the city's most famous squares, Place Royale and Place de Paris. Pause for lunch before touring the Musée de la Civilisation and the antiques district.

EXPLORING

TOP ATTRACTIONS

Église Notre-Dame-des-Victoires (*Our Lady of Victory Church*). The fortress shape of the altar is no accident; this small but beautiful stone church has a bellicose past. Grateful French colonists named it in honor of the Virgin Mary, whom they credited with helping French forces defeat two British invasions: one in 1690 by Admiral William Phipps and the other by Sir Hovendon Walker in 1711. The church itself was built in 1688, making it the city's oldest, and has been restored twice. Paintings by Van Dyck, Rubens, and Boyermans decorate the walls, and a model of *Le Brezé*, the boat that transported French soldiers to New France in 1664, hangs from the ceiling. The side chapel is dedicated to Ste. Geneviève, the patron saint of Paris. ⊠ *32 rue Sous-le-Fort, Lower Town* ☎ *418/692–1650* ⊕ *www. notredamedequebec.org* ⊑ *Free, C$2 for guided tours* ⊘ *Early May–late Oct., daily 9–5; late Oct.–early May, daily 10–4; closed to visitors during Mass (Sun. at 10:30 and noon), marriages, and funerals.*

L'Escalier du Casse-Cou. The steepness of the city's first iron stairway, an ambitious 1893 design by city architect and engineer Charles Baillairgé, is ample evidence of how it got its name: Breakneck Steps. The 59 steps were built on the site of the original 17th-century stairway that linked the Upper Town and Lower Town. There are shops and restaurants at various levels. ⊠ *Lower Town.*

Maison Chevalier. This old stone house (which is actually three houses brought together) was built in 1752 for ship owner Jean-Baptiste Chevalier. Its classic French style is one rich aspect of the urban architecture of New France. The double-thick walls, high chimneys, vaulted cellars, original wood beams, and stone fireplaces are noteworthy. An exhibition displays typical interior design from the 18th and 19th centuries, featuring artifacts from the Museum of Civilization vaults. ⊠ *50 rue du Marché-Champlain, Lower Town* ☎ *418/646–3167* ⊑ *C$5* ⊘ *June 24–early Sept., daily 9:30–5; early Sept.–June 23, Tues.–Sun. 10–5.*

Maison Louis-Jolliet. Louis Jolliet, the first European to see the Mississippi River, and his fellow explorers used this 1683 house as a base for westward journeys. Today it's the lower station of the funicular. A monument commemorating Louis Jolliet's 1672 trip to the Mississippi stands in the park next to the house. The house is at the foot of the famous **Escalier Casse-Cou** (Breakneck Staircase). ⊠ *16 rue du Petit-Champlain, Lower Town* ⊕ *www.funiculaire-quebec.com.*

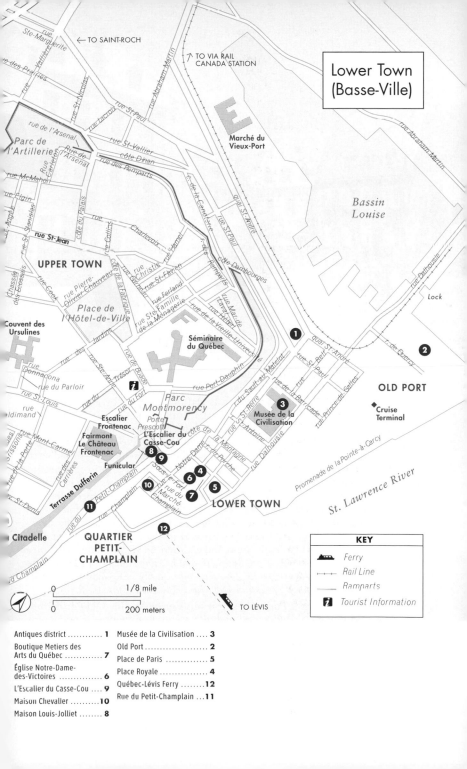

Lower Town (Basse-Ville)

← TO SAINT-ROCH

↑ TO VIA RAIL CANADA STATION

rue Ste-Marguerite
rue des Prairies
rue St-Nicolas
rue de l'Arsenal
Parc de l'Artillerie
rue de l'Arsenal
rue Carrière
rue McMahon
rue St-Vallier
côte Dinan
rue St-Paul
côte de la Canoterie
quai St-André
Marché du Vieux-Port

Bassin Louise

rue Dalhousie

Lock

rue Abraham-Martin

OLD PORT

UPPER TOWN

rue St-Jean
côte du Palais
rue des Glacis
rue Elgin
rue St-Stanislas
Chaussée des Écossais
rue Cook
rue Pierre-Olivier-Chauveau
rue Christie
rue St-Flavien
rue Ste-Famille
rue Ferland
rue Hôtel-Dieu
rue Garneau
rue de la Fabrique
rue Charlevoix
rue St-Jean
côte de la Fabrique
rue des Remparts
côte de la Montagne

Place de l'Hôtel-de-Ville

Couvent des Ursulines
rue Donnacona
rue du Parloir
rue St-Louis
rue Haldimand
rue Mont-Carmel
rue des Jardins
rue Ste-Anne
rue du Trésor
rue des Grisons
rue Ste-Ursule
rue Cook
rue du Fort
rue Buade
rue Port-Dauphin

Séminaire du Québec

rue de la Vieille-Université
rue Port-Dauphin
rue St-Pierre
rue Sault-au-Matelot
rue de la Barricade
rue St-Paul
rue Prince-de-Galles

1 Antiques district

quai St-André
2 Old Port
rue de Carazy

Parc Montmorency
Pointe Prescott

L'Escalier du Casse-Cou **8 9**

Escalier Frontenac

Fairmont Le Château Frontenac

Funicular

Terrasse Dufferin

Citadelle

QUARTIER PETIT-CHAMPLAIN

3 Musée de la Civilisation

rue Dalhousie
rue Sous-le-Fort
rue Notre-Dame
rue du Porche
rue de la Montagne
rue St-Antoine

Cruise Terminal

Promenade de la Pointe-à-Carcy

St. Lawrence River

6 4
7
5

10

LOWER TOWN

11

12

TO LÉVIS

0 —— 1/8 mile
0 —— 200 meters

KEY

⚓ Ferry
+ Rail Line
Ramparts
🛈 Tourist Information

One of Lower Town's top sights is the Place Royale, also one of the oldest public squares in the province.

Musée de la Civilisation (*Museum of Civilization*). Wedged between narrow streets at the foot of the cliff, this spacious museum with a striking limestone-and-glass facade was artfully designed by architect Moshe Safdie to blend into the landscape. Its campanile echoes the shape of the city's church steeples. Two excellent permanent exhibits at the museum examine Québec's history. "People of Québec, Now and Then" engagingly synthesizes 400 years of social and political history—including the role of the Catholic church and the rise of the separatist movement—with artifacts, time lines, original films and interviews, and news clips. It's a great introduction to the issues that face the province today. The "Nous, les Premières Nations" (We, the First Nations) exhibit looks at the 11 aboriginal nations that inhabit Québec. Several of the shows, with their imaginative use of artwork, video screens, computers, and sound, appeal to both adults and children. ✉ *85 rue Dalhousie, Lower Town* ☎ *418/643–2158, 866/710–8031* ⊕ *www.mcq.org* ⊡ *C$14; free Tues. Nov.–May* ⊗ *June 24–early Sept., daily 9:30–6:30; early Sept.– mid-Oct., daily 10–5; mid-Oct.–June 23, Tues.–Sun. 10–5.*

Old Port (*Vieux Port*). On warm summer nights, the Old Port harbors an interesting and varied nightlife scene. But daytime is no less fun. Stroll along the riverside promenade, where merchant and cruise ships dock. The old harbor dates from the 17th century, when ships brought supplies and settlers to the new colony. At one time this port was among the busiest on the continent: between 1797 and 1897, Québec shipyards turned out more than 2,500 ships, many of which passed the 1,000-ton mark. At the port's northern end, where the St. Charles meets the St. Lawrence, a lock protects the marina in the Louise Basin

Fodor's Choice
★

from the generous Atlantic tides that reach even this far up the St. Lawrence. ⊠ *Lower Town.*

At the port's northwestern tip, the **Marché du Vieux-Port** (*Old Port Market*) (⊠ *160 Quai St-André, Lower Town* ⊕ *www. marchevieuxport.com*) is where farmers sell fresh produce and cheese and artisans sell their handicrafts. The market, at quai St-André, is open weekdays from

WORD OF MOUTH

"If you like art, Le Musée des Beaux-Arts is well worth a visit. It doesn't limit itself to 'dead white guys'–type art but is quite all-encompassing. It includes First Nations and Inuit art as well as contemporary commercial pieces."
—knickerbocker

9–6 and weekends from 9–5 in summer. Some stalls stay open daily in winter, and the market is all dressed up for the Christmas season. Take a stroll through and taste some refreshing local produce, such as apples and berries.

Fodor's Choice **Place Royale.** The houses that encircle this cobblestone square, with steep
★ Normandy-style roofs, dormer windows, and chimneys, were once the homes of wealthy merchants. Until 1686 the area was called Place du Marché, but its name changed when a bust of Louis XIV was placed at its center. During the late 1600s and early 1700s, when Place Royale was continually under threat of British attack, the colonists moved progressively higher to safer quarters atop the cliff in Upper Town. After the French colony fell to British rule in 1759, Place Royale flourished again with shipbuilding, logging, fishing, and fur trading. The *Fresque des Québecois*, a 4,665-square-foot trompe-l'oeil mural depicting 400 years of Québec's history is to the east of the square, at the corner of rue Notre-Dame and côte de la Montagne. ⊠ *Lower Town.*

Centre d'Interprétation de Place Royale (⊠ *27 rue Notre-Dame, Lower Town* ☎ *418/646–3167* ⊕ *www.mcq.org* ☞ *C$7; free Tues. Nov.–May* ⊙ *June 24–early Sept., daily 9:30–5; mid-Sept.–June 23, Tues.–Sun. 10–5*), an information center, includes exhibits and a Discovery Hall with a replica of a 19th-century home, where children can try on period costumes. A clever multimedia presentation, good for kids, offers a brief history of Québec.

10

**OFF THE
BEATEN
PATH**

Québec–Lévis Ferry. En route to the opposite shore of the St. Lawrence River on this ferry, you get a striking view of the Québec City skyline, with the Château Frontenac and the Québec Seminary high atop the cliff. The view is even more impressive at night. Ferries generally run every 20 or 30 minutes from 7 am until 7 pm, and then every hour until 2:20 am; there are additional ferries from April through November. From late June to August you can combine a Québec–Lévis ferry ride with a bus tour of Lévis, getting off at such sights as the star-shaped Fort No. 1, one of three built by the British between 1865 and 1872 to defend Québec. ⊠ *10 rue des Traversiers, 1 block south of pl. de Paris, Lower Town* ☎ *418/643–8420, 877/787–7483* ⊕ *www.traversiers.gouv. qc.ca* ☞ *C$3.10.*

Rue du Petit-Champlain. The oldest street in the city was once the main street of a harbor village, with trading posts and the homes of rich merchants. Today it has pleasant boutiques and cafés, although on summer days the street is packed with tourists. Natural-fiber weaving, Inuit carvings, hand-painted silks, and enameled copper crafts are among local specialties for sale here. ⊠ *Lower Town* ⊕ *www. quartierpetitchamplain.com.*

QUICK
BITES

Bistrot Le Pape-Georges. For a respite from the shoppers on rue du Petit-Champlain, take a table outdoors at Bistrot Le Pape-Georges and cool off with a drink and creamy, tangy local cheeses and fruit. This stone-and-wood wine bar is also nice indoors; there's music on Thursday, Friday, and Saturday night. ⊠ *8 rue du Cul-de-Sac, Lower Town* ☎ *418/692–1320* ⊕ *www.papegeorges.com.*

Pizza Mag. For pizza lovers craving originality in their next slice, Pizza Mag, on rue St-Paul across from the train station, specializes in inventive (and fancy) toppings: Dijon mustard with tomatoes and onions; thinly sliced smoked meat with green peppers and pepperoni; duck with ginger and spinach. Seating is limited, especially on the outdoor terrace during summer. ⊠ *363, rue Saint-Paul, Lower Town* ☎ *418/692–1910* ⊕ *www.quebec.pizzamag.com.*

WORTH NOTING

Antiques district. Antiques shops cluster around rues St-Pierre and St-Paul, the latter once part of a business district packed with warehouses, stores, and businesses. After World War I, shipping and commercial activities plummeted and low rents attracted antiques dealers. Today their shops, together with numerous cafés, restaurants, boutique hotels, and art galleries, have made this one of the town's more fashionable areas. ⊠ *Lower Town.*

Boutique Metiers des Arts du Québec. Upon the sudden death of the legendary glassblower Jean Vallières, this location, formerly a workshop and museum known as Verriere La Mailloche under his watchful eye, was taken over by a nonprofit association dedicated to preserving Québec-made glass and the practice of the artform itself. Recognized worldwide by connoisseurs of glass art, the boutique carefully packages and ships collectibles anywhere. ⊠ *58 rue Sous-le-Fort, Lower Town* ☎ *418/694–3000* ⊕ *www.metiers-d-art.qc.ca* ☺ *Daily 10–5.*

Place de Paris. A much discussed (and sometimes ridiculed) black-and-white geometric sculpture, *Dialogue avec l'Histoire* (Dialogue with History) dominates this square. A 1987 gift from France, the sculpture is on the site where the first French settlers of Québec landed. ⊠ *rue Dalhousie, Lower Town.*

BEYOND THE WALLS

Venture outside the walls for a glimpse of the real Québec City. Bohemians frequent the St-Jean-Baptiste quarter, known for hipster hideouts and trendy shops. Grande-Allée and avenue Cartier buzz with clubs and bars inside Queen Anne–style mansions. Cafés, galleries, and good eateries are popping up regularly in St-Roch, the city's urban core. If you do have a car, it's a beautiful drive on boulevard Champlain, which runs from Lower Town all around the southern edge of Québec City, following the St. Lawrence River. Above are the cliffs that lead to the Plains of Abraham, and farther on you'll see the Sillery Coves. Any one of the steep hills will take you back toward the main roads that run east–west or the highways that cross north–south: Duplessis, the farthest west; Henri IV; Du Vallon; and Dufferin-Montmorency.

GETTING HERE AND AROUND

It's a 15-minute walk from the Old City to avenue Cartier, but the bus system is excellent here and easy to use. There are many bus stops throughout Upper Town, and a number of lines run up and down the Grande Allée—so many in fact that if you're waiting on rue St-Louis, which turns into the Grande Allée just outside the city walls, you can pretty much hop on whichever bus comes by. If you do choose to walk, take a detour to avenue Laurier or avenue Georges VI for a tour through leafy green streets with gorgeous homes.

St-Roch, on the other hand, is less convenient by bus and from the Old City. Plan to catch cabs, which aren't hard to find, to take you there and back.

TIMING

There's no need to dedicate more than half a day (at most) to see the area around Grande Allée or the St-Roch neighborhood. Both are great destinations for lunch, an afternoon browsing in the shops, or an evening out at a restaurant or bar.

EXPLORING

TOP ATTRACTIONS

★ **Avenue Cartier.** A mix of reasonably priced restaurants and bars, groceries and specialty food shops, hair salons, and stores, Cartier is a favorite lunchtime and after-work stop for many downtown office workers.

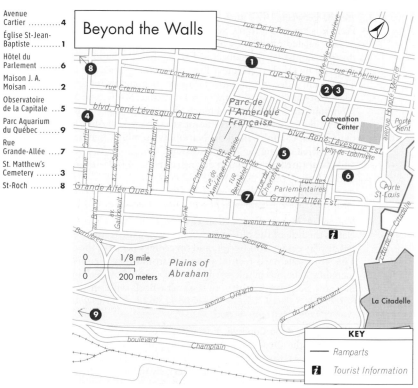

Beyond the Walls

After business hours the street hums with locals running errands or soaking up the sun on patios. When darkness falls, the avenue's patrons get noticeably younger. The attraction? A half dozen nightclubs and pubs that offer everything from cigars and quiet conversation to Latin music and earsplitting dance tunes. ⊠ *Montcalm.*

★ **Église St-Jean-Baptiste** (*St. John the Baptist Church*). Architect Joseph-Ferdinand Peachy's crowning glory in the "Second Empire" style, this church was inspired by the facade of the Église de la Trinité in Paris and rivals the Our Lady of Québec Basilica in beauty and size. The first church on the site, built in 1847, burned in the 1881 fire that destroyed much of the neighborhood. Seven varieties of Italian marble were used in the soaring columns, statues, and pulpit of the present church, which dates from 1884. Its 36 stained-glass windows consist of 30 sections each, and the organ, like the church, is classified as a historic monument. From October to the beginning of June and outside regular opening hours, knock at the **presbytery** at 490 rue St-Jean to see the church. ⊠ *400 rue St-Jean, St-Jean-Baptiste* ☎ *418/688–0350* ⊘ *June 23–Labor Day, weekdays noon–5, Sun. 9–4.*

★ **Hôtel du Parlement.** The only French-speaking legislature in continental North America, the 125-member Assemblée Nationale du Québec meets behind the stately walls of this Second Empire-style building erected between 1877 and 1886. If the Assemblée is sitting (and your French is up to scratch), see if you can get into the visitors gallery to hear heated exchanges between the federalist-leaning Liberals and the secessionist Parti Québecois. Failing that, the buildings themselves, designed by Québec architect Eugène-Étienne Taché, are worth a visit. The facade is decorated with statues of such important figures of Québec history as Cartier, Champlain, Frontenac, Wolfe, and Montcalm. A 30-minute tour (in English, French, or Spanish) takes in the President's Gallery, the Parlementaire restaurant (try the wild caribou), the Legislative Council Chamber, and the National Assembly Chamber. Tours may be restricted during legislative sessions. Outdoor tours of the gardens and statues are also available during summer. ☒ *1045 rue des Parlementaires, Upper Town* ☎ *418/643–7239, 866/337–8837* ⊕ *www.assnat. qc.ca* ☜ *Free* ☉ *Guided tours late June–early Sept. weekdays 9–4:15, weekends 10–4:30; early Sept.–late June, weekdays 9–4:15.*

★ **Maison J. A. Moisan.** Founded in 1871 by Jean-Alfred Moisan, this store claims the title of the oldest grocery store in North America. The original display cases, woodwork, and tin ceilings preserve the old-time feel. The store sells hard-to-find products from other regions of Québec, including delicious maple-syrup ale. The original owner's upstairs home has now been turned into a classic era B&B with all the trimmings. ☒ *699 rue St-Jean, Upper Town* ☎ *418/522–0685* ⊕ *www.jamoisan. com* ☉ *Daily 8:30 am–9 pm.*

Observatoire de la Capitale. For a bird's-eye view from 31 stories up, check out the Observatoire de la Capitale. Located atop the Edifice Marie-Guyart, the observation gallery offers a spectacular panorama of Québec City. The site features an overview of the city's history with 3-D imagery, audio-visual displays in both French and English, and a time-travel theme with a 1960s twist. ☒ *1037 rue de la Chevrotière, Upper Town* ☎ *418/644–9841* ⊕ *www.observatoirecapitale.org* ☜ *C$10* ☉ *Feb.–mid-Oct., daily 10–5; mid-Oct–late Jan., Tues.–Sun. 10–5.*

QUICK BITES

Halles du Petit-Cartier. This small but busy food and shopping mall on avenue Cartier has restaurants and shops that sell jewelry, fish, flowers, cheeses, pastries, breads, vegetables, fresh coffee, and candies. You'll find some excellent local cheeses, as well as a few Italian and other European specialties—there's no fast food here. If you're looking for picnic snacks for a day trip to the Plains of Abraham, plan to fill your basket here and then head up to the park. ☒ *1191 av. Cartier, Montcalm* ☎ *418/688–1635* ⊕ *www.hallesdupetitquartier.com.*

Rue Grande-Allée. One of the city's oldest streets, rue Grande Allée was the route people took from outlying areas to sell their furs in town. In the 19th century the wealthy built neo-Gothic and Queen Anne–style mansions here; they now house trendy cafés, clubs, and restaurants. The street actually has four names: inside the city walls it's rue St-Louis; outside the walls, Grande Allée Est; farther west, Grande Allée Ouest; then finally, boulevard Laurier. ☒ *Upper Town.*

St-Roch. Hip bars and trendy shops pepper St-Roch, a former industrial area-turned-technology hub. There's a fair selection of hotels, most of them catering to business clientele, and new ones pop up constantly. The "main drag" of the neighborhood is boulevard Charest—a mix of office buildings, lunch spots, and hangouts for the after-work crowd. Parc St-Roch, a large square on this street provides good people-watching opportunities and occasionally, street performances and art events.

Look for Église St-Roch, a massive stone church and you'll quickly find St-Joseph, the district's other major street, known for trendy shops and entertaining buskers. Shop for new duds here and follow it all by dining in one of the neighborhood's sleek new bistros. Food reigns in Québec, so dinner reservations are always recommended, but the popularity of the area has spawned many new eateries, so you'll have plenty of choices. When it comes time for an after-dinner drink, there's a plethora of pubs and terraces for a real taste of St-Roch life. Korrigane Brasserie Artisanale is a great example.

Art abounds in the neighborhood, from the famed graffiti viaduct to modern sculptures to outdoor theater and circus acts. Complexe Méduse on rue de St-Vallier is an avant-garde arts cooperative that houses multimedia artists, a community radio station, galleries, artists-in-residence, and performance spaces.

It's a long, but downhill jaunt from the Old City and walkable if you have the time. If you're not in the mood for exercise, the best way to reach this neighborhood is by cab. Plan to spend about C$8 each way. There are usually plenty of cabs available for the reverse trip. Taking the bus is also an option, but not a convenient one, as it likely involves a transfer. ⊠ *St-Roch.*

St. Matthew's Cemetery. The burial place of many of the earliest English settlers in Canada was established in 1771, and is the oldest cemetery remaining in Québec City. Also buried here is Robert Wood, the disavowed half-brother of Queen Victoria. Closed in 1860, the cemetery has been turned into a park. Next door is **St. Matthew's Anglican Church,** now a public library. It has a book listing most of the original tombstone inscriptions, including those on tombstones removed to make way for the city's modern convention center. ⊠ *755 rue St-Jean, Upper Town.*

10

WORTH NOTING

Ⓒ **Parc Aquarium du Québec.** Breakfast with the walruses, lunch (carefully) with the polar bears, and spend the afternoon watching the seals do their tricks. When you tire of the mammals, check out the thousands of species of fresh- and saltwater fish in the aquarium's massive, three-level aquatic gallery, or have some hands-on experiences with mollusks, starfish, and stingrays. Don't miss the jellyfish ballet or seahorse tanks in the new pavilion. It is the only aquarium in North America with examples of all five species of cold-water seals. The aquarium is on a cliff top overlooking the St. Lawrence and Québec City's two main bridges. ⊠ *1675 av. des Hôtels, Ste-Foy* ☎ *866/659–5264, 418/659–5264* ⊕ *www.aquariumduquebec.com* ⊠ *C$16.50* ☉ *June–Labor Day, daily 10–5; early Sept.–May, daily 10–4.*

WHERE TO EAT

A sea of bistros, sidewalk cafés, and chic, cutting-edge restaurants comprise the dining scene in Québec City. "Grab and go" is non-existent—be prepared to eat at a leisurely pace; dinner will usually take a few hours. Sample local fare—sip ice cider, indulge in *poutine*, and dive into sweet maple sugar pie. With cuisine ranging from traditional French dishes like foie gras and escargot to distinctly French-Canadian specialties such as *tourtière* (meat pie), Québec's thriving culinary community attracts tourists from around the globe.

With so many options, choosing where to go can be difficult. Many establishments post their *menu du jour* outside, so you can stroll along and let your cravings guide the way. However, bear in mind that reservations are a must at most restaurants during holidays, Winter Carnival, and in the summer months when the coveted outdoor terraces open. When ordering, remember that in the Francophone province, an *entrée* is an appetizer and the *plat principal* is the main course. Plan to tip at least 15% of the bill.

UPPER TOWN

$$$$
CANADIAN
✗**Aux Anciens Canadiens.** This establishment is named for a 19th-century book by Philippe-Aubert de Gaspé, who once resided here. The house, dating from 1675, has servers in period costume and five dining rooms with different themes. For example, the *vaisselier* (dish room) is bright and cheerful, with colorful antique dishes and a fireplace. People come for the authentic French-Canadian cooking; hearty specialties include sliced duck breast with a maple sauce, Lac St-Jean meat pie, and maple-syrup pie with fresh cream. One of the best deals is a three-course meal for C$18.95, available until 5:45 everyday. ⑤ *Average main: C$39* ✉ *34 rue St-Louis, Upper Town* ☎ *418/692–1627* ⊕ *www. auxancienscanadiens.qc.ca* ⌾ *Reservations essential* ⊙ *Closed for lunch weekdays in the fall and spring* ✛ *F3.*

$
CAFÉ
Fodor's Choice
★
✗**Café-Boulangerie Paillard.** Owned by Yves Simard and his partner Rebecca, this Certified Organic bakery, pastry counter, sandwich bar, pizza shop (summer only), and ice-cream parlor is known for its selection of nouvelle French pastries, whole-grain breads, gourmet sandwiches, and artisan gelato. Long wooden tables, designed to get customers talking to each other, create a convivial atmosphere. There might be a line while the locals buy their lunch, but it's well worth the wait. ⑤ *Average main: C$9* ✉ *1097 rue St-Jean, Upper Town* ☎ *418/692–1221* ⊕ *www. paillard.ca* ✛ *E2.*

$
CAFÉ
✗**Casse-Crêpe Breton.** Crepes in generous proportions are served in this busy café-style restaurant. From a menu of more than 20 fillings, pick your own chocolate or fruit combinations; design a larger meal with cheese, ham, and vegetables; or sip a bowl of Viennese coffee topped with whipped cream. Tables surround four round griddles at which you watch your creations being made. Crepes made with two to five fillings cost less than C$12. This place is popular with tourists and locals alike, and there can be lines to get in at peak hours and seasons. ⑤ *Average main: C$7* ✉ *1136 rue St-Jean, Upper Town*

BEST BETS FOR QUÉBEC CITY DINING

Fodor's Choice ★

Café-Boulangerie Paillard, p. 262

Joe Smoked Meat, p. 268

Laurie Raphaël Restaurant-Atelier-Boutique, p. 266

Le Café du Clocher Penché, p. 270

L'Initiale, p. 267

Panache, p. 267

Best By Price

$

Café-Boulangerie Paillard, p. 262

Casse-Crêpe Breton, p. 262

Chez Cora, p. 268

Chez Temporel, p. 263

Joe Smoked Meat, p. 268

Le Café Krieghoff, p. 270

Le Commensal, p. 270

$$

Chez Victor, p. 264

Le Cochon Dingue, p. 267

Le Parlementaire, p. 271

Le Petite Boîte Vietnamienne, p. 268

Simple Snack Sympathique, p. 268

$$$

Le Café du Clocher Penché, p. 270

Le Hobbit Bistro, p. 264

L'entrecôte Saint-Jean, p. 264

Louis Hébert, p. 271

Panache, p. 267

Restaurant Toast!, p. 268

$$$$

Chez Boulay Bistro Boréal, p. 263

Laurie Raphaël Restaurant-Atelier-Boutique, p. 266

Le Patriarche, p. 265

L'Initiale, p. 267

☎ 418/692–0438 ⊕ www.cassecrepebreton.com ⌂ Reservations not accepted ♦ E2.

$$$$ ✕ **Chez Boulay Bistro Boréal.** For something new in Old Québec, look no
SCANDINAVIAN further than Chez Boulay. Chefs Jean-Luc Boulay and Arnaud March-and, who are both revered in this town, delight patrons with elegant interpretations of Nordic cuisine inspired by the Boreal forest. A mix of locals celebrating special occasions and tourists fresh from shopping rue St-Jean dine on bison tartare, braised beef ravioli with candied red cabbage, and salmon in a flavorful cranberry glaze. Classic desserts have been reinvented in Nordic fashion: iced nougat with cloudberries is just one example. The somber color scheme, rustic-meets-modern graphics, and dark wood trim make this one of the more sophisticated bistros in the neighborhood. ⑤ Average main: C$35 ✉ 1110 rue St-Jean, Upper Town ☎ 418/380–8166 ⊕ www.chezboulay.com ⌂ Reservations essential ♦ E2.

$ ✕ **Chez Temporel.** At this small, bustling café, city dwellers of all sorts—
CAFÉ struggling writers, musicians, street-smart bohemians, bureaucrats, businessmen, and busy moms and dads—enjoy Wi-Fi and the city's best coffee, *croque monsieurs* (open-face French-bread sandwiches with ham, tomato, and broiled cheese), gazpacho, chili, tuna sandwiches, and soups. Good, modestly priced beer and wine are also served. Some patrons start their day here with croissants and coffee at 8 am and are back when the place closes at 10 pm. ⑤ Average main: C$6 ✉ 25 rue Couillard, Upper Town ☎ 418/694–1813 ⌂ Reservations not accepted ♦ F1.

10

$$ ✕ **Chez Victor.** It's no ordinary burger joint: this cozy café with brick-and-
MODERN   stone walls attracts an artsy crowd to rue St-Jean. Lettuce, tomatoes,
AMERICAN   onions, mushrooms, pickles, hot mustard, mayonnaise, and a choice
of cheeses (mozzarella, Swiss, blue, goat, and cream) top the hearty
burgers. French fries are served with a dollop of homemade mayon-
naise (there are five varieties to choose from) and poppy seeds. Sal-
ads, sandwiches, and a daily dessert made fresh by the pastry chef are
also available. ⑤ *Average main: C$14* ✉ *145 rue St-Jean, Upper Town*
☎ *418/529–7702* ⊕ *www.chezvictorburger.com* ✛ *A4.*

$ ✕ **Le Chic Shack.** A refreshing alternative to the Old City's ubiquitous
FAST FOOD   white-linen bistro, Le Chic Shack proves that fast food can be high
☺   quality. Burgers made from grass-fed cattle served on soft brioche from
an artisan baker make this a prime locale for lunch goers. With long
tables, red accents, and paper-towel rolls in place of napkin holders,
the interior has a touch of retro without feeling folksy or forced. Save
room for dessert, which includes heavenly dark-chocolate or salted-
caramel-maple milkshakes, chocolate ganache, or peanut-butter ice-
cream sandwiches. ⑤ *Average main: C$10* ✉ *15 rue du Fort, Upper
Town* ☎ *418/692–1485* ⊕ *www.chicshack.ca* ✛ *G2.*

$$$$ ✕ **Le Continental.** If Québec City had a dining hall of fame, Le Conti-
EUROPEAN   nental would be there among the best. Since 1956 this historic spot,
steps from the Château Frontenac, has been serving very good tradi-
tional dishes. Under the new ownership, the classic house specialties
continue to include orange duckling and filet mignon, flambéed right
at your table. Try the appetizer with foie gras, sweetbreads, scampi,
and snow crab delicately served on a square glass plate. A staple for
this place is the tender, velvety filet mignon "en boîte," flambéed in a
cognac sauce and then luxuriously covered in a gravy seasoned with
mustard and sage. ⑤ *Average main: C$60* ✉ *26 rue St-Louis, Upper
Town* ☎ *418/694–9995* ⊕ *www.restaurantlecontinental.com* ✛ *F2.*

$$$ ✕ **L'Entrecôte Saint-Jean.** *Steak frites* (steak with fries) is on menus every-
FRENCH   where in Québec City, but this lively establishment has a 30-year reputa-
tion as the master of the dish—*l'entrecôte* refers to a particular sirloin
cut, usually long and relatively thin. At this restaurant, it's all about
the sauce. Guests choose between three steak sizes, and each comes
smothered in the restaurant's signature peppery sauce with a heaping
pile of crispy fries. Other French fare graces the menu, such as tender
duck confit and smoked salmon salads. For C$25 and up, depending on
the size of the steak, the table d'hôte presents a good value. It ends with
decadent chocolate profiteroles, proving that this restaurant is more
than just l'entrecôte. This red-and-blue-trimmed house becomes packed
on weekends and it's wise to call ahead. ⑤ *Average main: C$25* ✉ *1080
rue St-Jean, Upper Town* ☎ *418/694–0234* ⊕ *www.entrecotesaintjean.
com* ☽ *Closed Sat. and Sun. lunch, Sept.–May* ✛ *E2.*

$$$ ✕ **Le Hobbit Bistro.** Inspired by Tolkien's famous creation, Le Hobbit Bis-
BISTRO   tro strives to one day become a legend, and a constant stream of well-
dressed patrons indicates that it's on its way. Tucked into a converted
house that was built in 1846, this little restaurant serves fresh, colorful
salads, juicy burgers, and delectable tartare. Highlights include duck
confit with a cranberry and orange compote or apple-and-beet salad

in a light vinaigrette. Order à la carte or from three different table d'hôte options, aptly named Hunger, Greed, and Decadence. Breakfast is just as good as dinner with tasty egg sandwiches and flaky croissants. Black-and-white prints of St-Jean-Baptiste create a true neighborhood-bistro vibe. $ *Average main: C$25* ✉ *700 rue St-Jean, St-Jean-Baptiste* ☎ *418/647–2677* ⊕ *www.hobbitbistro.com* ✍ *Reservations essential* ✛ *C3.*

$$$$
MODERN
CANADIAN

✕ **Le Patriarche.** A hit with foodies and wine connoisseurs, Le Patriarche serves its entire menu in triplicate. Chef Stephen Roth likes to play with food; he takes one ingredient and presents it in three very different styles, leading guests on an adventure in texture and taste. From the "symphony of foie gras," to Québec lamb and caribou, each morsel strives for perfection. Set in a converted 1827 house, the spacious upstairs dining room, intimate main level with comfy chairs and windowside tables, and wine cellar with over 200 bottles create an ambience that's romantic and contemporary without feeling forced. Save room because dessert is even sweeter when served as a trio. Guests can create their own five-course table d'hôte by adding C$28 to their main course selection. $ *Average main: C$40* ✉ *17 rue Saint-Stanislas, Upper Town* ☎ *418/692–5488* ⊕ *www.lepatriarche. com* ✍ *Reservations essential* ◯ *Closed Mon., except in July and Aug. Lunch by appointment only.* ✛ *E2*

$$$$
FRENCH

✕ **Le Saint-Amour.** Chef Jean-Luc Boulay entices diners with such creations as red-deer steak grilled with a wild-berry and peppercorn sauce, and filet mignon with port wine and local blue cheese at one of the city's most romantic restaurants. Sir Paul McCartney and Sting have been among Le Saint-Amour's patrons. Foie gras is the in-house signature delicacy. Sauces are generally light, with no flour or butter. Desserts are inspired; try the tasting plate of seven different kinds of Valrhona chocolate, served with a glass of vanilla-infused milk. The C$125 discovery menu has nine courses; the C$63 table d'hôte has five. More than 1,000 wines are available. $ *Average main: C$65* ✉ *48 rue Ste-Ursule, Upper Town* ☎ *418/694–0667* ⊕ *www.saint-amour.com* ✍ *Reservations essential* ◯ *No lunch weekends* ✛ *E3*

$$
BISTRO

✕ **Les Frères de la Côte.** With its central location, Mediterranean influence, and reasonable prices, this busy bistro is a favorite among politicians and the journalists who cover them. Attached to the Hôtel du Vieux-Québec, the outside tables are alive with bilingual chitchat. The menu, inspired by the south of France, changes constantly, but osso buco and a tender leg of lamb are among the regular choices. If you sit near the back, you can watch the chefs at work. This kitchen is often among those open latest. $ *Average main: C$18* ✉ *1190 rue St-Jean, Upper Town* ☎ *418/692–5445* ✛ *E1.*

$$$
ITALIAN

✕ **Portofino Bistro Italiano.** By joining two 18th-century houses, owners Francois Petit and Yves Moreau helm an Italian restaurant with a bistro flavor. The room is distinctive: burnt-sienna walls, a wood pizza oven set behind a semicircular bar, and caramel tablecloths and chairs. Don't miss the thin-crust pizza and its accompaniment of oils flavored with pepper and oregano. Chef Moreau's *pennini all'arrabbiata*—tubular pasta with a spicy tomato sauce—is also good. Save room for the

10

QUÉBEC CITY CRÊPES

Crepes—those delectable, paper-thin pancakes made of flour, eggs, and milk or cream—can be found on menus everywhere. But in Québec City you can order a crepe in French and know that what you're holding has been part of French gastronomy for centuries.

You'll want to plan your crepe tour carefully. These little folded-up packages of sweet or savory goodness are quite rich, and so it's not advisable to mix crepes in the same meal.

Chez Cora. Your first crepe of the day can be from the commercial but still yummy Chez Cora, which stays open from 6 am until 3 pm, so sleep in late or stay up late and make it a great brunch no matter which. ⊠ *545 rue du Parvis, St-Roch* ☎ *418/524-3232* ⊕ *www.chezcora.com.*

Casse-Crêpe Breton. Later in the day, you'll be ready for a salad and a decadent fruit- or ice-cream-filled crepe for dessert at Casse-Crêpe Breton. Expect to wait in line—even the locals do! ⊠ *1136 rue St-Jean, Upper Town* ☎ *418/692-0438.*

Le Billig. Continue your tour beyond the walls, where you'll find Le Billig, a crêperie that specializes in authentic buckwheat-flour crepes. Duck confit with onion marmalade or salted caramel with sweet Chantilly cream are two of the most popular options, but you also can't go wrong with simple ham and cheese. ⊠ *526 rue St-Jean, St-Jean-Baptiste* ☎ *418/524-8341.*

Take a deep breath—but not too deep—as you reminisce about all the wonderful crepes you encountered today.

homemade tiramisu. The kitchen closes at 11:30, and a musician performs nightly from 8 to 10:30. ⑤ *Average main: C$22* ⊠ *54 rue Couillard, Upper Town* ☎ *418/692-8888* ⊕ *www.portofino.qc.ca* ✤ *F1.*

LOWER TOWN

$$$$
FRENCH
Fodor's Choice
★
✕ **Laurie Raphaël Restaurant-Atelier-Boutique.** Local and regional products are at the heart of fine cuisine here. Among Chef Daniel Vézina's creations are crystallized foie gras with truffle snow, and venison tartare. There's a C$100 eight-course menu dégustation, and for another C$60 you'll get a glass of wine with each course, chosen to perfectly complement each dish. If you're seeking adventure, opt for the Chef Chef menu—for C$60 a surprise meal will be delivered to your table. Lunch is C$29. If that's not enough, sign up for a private cooking class. Don't miss the exclusive food and product lines available at the Laurie Raphaël boutique. ⑤ *Average main: C$60* ⊠ *117 rue Dalhousie, Lower Town* ☎ *418/692-4555* ⊕ *www.laurieraphael.com* ⊘ *Closed Sun., Mon., and Jan. 1–15* ✤ *G1.*

$$$
CAFÉ
✕ **Le Café du Monde.** Next to the cruise terminal in the Old Port, this massive restaurant has a spectacular view to equal its food. The outdoor terrace in front overlooks the St. Lawrence River, while the side *verrière* (glass atrium) looks onto l'Agora amphitheater and the old stone Customs House. Etched-glass dividers, wicker chairs, and palm trees set the scene for the Parisian-bistro-style menu, which includes such

classics as steak frites, rotisserie chicken, calamari, and duck liver pâté with raisin jam. ⑤ *Average main: C$30* ✉ *84 rue Dalhousie, Suite 140, Lower Town* ☎ *418/692–4455* ⊕ *www.lecafedumonde.com* ⚓ *Reservations essential* ✛ *H1.*

$$ ✕**Le Cochon Dingue.** The café fare at this cheerful chain, whose name
CAFÉ translates into the Crazy Pig, includes delicious mussels, steak with fries, thick soups, and apple pie with vanilla cream. At the boulevard Champlain restaurant location, sidewalk tables and indoor dining rooms artfully blend the chic and the antique; black-and-white checkerboard floors contrast with ancient stone walls. The best-kept secret in Québec City is the full breakfast served here all week. Meanwhile, a few doors away, you'll find their fresh pastry, sandwich, and pizza shop: Le Petit Cochon Dingue. ⑤ *Average main: C$14* ✉ *46 boul. Champlain, Lower Town* ☎ *418/692–2013* ⊕ *www.cochondingue.com* ✛ *G3.*

$$$ ✕**L'Echaudé.** A mix of businesspeople and tourists frequent L'Echaudé
FRENCH because of its location between the financial and antiques districts. The mahogany lobby and green-and-beige interior creates a warm atmosphere, as does the open kitchen. For lunch, try duck confit with fries and fresh salad. Every day there's a meat dish, a fish plate, a steak, and pasta on the menu. Highlights of the three-course brunch are eggs Benedict and tantalizing desserts. The interior is modern, with hardwood floors, a mirrored wall, and a stainless-steel bar with back-lighted river stones underneath. ⑤ *Average main: C$25* ✉ *73 rue Sault-au-Matelot, Lower Town* ☎ *418/692–1299* ⊕ *www.echaude.com* ✛ *G1.*

$$$$ ✕**L'Initiale.** A contemporary setting and gracious service place L'Initiale
FRENCH in the upper echelon of restaurants in this city; it's a member of the
Fodor's Choice Relais & Châteaux group. Widely spaced tables favor intimate dining,
★ and the warm brown-and-cream interior is cozy. But don't rush to your table. Begin your night in the lounge, where you can peruse the menu at your leisure. Chef Yvan Lebrun roasts many of the meats over a spit: this produces a unique taste, particularly with lamb. The constantly changing menu follows the whims of the chef and the season. Try the foie gras or the lamb. There's also a C$129 eight-course menu dégustation. For dessert, many small treats are arranged attractively on a single plate. After dinner, return to the lounge for your coffee. ⑤ *Average main: C$65* ✉ *54 rue St-Pierre, Lower Town* ☎ *418/694–1818* ⊕ *www. restaurantinitiale.com* ⊙ *Closed Sun., Mon., and early Jan.* ✛ *G2*

$$$ ✕**Panache.** This restaurant, nestled in the museum-like Auberge Saint-
CANADIAN Antoine, has enchanting wooden floors and exposed beams from the
Fodor's Choice building's warehouse days. Chef Jean-Francois Bédard has taken tradi-
★ tional French-Canadian cuisine and tweaked it for the modern palate. The menus change with the seasons, but you'll find candied duck legs or maple-glazed breast of duck any day. A family-owned farm supplies ingredients for the restaurant's recipes. For a true feast, your table can order the Signature Menu, a six-course meal for C$105 per person with a classic wine pairing for an additional C$95. Québec and other Canadian wines top their list, starting at C$50 a bottle, but they also carry some exclusive imports from Australia, France, and Italy. ⑤ *Average main: C$30* ✉ *10 rue St-Antoine, Lower Town* ☎ *418/692–1022* ⊕ *www.saint-antoine.com* ✛ *G2.*

10

$$$ ✕**Restaurant Toast!** This very chic, very intimate restaurant in Le Priori
MODERN   hotel is the talk of the town. Under mod light fixtures set against stone-
CANADIAN   and-brick walls, dine on grilled octopus, rabbit stuffed with blood sau-
sage, or smoked salmon risotto. Most of the tasty dishes are served
as appetizers for C$15, so mix and match or share to make a full
meal. A secret garden terrace removes all street noise out back, perfect
for meeting friends for cocktails or relaxing. $ *Average main: C$30*
✉ *17 rue Sault-au-Matelot, Lower Town* ☎ *418/692–1334* ⊕ *www.
restauranttoast.com* ⚱ *Reservations essential* ✢ *G2.*

$$ ✕**Simple Snack Sympathique** (*SSS*). Throngs of professionals and young
ECLECTIC   urbanites pack restaurant Simple Snack Sympathique (SSS) to dine on
artfully prepared dishes, from angel hair pasta with succulent duck
confit to tender ribs served alongside crispy fries. Owned by Stéphane
D'Anjou and Christian Lemelin, proprietors of Restaurant Toast!, this
chic establishment is quickly becoming the place to be on Saturday night.
Two distinct dining areas let patrons choose between sass and sophistication; one features high tables, "mouthy" wallpaper, and techno
music. Just through the curtain is a more relaxed space with a flicker-
ing fireplace and exposed brick wall. Come for lunch (weekdays only),
or stop by for late-night grub—SSS is one of the few restaurants open
daily until midnight, and they have a special snack menu for night-owls.
$ *Average main: C$20* ✉ *71 rue St-Paul, Lower Town* ☎ *418/692–1991*
⊕ *www.restaurantsss.com* ☯ *No lunch weekends* ✢ *G1.*

OUTSIDE THE WALLS

$ ✕**Chez Cora.** Spectacular breakfasts with mounds of fresh fruit are the
ECLECTIC   specialty at this sunny chain restaurant. Whimsy is everywhere, from
☺   the plastic chicken decorations to the inventive dishes, often named after
customers and family members who inspired them. Try the Eggs Ben et
Dictine, which has smoked salmon, or the Gargantua—two eggs, sausage, ham, fruit, pancakes, *cretons* (pâtés), and baked beans. Kids love
the Banana Surprise, a banana wrapped in a pancake with chocolate
or peanut butter and honey. The restaurant also serves light lunch fare,
such as salmon bagels, salads, and club sandwiches. $ *Average main:*
C$9 ✉ *545 rue du Parvis, St-Roch* ☎ *418/524–3232* ⊕ *www.chezcora.
com* ☯ *No dinner* ✢ *B2.*

$ ✕**Joe Smoked Meat.** There are plenty of smoked meat places in Québec,
DELI   but Joe Smoked Meat manages to impress—and that's saying something
Fodor's Choice   in a city of aficionados. They pile it high here and serve it with a side of
★   chips, coleslaw, and a pickle. Frequented by lunching locals and families seeking a budget-friendly meal, the restaurant is on a quiet street
behind a cluster of offices in St-Roch. The bright, casual interior seems
slightly out of place in this trendy neighborhood, but the fast, friendly
service makes patrons feel right at home. In addition to the smoked
meat sandwiches, salads and spaghetti are also on the menu. $ *Average*
main: C$12 ✉ *275 rue St-Vallier Est, St-Roch* ☎ *418/523–4545* ⊕ *www.
joesmokedmeat.com* ☯ *Closed Sun.* ✢ *A2*

$$ ✕**La Petite Boîte Vietnamienne.** Red walls, dark furnishings, and flick-
VIETNAMESE   ering tea lights make this little hideaway a favorite for date night,
but the magic doesn't end with the romantic setting—the "Little

Vietnamese Box" is making big waves in the Québec culinary scene. Owner and chef Nhung Le swirls influences from both "here" and "home"—smoked salmon tucked in a spring roll; duck breast with Hanoi flavor; even a spicy Asian fondue. For traditionalists, it's one of the better places hereabouts to try *pho*—a hearty soup made with rice noodles and served with fresh basil, bean sprouts, and lime. Save room to sample Eastern-inspired desserts, such as fruit fritters with maple syrup or green tapioca pudding. $ *Average main: C$15* ✉ *281 rue de la Couronne, St-Roch* ☎ *418/204–6323* ⊕ *www.chefle.com* ⊘ *Closed Sun. and Mon.* ✛ *A1*

$$$
FRENCH
Fodor'sChoice
★

✘ **Le Café du Clocher Penché.** An amiable staff and inventive bistro cuisine (sans pretentious fluff) make this establishment a local favorite. The high ceilings and imposing vault-door give away the neighborhood's worst-kept secret: the building once was a bank. Grilled cheese sandwich raclettes and salmon tartare with grapefruit dressing grace the popular C$16 weekend brunch menu. During lunch, the restaurant is packed with suits and skirts who munch on well-prepared salads and pasta. Dinner draws the date-night crowd. The menu changes often but the ingredients are always fresh and from Québec. $ *Average main: C$22* ✉ *203 rue St-Joseph Est, St-Roch* ☎ *418/640–0597* ⊕ *www. clocherpenche.ca* ⊘ *Closed Sun. dinner, Mon.* ✛ *A2*

$$
BISTRO

✘ **Le Café Krieghoff.** Modeled after a typical Paris bistro and named for a Canadian painter who lived just up the street (and whose prints hang on the walls), this busy, noisy restaurant with patios in front and back is a popular place with the locals. Open every day from 7 am to midnight, Krieghoff serves specialties that include salmon, quiche, "la Toulouse" (big French sausage with sauerkraut), steak with french fries, *boudin* (pig-blood sausage), and "la Bavette" (a French-style minute steak). This place is a big local literary hangout, with great coffee, tea, and desserts. There's a seven-room auberge upstairs catering to upscale families. $ *Average main: C$15* ✉ *1089 rue Cartier, Upper Town* ☎ *418/522–3711* ⊕ *www.cafekrieghoff.qc.ca* ✛ *A6.*

$$$
MODERN
EUROPEAN

✘ **Le Cercle.** Frequented by the area's artsy types, this contemporary venue-cum–urban eatery—a unique hybrid of bar, restaurant, and theater—serves delectable tapas, lasagna, and short ribs. Movie clips are projected onto the walls and a garage door lets in city sounds, creating a lively setting, especially during summer. The tapas menu presents ample sharing opportunities with smoked mussels, marinated olives, and cured ham. If Italian fare appeals, try the dried-tomato gnocchi or the lasagna bolognaise. Even the simple grilled cheese tastes exceptional here. $ *Average main: C$22* ✉ *228 & 226 St-Joseph Est, St-Roch* ☎ *418/948–8648* ⊕ *www.le-cercle.ca* ⊘ *No lunch Sat.–Wed.; brunch weekends only* ✛ *A2.*

$
VEGETARIAN

✘ **Le Commensal.** At this upscale cafeteria you serve yourself from an outstanding informal vegetarian buffet and then grab a table in the vast dining room, where brick walls and decorative plants create an inviting setting. Plates are weighed to determine the price, but a maximum price policy pegs the top charge at C$12.95 for lunch and C$15.95 for dinner, not counting desserts, soups, or beverages. Hot and cold dishes, all health-conscious in some way, include stir-fry tofu and ratatouille with couscous, seitan, pizza, hazelnut cake, sugar pie, and fruitcake. $ *Average main: C$12* ✉ *860 rue St-Jean, St-Jean-Baptiste* ☎ *418/647–3733* ⊕ *www.commensal.com* ✛ *D3.*

$$ ✕ **Le Parlementaire.** Despite its magnificent beaux arts interior and its
MODERN reasonable prices, the National Assembly's restaurant remains one of
CANADIAN the best-kept secrets in town. Chef Réal Therrien prepares contemporary cuisine with products from Québec's various regions. In summer, for example, the three-course lunch menu includes everything from mini-fondues made with Charlevoix cheese to ravioli made from lobster caught in the Gaspé. Other dishes might include pork from the Beauce region, trout from the Magdalen Islands, and candied-duck salad. Opening hours vary, but it routinely serves lunch weekdays from 11:30–2. Depending on the time of year, the restaurant also opens for breakfast and occasionally, Sunday brunch. $ *Average main: C$17* ✉ *1045 rue des Parlementaires, Montcalm* ☎ *418/643–6640* ⊕ *www. assnat.qc.ca* ⊘ *Closed weekends July–Labor Day; closed Sat.–Mon., Labor Day–June. No dinner.* ✛ *D4*

$$$ ✕ **Louis Hébert.** With its fine French cuisine and convenient location in
FRENCH a 95-year-old home on the bustling Grande Allée, this restaurant has long been popular with many of Québec's top decision makers. Dining areas range from the very public summer terrace to discreet second-floor meeting rooms, a solarium with bamboo chairs, and a cozy dining room with exposed stone walls and warm wood accents. Chef Hervé Toussaint's dazzlers are, along with his rack of lamb, seafood dishes such as shelled lobster, as well as fresh pasta. With more than 5,000 bottles of wine on hand, nobody goes thirsty, and the owner checks in on diners in person. $ *Average main: C$30* ✉ *668 Grande Allée Est, Montcalm* ☎ *418/525–7812* ⊕ *www.louishebert.com* ⊘ *No lunch weekends Oct.–Apr.* ✛ *D4*

WHERE TO STAY

More than 35 hotels are within Québec City's walls, and there's also an abundance of family-run bed-and-breakfasts.

Landmark hotels are as prominent as the city's most historic sights, while modern high-rises outside the ramparts have spectacular views of the Old City. Another option is to immerse yourself in the city's historic charm by staying in an old-fashioned inn, where no two rooms are alike.

Be sure to make a reservation if you visit during peak season (May through September) or during the Winter Carnival, in January and/or February.

During especially busy times, hotel rates usually rise 30%. From November through April, many lodgings offer weekend discounts and other promotions.

For expanded hotel reviews, visit Fodors.com.

10

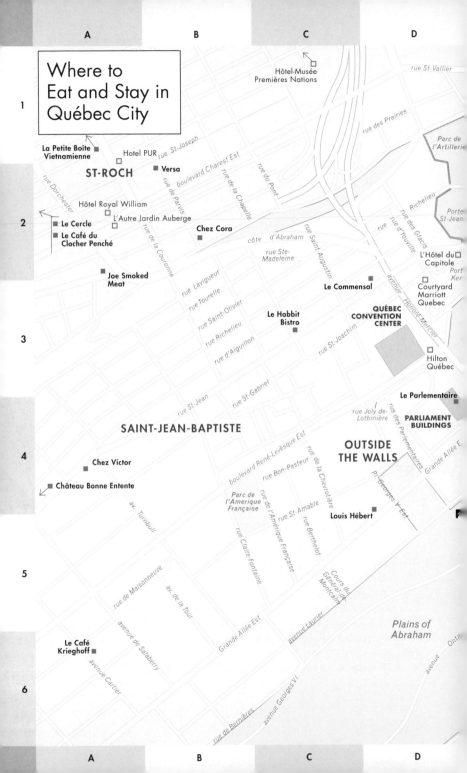

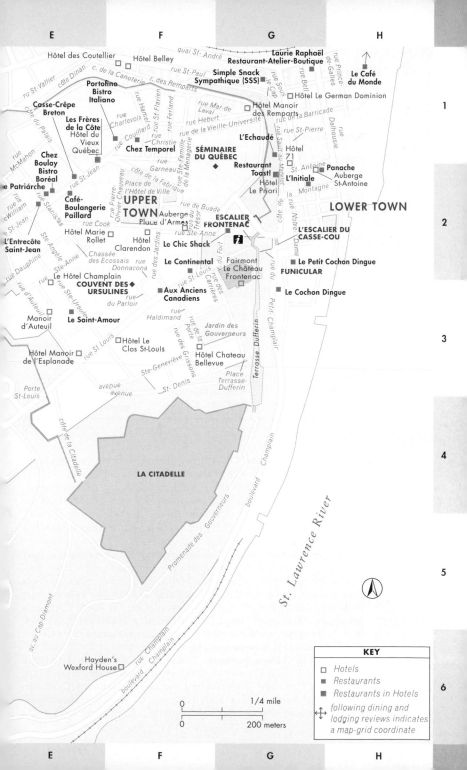

BEST BETS FOR QUÉBEC CITY LODGING

Fodor's Choice ★

Auberge St-Antoine, p. 276

Fairmont Le Château Frontenac, p. 274

Hôtel des Coutellier, p. 277

Hôtel du Vieux-Québec, p. 275

Hôtel Le Germain Dominion, p. 277

Best by Price

$

Hôtel Belley, p. 277

Hôtel Manoir de l'Esplanade, p. 276

Hôtel Manoir des Remparts, p. 276

L'Autre Jardin Auberge, p. 280

Manoir d'Auteuil, p. 276

$$

Hôtel Château Bellevue, p. 275

Hôtel du Vieux Québec, p. 275

Hôtel Le Priori, p. 277

Hôtel PUR, p. 280

Hôtel Royal William, p. 280

$$$

Hilton Québec, p. 275

Hôtel 71, p. 277

Hôtel des Coutellier, p. 277

Hôtel Le Germain Dominion, p. 277

$$$$

Auberge St-Antoine, p. 276

Fairmont Le Château Frontenac, p. 274

Best by Experience

BEST GRAND DAME HOTELS

Fairmont Le Château Frontenac, p. 274

BEST VIEWS

Fairmont Le Château Frontenac, p. 274

Hilton Québec, p. 275

Hôtel Le Germain Dominion, p. 277

UPPER TOWN

$$ ⚐**Auberge Place d'Armes.** Old Québec charm meets new world conve-
HOTEL nience at this property, which attracts a mix of couples and business
clientele. **Pros:** central location; historic building creates a romantic
atmosphere. **Cons:** no elevator means working off breakfast on the
stairs; no on-site parking. ⑤ *Rooms from: C$200* ✉ *24 rue St-Anne,
Upper Town* ☎ *418/694–9485* ⊕ *www.aubergeplacedarmes.com* ⟿ *21
rooms* ⓘⓞⓘ *Breakfast* ✛ *F2.*

$$ ⚐**Courtyard Marriott Québec.** This former bank building exudes a quiet
HOTEL elegance, with stained-glass windows, two fireplaces, and a tiny wood-
lined corner bar in the lobby. **Pros:** French gastronomy from Que Sera
Sera restaurant's open kitchen; thoughtful facilities like coffeemakers
and cribs; laundry machines are a bonus. **Cons:** it doesn't inspire a
lusty romp. ⑤ *Rooms from: C$199* ✉ *850 pl. d'Youville, Upper Town*
☎ *418/694–4004, 866/694–4004* ⊕ *www.marriott-quebec.com* ⟿ *103
rooms, 8 suites* ⓘⓞⓘ *No meals* ✛ *D3.*

$$$$ ⚐**Fairmont Le Château Frontenac.** Towering above the St. Lawrence
HOTEL River, the Château Frontenac is the most photographed landmark
ⓒ in Québec City, and is considered the Grand Dame of Canadian
Fodor's Choice hotels.**Pros:** historic aura adds romance to incomparable views;
★ pets are treated like royalty; food is divine. **Cons:** high foot traffic

in public spaces; some rooms are smallish for the price. $ *Rooms from: C$259* ✉ *1 rue des Carrières, Upper Town* ☎ *418/692–3861, 800/441–1414* ⊕ *www.fairmont.com/frontenac* ⇆ *618 rooms, 30 suites* †○† *No meals* ✛ *G3.*

$$$ ⊞ **Hilton Québec.** Just opposite the National Assembly, the Hilton rises from the shadow of Parliament Hill and rooms on the upper floors have fine views of Vieux-Québec. **Pros:** direct access to the convention center; amazing Executive Lounge; connected to a shopping mall. **Cons:** blocky exterior lacks pizzazz. $ *Rooms from: C$199* ✉ *1100 boul. René-Lévesque Est, Upper Town* ☎ *418/647–2411, 800/447–2411 in Canada* ⊕ *www.hiltonquebec.com* ⇆ *538 rooms, 33 suites* †○† *No meals* ✛ *D3.*

$$
HOTEL
⊞ **Hôtel Champlain.** Tucked away on a quiet street in the Old City, this three-star hotel is a good fit for middle-of-the-road travelers looking for attentive service, boutique charm, and a central location. **Pros:** within walking distance to main attractions; on-site parking—a rare find in this part of town. **Cons:** bathrooms are on the small side; no in-room coffee pots means waiting for the communal espresso machine. $ *Rooms from: C$179* ✉ *115 rue Ste-Anne, Upper Town* ☎ *418/694–0106* ⊕ *www.champlainhotel.com* ⇆ *47 rooms, 5 suites* †○† *Breakfast* ✛ *E2.*

$
HOTEL
⊞ **Hôtel Château Bellevue.** Behind the Château Frontenac, this 1898 hotel occupies four heritage homes with the same green roofing, and offers comfortable accommodations at reasonable prices in a good location. **Pros:** fun package deals offered with museums, aquariums, restaurants. **Cons:** smallish rooms lack pizzazz. $ *Rooms from: C$139* ✉ *16 rue de la Porte, Upper Town* ☎ *418/692–2573, 800/463–2617* ⊕ *www.hotelchateaubellevue.com* ⇆ *48 rooms, 1 suite* †○† *Breakfast* ✛ *F3.*

$$
HOTEL
⊞ **Hôtel Clarendon.** Built in 1870, the Clarendon is the oldest operating hotel in Québec City and half the rooms have excellent views over Old Québec; the others overlook a courtyard. **Pros:** the piano in the lounge attracts merrymakers; interesting historic features. **Cons:** brassy acoustics on the reception level. $ *Rooms from: C$164* ✉ *57, rue Ste-Anne, Upper Town* ☎ *418/692–2480, 888/554–6001* ⊕ *www.hotelclarendon.com* ⇆ *143 rooms* †○† *No meals* ✛ *F2.*

$$
HOTEL
Fodor's Choice
★
⊞ **Hôtel du Vieux Québec.** Visiting students make tracks to this award-winning hotel, with its signature red roof and stone walls. **Pros:** lively location; breakfast delivered to your door with a weather report. **Cons:** with student guests come occasional shenanigans. $ *Rooms from: C$168* ✉ *1190 rue St-Jean, Upper Town* ☎ *418/692–1850, 800/361–7787* ⊕ *www.hvq.com* ⇆ *45 rooms* †○† *Breakfast* ✛ *E1.*

$$
HOTEL
⊞ **Hôtel Le Clos St-Louis.** Winding staircases and crystal chandeliers add to the Victorian elegance of this central, four-star inn made up of two updated 1845-era houses. **Pros:** period interiors; cheery breakfast room; great location near wonderful eateries and shops. **Cons:** Victorian ruffles around the beds won't appeal to young hipsters; no elevator to whisk guests up to their rooms. $ *Rooms from: C$195* ✉ *69 rue St-Louis, Upper Town* ☎ *418/694–1311, 800/461–1311* ⊕ *www.clossaintlouis.com* ⇆ *16 rooms, 2 suites* †○† *Breakfast* ✛ *F3.*

10

$ ▦ **Hôtel Manoir de l'Esplanade.** The four 1845 stone houses at the corner
HOTEL   of rues d'Auteuil and St-Louis conceal one of the city's good deals: a
charming hotel with well-appointed rooms, and an expanded continental breakfast with fruit, cheese, and yogurt is included. **Pros:** ancestral
fireplaces and dormer windows add to the charm; elevator is a luxury in this part of town; all rooms come with full private bathrooms.
Cons: central location means some nighttime noise. ⑤ *Rooms from:*
C$150 ✉ *83 rue d'Auteuil, Upper Town* ☎ *418/694–0834* ⊕ *www.*
manoiresplanade.ca ➷ *34 rooms, 2 suites* ⊙| *Breakfast* ✛ *E3.*

$ ▦ **Hôtel Manoir des Remparts.** With its homey furnishings, basic but cheery
HOTEL   rooms, and reasonable rates, this serviceable central hotel attracts many
teachers and travelers who can't bring themselves to stay in a hostel.
Pros: good for people who want to escape antiques-filled B&Bs. **Cons:**
no "wow" factor; no elevator. ⑤ *Rooms from: C$110* ✉ *3½ rue des*
Remparts, Upper Town ☎ *418/692–2056* ⊕ *www.manoirdesremparts.*
com ➷ *34 rooms, 24 with bath* ⊙| *Breakfast* ✛ *G1.*

$ ▦ **Hôtel Marie Rollet.** In the heart of Vieux-Québec, this intimate little inn
B&B/INN   built in 1876 by the Ursuline Order has warm woodwork and antiques
to match its surroundings. **Pros:** central location; remote-controlled
air-conditioning; private bathroom in every room. **Cons:** no elevator;
steep stairs. ⑤ *Rooms from: C$135* ✉ *81 rue Ste-Anne, Upper Town*
☎ *418/694–9271, 800/275–0338* ⊕ *www.hotelmarierollet.com* ➷ *11*
rooms ⊙| *No meals* ✛ *F2.*

$$ ▦ **L'Hôtel du Capitole.** This turn-of-the-20th-century structure just out-
HOTEL   side the St-Jean Gate is a fancy hotel, an Italian bistro, and a 1920s
cabaret-style dinner theater (the Théâtre Capitole) all rolled into one.
Pros: whirlpool tubs and fluffy white towels. **Cons:** lively theater/hotel
complex isn't ideal for cocooning. ⑤ *Rooms from: C$195* ✉ *972, rue St-*
Jean, Upper Town ☎ *418/694–4040, 800/363–4040* ⊕ *www.lecapitole.*
com ➷ *39 rooms, 1 suite* ⊙| *No meals* ✛ *D2.*

$ ▦ **Manoir d'Auteuil.** Art deco and art nouveau combine in this hotel,
HOTEL   converted from a private house in the 1950s, and 2012 saw a major
update that included individual climate-control systems and other fea-
tures. **Pros:** direct view of the Parliament building; close to the conven-
tion center; deco charm. **Cons:** midweek business guests do not invite
much chitchat in the lobby; no elevator. ⑤ *Rooms from: C$159* ✉ *49*
rue d'Auteuil, Upper Town ☎ *418/694–1173, 866/662–6647* ⊕ *www.*
manoirdauteuil.com ➷ *22 rooms, 5 suites* ⊙| *Breakfast* ✛ *E3.*

LOWER TOWN

$$$$ ▦ **Auberge St-Antoine.** On the site of a 19th-century maritime ware-
Fodor's Choice   house, this charming hotel incorporates the historic stone walls of the
★   old building along with artifacts dating to the 1600s, many of which
were found during expansion excavation, and are encased in glass dis-
plays in the public areas and guest rooms. **Pros:** historic architectural
accents and exhibits are unique. **Cons:** low vacancy rate means guests
must plan well in advance. ⑤ *Rooms from: C$269* ✉ *8 rue St-Antoine,*
Lower Town ☎ *418/692–2211, 888/692–2211* ⊕ *www.saint-antoine.*
com ➷ *84 rooms, 11 suites* ⊙| *Multiple meal plans* ✛ *G2.*

$ ⚐ **Hayden's Wexford House.** This charming B&B is comfortably removed
B&B/INN from the torrent of tourists, but it's only a scenic 15-minute walk from
all the Lower Town sites. **Pros:** big breakfast; quiet location near the
river with ample street parking. **Cons:** no TVs or telephones means
you're truly getting away from it all; books up fast in the summer
months. Ⓢ *Rooms from: C$140* ✉ *450 rue Champlain, Lower Town*
☎ *418/524–0524* ⊕ *www.haydenwexfordhouse.com* ⟿ *3 rooms*
⦿ *Breakfast* ✛ *F6.*

$$$ ⚐ **Hôtel 71.** This four-star luxury hotel is in the founding building of
the National Bank of Canada and its guest rooms have 12-foot-high
ceilings and stunning views of Old Québec. **Pros:** fabulous Golden
Key concierge service; luxurious packages. **Cons:** chic interiors might
make parents of active kids nervous; valet service is steep at C$21
per day. Ⓢ *Rooms from: C$225* ✉ *71 rue St-Pierre, Lower Town*
☎ *418/692–1171, 888/692–1171* ⊕ *www.hotel71.ca* ⟿ *60 rooms, 9*
suites ⦿ *Breakfast* ✛ *G1.*

$ ⚐ **Hôtel Belley.** Modern artwork by local artists is everywhere in this
HOTEL modest little hotel up the stairs above Belley Tavern, a stone's throw
from the train station, Marché du Vieux-Port, and the antiques district.
Pros: unique establishment; close to antiques district; hip tourists meet
at the tavern downstairs. **Cons:** small capacity means high occupancy;
no elevator. Ⓢ *Rooms from: C$110* ✉ *249 rue St-Paul, Lower Town*
☎ *418/692–1694, 888/692–1694* ⊕ *www.hotelbelley.com* ⟿ *8 rooms*
⦿ *No meals* ✛ *F1.*

$$$ ⚐ **Hôtel des Coutellier.** Charming details like buttery croissants delivered
HOTEL to the room each morning, exposed brick walls, and lush linens make
Fodor's Choice this boutique hotel a popular roosting spot for lovebirds. **Pros:** elevator,
★ a rarity in this historic part of town; breakfast delivered to the door
each morning. **Cons:** bathrooms are snug; in-room temperature controls
aren't intuitive. Ⓢ *Rooms from: C$205* ✉ *253 rue St. Paul, Lower Town*
☎ *418/692–9696, 888/523–9696* ⊕ *www.hoteldescoutellier.com* ⟿ *21*
rooms, 3 suites ⦿ *Breakfast* ✛ *F1.*

$$$$ ⚐ **Hôtel Le Germain Dominion.** Sophistication and attention to the smallest
HOTEL detail prevail in the modern rooms of this completely renovated four-
Fodor's Choice star boutique hotel, part of the Germain family hotel legacy—from
★ the custom-designed swing-out night tables to the white goose-down
duvets and custom umbrellas. **Pros:** designer's delight; great concierge
service; pets welcome. **Cons:** minimal chic interior is perhaps not well
suited to families with small children. Ⓢ *Rooms from: C$255* ✉ *126*
rue St-Pierre, Lower Town ☎ *418/692–2224, 888/833–5253* ⊕ *www.*
germaindominion.com ⟿ *60 rooms* ⦿ *Breakfast* ✛ *G1.*

$$ ⚐ **Hôtel Le Priori.** A dazzling four-star boutique hotel, Le Priori's build-
HOTEL ing may be 300 years old, with stone and brick walls, but the style is
rigorously modern, with custom leather beds, stainless steel sinks, slate
floors, and three-head shower jets. **Pros:** both hot and cold food at the
buffet breakfast; new desks and mirrors update the rooms. **Cons:** spon-
taneous trips to Le Priori are curbed by high occupancy rates. Ⓢ *Rooms*
from: C$199 ✉ *15 rue Sault-au-Matelot, Lower Town* ☎ *418/692–*
3992, 800/351 3992 ⊕ *www.hotellepriori.com* ⟿ *20 rooms, 8 suites*
⦿ *Breakfast* ✛ *G2.*

10

Fairmont Le Château Frontenac

Hôtel Le Germain Dominion

Auberge St-Antoine

Hôtel des Coutellier

OUTSIDE THE WALLS

$$$ **⚇ Château Bonne Entente.** The Château Bonne Entente offers modern
HOTEL simplicity at its finest, with classic rooms featuring white duvets, marble
bathrooms, and refinished wood furniture and boutique rooms right out
of a design magazine. **Pros:** cutting-edge design; heated bathroom floors
in Espace Terzo. **Cons:** chic interiors not practical for kids without
attentive nannies. ⑤ *Rooms from: C$179 ✉ 3400, chemin Ste-Foy, Ste-
Foy ☎ 418/653–5221, 800/463–4390 ⊕ www.chateaubonneentente.
com ⤳ 120 rooms, 45 suites* ⎮⎮ *No meals ✦ A4.*

$$ **⚇ Hôtel-Musée Premières Nations.** A warm "Kwe" welcome, spacious
HOTEL rooms outfitted with real pelts, and river views await at this lodging,
☾ restaurant, and museum complex in Wendake, a 15-minute drive north
of the city. **Pros:** ample free parking; trails and nature activities nearby.
Cons: rustic-meets-contemporary style might not appeal to squeamish
animal lovers; out-of-the-way locale is not for city slickers. ⑤ *Rooms
from: C$179 ✉ 5 place de la Rencontre, Wendake ☎ 418/847–2222
⊕ www.maisondespremieresnations.com ⤳ 53 rooms, 2 suites ✦ C1.*

$$ **⚇ Hotel PUR.** For choosy travelers with an image to maintain, this ultra-
HOTEL chic boutique hotel, owned by New York hoteliers with a mandate for
minimalism, is worthy of your Prada luggage. **Pros:** aesthetic perfection;
fabulous dining room doubles as a bar late evenings. **Cons:** minimal
design may not appeal to conservative tastes. ⑤ *Rooms from: C$180
✉ 395 rue de la Couronne, St-Roch ☎ 418/647–2611 ⊕ www.hotelpur.
com ⤳ 235 rooms, 7 suites* ⎮⎮ *No meals ✦ A1.*

$$ **⚇ Hôtel Royal William.** Like its namesake, the first Canadian steamship
HOTEL to cross the Atlantic (in 1833), the Royal William brings the spirit of
technology and innovation to this hotel designed with the business
traveler in mind. **Pros:** friendly staff; brand-new Presse Café in building serves strong coffee and great eats. **Cons:** banquet-hall ambience in
the public areas is uninspired; the business travelers aren't big minglers.
⑤ *Rooms from: C$160 ✉ 360, boul. Charest Est, St-Roch ☎ 418/521–
4488, 888/541–0405 ⊕ www.royalwilliam.com ⤳ 36 rooms, 8 suites*
⎮⎮ *Breakfast ✦ A2.*

$ **⚇ L'Autre Jardin Auberge.** In the heart of the burgeoning St-Roch dis-
B&B/INN trict in downtown Québec, this modern, pleasant inn is geared toward
the academics, high-tech entrepreneurs, and others who visit the many
office and administrative buildings that surround it. **Pros:** one of the
best buffet breakfasts in town; superlative use of sustainable business
practices. **Cons:** rooms are a bit spartan; no elevator. ⑤ *Rooms from:
C$135 ✉ 365 boul. Charest Est, St-Roch ☎ 418/523–1790, 877/747–
0447 ⊕ www.autrejardin.com ⤳ 25 rooms, 3 suites* ⎮⎮ *Breakfast ✦ A2.*

NIGHTLIFE AND THE ARTS

Québec City has a good variety of cultural institutions for a town of
its size, from its renowned symphony orchestra to several small theater
companies. The arts scene changes with the seasons. From September
through May a steady repertoire of concerts, plays, and performances
is presented in theaters and halls. In summer, indoor theaters close,
making room for outdoor stages.

Billetech. Tickets for most shows are sold at Billetech. ⊠ *Colisée Pepsi, Parc de l'Expocité, 250 boul. Wilfrid-Hamel, Limoilou* ☎ *418/ 691–7211.* ✉ *Grand Théâtre de Québec, 269 boul. René-Lévesque Est, Upper Town* ☎ *418/643–8131, 877/643–8131* ✉ *Salle Albert-Rousseau, 2410 chemin Ste-Foy, Ste-Foy* ☎ *418/659–6710* ✉ *Théâtre Capitole, 972 rue St-Jean, Upper Town* ☎ *418/694–4444.*

NIGHTLIFE

Québec City nightlife centers on the clubs and cafés of rue St-Jean, avenue Cartier, and Grande-Allée, and to a lesser extent in the Lower Town. In winter, evening activity grows livelier as the week nears its end, beginning on Wednesday. As warmer temperatures set in, the café-terrace crowd emerges, and bars are active seven days a week. Most bars and clubs stay open until 3 am.

UPPER TOWN
BARS AND LOUNGES

Bar Les Voûtes Napoléon. The brick walls and wine cellar–like atmosphere help make Les Voûtes a popular place to listen to Québecois music and sample beer from local microbreweries. ⊠ *680 rue Grande-Allée Est, Upper Town* ☎ *418/640–9388* ⊕ *www.voutesdenapoleon.com.*

Bar St-Laurent. One of the city's most romantic spots is the Château Frontenac's bar, with its soft lights, a panoramic view of the St. Lawrence, and a fireplace. ⊠ *1 rue des Carrières, Upper Town* ☎ *418/266–3906.*

★ **Cosmos Café.** This trendy restaurant and lively club is on the ground floor under Chez Maurice. Great chandeliers, art, and loud music round out the atmosphere. ⊠ *575 rue Grande-Allée Est, Upper Town* ☎ *418/640–0606* ⊕ *www.lecosmos.com.*

La Ninkasi. A bohemian favorite just outside the walls, La Ninkasi has an art-exhibition space, plasma screen TVs often tuned to hockey, and several gaming tables. Sample from an expansive collection of local brews and find out what's going on in the area's thriving art scene. ⊠ *811 rue St-Jean, Upper Town* ☎ *418/529–8538* ⊕ *www.ninkasi.ca.*

Le Chantauteuil. Established in 1968, this restaurant-pub is a hit with the locals. The kitchen sometimes closes early, but people stay late into the evening for drinking and discussion. ⊠ *1001 rue St-Jean, Upper Town* ☎ *418/692–2030* ⊕ *lechantauteuil.com.*

Le Pub Saint-Alexandre. This popular English-style pub serves 45 kinds of single-malt scotch and 250 kinds of beer, 30 of which are on tap. ⊠ *1087 rue St-Jean, Upper Town* ☎ *418/694–0015* ⊕ *www. pubstalexandre.com.*

L'Inox. A popular Upper Town brewpub, L'Inox serves beers that have been brewed on-site, like Montagnais and Coulée-Douce. Some, like Transat and Viking, were developed to mark special events. Inside are billiard tables and excellent European-style hot dogs; outside there's a summer terrace. ⊠ *655 rue Grande-Allée Est, Upper Town* ☎ *418/692–2877* ⊕ *www.inox.qc.ca.*

10

Maurice Nightclub. This is a bar complex named after the former premier of Québec, Maurice Duplessis. The crowd is young, and the atmosphere is racy, provocative, and sexually charged. ✉ *575 rue Grande-Allée Est, 2nd fl., Upper Town* ☎ *418/647–2000* ⊕ *www.mauricenightclub.com.*

FOLK, JAZZ, AND BLUES
Bar Le Sacrilège. Nightly live music is the main draw at Le Sacrilège. This place bears its name well, with a couple of church pews and religious icons; ironically, it's also located across the street from Église St-Jean-Baptiste. Le Sacrilège has Québec-crafted McAuslan and Boréale microbrew products in bottles and on tap, and the special changes daily. It also has the best terrace in the city. ✉ *447 rue St-Jean, Upper Town* ☎ *418/649–1985* ⊕ *www.lesacrilege.net.*

Bar Ste-Angèle. This cozy hipster hideaway features live jazz some nights, a variety of delicious cocktails, and a vintage Hollywood theme. Enjoy drink specials on Tuesday. ✉ *26 rue Ste-Angèle, Upper Town* ☎ *418/692–2171.*

OUTSIDE THE WALLS
BARS AND LOUNGES
Korrigane Brasserie Artisanale. A popular after-work spot with the locals, this brewery crafts high-quality beer and offers pairings with tapas-inspired pub fare. A friendly vibe and ample seating make Korrigane the ideal spot for a *cinq à sept* or a low-key night out. In addition to numerous house brews, they highlight other artisan beers from Québec. ✉ *380 rue Dorchester, St-Roch* ☎ *418/614–0932* ⊕ *www.korrigane.ca.*

Le Boudoir. Some say this is Québec's best and classiest bar for singles and younger couples. The lower-level dance floor is DJ-powered from Thursday to Sunday, and you'll hear all the latest beats. Le Boudoir's martinis are popular, and a menu of comfort food and side dishes rounds out the supper club's offerings. ✉ *441 rue d'Eglise, St-Roch* ☎ *418/524–2777* ⊕ *www.boudoirlounge.com.*

Les Salons d'Edgar. In an old movie theater, this popular club is perched on the cliff just above the St-Roch district and attracts people in their 30s with its eclectic music, which includes everything from salsa beats and Sunday-night tango to jazz, techno, and beyond. ✉ *263 rue St-Vallier Est, St-Roch* ☎ *418/523–7811* ⊘ *Closed July and Aug.*

CLUBS
Le Boudoir. You can boogie down to live musicians or a DJ's picks at this bar, the hub of St-Roch's singles scene. Two distinct atmospheres—a restaurant-lounge on the first floor and expansive dance area on the second—make this a popular hangout for the neighborhood's young professionals. ✉ *441 rue du Parvis, St-Roch* ☎ *418/524–2777.*

THE ARTS

Art is everywhere in Québec City—from theater to chic galleries to accordion street performers and statue mimes in the parks. On summer nights, the old grain elevator is transformed into a multimedia projector and the colorful viaduct in St-Roch turns into a stage for the Cirque du Soleil.

The rue du Trésor in Upper Town is an alleyway lined with local artists selling their paintings and sketches.

ARTS CENTERS

Fodor's Choice ★   **Grand Théâtre de Québec.** This is Québec City's main theater, with two stages for symphonic concerts, opera, plays, dance performances, and touring companies of all sorts. A three-wall mural by Québec sculptor Jordi Bonet depicts Death, Life, and Liberty. Bonet wrote "La Liberté" on one wall to bring attention to the Québecois struggle for freedom and cultural distinction. ✉ *269, blvd. René-Lévesque Est, Upper Town* ☎ *418/643–8131* ⊕ *www.grandtheatre.qc.ca.*

DANCE

Grand Théâtre de Québec. Dancers appear at the Bibliothèque Gabrielle-Roy, Salle Albert-Rousseau, and Complexe Méduse. The Grand Théâtre presents a dance series with Canadian and international companies. ✉ *269 blvd. René-Lévesque Est, Montcalm* ☎ *418/643–8131* ⊕ *www.grandtheatre.qc.ca.*

MUSIC

Fodor's Choice ★   **Orchestre Symphonique de Québec** (*Québec Symphony Orchestra*). Canada's oldest symphony orchestra, renowned for its musicians and conductor Yoav Talmi, performs at Louis-Frechette Hall in the Grand Théâtre de Québec. ✉ *269 boul. René-Lévesque Est, Upper Town* ☎ *418/643–8486* ⊕ *www.osq.org.*

Théâtre Petit-Champlain. A charming intimate theater, this is a fine spot to hear contemporary francophone music during the year and take in a play in summer. ✉ *68 rue du Petit-Champlain, Lower Town* ☎ *418/692–2631* ⊕ *www.theatrepetitchamplain.com.*

THEATER

Most theater productions are in French. *The theaters listed below schedule shows from September to May.*

In summer, open-air concerts are presented at Place d'Youville (just outside St-Jean Gate) and on the Plains of Abraham.

Carrefour international de théâtre de Québec. This international theatrical adventure takes over several spaces during the month of May: Salle Albert-Rousseau, Grand Théâtre de Québec, Théâtre Périscope (near avenue Cartier), and Complexe Méduse. There are usually at least one or two productions in English or with English subtitles. ☎ *418/692–3131* ⊕ *www.carrefourtheatre.qc.ca.*

Coopérative Méduse. This multidisciplinary arts center is a hub for local artists, and presents installations and live shows. ⊠ *541 rue de St-Vallier Est, St-Roch* ☎ *418/640–9218* ⊕ *www.meduse.org.*

École de Cirque. Every year, for three weeks starting in May, students of this circus school and others take to the trapeze to promote their art form in the Circus Days festival. Throughout the year, students and teachers put on various shows, training camps, and workshops in the historic church that now houses their school. ⊠ *750 ave. 2e, Limoilou* ☎ *418/425–0101* ⊕ *www.ecoledecirque.com.*

Grand Théâtre de Québec. Classic and contemporary plays are staged here by the leading local company, le Théâtre du Trident. ⊠ *269 blvd. René-Lévesque Est, Montcalm* ☎ *418/643–8131* ⊕ *www.grandtheatre.qc.ca.*

Théâtre Périscope. This multipurpose theater hosts about 125 shows a year, staged by several different theater companies. ⊠ *2, rue Crémazie Est, Montcalm* ☎ *418/529–2183* ⊕ *www.theatreperiscope.qc.ca.*

SPORTS AND OUTDOOR ACTIVITIES

Scenic rivers and nearby mountains (no more than 30 minutes away by car) make Québec City a great place for the sporting life.

Billetech. You can order tickets for many events through this company. ⊕ *www.billetech.com.*

Colisée Pepsi. Tickets for sporting events can be bought at Colisée Pepsi. ⊠ *Parc de l'Expocité, 250 boul. Wilfrid-Hamel, Limoilou* ☎ *418/691–7211.*

Québec City Bureau of Recreation and Community Life. This is a good source for information about municipal facilities. ⊠ *160 76th rue E, St-Roch* ☎ *418/641–6224* ⊕ *www.ville.quebec.qc.ca.*

Québec City Tourist Information. For information about sports and fitness activities around the city, contact Québec City Tourist Information. ⊠ *399 rue St-Joseph Est., St-Roch* ☎ *418/641–6654, 877/783–1608* ⊕ *www.quebecregion.com.*

QUÉBEC SUMMER FESTIVAL

Festival d'Été International de Québec (*Québec City Summer Festival*). An annual highlight in mid-July is Québec City's Summer Festival, an exuberant, 11-day music festival with rock, folk, hip-hop, world music, and more (the website has a detailed program). It's a great event for hearing unfamiliar performers and expanding your musical horizons. The main concerts take place each evening on three outdoor stages in or near the Old City, including one on the Plains of Abraham. A pass (C$65) admits you to all events throughout the festival and single-show passes, for around C$30, are also available. Some concerts at indoor theaters cost extra, but free music and activities are also plentiful, such as family concerts and street performers during the day. At night rue St-Jean near the city gate turns into a free street theater, with drummers, dancers, and skits. Book lodging several months in advance if you plan to attend this popular event. ☎ 418/523–4540, 888/992–5200 ⊕ www.infofestival.com.

BIKING

There are 64 km (40 miles) of fairly flat, well-maintained bike paths on Québec City's side of the St. Lawrence River and an equal amount on the south shore. Detailed route maps are available through tourism offices. The best and most scenic of the bike paths is the one that follows the old railway bed in Lévis. Take the Québec–Lévis ferry to reach the marvelous views along this 10-km-long (6-mile-long) trail. It's now part of the province-wide Route Verte, a government-funded, 4,000-km-long (2,500-mile-long) circuit of long-distance bicycle paths and road routes.

Corridor des Cheminots. Ambitious cyclists can embark on the 22-km-long (14-mile-long) trail that runs from Québec City near Old City to the town of Shannon.

Côte de Beaupré. Paths along the beginning of this coast, at the confluence of the St. Charles and St. Lawrence rivers, are especially scenic. They begin northeast of the city at rue de la Vérandrye and boulevard Montmorency or rue Abraham-Martin and Pont Samson (Samson Bridge) and continue 10 km (6 miles) along the coast to Montmorency Falls.

Mont-Ste-Anne. The site of the 1998 world mountain-biking championship and races for the annual World Cup has 150 km (93 miles) of mountain-bike trails and an extreme-mountain-biking park.

DOG SLEDDING

For centuries dog sledding has been a part of the Canadian winter experience. Outfitters around Québec City generally offer excursions from January through March.

Aventures Nord-Bec Stoneham. A 30-minute drive from Old City, Aventures Nord-Bec Stoneham will teach you how to mush in the forest. A

10

half-day expedition, which includes initiation, dog sledding, a guided tour of kennels, and a snack, costs C$110 per person. Overnight camping trips, snowshoeing, and ice fishing are also available. In summer this location offers mountain biking and kennel tours. Transportation between Stoneham and your hotel can be provided for a fee and some packages include entry to the Ice Hotel. ⊠ *4 ch. des Anémones, Stoneham* ☎ *418/848–3732* ⊕ *www.traineaux-chiens.com.*

GOLF

The Québec City region has 18 golf courses, and most are open to the public. Reservations are essential in summer.

Club de Golf de Cap-Rouge. This is one of the closest courses to the city center, just 25 minutes by car from Vieux-Québec, with women's, men's (blue), and advanced courses of varying lengths. Chef Pierre Gelly prepares gastronomic delights in the dining room, and François Sauvé is the on-site pro. ⊠ *4600 rue St-Felix, Cap-Rouge* ☎ *418/653–9381* ⊕ *www. golfcap-rouge.qc.ca* 🏌 *18 holes. 6756 yds. Par 72. Slope 125. Greens fee: C$85* ⚲ *Driving range, putting green, golf carts, rental clubs, proshop, lessons, restaurant.*

Club de Golf de Mont Tourbillon. The Mont Tourbillon is 20 minutes from the city by car via Route 73 North (Lac Beauport exit) and features three courses and an elegant bistro, set next to the mountains with views of the rolling hillside and Lac Beauport. ⊠ *55 montée du Golf, Lac Beauport* ☎ *418/849–4418* ⊕ *www.monttourbillon.com* 🏌 *Blue Course: 18 holes. 6090 yards. Par 70. Slope 121. White Course: 18 holes. 5590 yards. Par 70. Slope 117. Red Course: 18 holes. 4625 yards. Par 70. Slope 113. Greens fee: C$49 weekends, C$41 weekdays* ⚲ *Facilities: Driving range, putting green, golf carts, rental clubs, lessons, restaurant, bar.*

Le Saint-Ferréol. This course is a half-hour drive north of Québec City, across from Mont Sainte-Anne, and has one of the best and best-priced courses in the region, fine-tuned by pro Denis Gagné. ⊠ *1700 blvd. les Neiges, St-Ferréol* ☎ *418/827–3778* ⊕ *www.golfstferreol.com* 🏌 *18 holes. 6445 yds. Par 72. Slope 115. Greens fee: C$44* ⚲ *Facilities: Driving range, golf carts, rental clubs, pro-shop, lessons, restaurant, bar.*

ICE-SKATING

Come winter, ice-skating is one of Canada's most popular activities.

Place d'Youville. This well-known outdoor rink just outside St-Jean Gate is open daily October through the end of March, from noon to 10 pm. Skate rental is about C$5, and skating itself is free. A locker will run you C$1. ☎ *418/641–6256.*

Village Vacances Valcartier. You can go skating at night here, although closing times vary. It's located approximately 20 minutes from the city and driving is the best option. The price for skating is about C$7 or included with park admission ticket (C$32). ⊠ *1860 blvd. Valcartier, Valcartier* ☎ *418/844–2200, 888/384–5524* ⊕ *www.valcartier.com.*

RAFTING

Just outside the city, the Jacques-Cartier River (to the west) and Riviére Malbaie (to the east) both make for an easy white-water rafting day-trip.

Excursions et Mechoui Jacques Cartier. This outfitter runs rafting trips on the Jacques Cartier River, about 48 km (30 miles) northwest of Québec City, from May through October. Tours originate from Tewkesbury, a half-hour drive from Québec City. A half-day trip ranges from C$58 per person on weekdays to C$78 on weekends, wet suits included. Horseback riding is also available at this location. ⊠ *860 av. Jacques-Cartier Nord, Tewkesbury* ☎ *418/848–7238* ⊕ *www.excursionsj-cartier.com.*

Village Vacances Valcartier. This center runs rafting excursions on the Jacques Cartier River from May through September. A three-hour excursion costs approximately C$50 plus C$16 to rent a wet suit (call first to check prices). Also available are hydro-speeding—running the rapids on surfboards—and quieter family river tours. ⊠ *1860 boul. Valcartier, Valcartier* ☎ *418/844–2200, 888/384–5524* ⊕ *www.valcartier.com.*

SKIING

Skiing is very popular here, whether it's downhill on one of the mountains surrounding the city or cross-country in an urban park. A dynamic landscape, top-notch ski resorts, and lots of fresh powder create a winter wonderland and the ideal training area for some of Canada's top athletes.

⇨ *For more cross-country and downhill skiing options near Québec City, see the Side Trips from Québec City chapter.*

Ski Express. In winter, this shuttle runs between major hotels in Old City and major ski centers. It leaves hotels in Old City at 8 and 10 am for the ski hills and returns at 2:30 and 4:30 pm. The cost is C$63–C$140; reserve and pay in advance at hotels. ☎ *418/525–5191* ⊕ *www.taxicoop-quebec.com.*

Québec Tourism and Convention Bureau. Brochures offering general information about ski centers in Québec are available from the Québec Tourism and Convention Bureau. ☎ *877/266–5687* ⊕ *www.bonjourquebec.com.*

CROSS-COUNTRY

Regroupement des Stations de Ski de Fond. Thirty-seven cross-country ski centers in the Québec area have 2,000 km (1,240 miles) of groomed trails and heated shelters between them; for information, contact the Regroupement des Stations de Ski de Fond. ⊕ *www.skidefondraquette.com.*

SKI CENTERS

Les Sentiers du Moulin. This center is 19 km (12 miles) north of the city, and it has more than 20 marked trails covering 12 km (7 miles) single-track, and 15 km (9 miles) multitrack. ⊠ *99 chemin du Moulin, Lac Beauport* ☎ *418/849–9652.*

10

Parc des Champs-de-Bataille (*Battlefields Park*). You can reach the park from Place Montcalm. It has more than 10 km (6 miles) of scenic, marked, cross-country skiing trails. ⊠ *835 av. Wilfrid-Laurier, Montcalm.*

DOWNHILL

Choose from multiple downhill ski resorts, all with night skiing, within a 30-minute drive of Québec City. ⇨ *For more information on Le Massif and Mont-Ste-Anne, see the Côte-de-Beaupré section in Chapter 11, Side Trips from Québec City.*

Le Relais. There are 25 trails and a vertical drop of 734 feet at this relatively small ski center, where you can buy lift tickets by the hour. Le Relais is about 20 minutes from downtown Québec City. ⊠ *1084 boul. du Lac, Lac Beauport* ☎ *418/849–1851* ⊕ *www.skirelais.com.*

Station Touristique Stoneham. Stoneham is 20 minutes north of Old Québec. The hill has a vertical drop of 1,380 feet and is known for its long, easy slopes. It has 32 downhill runs and 10 lifts, plus three terrain parks and one super-half-pipe. ⊠ *1420 av. du Hibou, Stoneham* ☎ *418/848–2411, 800/463–6888* ⊕ *www.ski-stoneham.com.*

SNOW SLIDES

Growing in popularity each year, the snow slide from Dufferin Terrace is easily one of the most exciting winter activities in Québec.

☼ **Glissades de la Terrasse.** A wooden toboggan takes you down a 270-feet-high snow slide that's adjacent to the Château Frontenac. Three rides cost C$10. ☎ *418/829–9898.*

☼ **Village Vacances Valcartier.** Hop on an inner tube or carpet and shoot down one of more than 35 snow slides here. Or join 6 to 12 others for a snow-raft ride on one of three groomed trails. You can also take a dizzying ride on the Tornado, a giant inner tube that seats eight and spins down the slopes. Rafting and sliding cost C$34 per day, C$36 with skating and the Tornado. Trails open daily at 10 am; closing times vary. ⊠ *1860 boul. Valcartier, Valcartier* ☎ *418/844–2200, 888/384–5524* ⊕ *www.valcartier.com.*

SNOWMOBILING

Québec is the birthplace of the snowmobile, and with 32,000 km (19,840 miles) of trails, it's one of the best places in the world for the sport. Two major trails, the 2,000-km (1,250-mile) Trans-Québec Snowmobile Trail and the 1,300-km (806-mile) Fur Traders Tour, run just north of Québec City. Trail maps are available at tourist offices.

SM Sport. Snowmobile rentals with this company begin at C$45 per hour, or C$118 per day, plus tax and the cost of gas. These folks will also pick up from several downtown hotels for an additional price, starting at C$20 per person. ⊠ *11337 blvd. Valcartier, Loretteville* ☎ *418/842–2703* ⊕ *www.smsport.ca.*

WATER PARKS

Québec's water parks provide refreshing relief from hot summer days.

☺ **Village Vacances Valcartier.** The largest water park in Canada has a wave pool, a 1-km (½-mile) tropical-river adventure called the Amazon, more than 35 waterslides, and a 100-foot accelerating slide on which bathers reach a speed of up to 80 kph (50 mph). Mirage, the park's newest addition, features a heated pool and a huge number of water games. There's also a winding indoor river in a medieval setting. Admission is C$33.05 a day for those at least 52 inches tall, C$26.09 for those under 52 inches. ⊠ *1860 blvd. Valcartier, Valcartier* ☎ *418/844–2200, 888/384–5524* ⊕ *www.valcartier.com.*

WINTER CARNIVAL

For three weekends in January or February, Québec City throws one of the biggest winter parties in the world. Each year, an Ice Palace is built as the center of the festivities, which include dog sled races and several parades. Ice bars are plentiful on the Grande Allée and the streets fill with families and visitors singing songs and blowing into trumpets.

☺ **Carnaval de Québec.** A flurry of activity, mainly on the Plains of Abraham,
Fodor's Choice surrounds Carnaval de Québec, which occurs over three weekends every
★ January or February. Snow and ice sculpture contests, dog sled relays, and canoe races in the St. Lawrence chase away winter doldrums. Visitors brave the cold to get a glimpse of Bonhomme, the friendly Carnival Master, and tour his Ice Palace, which is rebuilt each year. Caribou, a strong mixture of red wine, hard liquor, and maple syrup is a popular libation during the festivities. ⊕ *www.carnaval.qc.ca.*

SHOPPING

On the fashionable streets of Old City shopping has a European tinge. The boutiques and specialty shops clustered along narrow streets such as rue du Petit-Champlain, and rues de Buade and St-Jean are like trips back in time.

Stores are generally open Monday–Wednesday 9:30–5:30, Thursday and Friday until 9, Saturday until 5, and Sunday noon–5. In summer most shops have later evening hours.

UPPER TOWN

ART GALLERIES

★ **Galerie Brousseau et Brousseau.** High-quality Inuit art is the specialty of this large, well-known gallery. The gallery director, Jean-Francois Brousseau, selects works by artists represented by the North Canadian Inuit cooperatives and the gallery receives much praise for improving life in the Canadian Arctic. ⊠ *35 rue St-Louis, Upper Town* ☎ *418/694–1828* ⊕ *www.sculpture.artinuit.ca.*

CLOTHING

Bedo. A popular chain with trendy, well-priced items to round out your work wardrobe, Bedo also has great sales racks to sort through at the end of seasons. ⊠ *1161 rue St-Jean, Upper Town* ☎ *418/692–0761* ⊕ *www.bedo.ca.*

Jacob. A Montréal-based chain, Jacob sells well-priced work and play clothes with a clean, sophisticated edge. ⊠ *1160–1170 rue St-Jean, Upper Town* ☎ *418/694–0580* ⊕ *www.jacob.ca.*

CRAFTS

Les Trois Colombes. Handmade items, including clothing made from handwoven fabric, native and Inuit carvings, furs, and ceramics, are available at this interesting shop. ⊠ *46 rue St-Louis, Upper Town* ☎ *418/694–1114.*

DEPARTMENT STORES

★ **La Maison Simons.** A large Canadian chain store operation started here in Québec City, Simons used to be the city's only source for fine British woolens and tweeds. Now the store also carries designer clothing, linens, and other household items. ⊠ *20 côte de la Fabrique, Upper Town* ☎ *418/692–3630* ⊕ *www.simons.ca/.*

FOOD

Les Délices de l'Érable. Find a sweet souvenir at this maple syrup shop, which has everything from maple cookies to muffins and serves the best gelato in town. ⊠ *1044 rue St-Jean, Upper Town* ☎ *418/692–3245* ⊕ *www.mapledelights.com.*

GIFTS

★ **Point d'Exclamation!.** Handcrafted bags, jewelry, hair accessories, paper, notebooks, cards, and paintings by 140 Québecois artisans fill Diane Bergeron's shop. ⊠ *762 rue St-Jean, Upper Town* ☎ *418/525–8053.*

JEWELRY

Zimmermann. Exclusive handmade jewelry can be found at this Upper Town shop, a landmark in the city for many years. ⊠ *46 côte de la Fabrique, Upper Town* ☎ *418/692–2672* ⊕ *www.zimmermann-quebec.com.*

SHOPPING MALLS

Les Promenades du Vieux-Québec. You'll find high-end items—clothing, perfume, and art—great for packaging as gifts or tucking away as souvenirs of this unique little shopping corner's boutiques. There's also a restaurant, a 3-D multimedia show on the history of Québec, and a change bureau. ⊠ *43, rue de Buade, Upper Town* ☎ *418/692–6000.*

LOWER TOWN

ANTIQUES

French-Canadian, Victorian, and art deco furniture, clocks, silverware, and porcelain, are some of the rare collectibles found here. Authentic Québec pine furniture, characterized by simple forms and lines, is rare—and costly.

10

Antiquités Bolduc. The largest antiques store on rue St-Paul features furniture, household items, old paintings, and knickknacks. ⊠ *89 rue St-Paul, Lower Town* ☎ *418/694–9558* ⊕ *www.lesantiquitesbolduc.com.*

Argus Livres Anciens. Antique books, most of them in French, draw bibliophiles to this store. ⊠ *399 chemin de la Canadière, Lower Town* ☎ *418/694–2122.*

Gérard Bourguet Antiquaire. You're not likely to find any bargains here, but this shop has a very good selection of authentic 18th- and 19th-century Québec pine furniture. ⊠ *97 rue St-Paul, Lower Town* ☎ *418/ 694–0896* ⊕ *www.gerardbourguet.com.*

L'Héritage Antiquité. This is probably the best place in the antiques district to find good Québecois furniture, clocks, oil lamps, porcelain, and ceramics. It's a very welcoming store as well. ⊠ *109 rue St-Paul, Lower Town* ☎ *418/692–1681.*

ART GALLERIES

Galerie Madeleine Lacerte. Head to this gallery in an old car-repair garage for contemporary art and sculpture. ⊠ *1 côte Dinan, Lower Town* ☎ *418/692–1566* ⊕ *www.galerielacerte.com.*

CLOTHING

Le Blanc Mouton. Locally designed creations for women, including accessories and jewelry, fill this boutique in Quartier Petit-Champlain. ⊠ *51 Sous le Fort, Lower Town* ☎ *418/692–2880.*

FURS

Fourrures Richard Robitaille. This furrier has an on-site workshop that produces custom designs, and as a part of the exciting international network called Economuseums, invites participation from clients. ⊠ *329 rue St-Paul, Lower Town* ☎ *418/692–9699* ⊕ *www.economusees.com.*

SHOPPING MALLS

Fodor's Choice ★ **Quartier Petit-Champlain.** A pedestrian mall in Lower Town, surrounded by rues Champlain and du Marché-Champlain, Quartier Petit-Champlain has some 50 boutiques, local businesses, and restaurants. This popular district is the best area for native Québec wood sculptures, weavings, ceramics, and jewelry. ⊠ *Lower Town* ☎ *418/692–2613* ⊕ *www.quartierpetitchamplain.com.*

OUTSIDE THE WALLS

CLOTHING

Boutique Flirt. The name of the game is pleasure at this brightly colored boutique where lingerie for men and women cohabit, and fun meets femme fatale. Flirt specializes in hard-to-find sizes. They carry Aubade, Punto Blanco, Freya, Parah, Simone Perèle, Prima Donna, Marie Jo, and Empreinte. ⊠ *525 rue St-Joseph Est, St-Roch* ☎ *418/529–5221* ⊕ *www. lingerieflirt.com.*

Signatures Québécoises. Those who think of fashion as religion should make their way to Église St-Roch. The belly of this immense, Gothic-style church holds a large collection of wardrobe items and accessories from burgeoning Québec designers. ⊠ *560 rue St-Joseph Est, St-Roch* ☎ *418/628–9976* ⊕ *www.signaturesquebecoises.com.*

DEPARTMENT STORES

Large department stores can be found in the malls of suburban Ste-Foy.

La Baie. Part of the historic Hudson's Bay Company chain, La Baie carries clothing for the entire family, as well as household wares. ⊠ *Pl. Laurier, Ste-Foy* ☎ *418/627–5959.*

FOOD

Camellia Sinensis Maison de Thé. This modest space stocks 150 different teas from China, Japan, Africa, and beyond and you can sign up for a tea-tasting session on weekends at 10 am. ⊠ *624 St-Joseph Est, St-Roch* ☎ *418/525–0247* ⊕ *www.camellia-sinensis.com.*

La Boîte à Pain. Baker Patrick Nisot offers a selection of baguettes, multigrain breads (pumpernickel, rye), special flavors (olive, tomato and pesto, Sicilian), and dessert breads. No credit cards are accepted. ⊠ *289 St-Joseph Est, St-Roch* ☎ *418/647–3666.*

FURS

J.B. Laliberté. In business since 1867, the well-established Laliberté carries men's and women's furs and accessories. ⊠ *595 rue St-Joseph Est, St-Roch* ☎ *418/525–4841.*

GIFTS

Baltazar. Hip urban housewares can be found at this local favorite. Neon soap dishes, vases, and utensils, as well as unique cookbooks, wall decorations, and gifts in a range of prices make Baltazar a good place to find your next conversation piece. ⊠ *461 rue St-Joseph, St-Roch* ☎ *418/524–1991* ⊕ *www.baltazar.ca.*

SHOPPING MALLS

☾ **Galeries de la Capitale.** Thirty-five restaurants, roughly 280 shops, an IMAX theater, and an adjacent indoor amusement park make this an ideal shopping center for a whole day of family retail therapy. ⊠ *5401 blvd. des Galeries, Lebourgneuf* ☎ *418/627–5800* ⊕ *www. galeriesdelacapitale.com.*

TOYS/GAMES

☾ **Benjo.** Whimsy runs wild at Benjo. This store features games and toys, kids clothes, a large café with thrones for little princes and princesses, and an ample bookstore filled with French storybooks. It's loved by young ones and the young at heart. ⊠ *550 blvd. Charest Est, St-Roch* ☎ *418/640–0001* ⊕ *www.benjo.ca.*

EXCURSIONS

Huron-Wendat Village. A 15-minute drive outside city limits takes you into another world. The Huron Nation, a part of the native Canadian First Nations people, is famous for its handcrafted clothing, decorations, and hunting tools, which are on display at Huron-Wendat. This community encompasses a fascinating traditional village exhibition, complete with longhouse, dances, and storytelling. Visitors can take guided tours and discover stunning handmade crafts in the huge gift

10

North America's first ice hotel, rebuilt each winter, is only 10 minutes from Québec City by car, and worth a tour even if you don't spend the night.

shop. Traditional meals are served in an on-site restaurant. ✉ *575 rue Stanislas-Kosca, Village-de-Hurons (Wendake)* ☎ *418/842–4308* ⊕ *www.huron-wendat.qc.ca* ✉ *Guided tour C$12.50* ☉ *Daily 9–5.*

Ice Hotel (*Hôtel de Glace*). At this hotel constructed completely of ice and snow—the first of its kind in North America—you can tour the art galleries of ice sculptures, get married in the chapel, lounge in the hot tub, have a drink in a glass made of ice at the bar made of ice, dance in the ice club, then nestle into a bed lined with deerskin. The icy abode is rebuilt each year and is open from the first week in January to the end of March. The standard overnight stay packages start at C$199 per person and include a welcome cocktail served in an ice glass, access to the Nordic area's hot tubs and sauna, and a hot breakfast. If you'd rather not brave the frigid temperatures for a whole night, take a tour of the facilities for C$17.50. ✉ *9530 rue de la Faune, about 10 minutes from downtown Québec City* ☎ *418/623–2888, 877/505–0423* ⊕ *www.hoteldeglace-canada.com.*

Side Trips from Québec City

WORD OF MOUTH

"Baie-Ste.-Paul is a quaint little city [with] a beautiful setting in a cove surrounded by mountains."

—tomarket

SIDE TRIPS FROM QUÉBEC CITY

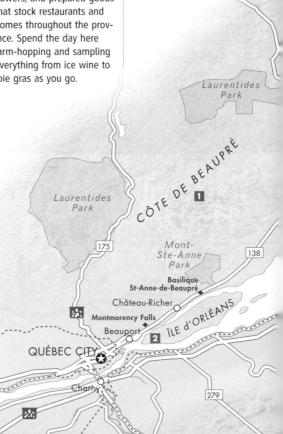

TOP REASONS TO GO

★ **Ski at Le Massif:** This three-peak ski resort has the largest vertical drop east of the Rocky Mountains at just over 2,500 feet.

★ **Farm-hop on Île d'Orléans:** The "Garden of Québec" is covered with farmland and bed-and-breakfasts, and makes for the perfect overnight trip from Québec City.

★ **Whale-watch in Tadoussac:** A few hours north of Charlevoix, you can see small, white beluga whales—an endangered species—year-round in Saguenay River.

★ **See Basilique Ste-Anne-de-Beaupré:** More than a million people a year make pilgrimages to this church, named after the patron saint of Québec.

★ **Take the bridge across Montmorency Falls:** These waterfalls on the Côte-de-Beaupré are double the height of Niagara Falls, and a pedestrian bridge will take you from one side to the other.

1 Côte-de-Beaupré. Driving along this coast offers views of Île d'Orléans, as well as Montmorency Falls and the famous pilgrimage site, Ste-Anne-de-Beaupré.

2 Île d'Orléans. This island is called the "Garden of Québec" for all the produce, flowers, and prepared goods that stock restaurants and homes throughout the province. Spend the day here farm-hopping and sampling everything from ice wine to foie gras as you go.

3 Charlevoix. People refer to Charlevoix as the "Switzerland of Québec" due to its terrain of mountains, valleys, streams, and waterfalls. Charlevoix's charming villages line the shore of the St. Lawrence River for about 200 km (125 miles).

GETTING ORIENTED

Île d'Orléans and the Côte-de-Beaupré are about 40 km (25 miles) east of Québec City. The Charlevoix region is about 113 km (70 miles) northeast of Île d'Orléans and Côte-de-Beaupré, so consider spending the night.

Experience a deeper understanding of this region's history and culture by venturing outside the city. In addition to the beauty of Montmorency Falls and Côte-de-Beaupré, get acquainted with rural life on the charming Île d'Orléans, known as "the Garden of Québec." There's much to see and do in the Charlevoix area—a diverse landscape of mountains, pristine lakes, and rolling valleys. Shops and galleries make Baie-St-Paul a hub for art lovers. Tadoussac offers rustic excursions, such as whale-watching and fjord tours.

Updated by
Amanda Halm

Montmorency Falls is an excellent first stop in any adventure outside the city. From there, you can cruise up Québec's Côte-de-Beaupré and eventually make your way to Ste-Anne-de-Beaupré, an immense neo-Roman church. Or take the bridge to Île d'Orléans where you can pick fresh berries, sample iced cider, and shop for antiques. A leisurely drive around the island can be done in a day.

Charlevoix, a few hours from Québec City, takes more planning and probably an overnight stay, but is well worth the drive. There are plenty of postcard-worthy villages and picnic spots along the way. Artists of all disciplines draw inspiration from this region, which is steeped in natural beauty and Algonquin history. In Tadoussac, the far-reaches of Charlevoix, the river begins to widen and mingle with the open sea. Slicing into the land is the dramatic Saguenay Fjord, touted as one of the largest fjords in the world.

QUÉBEC CITY SIDE TRIPS PLANNER

WHEN TO GO

Côte-de-Beaupré, Île d'Orléans, and Charlevoix are spectacular in fall, when you can leaf-peep and go apple picking. Summer means roadside stands featuring fresh-from-the-farm produce on Île d'Orléans or Côte-de-Beaupré. Artists flock to Baie-St-Paul in Charlevoix for festivals and gallery openings. It's also the perfect time to see beluga whales in Tadoussac. In winter, in all regions, there are plenty of cold-weather activities: cross-country skiing, snowshoeing, and ice fishing, among others. The area's best downhill skiing can be found in Charlevoix, but the roads can be tough to maneuver—consider taking Le Massif train or a shuttle. Spring has its own magic, when the ice begins to melt and the maple syrup starts to flow.

GETTING HERE AND AROUND

To reach Montmorency Falls, take Route 440 (Autoroute Dufferin–Montmorency) east from Québec City approximately 9½ km (6 miles) to the exit for Montmorency Falls. For Ste-Anne-de-Beaupré, take Route 440 (Autoroute Dufferin–Montmorency) east from Québec City approximately 23 km (14 miles). To get to Île d'Orléans, take Route 440 (Autoroute Dufferin–Montmorency) northeast. After a drive of about 10 km (6 miles) take the Pont de l'Île d'Orléans (a bridge) to the island. The main road, chemin Royal (Route 368), circles the island, extending 67 km (42 miles) through the island's six villages; the route turns into chemin du Bout de l'Île in Ste-Pétronille.

To get to Charlevoix from Québec City, take Route 440 (Autoroute Dufferin–Montmorency) northeast and then continue past the Côte-de-Beaupré on Route 138. From there you'll be able to branch out for destinations such as Petit-Rivière-St-François or Baie-St-Paul. Though a half hour longer from Québec City, Route 362 between Baie-St-Paul and La Malbaie is more scenic.

Another way to explore the exceptional beauty of the region is to hop aboard the new train of Le Massif Charlevoix, which offers a 7-hour cruise along the shoreline from Parc de la Chute-Montmorency station to La Malbaie and back for C$275, including lunch and dinner.

Train Information Le Massif Train ☎ *418/632–5876, 877/536–2774* ⊕ *www.lemassif.com/train.*

That said, most people traveling to this region do so by car, making it easy to spend as much or as little time in any given area as desired. However, Québec is in the process of expanding the Route Verte, or the Green Route, a 3,600-km (2,230-mile) network of bike trails in the southern part of the province.

⇨ *For more information on getting here and around, refer to Travel Smart.*

RESTAURANTS

Most of the restaurants on the Côte-de-Beaupré and Île d'Orléans are open only during high season, May to October, so check ahead. But visitors who do arrive in season won't be disappointed by the overall quality of dining options here. With nary a fast-food or chain outlet for miles around, your best—and most widely available—option is to sample some of the regional cuisine on offer. And while fine dining is the order of the day on Île d'Orléans, those traveling on a budget won't go hungry, as there are some good pubs and family-style restaurants with fairly reasonable prices.

In Charlevoix, the same rules apply—call ahead if you're visiting from November through April. During summer, Charlevoix is a food-lover's haven with fresh berries and cheeses sold roadside and plenty of bistros in the towns. Pick up a map of *La Route des Saveurs*, a route through the region dotted with restaurants and farms, and taste your way to Tadoussac.

Prices in the reviews are the average cost of a main course at dinner or, if dinner is not served, at lunch.

HOTELS

Reservations at hotels are highly recommended, although off-season it's possible to book a room same-day. B&Bs are the most common lodging options on Île d'Orléans, although there are a handful of inns and one motel as well. Côte-de-Beaupré, on the other hand, not only has plenty of inns and B&Bs, but several hotel/motel establishments as well, ranging from budget accommodations to four-star luxury resorts.

Given its status as one of Québec's premier summer vacation destinations, the Charlevoix region offers a plethora of lodging options, catering to travelers on almost any budget. Nevertheless, it's wise to book ahead in high season, especially if you're looking for one of the less expensive accommodations, which tend to fill up pretty quickly during the summer months.

Prices in the reviews are the lowest cost of a standard double room in high season.

VISITOR INFORMATION

Association Touristique Régionale de Charlevoix ✉ *495 blvd. de Comporté, C.P. 275, La Malbaie* ☎ *418/665–4454, 800/667–2276* ⊕ *www.tourisme-charlevoix.com.*

Beaupré Coast Interpretation Center ✉ *7976 av. Royale, C.P. 40, Château-Richer* ☎ *418/824–3677* ⊕ *www.histoire-cotedebeaupre.org.*

CÔTE-DE-BEAUPRÉ

As legend has it, when explorer Jacques Cartier first caught sight of the north shore of the St. Lawrence River in 1535, he exclaimed, "*Quel beau pré!*" ("What a lovely meadow!"), because the area was the first inviting piece of land he had spotted since leaving France. Today the Côte-de-Beaupré (Beaupré Coast), first settled by French farmers, stretches 40 km (25 miles) east from Québec City to the famous pilgrimage site of Ste-Anne-de-Beaupré. Historic Route 360, or avenue Royale, winds its way from Beauport to St-Joachim, east of Ste-Anne-de-Beaupré. The impressive Montmorency Falls lie midway between Québec City and Ste-Anne-de-Beaupré.

EXPLORING

TOP ATTRACTIONS

Fodor's Choice ★ **Basilique Ste-Anne-de-Beaupré.** On Route 138, east of Québec City, is the tiny town Ste-Anne-de-Beaupré, named for Québec's patron saint, and each year more than a million pilgrims visit the region's most famous religious site here, dedicated to the mother of the Virgin Mary.

The French brought their devotion to St. Anne (the patron saint of shipwrecked sailors) when they sailed across the Atlantic to New France. According to local legend, St. Anne was responsible over the years for saving voyagers from shipwrecks in the harsh waters of the St. Lawrence. In 1650 Breton sailors caught in a storm vowed to erect a chapel in honor of this patron saint at the exact spot where they landed.

The present neo-Roman basilica, constructed in 1923, is the fifth to be built on the site where the sailors first touched ground. The original 17th-century wood chapel was built too close to the St. Lawrence and was swept away by river flooding.

The gigantic structure is in the shape of a Latin cross, and has two imposing granite steeples. The interior has 22 chapels and 18 altars, as well as rounded arches and numerous ornaments in the Romanesque style. The 214 stained-glass windows, completed in 1949, are by Frenchmen Auguste Labouret and Pierre Chaudière.

Tributes to St. Anne can be seen in the shrine's mosaics, murals, altars, and ceilings. A bas-relief at the entrance depicts St. Anne welcoming her pilgrims, and ceiling mosaics represent her life. Numerous crutches and braces posted on the back pillars have been left by those who have felt the saint's healing powers.

In the basilica parking lot, the **Musée de Sainte Anne** (☎ 418/827–6873 💲 C$2 ☉ Early June–mid-Oct., daily 9:30–4:30) exhibits church treasures, including an impressive collection of votive offerings, many works of art, and donations made by pilgrims. ⊠ 10018 av. Royale, Ste-Anne-de-Beaupré ☎ 418/827–3781 ⊕ www.ssadb.qc.ca 💲 C$2 ☉ June–Sept., daily 8–8; Oct.–May, daily 8–5. Guided tours June–Sept. 4.

★ **Montmorency Falls.** The Montmorency River was named for Charles de Montmorency, viceroy of New France in the 1620s and explorer Samuel de Champlain's immediate commander. The river cascading over a cliff into the St. Lawrence is one of the most beautiful sights in the province—and at 27 stories high, the falls are double the height of Niagara Falls. A cable car runs to the top of the falls in **Parc de la Chute-Montmorency** (Montmorency Falls Park) from late April to late October. During very cold weather the falls' heavy spray freezes and forms a giant loaf-shape ice cone known to Québecois as the Pain du Sucre (Sugarloaf); this phenomenon attracts sledders and sliders from Québec City.

The park also has a historic side. The British general James Wolfe, on his way to conquer New France, camped here in 1759. In 1780 Sir Fredcrick Haldimand, then the governor of Canada, built a summer home atop the cliff. The structure burned down, however, and what stands today is a re-creation, now a good restaurant called Manoir Montmorency. It's open year-round, with a terrace in summertime that offers a

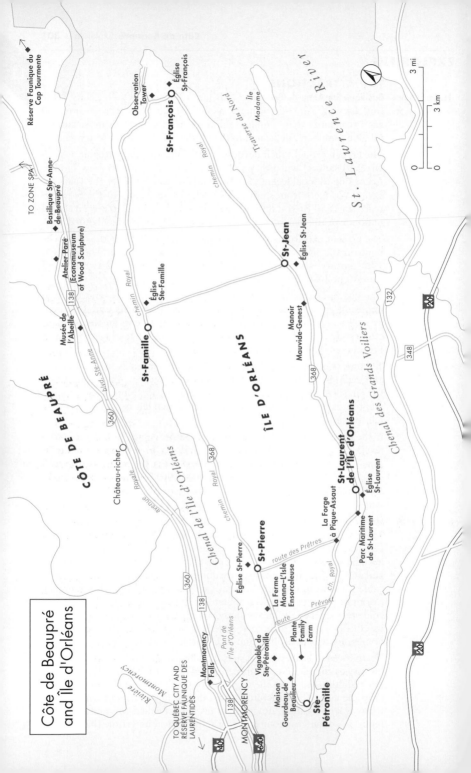

Côte de Beaupré and Île d'Orléans

Réserve Faunique du Cap Tourmente

TO ZONE SPA

Basilique Ste-Anne-de-Beaupré

Atelier Paré (Economuseum of Wood Sculpture)

138

Musée de l'Abeille

CÔTE DE BEAUPRÉ

360

Château-richer

avenue Royale

boul. Ste-Anne

Chenal de l'île d'Orléans

chemin Royal 368

St-Famille

Église Ste-Famille

chemin Royal

Observation Tower

St-François

Église St-François

chemin Royal

Île Madame

Traverse du Nord

St. Lawrence River

3 mi

3 km

St-Jean

Église St-Jean

Manoir Mauvide-Genest

132

20

348

ÎLE D'ORLÉANS

368

St-Laurent de l'île d'Orléans

Église St-Laurent

La Forge à Pique-Assaut

Parc Maritime de St-Laurent

ch. Royal

Chenal des Grands Voiliers

route des Prêtres

St-Pierre

Église St-Pierre

La Ferme Monna–L'Isle Ensorceleuse

route Prévost

Plante Family Farm

138

360

Montmorency Falls

Pont de l'île d'Orléans

Vignoble de Ste-Pétronille

Maison Gourdeau de Beaulieu

Ste-Pétronille

MONTMORENCY

Rivière Montmorency

TO QUÉBEC CITY AND RÉSERVE FAUNIQUE DES LAURENTIDES

440

40

20

stunning view of the falls and river below. ⊠ *2490 av. Royale, Beauport* ☏ *418/663–3330* ⊕ *www.sepaq.com* ⊠ *Cable car C$10.36 round-trip; parking C$9.75* ⊙ *Site open year round. Cable car Apr. 6–June 23 and Aug. 27–Oct., daily 9–6; June 24–Aug. 26, daily 8:30–7:30; Dec. 26– Apr. 5, weekends 10–4. Closed Nov. –Dec.25.*

WORTH NOTING

Atelier Paré (Economuseum of Wood Sculpture). This economuseum and workshop represents two centuries of wood sculpture. Visitors may watch artisans at work, tour the outdoor museum, see a 13-minute video presentation (in English and French), or learn about key personages in Québec's history through the Legend Theatre Workshop. There is also a boutique. ⊠ *9269 av. Royale, Ste-Anne-de-Beaupré* ☏ *418/827–3992* ⊕ *www.atelierpare.com* ⊠ *Free; guided tour C$4* ⊙ *late May–early Oct., daily 9–5; early Oct.–late May, Wed.–Sun. 1–4.*

🐝 **Musée de L'Abeille.** Things are buzzing at this economuseum (part of an organization of museums focusing on traditional trades) devoted to bees and honey. A giant glassed-in hive with a tube leading outdoors allows you to take a close look at life inside a beehive. You can taste honey and honey wine made by bees that have fed on different kinds of flowers, from clover to blueberry. The museum is a 10-minute drive east of Montmorency Falls. ⊠ *8862 blvd. Ste-Anne, Château-Richer* ☏ *418/824–4411* ⊕ *www.musee-abeille.com* ⊠ *Museum free* ⊙ *June 24–Sept. 3, daily 9–6; Sept. 4–June 23, daily 9–5.*

Réserve Faunique du Cap Tourmente (*Cap Tourmente Wildlife Reserve*). About 8 km (5 miles) northeast of Ste-Anne-de-Beaupré, this nature reserve sees gatherings of more than 800,000 greater snow geese every October and May, with an average of 100,000 birds coming per day. The park harbors hundreds of kinds of birds and mammals, and more than 700 plant species. This enclave on the north shore of the St. Lawrence River also has 18 km (11 miles) of hiking trails; naturalists give guided tours. ⊠ *570 chemin du Cap Tourmente, St-Joachim* ☏ *418/827–4591* ⊠ *C$6* ⊙ *Mid-Apr.–Oct., daily 8:30–5.*

OFF THE
BEATEN
PATH
Réserve Faunique des Laurentides. The wildlife reserve, approximately 80 km (49 miles) north of Québec City via Route 175, which leads to the Saguenay region, has good lakes for fishing. It's advisable to reserve a time slot 48 hours ahead by phone. ☏ *418/528–6868, 418/890–6527 fishing reservations* ⊕ *www.sepaq.com.*

Zone Spa. At the foot of Mont-Sainte-Anne, this spa is a great après-sport stop. After steeping in Nordic baths, try a "muscular tonic massage" employing peppermint as an anti-inflammatory. Gentle children's massages use aloe with the aroma of bubble gum. Nordic baths start at C$25 and massage prices begin at C$50 for 30 minutes. ⊠ *186 rang St-Julien, St-Ferréol-les-Neiges* ☏ *866/353–1772* ⊕ *www.zonespa.com* ⊙ *Dec. 15–Apr. 12, Mon.–Wed. 10–7, Thurs.–Sun. 10–9; Apr. 13–Dec. 14, Mon.–Wed., 10–6, Thurs.–Sun. 10–7.*

WHERE TO EAT

$$$$ ✕ **Auberge Baker.** The best of old and new blend at this restaurant in
CANADIAN an 1840 French-Canadian farmhouse, built by the owners' ancestors,
which lies just 4 km (2½ miles) west of St. Anne's Basilica. Antiques
and old-fashioned woodstoves decorate the dining rooms, where you
can sample traditional Québec fare, from *tourtière* (meat pie) and pork
hocks to maple-sugar pie. Or opt for contemporary dishes such as the
excellent herbed-and-breaded grilled lamb loin and pastry-wrapped
"Ferme d'Oc" goose leg confit and prosciutto. The lower-priced lunch
menu is served until 4. Upstairs is a five-room B&B, also decorated in
Canadiana; two exterior buildings hold two additional rooms. ⑤ *Average main: C$35* ✉ *8790 av. Royale, Château-Richer* ☎ *418/824–4478,
866/824–4478* ⊕ *www.auberge-baker.qc.ca.*

SPORTS AND THE OUTDOORS

Le Massif. This three-peak ski resort has Canada's longest vertical drop
east of the Rockies—2,526 feet. Owned by Daniel Gauthier, cofounder
of Le Cirque du Soleil, the resort has two multiservice chalets at the top
and bottom. Six lifts and one gondola service the 53 trails, which are
divided into runs for different levels; the longest run is 4.8 km (2.98
miles). Equipment can be rented on-site, and the resort offers daycare
for younger children and shuttles from Québec City, Beaupré, Baie-St-
Paul, and the Montréal area. ✉ *1350 rue Principale, Petit-Rivière-St-
François* ☎ *418/632–5876, 877/536–2774* ⊕ *www.lemassif.com.*

Mont-Ste-Anne. Part of the World Cup downhill circuit, Mont-Ste-Anne
is one of the largest resorts in eastern Canada, with a vertical drop
of 2,050 feet, 66 downhill trails, two half-pipes for snowboarders, a
terrain park, and 13 lifts, including a gondola. The mountain stays
active even after the sun goes down with 18 lighted downhill trails.
Cross-country skiing is also a draw here, with 21 trails totaling 224
km (139 miles). When the weather warms, mountain biking becomes
the sport of choice. Enthusiasts can choose from 150 km (93 miles) of
mountain-bike trails and 14 downhill runs (and a gondola up to the
top). Three bike runs are designated "extreme zones." ✉ *2000 blvd.
du Beau-Pré, Beaupré* ☎ *418/827–4561, 888/827–4579* ⊕ *www.mont-
sainte-anne.com.*

ÎLE D'ORLÉANS

The Algonquins called it Minigo, the "Bewitched Place," and over the
years the island's tranquil rural beauty has inspired poets and painters.
Île d'Orléans is only 15 minutes by car from downtown Québec City,
but a visit here is one of the best ways to get a feel for traditional life
in rural Québec. Centuries-old homes and some of the oldest churches
in the region dot the road that rings the island.

Île d'Orléans is at its best in summer, when the boughs of trees in lush
orchards bend under the weight of apples, plums, or pears, and the
fields burst with strawberries and raspberries. Roadside stands sell

woven articles, maple syrup, baked goods, jams, fruits, and vegetables. You can also pick your own produce at about two dozen farms. The island, immortalized by one of its most famous residents, the poet and songwriter Félix Leclerc (1914–88), is still fertile ground for artists and artisans.

The island was discovered at about the same time as the future site of Québec City, in 1535. Explorer Jacques Cartier noticed an abundance of vines and called it the Island of Bacchus, after the Greek god of wine. (Today native vines are being crossbred with European varieties at Ste-Pétronille's fledgling vineyard.) In 1536 Cartier renamed the island in honor of the duke of Orléans, son of the French king François I. Its fertile soil and abundant fishing made it so attractive to settlers that at one time there were more people living here than in Québec City.

> ### WORD OF MOUTH
>
> "In the summer I just love Île d'Orléans, the island on the St. Lawrence, with its galleries, farms, and cideries. . . . If you wanted to go much farther afield, go east to Baie St. Paul (home town to the founder of Cirque de Soleil) an hour or so. It's a beautiful little town full of great galleries and restaurants and has fantastic Le Massif skiing next door during the winter."
> —MsLizzy

About 8 km (5 miles) wide and 35 km (22 miles) long, Île d'Orléans is made up of six small villages that have sought over the years to retain their identities. The bridge to the mainland was built in 1935, and in 1970 the island was declared a historic area to protect it from most sorts of development.

ESSENTIALS

Tourist Information Center Île d'Orléans ⊠ 490 Côte du Pont, St-Pierre-de-Île d'Orleans 🕾 418/828–9411, 866/941–9411.

STE-PÉTRONILLE

17 km (10½ miles) northeast of Québec City.

The lovely village of Ste-Pétronille, the first to be settled on Île d'Orléans, is west of the bridge to the island. Founded in 1648, the community was chosen in 1759 by British general James Wolfe for his headquarters. With 40,000 soldiers and a hundred ships, the English bombarded French-occupied Québec City and Côte-de-Beaupré.

In the late 19th century the English population of Québec developed Ste-Pétronille into a resort village. This area is considered to be the island's most beautiful, not only because of its spectacular views of Montmorency Falls and Québec City but also for its Regency-style English villas and exquisitely tended gardens.

EXPLORING

Maison Gourdeau de Beaulieu. The island's first home was built in 1648 for Jacques Gourdeau de Beaulieu, the first seigneur (a landholder who distributed lots to tenant farmers) of Ste-Pétronille. Remodeled over the years, this white house with blue shutters now incorporates both French

Montmorency Falls along the Côte-de-Beaupré might not be as wide, but it's nearly twice as tall as Niagara Falls.

and Québec styles. Its thick walls and dormer windows are characteristic of Breton architecture, but its sloping, bell-shape roof, designed to protect buildings from large amounts of snow, is typical Québec style. The house is not open to the public. ✉ *137 chemin du Bout de l'Île.*

Plante family farm. Pick apples and strawberries (in season) or buy fresh fruits, vegetables, and apple cider at this family farm. In winter, enjoy maple-sugar treats from the roadside sugar shack. ✉ *20 chemin du Bout de l'Île* ☎ *418/828–9603.*

Vignoble de Ste-Pétronille. Hardy native Québec vines have been crossbred with three types of European grapes to produce a surprisingly good dry white wine as well as a red, a rosé, and a locally created ice wine called Vandal. A guided tour of the vineyard includes a tasting. ✉ *1A chemin du Bout de l'Île* ☎ *418/828–9554* ⊕ *www. vignobleorleans.com* ✉ *Guided tour C$6* ⊙ *May–Nov., daily; times vary, call for up-to-date schedule.*

WHERE TO STAY

For expanded hotel reviews, visit fodors.com.

$$ 🏨 **Auberge La Goéliche.** This English-style country manor (rebuilt in
B&B/INN 1996–97 following a fire) is steps away from the St. Lawrence River, and the small but elegant rooms, decorated with antiques, all have river views. **Pros:** spectacular location; notably pleasant staff celebrated for their hospitality. **Cons:** riverfront but no access to the water; some rooms only have very small TVs with no remote. ⑤ *Rooms from: C$188* ✉ *22 chemin du Quai* ☎ *418/828–2248, 888/511–2248* ⊕ *www. goeliche.ca* ⤴ *16 rooms, 3 suites* ⧖ *Breakfast.*

SHOPPING

Chocolaterie de l'Île d'Orléans. This chocolatier combines Belgian chocolate with local ingredients to create handmade treats—chocolates filled with maple butter, for example, or *framboisette*, made from raspberries. In summer try the homemade ice creams and sherbets. ⊠ *150 chemin du Bout de l'Île* ☎ *418/828–2250.*

ST-LAURENT DE L'ÎLE D'ORLÉANS

9 km (5½ miles) east of Ste-Pétronille.

Founded in 1679, St-Laurent is one of the island's maritime villages. Until as late as 1935, residents here used boats as their main means of transportation. St-Laurent has a rich history in farming and fishing. Work is under way to help bring back to the island some of the species of fish that were once abundant here.

EXPLORING

Église St-Laurent. The tall, inspiring church that stands next to the village marina on chemin Royal was built in 1860 on the site of an 18th-century church that had to be torn down. One of the church's procession chapels is a miniature stone reproduction of the original. ⊠ *1532 chemin Royal* ☎ *418/828–2551* ⬚ *Free* ☉ *Mid-June–Oct., daily 10–5.*

La Forge à Pique-Assaut. This forge belongs to the talented local artisan Guy Bel, who has done ironwork restoration for Québec City. He was born in Lyon, France, and studied there at the École des Beaux-Arts. You can watch him and his team at work; his stylish candlesticks, chandeliers, fireplace tools, and other ironwork are for sale. ⊠ *2200 chemin Royal* ☎ *418/828–9300* ⊕ *www.forge-pique-assaut.com* ☉ *June 24–Sept. 3, daily 10–5; Sept. 4–June 23, call for reservations.*

Parc Maritime de St-Laurent. This former boatyard includes the Chalouperie Godbout (Godbout Longboat), which holds a collection of tools used by specialist craftsmen during the golden era of boatbuilding. You can picnic here and watch fishermen at work trapping eels in tall nets at low tide. ⊠ *120 chemin de la Chalouperie* ☎ *418/828–9672* ⊕ *www.parcmaritime.ca* ⬚ *C$5* ☉ *June 9–Oct. 8, daily 10–5.*

WHERE TO EAT AND STAY

For expanded hotel reviews, visit Fodors.com.

$$
CAFÉ ✕ **Moulin de St-Laurent.** You can dine inside or outside at the foot of a tiny, yet delightfully peaceful waterfall at this restaurant, converted from an early-18th-century stone mill. Scrumptious snacks, such as quiche and salads, are available on the terrace, and evening dishes include regional salmon and sweetbreads. You can stay overnight at one of the Moulin de St-Laurent's chalets—nine available in summer; six in winter—on the edge of the St. Lawrence. Lodging packages are also available,

starting at C$460 fo two nights, including some meals. ⑤ *Average main: C$20* ✉ *754 chemin Royal* ☎ *418/829–3888, 888/629–3888* ⊕ *www. moulinstlaurent.qc.ca* ⊙ *Restaurant closed mid-Oct.–May.*

$ ⊡ **Le Canard Huppé.** While the food here is among the best the island has
B&B/INN to offer, and is the property's main attraction, the inn itself shouldn't be overlooked, featuring large, unique, and comfortable rooms in a beautiful location between the St. Lawrence River and the island's lush, verdant fields. **Pros:** ideal spot for gourmands; inventive cuisine; many sights and areas of interest very nearby; good for cyclists. **Cons:** no pool. ⑤ *Rooms from: C$140* ✉ *2198 chemin Royal* ☎ *418/828–2292, 800/838–2292* ⊕ *www.canard-huppe.com* ↝ *9 rooms, 1 suite* ⊙ *Restaurant by reservation only Nov.–May* ⏐⃝*Breakfast.*

ST-JEAN

12 km (7 miles) northeast of St-Laurent.

The village of St-Jean used to be occupied by river pilots and navigators. At sea most of the time, the sailors didn't need the large homes and plots of land that the farmers did. Often richer than farmers, they displayed their affluence by building their houses with bricks brought back from Scotland as ballast. Most of St-Jean's small, homogeneous row houses were built between 1840 and 1860.

EXPLORING

Église St-Jean. At the eastern end of the village sits a massive granite structure built in 1749, with large red doors and a towering steeple. The church resembles a ship; it's big and round and appears to be sitting right on the river. Paintings of the patron saints of seamen line the interior walls. The church's cemetery is also intriguing, especially if you can read French. Back in the 1700s, piloting the St. Lawrence was a dangerous profession; the cemetery tombstones recall the many lives lost in these harsh waters. ✉ *2001 chemin Royal* ☎ *418/828–2551* ▱ *Free* ⊙ *Late May–early Oct., daily 10–5.*

Manoir Mauvide-Genest. St-Jean's beautiful Normandy-style manor was built in 1734 for Jean Mauvide, surgeon to Louis XV, and his wife, Marie-Anne Genest. The most notable thing about this house, which still has its original thick walls, ceiling beams, and fireplaces, is the degree to which it has held up over the years. The house serves as an interpretation center of New France's seigneurial regime, with 18th-century furniture, a multimedia presentation, and tours with guides dressed in 18th-century costumes. ✉ *1451 chemin Royal* ☎ *418/829– 2630* ⊕ *www.manoirmauvidegenest.com* ▱ *C$6 (nonguided tour), C$8 (guided tour)* ⊙ *May 15–Oct. 23., daily 10–5.*

ST-FRANÇOIS

12 km (7 miles) northeast of St-Jean.

Sprawling open fields separate 17th-century farmhouses in St-François, the island's least-toured and most rustic village. This community at the eastern tip of the island was settled mainly by farmers. St-François is the perfect place to visit one of the island's *cabanes à sucre* (maple-sugaring shacks), found along chemin Royal. Stop at a hut for a tasting tour; sap is gathered from the maple groves and boiled until it turns to syrup. When it's poured on ice, it tastes like toffee. The maple-syrup season is from late March through April.

EXPLORING

Église St-François. Built in 1734, St-François is one of eight extant provincial churches dating from the French regime. At the time the English seized Québec City in 1759, General James Wolfe knew St-François to be a strategic point along the St. Lawrence. Consequently, he stationed British troops here and used the church as a military hospital. In 1988 a car crash set the church on fire, and most of the interior treasures were lost. A separate children's cemetery stands as a silent witness to the difficult life of early residents. ✉ *341 chemin Royal* ☎ *418/828–2551* ✎ *Free* ☉ *June 24–Sept. 5, daily noon–5.*

Observation Tower. This picnic area with a wooden tower is well situated for viewing the majestic St. Lawrence. In spring and fall wild Canada geese can be seen here. The area is about 2 km (1 mile) north of Église St-François on chemin Royal.

STE-FAMILLE

14 km (9 miles) west of St-François.

The village of Ste-Famille, founded in 1661, has exquisite scenery, including abundant apple orchards and strawberry fields with views of Côte-de-Beaupré and Mont-Ste-Anne in the distance. But it also has plenty of historic charm, with the area's highest concentration of stone houses dating from the French regime.

EXPLORING

Église Ste-Famille. This impressive church, constructed in 1749, is the only one in Québec province to have three bell towers at its front. The ceiling was redone in the mid-19th century with elaborate designs in wood and gold. The church also holds a famous painting, *L'Enfant Jésus Voyant la Croix* (Baby Jesus Looking at the Cross). It was done in 1670 by Frère Luc (Father Luc), sent from France to decorate churches in the area. ✉ *3915 chemin Royal* ☎ *418/828–2656* ✎ *Free* ☉ *Late June–early Sept., daily 10–5.*

ST-PIERRE

14 km (9 miles) southwest of Ste-Famille.

St-Pierre, established in 1679, is set on a plateau that has the island's most fertile land. The town has long been the center of traditional farming industries. The best products grown here are potatoes, asparagus, and corn. In 2002 the Espace Félix Leclerc—an exhibit by day and a *boîte à chansons* (combination coffeehouse and bar with live performances) by night—was opened to honor the late singer and songwriter who made St-Pierre his home. If you continue west on chemin Royal, just ahead is the bridge to the mainland and Route 440.

EXPLORING

Église St-Pierre. The oldest church on the island dates from 1717. It's no longer used for worship, but it was restored during the 1960s and is open to visitors. Many original components are still intact, such as benches with compartments below where hot bricks and stones were placed to keep people warm in winter. Félix Leclerc, the first Québecois singer to make a mark in Europe, is buried in the cemetery nearby. ✉ *1249 chemin Royal* ☎ *418/828–9824* 🎫 *Free* ⏱ *May, daily 10–4; June, Sept., and Oct., daily 10–5; July and Aug., daily 9:30–5.*

La Ferme Monna–L'Isle Ensorceleuse. This family farm has won international awards for its *crème de cassis de l'Île d'Orléans,* a liqueur made from black currants. The farm offers free samples of the strong, sweet cassis or one of its black-currant wines; the tour explains how they are made. In summer you can sample foods made with cassis on a terrace overlooking the river. ✉ *726 chemin Royal* ☎ *418/828–1057* ⊕ *www.cassismonna.com* 🎫 *Free, guided tour C$5* ⏱ *June–Nov., daily 10–7.*

SHOPPING

Poissonnerie Joseph Paquet. The only remaining commercial fisherman on the island smokes his fish and sells it from a tiny shack. You can sample surprisingly tasty smoked eel as well as smoked trout and salmon. Also on sale are fresh and smoked walleye pike and sturgeon, all from the St. Lawrence River. New products include a sturgeon mousse and, a most rare treat—sturgeon *méchoui*: the fish is marinated in salt the traditional way, and then roasted on a spit. ✉ *2705 chemin Royal* ☎ *418/828–2670* ⊕ *www.poissonneriejospaquet.com* ⏱ *June 24–Oct. 8, daily 10–6; Oct. 9–Dec. and Mar.–June 23, daily 9–6. Jan. and Feb. on request.*

CHARLEVOIX

Bordered by the Laurentian Mountains to the north, the Saguenay River to the east, and the St. Lawrence River to the south, the Charlevoix region is famous for awe-inspiring vistas and kaleidoscopes of color that change throughout the day. The region also has rich historical significance for both French Canadians and English Canadians.

The "discoverer" of Canada, Jacques Cartier, is believed to have set foot in the area in 1535. More certain is a visit 73 years later by Samuel de Champlain.

New France's first historian, the Jesuit priest François-Xavier de Charlevoix (pronounced shar-le-*vwah*), is the region's namesake. The area's first white inhabitants arrived in the early 1700s. Among other things, they developed a small shipbuilding industry that specialized in sturdy schooners called *goélettes,* which were used to haul everything from logs to lobsters up and down the coast in the days before rail and paved roads. In the 19th century, as steamships plied the St. Lawrence, Charlevoix became a popular tourist destination for well-to-do English Canadians and British colonial administrators from Montréal and Québec City. Since then, tourism—and hospitality—has become Charlevoix's trademark.

The region has attracted and inspired generations of painters, poets, writers, and musicians from across Québec and Canada, and became a UNESCO World Biosphere Reserve in 1989. In summer, hiking, fishing, picnicking, sightseeing, and whale-watching are the area's main attractions. Winter activities include downhill and cross-country skiing, snowmobiling, ice fishing, dogsledding, and snowshoeing.

BAIE-ST-PAUL

120 km (72 miles) northeast of Québec City.

Baie-St-Paul, one of the oldest towns in the province, is popular with craftspeople and artists. With its centuries-old mansard-roof houses, the village is on the banks of a winding river, on a wide plain encircled by high hills. Boutiques and a handful of commercial galleries line the historic narrow streets in the town center; most have original artwork and crafts for sale. In addition, each August more than a dozen artists from across Canada take part in the "Symposium of Modern Art." The artists work together to create a giant canvas about the year's theme.

EXPLORING

Maison René Richard. Jean-Paul Lemieux, Clarence Gagnon, and many more of Québec's greatest landscape artists have depicted the area, and some of these works are on show (some also for sale) at this gallery, which also houses Gagnon's old studio. Guided tours of the studio are available for groups. ⊠ *58 rue St-Jean-Baptiste* ☎ *418/435–5571* 🖾 *Free; guided tours C$75, or C$6 per person for groups of more than 15* ⊙ *Daily 10–6.*

Musée d'Art Contemporain de Baie-St-Paul. Recognized as a museum in 2008, this center highlights modern and contemporary art created by Charlevoix artists from 1920 to 1970. It also has a robust collection from the province in general, with works from Georges D. Pepper, Kathleen Daly, René Richard, the Bolduc sisters, and many more. The modern building was awarded a provincial architectural prize in 1992. ⊠ *23 rue Ambroise-Fafard* ☎ *418/435–3681* ⊕ *www.macbsp.com* 🖾 *C$7* ⊙ *June 24–Sept. 5, daily 10–5; Sept. 6–June 23, Tues.–Sun. 11–5.*

WHERE TO STAY

For expanded hotel reviews, visit Fodors.com.

$$
HOTEL

Hôtel La Ferme. For something more luxurious than the standard sleepy inns of Baie-St-Paul, the new Gauthier venture opened in 2012 consists of five distinct pavilions housing rooms in various styles, including lofts and dormitories. **Pros:** location with on-site train station and public square; in-room espresso makers. **Cons:** new hotel means they're still working out the kinks. 🖼 *Rooms from: C$175* ⊠ *50 rue de la Ferme, Baie-St-Paul* ☎ *418/240–4100, 877/536–2774* ⊕ *www.lemassif. com* 🛏 *145 rooms, 7 suites* ⍩ *No meals.*

EN
ROUTE

Route 362. From Baie-St-Paul, instead of the faster Route 138 to La Malbaie, drivers can choose the open, scenic coastal drive on Route 362. This section of road has memorable views of rolling hills—green, white, or ablaze with fiery hues, depending on the season—meeting the broad expanse of the "sea," as the locals like to call the St. Lawrence estuary.

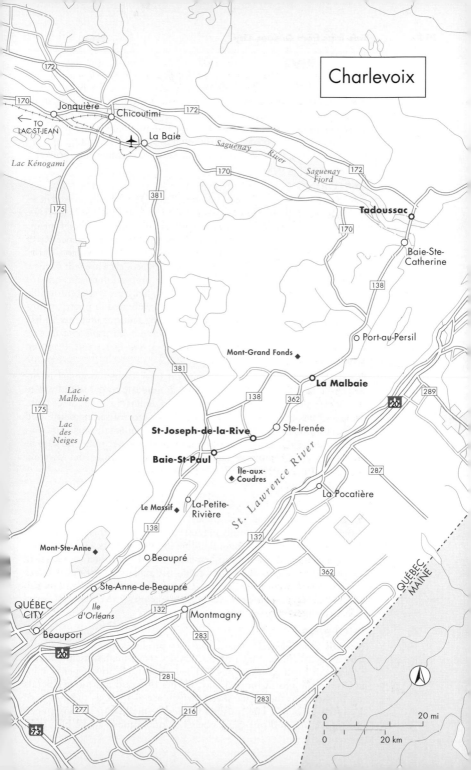

ST-JOSEPH-DE-LA-RIVE

19 km (12 miles) northeast of Baie-St-Paul.

A secondary road descends sharply into St-Joseph-de-la-Rive, with its line of old houses hugging the mountain base on a narrow shore route. The town has a number of peaceful inns and inviting restaurants. Drive through and see the traces of early town life and the beginning of local industry: an old firehouse and a hydroelectric building that houses a generator dating back to 1928.

EXPLORING

Exposition Maritime (*Maritime Museum*). This small exhibit, housed in an old, still-active shipyard, commemorates the days of the St. Lawrence *goélettes*, the feisty little wooden freighters that were the chief means of transporting goods along the north shore of the St. Lawrence River well into the 1960s. In the mid-20th century the roads through Charlevoix were little more than rugged tracks. (Indeed, they are still narrow and winding.) Very large families lived in cramped conditions aboard the boats. To modern eyes, it doesn't look like it was a comfortable existence, but the folklore of the goélettes, celebrated in poetry, paintings, and song, is part of the region's strong cultural identity. ⊠ *305 rue de l'Église* ☎ *418/635–1131* ⊕ *www.musee-maritime-charlevoix. com* ⊠ *C$5* ⊗ *Mid-May–mid-Oct., daily 9–5; mid-Oct.–Nov., by group reservation only.*

Île-aux-Coudres. A free, government-run ferry from the wharf in St-Joseph-de-la-Rive takes you on the 15-minute trip to the island where Jacques Cartier's men gathered *coudres* (hazelnuts) in 1535. Since then, the island has produced many a *goélette* (a type of sailing ship), and the families of former captains now run several small inns. You can bike around the island and see windmills and water mills, or stop at boutiques selling paintings and crafts such as traditional handwoven household linens. ☎ *877/787–7483 ferry schedules.*

WHERE TO STAY

For expanded hotel reviews, visit fodors.com.

$ ⊞ **Hôtel Cap-aux-Pierres.** One of several properties established by the
HOTEL entrepreneurial Dufour family in the 1930s to support their 17 children, the traditional Canadian main building of this hotel has a long veranda with river views. **Pros:** beautiful environment. **Cons:** hotel rooms fairly unspectacular and motel rooms could use updating. ⑤ *Rooms from: C$129* ⊠ *444 chemin la Baleine, Île-aux-Coudres* ☎ *888/554–6003, 418/438–2711* ⊕ *www.hotelcapauxpierres.com* ↷ *98 rooms* ⊗ *Closed mid-Oct.–Apr.* ⑩ *No meals.*

SHOPPING

Papeterie Saint-Gilles. This paper factory produces handcrafted stationery using a 17th-century process. There's also a small museum, which explains through photographs and demonstrations how paper is manufactured the old-fashioned way. Slivers of wood and flower petals are pressed into the paper sheets, which are as thick as the covers of a paperback book. The finished products—made into writing paper, greeting cards, and one-page poems or quotations—make beautiful,

Baie-St-Paul is a charming small town popular with writers and artists. Each August It hosts a modern art show.

if pricey, gifts. Visitors can wander through the museum for free and guided tours can be arranged for groups (of 15 or more) for C$3.25 per person. ✉ *354 rue F.A. Savard* ☎ *418/635–2430, 866/635–2430* ⊕ *www.papeteriesaintgilles.com.*

LA MALBAIE

35 km (22 miles) northeast of St-Joseph-de-la-Rive.

La Malbaie, one of the province's most elegant and historically interesting resort towns, was known as Murray Bay when wealthy Anglophones summered here. The area became popular with American and Canadian politicians in the late 1800s, when Ottawa Liberals and Washington Republicans partied decorously all summer with members of the Québec judiciary. William Howard Taft built the "summer White House," the first of three summer residences, in 1894, when he was the American civil governor of the Philippines. He became the 27th president of the United States in 1908.

Many Taft-era homes now serve as handsome inns, offering old-fashioned coddling with such extras as breakfast in bed, whirlpool baths, and free shuttles to the ski areas in winter. Many serve lunch and dinner to nonresidents, so you can tour the area going from one gourmet delight to the next. The cuisine, as elsewhere in Québec, is genuine French or regional fare.

A hiker takes in the view of an ancient glacial valley in Hautes-Gorges-de-la-Rivière-Malbaie National Park.

EXPLORING

Casino de Charlevoix. The casino is one of three gaming halls in Québec (the others are in Montréal and Gatineau) owned and operated by Loto-Québec. The smallest of the three, it still draws more than 1 million visitors a year—some of whom stay at the Fairmont Le Manoir Richelieu, which is connected to the casino by a tunnel. There are 21 gaming tables and more than 900 slot machines. The minimum gambling age is 18. Photo ID is required to enter the casino. ⊠ *183 rue Richelieu, Pointe-au-Pic* ☎ *418/665–5300, 800/665–2274* ⊕ *www.casino-de-charlevoix.com* ⊗ *June 22–Sept 2., Sun.–Thurs. 9 am–2 am, Fri. and Sat. 10 am–3 am; Sept 3.–late Oct., Sun.–Thurs. 10 am–1 am, Fri. and Sat. 10 am–3 am.*

Musée de Charlevoix. The museum traces the region's history through a major permanent exhibit called "Appartenances" (Belonging). Folk art, paintings, and artifacts recount the past, starting with the French, then the Scottish settlers, and the area's evolution into a vacation spot and artists' haven. ⊠ *10 chemin du Havre, Pointe-au-Pic* ☎ *418/665–4411* ⊕ *www.museedecharlevoix.qc.ca* ⊠ *C$7* ⊗ *June–mid-Oct., daily 9–5; mid-Oct.–May, weekdays 10–5, weekends 1–5.*

OFF THE
BEATEN
PATH

Poterie de Port-au-Persil. Visiting potters, many from France, study Canadian ceramic techniques at this pottery studio, about 25 km (15½ miles) east of La Malbaie. Classes for amateurs are available from late June through August (by the hour or longer starting at C$12). Half of the bright yellow barn housing the studio is a store, with ceramics and other crafts made by Québec artists. ⊠ *1001 rue St-Laurent(Rte.*

138), St-Siméon ☎ *418/638–2349* ⊕ *www.poteriedeportaupersil.com* ⊙ *June–Labor Day, daily 9–6; Labor Day–mid-Oct., daily 10–4.*

WHERE TO STAY

For expanded hotel reviews, visit Fodors.com.

$ ⊡ **Auberge des Peupliers.** About half the guest rooms at this hilltop inn
B&B/INN   overlook the St. Lawrence River, and the country-style accommodations are spread among three buildings, including a farmhouse more than two centuries old. **Pros:** lounge with fireplace and bar perfect for relaxing; excellent food and service. **Cons:** location is not a convenient walk to downtown La Malbaie. ⑤ *Rooms from: C$129* ⊠ *381 rue St-Raphaël, Cap-à-l'Aigle* ☎ *418/665–4423, 888/282–3743* ⊕ *www. aubergedespeupliers.com* ⟿ *22 rooms* ⓧ *Breakfast.*

$$$$ ⊡ **Auberge la Pinsonnière.** An atmosphere of country luxury prevails
HOTEL   at this Relais & Châteaux inn, which has an impressive art collection. **Pros:** friendly staff; fireplaces in every room; views of Murray Bay; luxurious surroundings in a remote environment; a wonderful, albeit very steep, trail leading down to the river. **Cons:** not vegetarian friendly. ⑤ *Rooms from: C$295* ⊠ *124 rue St-Raphaël, Cap-à-l'Aigle* ☎ *418/665–4431, 800/387–4431* ⊕ *www.lapinsonniere.com* ⟿ *18 rooms* ⓧ *No meals.*

$$$ ⊡ **Fairmont Le Manoir Richelieu.** Constructed in 1929, this castlelike build-
RESORT   ing and its sweeping grounds underwent a C$100 million restoration
⟳   in the late 1990s. **Pros:** stunning views; variety of dining options on-site. **Cons:** rooms could use updating. ⑤ *Rooms from: C$219* ⊠ *181 rue Richelieu, Pointe-au-Pic* ☎ *418/665–3703, 800/463–2613* ⊕ *www. fairmont.com* ⟿ *405 rooms, 17 suites* ⓧ *Breakfast.*

THE ARTS

Domaine Forget. The music and dance academy has a 604-seat hall in Ste-Irenée, 15 km (9 miles) south of La Malbaie. Fine musicians from around the world, many of whom teach or study at the school, perform during its International Festival. The festival, which runs from mid-June to late August, includes Sunday musical brunches with a variety of music, a buffet lunch, and a view of the St. Lawrence. ⊠ *5 rang St-Antoine, Ste-Irenée* ☎ *418/452–3535, 888/336–7438* ⊕ *www. domaineforget.com.*

SPORTS AND THE OUTDOORS

Club de Golf de Manoir Richelieu. This is a links-style course with three nine-hole courses and views of the St. Lawrence River. ⊠ *181 rue Richelieu, Pointe-au-Pic* ☎ *418/665–2526, 800/665–8082* ⊕ *www. fairmont.com* ⚐ *St-Laurent Course: 9 holes. 3128 yds. Par 36. Slope 123. Richelieu Course: 9 holes. 3148 yds. Par 36. Slope 124. Tadoussac Course: 9 holes. 2918 yds. Par 35. Slope 120. Greens Fee: C$65–C$114* ⚐ *Facilities: driving range, putting green, golf carts, rental clubs, restaurant, bar.*

Mont-Grand Fonds. This winter-sports center 12 km (7 miles) north of La Malbaie has 14 downhill slopes, a 1,105-foot vertical drop, and three lifts. It also has 160 km (99 miles) of cross-country trails. Two trails meet International Ski Federation standards, and the ski center occasionally hosts major competitions. You may also go dog

In Tadoussac from May to October, you can see whales living in the Saguenay River.

sledding, sleigh riding, ice-skating, and tobogganing here. ✉ *1000 chemin des Loisirs, La Malbaie* ☎ *418/665–0095, 877/665–0095* ⊕ *www.montgrandfonds.com.*

TADOUSSAC

71 km (44 miles) north of La Malbaie.

The small town of Tadoussac shares the view up the magnificent Saguenay Fjord with Baie-Ste-Catherine, across the Saguenay River. The drive here from La Malbaie, along Route 138, leads past lovely villages and views along the St. Lawrence. Jacques Cartier made a stop at this point in 1535, and from 1600 to the mid-19th century it was an important meeting site for fur traders. Whale-watching excursions and fjord cruises now depart from Tadoussac, as well as from Chicoutimi, farther up the deep fjord.

As the Saguenay River flows from Lac St-Jean south toward the St. Lawrence, it has a dual character: between Alma and Chicoutimi, the once rapidly flowing river has been harnessed for hydroelectric power; in its lower section, it becomes wider and deeper and flows by steep mountains and cliffs en route to the St. Lawrence. Beluga whales, highly recognizable because of their all-white color, small size, and high-pitch call, live here year-round, and breed in the lower portion of the Saguenay in summer. The many marine species that live in the confluence of the fjord and the seaway attract other whales, too, such as pilots, finbacks, and humpbacks.

Sadly, the beluga is an endangered species; the whales, with 35 other species of mammals and birds and 21 species of fish, are threatened by pollution in the St. Lawrence River. This has spurred a C$100 million project (funded by the federal and provincial governments) aimed at removing or capping sediment in the most polluted areas, stopping industrial and residential emissions into the river, and restoring natural

habitat. And while there's still much work to be done, most experts agree that the St. Lawrence River's ecosystem is healthier now than it has been anytime in the past 50 years.

GETTING HERE AND AROUND

You must take a free 10-minute ferry ride from Baie-Ste-Catherine to get to Tadoussac. The ferries leave every 20 minutes, 24 hours a day, except from midnight until 4 am, when they depart every half hour. For more information on ferry schedules call ☎418/643–2019.

ESSENTIALS

Tourist Information Center Tadoussac ✉ 197 rue des Pionniers ☎418/235–4744, 866/235–4744.

EXPLORING

Centre d'Interprétation des Mammifères Marins. You can learn more about the whales and their habitat at this interpretation center run by members of a locally based research team. They're only too glad to answer questions. In addition, explanatory videos and exhibits (including a collection of whale skeletons) tell you everything there is to know about the mighty cetaceans. ✉ 108 rue de la Cale-Sèche ☎418/235–4701 ⊕ www. gremm.org ⊠ C$12 ☉ Mid-May–mid-June and mid-Sept.–mid-Oct., daily noon–5; mid-June–mid-Sept., daily 9–8.

Parc Marin du Saguenay–St-Laurent. The 800-square-km (309-square-mile) marine park, at the confluence of the Saguenay and St. Lawrence rivers, has been created to protect the latter's fragile ecosystem. ✉ Park office, 182 rue de l'Église ☎418/235–4703 ⊕ www.parcmarin.qc.ca.

WHERE TO STAY

For expanded hotel reviews, visit Fodors.com.

$$$ 🛏 **Hôtel Tadoussac.** The rambling white Victorian-style hotel with a
HOTEL red mansard roof is as much a symbol of Tadoussac as the Château Frontenac is of Québec City. **Pros:** they have an ongoing sustainability program and strive to be eco-friendly; stunning natural environment; restaurants suit different tastes and budgets. **Cons:** no air-conditioning in rooms. ⑤ *Rooms from: C$215* ✉ *165 rue Bord d'Eau* ☎ *418/235–4421, 800/561–0718* ⊕ *www.hoteltadoussac.com* ⇱ *149 rooms* ☉ *Closed mid-Oct.–early May* ⑩ *No meals.*

SPORTS AND THE OUTDOORS

The best months for seeing whales are August and September, although some operators extend the season at either end if whales are around. Fjord tours are also available.

Croisières AML. This outfitter offers two- to three-hour whale-watching tours starting at C$69. The tours, in Zodiacs or larger boats, depart from Baie-Ste-Catherine and Tadoussac. ☎ *418/692–1159, 800/463–1292* ⊕ *www.croisieresaml.com.*

Croisières Dufour. This company offers daylong cruises combined with whale-watching from Québec City as well as 2¼- and 3-hour whale-watching cruises (C$79) from Baie-Ste-Catherine and Tadoussac. Tours, some of which cruise up the Saguenay Fjord, use Zodiacs or larger boats. ☎ *800/463–5250* ⊕ *www.dufour.ca.*

FRENCH VOCABULARY

One of the trickiest French sounds to pronounce is the nasal final *n* sound (whether or not the n is actually the last letter of the word). You should try to pronounce it as a sort of nasal grunt—as in "huh." The vowel that precedes the *n* will govern the vowel sound of the word, and in this list we precede the final *n* with an *h* to remind you to be nasal.

Another problem sound is the ubiquitous but untransliterable eu, as in bleu (blue) or deux (two), and the very similar sound in je (I), ce (this), and de (of). The closest equivalent might be the vowel sound in "put," but rounded. The famous rolled *r* is a glottal sound. Consonants at the ends of words are usually silent; when the following word begins with a vowel, however, the two are run together by sounding the consonant. There are two forms of "you" in French: vous (formal and plural) and tu (a singular, personal form). When addressing an adult you don't know, vous is always best.

	ENGLISH	FRENCH	PRONUNCIATION
BASICS			
	Yes/no	Oui/non	wee/nohn
	Please	S'il vous plaît	seel voo play
	Thank you	Merci	mair **see**
	You're welcome	De rien	deh ree-**ehn**
	Excuse me, sorry	Pardon	pahr-**don**
	Good morning/ afternoon	Bonjour	bohn-**zhoor**
	Good evening	Bonsoir	bohn-**swahr**
	Good-bye	Au revoir	o ruh-**vwahr**
	Mr. (Sir)	Monsieur	muh-**syuh**
	Mrs. (Ma'am)	Madame	ma-**dam**
	Miss	Mademoiselle	mad-mwa-**zel**
	Pleased to meet you	Enchanté(e)	ohn-shahn-**tay**
	How are you?	Comment allez-vous?	kuh-mahn- tahl-ay **voo**
	Very well, thanks	Très bien, merci	tray bee-ehn, mair-**see**
	And you?	Et vous?	ay voo?
NUMBERS			
	one	un	uhn
	two	deux	deuh
	three	trois	twah

ENGLISH	FRENCH	PRONUNCIATION
four	quatre	**kaht**-ruh
five	cinq	sank
six	six	seess
seven	sept	set
eight	huit	wheat
nine	neuf	nuf
ten	dix	deess
eleven	onze	ohnz
twelve	douze	dooz
thirteen	treize	trehz
fourteen	quatorze	kah-torz
fifteen	quinze	kanz
sixteen	seize	sez
seventeen	dix-sept	deez-**set**
eighteen	dix-huit	deez-**wheat**
nineteen	dix-neuf	deez-**nuf**
twenty	vingt	vehn
twenty-one	vingt-et-un	vehnt-ay-**uhn**
thirty	trente	trahnt
forty	quarante	ka-**rahnt**
fifty	cinquante	sang-**kahnt**
sixty	soixante	swa-**sahnt**
seventy	soixante-dix	swa-sahnt-**deess**
eighty	quatre-vingts	kaht-ruh-**vehn**
ninety	quatre-vingt-dix	kaht-ruh-vehn-**deess**
one hundred	cent	sahn
one thousand	mille	meel

COLORS

black	noir	nwahr
blue	bleu	bleuh
brown	brun/marron	bruhn/mar-**rohn**

ENGLISH	FRENCH	PRONUNCIATION
green	vert	vair
orange	orange	o-**rahnj**
pink	rose	rose
red	rouge	rouge
violet	violette	vee-o-**let**
white	blanc	blahnk
yellow	jaune	zhone

DAYS OF THE WEEK

Sunday	dimanche	dee-**mahnsh**
Monday	lundi	luhn-**dee**
Tuesday	mardi	mahr-**dee**
Wednesday	mercredi	mair-kruh-**dee**
Thursday	jeudi	zhuh-**dee**
Friday	vendredi	vawn-druh-**dee**
Saturday	samedi	sahm-**dee**

MONTHS

January	janvier	zhahn-vee-**ay**
February	février	feh-vree-**ay**
March	mars	marce
April	avril	a-**vreel**
May	mai	meh
June	juin	zhwehn
July	juillet	zhwee-**ay**
August	août	ah-**oo**
September	septembre	sep-**tahm**-bruh
October	octobre	awk-**to**-bruh
November	novembre	no-**vahm**-bruh
December	décembre	day-**sahm**-bruh

ENGLISH	FRENCH	PRONUNCIATION

USEFUL PHRASES

Do you speak English?	Parlez-vous anglais?	par-lay **voo ahn**-glay
I don't speak . . .	Je ne parle pas . . .	zhuh nuh parl pah
French	français	frahn-**say**
I don't understand.	Je ne comprends pas.	zhuh nuh kohm-**prahn** pah
I understand.	Je comprends.	zhuh kohm-**prahn**
I don't know.	Je ne sais pas.	zhuh nuh say **pah**
I'm American/ British.	Je suis américain/ anglais.	a-may-ree-**kehn**/ ahn-**glay**
What's your name?	Comment vous appelez-vous?	ko-mahn voo za-pell-ay-**voo**
My name is . . .	Je m'appelle . . .	zhuh ma-**pell** . . .
What time is it?	Quelle heure est-il?	kel air eh-**teel**
How?	Comment?	ko-**mahn**
When?	Quand?	kahn
Yesterday	Hier	yair
Today	Aujourd'hui	o-zhoor-**dwee**
Tomorrow	Demain	duh-**mehn**
Tonight	Ce soir	suh **swahr**
What?	Quoi?	kwah
What is it?	Qu'est-ce que c'est?	kess-kuh-**say**
Why?	Pourquoi?	**poor**-kwa
Who?	Qui?	kee
Where is . . .	Où est . . .	oo ay
the train station?	la gare?	la gar
the subway station?	la station de métro?	la sta-**syon** duh may-**tro**
the bus stop?	l'arrêt de bus?	la-**ray** duh **booss**
the post office?	la poste?	la post
the bank?	la banque?	la bahnk
the . . . hotel?	l'hôtel . . .?	lo-**tel**

ENGLISH	FRENCH	PRONUNCIATION
the store?	le magasin?	luh ma-ga-**zehn**
the cashier?	la caisse?	la **kess**
the . . . museum?	le musée . . .?	luh mew-**zay**
the hospital?	l'hôpital?	lo-pee-**tahl**
the elevator?	l'ascenseur?	la-sahn-**seuhr**
the telephone?	le téléphone?	luh tay-lay-**phone**
Where are the restrooms?	Où sont les toilettes?	oo sohn lay twah-**let**
(men/women)	(hommes/femmes)	(**oh**-mmm/**fah**-mm)
Here/there	Ici/là	ee-**see**/la
Left/right	A gauche/à droite	a goash/a draht
Straight ahead	Tout droit	too drwah
Is it near/far?	C'est près/loin?	say pray/lwehn
I'd like . . .	Je voudrais . . .	zhuh voo-**dray**
a room	une chambre	ewn **shahm**-bruh
the key	la clé	la clay
a newspaper	un journal	uhn zhoor-**nahl**
a stamp	un timbre	uhn **tam**-bruh
I'd like to buy . . .	Je voudrais acheter . . .	zhuh voo-**dray ahsh**-tay
cigarettes	des cigarettes	day see-ga-**ret**
matches	des allumettes	days a-loo-**met**
soap	du savon	dew sah-**vohn**
city map	un plan de ville	uhn plahn de **veel**
road map	une carte routière	ewn cart roo-tee-**air**
magazine	une revue	ewn reh-**vu**
envelopes	des enveloppes	dayz ahn-veh-**lope**
writing paper	du papier à lettres	dew pa-pee-**ay** a **let**-ruh
postcard	une carte postale	ewn cart pos-**tal**
How much is it?	C'est combien?	say comb-bee-**ehn**
A little/a lot	Un peu/beaucoup	uhn peuh/bo-**koo**
More/less	Plus/moins	plu/mwehn

ENGLISH	FRENCH	PRONUNCIATION
Enough/too (much)	Assez/trop	a-say/tro
I am ill/sick.	Je suis malade.	zhuh swee ma-**lahd**
Call a . . .	Appelez un . . .	a-play uhn
doctor	Docteur	dohk-**tehr**
Help!	Au secours!	o suh-**koor**
Stop!	Arrêtez!	a-reh-**tay**
Fire!	Au feu!	o fuh
Caution!/Look out!	Attention!	a-tahn-see-**ohn**

DINING OUT

A bottle of . . .	une bouteille de . . .	ewn boo-**tay** duh
A cup of . . .	une tasse de . . .	ewn tass duh
A glass of . . .	un verre de . . .	uhn vair duh
Bill/check	l'addition	la-dee-see-**ohn**
Bread	du pain	dew pan
Breakfast	le petit-déjeuner	luh puh-**tee** day-zhuh-**nay**
Butter	du beurre	dew burr
Cheers!	A votre santé!	ah vo-truh sahn-**tay**
Cocktail/aperitif	un apéritif	uhn ah-pay-ree-**teef**
Dinner	le dîner	luh dee-**nay**
Dish of the day	le plat du jour	luh plah dew **zhoor**
Enjoy!	Bon appétit!	bohn a-pay-**tee**
Fixed-price menu	le menu	luh may-**new**
Fork	une fourchette	ewn four-**shet**
I am diabetic.	Je suis diabétique.	zhuh swee dee-ah- bay-**teek**
I am vegetarian.	Je suis végétarien(ne).	zhuh swee vay-zhay-ta-ree-**en**
I cannot eat . . .	Je ne peux pas manger de . . .	zhuh nuh **puh** pah mahn-**jay** deh
I'd like to order.	Je voudrais commander.	zhuh voo-**dray** ko-mahn-**day**

ENGLISH	FRENCH	PRONUNCIATION
Is service/the tip included?	Est-ce que le service est compris?	ess kuh luh sair-**veess** ay comb-**pree**
It's good/bad.	C'est bon/mauvais.	say bohn/mo-**vay**
It's hot/cold.	C'est chaud/froid.	Say sho/frwah
Knife	un couteau	uhn koo-**toe**
Lunch	le déjeuner	luh day-zhuh-**nay**
Menu	la carte	la cart
Napkin	une serviette	ewn sair-vee-**et**
Pepper	du poivre	dew **pwah**-vruh
Plate	une assiette	ewn a-see-**et**
Please give me . . .	Donnez-moi . . .	doe-nay-**mwah**
Salt	du sel	dew sell
Spoon	une cuillère	ewn kwee-air
Sugar	du sucre	dew **sook**-ruh
Waiter!/Waitress!	Monsieur!/ Mademoiselle!	muh-**syuh**/ mad-mwa-**zel**
Wine list	la carte des vins	la cart day vehn

MENU GUIDE

FRENCH	ENGLISH

GENERAL DINING

Entrée	Appetizer/Starter
Garniture au choix	Choice of vegetable side
Plat du jour	Dish of the day
Selon arrivage	When available
Supplément/En sus	Extra charge
Sur commande	Made to order

PETIT DÉJEUNER (BREAKFAST)

Confiture	Jam
Miel	Honey
Oeuf à la coque	Boiled egg

FRENCH	ENGLISH
Oeufs sur le plat	Fried eggs
Oeufs brouillés	Scrambled eggs
Tartine	Bread with butter

POISSONS/FRUITS DE MER (FISH/SEAFOOD)

Anchois	Anchovies
Bar	Bass
Brandade de morue	Creamed salt cod
Brochet	Pike
Cabillaud/Morue	Fresh cod
Calmar	Squid
Coquilles St-Jacques	Scallops
Crevettes	Shrimp
Daurade	Sea bream
Ecrevisses	Prawns/Crayfish
Harengs	Herring
Homard	Lobster
Huîtres	Oysters
Langoustine	Prawn/Lobster
Lotte	Monkfish
Moules	Mussels
Palourdes	Clams
Saumon	Salmon
Thon	Tuna
Truite	Trout

VIANDE (MEAT)

Agneau	Lamb
Boeuf	Beef
Boudin	Sausage
Boulettes de viande	Meatballs
Brochettes	Kebabs

FRENCH	ENGLISH
Cassoulet	Casserole of white beans, meat
Cervelle	Brains
Chateaubriand	Double fillet steak
Choucroute garnie	Sausages with sauerkraut
Côtelettes	Chops
Côte/Côte de boeuf	Rib/T-bone steak
Cuisses de grenouilles	Frogs' legs
Entrecôte	Rib or rib-eye steak
Épaule	Shoulder
Escalope	Cutlet
Foie	Liver
Gigot	Leg
Porc	Pork
Ris de veau	Veal sweetbreads
Rognons	Kidneys
Saucisses	Sausages
Selle	Saddle
Tournedos	Tenderloin of T-bone steak
Veau	Veal

METHODS OF PREPARATION

A point	Medium
A l'étouffée	Stewed
Au four	Baked
Ballotine	Boned, stuffed, and rolled
Bien cuit	Well-done
Bleu	Very rare
Frit	Fried
Grillé	Grilled
Rôti	Roast
Saignant	Rare

FRENCH	ENGLISH
VOLAILLES/GIBIER (POULTRY/GAME)	
Blanc de volaille	Chicken breast
Canard/Caneton	Duck/Duckling
Cerf/Chevreuil	Venison (red/roe)
Coq au vin	Chicken stewed in red wine
Dinde/Dindonneau	Turkey/Young turkey
Faisan	Pheasant
Lapin/Lièvre	Rabbit/Wild hare
Oie	Goose
Pintade/Pintadeau	Guinea fowl/Young guinea fowl
Poulet/Poussin	Chicken/Spring chicken
LÉGUMES (VEGETABLES)	
Artichaut	Artichoke
Asperge	Asparagus
Aubergine	Eggplant
Carottes	Carrots
Champignons	Mushrooms
Chou-fleur	Cauliflower
Chou (rouge)	Cabbage (red)
Laitue	Lettuce
Oignons	Onions
Petits pois	Peas
Pomme de terre	Potato
Tomates	Tomatoes

Travel Smart Montréal and Québec City

WORD OF MOUTH

"Has anyone taken a bicycle tour in Montreal?"
—samejia

"As a Montrealer who cycles regularly . . . [I would] always be alert and cycle defensively. This said the cycling network is extensive and among the best I've seen in North America. . . . If you're actually interested in a tour, Vélo Québec is a good place to check out."
—Daniel_Williams

GETTING HERE AND AROUND

■ AIR TRAVEL

Flying time (gate-to-gate) to Montréal is about 1½ hours from New York, 2½ hours from Chicago, 4 hours from Dallas, and 6 hours from Los Angeles. Flying time to Québec City is about 2 hours from New York, 3 hours from Chicago, 5 hours from Dallas, and 7 hours from Los Angeles.

Trudeau Airport offers self-serve check-in and boarding passes at electronic kiosks throughout the airport. Make sure you arrive at the airport two hours before your flight's scheduled departure.

Security measures at Canadian airports are similar to those in the United States.

Airport Security Issues Transportation **Security Administration** ⊕ www.tsa.gov.

AIRPORTS

For service to Montréal, Montréal–Pierre Elliott Trudeau International Airport (also known by its previous name, Dorval International Airport, airport code YUL) is 22½ km (14 miles) west of the city. Québec City's Jean Lesage International Airport (YQB) is about 19 km (12 miles) northwest of downtown. Both airports handle domestic and international flights.

Airport Information Aéroports de Montréal ⊠ 800 Leigh-Capreol, Suite 1000, Dorval ☎ 514/394–7200 ⊕ www.admtl. com. **Jean Lesage International Airport** ☎ 418/640–3300, 877/769–2700 ⊕ www.aeroportdequebec.com. **Montréal– Pierre Elliott Trudeau International Airport** ☎ 800/465–1213, 514/394–7377 ⊕ www.admtl.com.

GROUND TRANSPORTATION

In Montréal, a taxi from Trudeau International to downtown costs C$38. All taxi companies must charge the same rate for travel between the airport and downtown.

The least expensive way to get from Trudeau International Airport into the city is to take the 747 Express Bus, operated by Société de transport de Montréal. Shuttles leave from Montréal Central Bus Station and run every 20 minutes all day long, except during evening and morning rush hours, 6 am–9 am and 4 pm–8 pm, when they leave every 10 to 15 minutes. The cost is C$8 one-way. Also available at the Currency Exchange kiosk in the airport are C$8 day bus passes, which not only buys you a ticket for the airport shuttle but also unlimited travel on the entire Montréal bus and métro system for a 24-hour period.

In Québec City, taxis are available immediately outside the airport exit near the baggage-claim area. A ride into the city costs about C$37. Two local taxi firms are Taxi Coop de Québec, the largest company in the city, and Taxi Québec. Private limo service is expensive, starting at C$65 for the ride from the airport into the city. Try Groupe Limousine A-1.

Montréal Contacts Société de transport de Montréal ☎ 514/786–4636 ⊕ www.stum.qc.ca.

Québec City Contacts Groupe Limousine A-1 ⊠ 160 boul. des Cedres, Québec City ☎ 418/523–5059, 866/523–5059. **Taxi Coop de Québec** ⊠ 496 2e av., Québec City ☎ 418/525–5191 ⊕ www.taxicoop-quebec. com. **Taxi Québec** ⊠ 975 8e av., Québec City ☎ 418/525–8123.

FLIGHTS

Of the major U.S. airlines, American, Continental, Delta, United, and US Airways serve Montréal; Delta also flies to Québec City.

Regularly scheduled flights from the United States to Montréal and Québec City as well as flights within Canada are available on Air Canada and the regional airlines associated with it, including Air Canada Jazz (reservations are made through Air Canada). Air Canada has the most nonstop flights to Montréal and Québec City from some 30 U.S. cities.

Porter Airlines also has connecting service to Montréal and Québec City from select U.S. cities, via Toronto.

Airline Contacts Air Canada ☎ *888/247-2262* ⊕ *www.aircanada.ca.* **American Airlines** ☎ *800/433-7300* ⊕ *www.aa.com.*

Delta Airlines ☎ *800/221-1212 for U.S. reservations, 800/241-4141 for international reservations* ⊕ *www.delta.com.*

Porter Airlines ☎ *888/619-8622* ⊕ *www.flyporter.com.*

US Airways ☎ *800/428-4322 for U.S. and Canada reservations, 800/622-1015 for international reservations* ⊕ *www.usairways.com.*

▌ BIKE TRAVEL

Québec is in the process of developing the Route Verte, or the Green Route, a network of bike trails covering the southern half of the province, which will eventually link with trails in New England and New York. More than half of the marked trails are already open, and when the project is completed, it will comprise 4,300 km (more than 2,600 miles) of bikeways. For information and a map, contact Vélo Québec.

Contact Vélo Québec ☎ *514/521-8356, 800/567-8356* ⊕ *www.velo.qc.ca.*

▌ BOAT AND FERRY TRAVEL

The Québec–Lévis ferry crosses the St. Lawrence River to the town of Lévis and gives you a magnificent panorama of Old Québec. Although the crossing takes 15 minutes, waiting time can increase the trip to an hour. The cost is C$3. The first ferry from Québec City leaves weekdays at 6:20 am from the pier at rue Dalhousie, opposite Place Royale. Crossings run every 20 minutes during weekday rush hours, from 6:20 am to 9 am and 3 pm to 6 pm. At other times it runs every 30 minutes until 2:20 am. On weekends and holidays, the ferry leaves every 30 minutes from 6:30 am to 2:20 am. Schedules

can change, so be sure to check the ferry website or call ahead.

Boat and Ferry Information
Québec–Lévis ferry ☎ *877/787-7483* ⊕ *www.traversiers.gouv.qc.ca.*

▌ BUS TRAVEL

Approximately 10 private bus lines serve the province. Orléans Express is probably the most convenient, as it offers regular service between Montréal and Québec City with a fairly new fleet of clean, comfortable buses. The trip takes three hours. Limocar, another bus line, serves the ski resorts of the Laurentians and Eastern Townships. Greyhound Lines and Voyageur offer interprovincial service and are timely and comfortable, if not exactly plush. Smoking isn't permitted on any buses.

Bus terminals in Montréal and Québec City are usually efficient operations, with service all week and plenty of agents on hand to handle ticket sales. In villages and some small towns the bus station is simply a counter in a local convenience store, gas station, or snack bar. Getting information on schedules beyond the local ones is sometimes difficult in these places. In rural Québec it's a good idea to bring along a French–English dictionary, although most merchants and clerks can handle a simple ticket sale in English.

Buses from Montréal to Québec City depart daily every hour on the hour from 6 am to 8 pm, with additional departures at 9:30 pm and 11 pm. A one-way ticket costs C$56.80, taxes included; round-trip costs C$90.89. Tickets can be purchased only at terminals. All intercity bus lines servicing Montréal arrive at and depart from the city's downtown bus terminal, the Station Centrale d'Autobus Montréal, which is built on top of the Berri-UQÀM métro station. The staff has schedule and fare information for all bus companies at the station.

Many bus companies offer discounts if you book in advance, usually either 7 or 14 days ahead. Discounts are also often available for kids (children ages 15 and under can travel for free on most bus lines if tickets are booked three days in advance).

In major bus terminals, most bus lines accept at least some of the major credit cards. Some smaller lines require cash or take only Visa or MasterCard. All accept traveler's checks in U.S. or Canadian currency with suitable identification, but it's advisable to exchange foreign currency (including U.S. currency) at a bank or exchange office. Be prepared to use cash to buy a ticket in really small towns.

Most bus lines don't accept reservations for specific seats. You should plan on picking up your tickets at least 45 minutes before the bus's scheduled departure time.

While it's still in the same location, there were some renovations done to Central Station recently and they now have a new official address, which is: 1717 rue Berri, Montréal Québec, Canada, H2L 4E9.

Bus Information Central Bus Station
✉ *1717 rue Berri, Montréal* ☎ *514/842–2281.*
Gare du Palais Bus Station ✉ *320 rue Abraham-Martin, Québec City* ☎ *418/525–3000.* **Greyhound Lines** ☎ *800/231–2222, 800/661–8747 in Canada* ⊕ *www.greyhound. com.* **Limocar** ☎ *514/842–2281* ⊕ *www. transdev.ca.* **Orléans Express** ☎ *888/999–3977, 514/395–4000* ⊕ *www.orleansexpress. com.* **Voyageur/Greyhound Canada** ☎ *514/842–2281* ⊕ *www.greyhound.ca.*

■ CAR TRAVEL

Montréal is accessible from the rest of Canada via the Trans-Canada Highway, which crosses the southern part of the island as Route 20, with Route 720 leading into downtown. Route 40 parallels Route 20 to the north; exits to downtown include St-Laurent and St-Denis. From New York, take I–87 north until it becomes Route 15 at the Canadian border; continue for another 47 km (29 miles) to the outskirts of Montréal. You can also follow U.S. I–89 north until it becomes two-lane Route 133, which eventually joins Route 10, an east–west highway that leads west across the Champlain Bridge and right into downtown. From I–91 through Massachusetts via New Hampshire and Vermont, you can take Route 55 to Route 10. Again, turn west to reach Montréal.

At the border you must clear Canadian Customs, so be prepared with your passport and car registration. On holidays and during the peak summer season, expect to wait a half hour or more at the major crossings.

Montréal and Québec City are linked by Route 20 on the south shore of the St. Lawrence River and by Route 40 on the north shore. On both highways, the ride between the two cities is about 240 km (149 miles) and takes about three hours. U.S. I–87 in New York, U.S. I–89 in Vermont, and U.S. I–91 in New Hampshire connect with Route 20, as does Highway 401 from Toronto.

Driving northeast from Montréal on Route 20, follow signs for Pont Pierre-Laporte (Pierre Laporte Bridge) as you approach Québec City. After you've crossed the bridge, turn right onto boulevard Laurier (Route 175), which becomes the Grande Allée.

The speed limit is posted in kilometers; on highways the limit is 100 kph (about 62 mph), and the use of radar-detection devices is prohibited.

In Québec the road signs are in French, but the important ones have pictograms. Signs with a red circle and a slash indicate that something, such as a left or right turn, is prohibited. Those with a green circle show what's permitted. Parking signs display a green-circled "P" with either the number of hours you can park or a clock showing the hours parking is permitted. It's not unusual to have two or three road signs all together to indicate several different strictures. Keep in mind the following terms: *centre-ville* (downtown), *arrêt* (stop), *détenteurs de permis* (permit holders only), *gauche* (left), *droit* (right), *ouest* (west), and *est* (east).

Drivers must carry owner registration and proof of insurance coverage, which is compulsory in Canada. Québec drivers are covered by the Québec government no-fault insurance plan. Drivers from outside Québec can obtain a Canadian Non-Resident Inter-Provincial Motor Vehicle Liability Insurance Card, available from any U.S. insurance company. The card is accepted as evidence of financial responsibility in Canada, but you're not required to have one. The minimum liability in Québec is C$50,000. If you are driving a car that isn't registered in your name, carry a letter from the owner that authorizes your use of the vehicle.

GASOLINE

Gasoline is always sold in liters; 3.8 liters make a gallon. At this writing, gas prices in Canada are fluctuating considerably, ranging from C$1.15 to C$1.40 per liter (this works out to about $4.73 to $5.32 per gallon U.S.). Unleaded gas is called *sans plomb* or *ordinaire* (gas stations don't sell leaded gasoline). Fuel comes in several grades, denoted as *regulière*, *supérieure*, and *prémium*.

PARKING

Expect on-street parking in Montréal to be just as difficult as in any major city; your best bet is to leave the car at your hotel garage and take public transportation or a cab. If you must drive, ask your concierge to recommend a garage near your destination. Be extra careful where you park if it snows, to avoid getting towed. Parking in Québec City is much less stressful, although it's also advisable to leave the car at the hotel and walk—especially if you're heading to Vieux-Québec.

ROAD CONDITIONS

In winter, be aware of changing road conditions: Montréal streets are kept mostly clear of snow and ice, but outside the city the situation can deteriorate. Locals are notorious for exceeding the speed limit, so keep an eye on your mirrors. For up to

date reports on road conditions throughout the province, go to Transport Quebec's website.

Contact Transport Quebec ⊕ *www.quebec511.gouv.qc.ca.*

ROADSIDE EMERGENCIES

Dial 911 in an emergency. Contact CAA, the Canadian Automobile Association, in the event of a flat tire, dead battery, empty gas tank, or other car-related mishap. Automobile Association of America membership includes CAA service.

Emergency Services CAA ☎ *800/222-4357, 514/861-1313* ⊕ *www.caa.ca.*

Insurance Information Insurance Bureau of Canada ☎ *514/288-4321, 877/288-4321 in Québec* ⊕ *www.ibc.ca.* **Société de l'assurance automobile du Québec** ☎ *800/361-7620, 514/873-7620, 418/643-7620* ⊕ *www.saaq.gouv.qc.ca.*

RULES OF THE ROAD

By law, you're required to wear seat belts even in the backseat. Infant seats also are required. Radar-detection devices are illegal in Québec; just having one in your car is illegal. Speed limits, given in kilometers, are usually within the 90 kph–100 kph (50 mph–60 mph) range outside the cities.

Right turns on red signals are allowed in the province, excluding the island of Montréal, where they're prohibited. Driving with a blood-alcohol content of 0.08% or higher is illegal and can earn you a stiff fine and jail time. Headlights are compulsory in inclement weather. Drivers aren't permitted to use handheld cell phones. The laws here are similar to the rest of North America; to consult Québec's Highway Code go to the Société de l'assurance automobile du Québec's website.

Contact Ministère des Transports du Québec ☎ *888/355-0511* ⊕ *www.mtq.gouv.qc.ca.* **Société de l'assurance automobile du Québec** ☎ *800/361-7620, 514/873-7620, 418/643-7620* ⊕ *www.saaq.gouv.qc.ca.*

CAR RENTAL

Rates in Montréal run from about C$34 to C$60 a day for an economy car with air-conditioning and unlimited kilometers. If you prefer a manual-transmission car, check whether the rental agency of your choice offers stick shifts; many agencies in Canada don't.

You must be at least 21 years old to rent a car in Québec, and some car-rental agencies don't rent to drivers under 25. Most rental companies don't allow you to drive on gravel roads. Child seats are compulsory for children ages five and under. In Québec, drivers under age 25 often have to pay a surcharge of C$10 a day.

Rentals at the airports near Québec City and Montréal are usually more expensive than rentals elsewhere in the area.

Major Rental Agencies Alamo
☏ *877/222–9075* ⊕ *www.alamo.com.*
Avis ☏ *800/331–1084* ⊕ *www.avis.com.*
Budget ☏ *800/472–3325 for calls in Canada, 800/527–0700 for calls in the U.S.*
⊕ *www.budget.com.* **Hertz** ☏ *800/654–3001*
⊕ *www.hertz.com.* **National Car Rental**
☏ *877/222–9058* ⊕ *www.nationalcar.com.*

▌ TRAIN TRAVEL

Amtrak has daily service from New York City's Penn Station to Montréal, although the train sometimes arrives too late to make any connecting trains that evening. Connections are available, often the next day, to Canadian rail line VIA Rail's Canadian routes. The ride takes up to 10 hours, and one-way tickets cost C$63. VIA Rail trains run from Montréal to Québec City often and take three hours. Smoking isn't allowed on these trains.

The train arrives at the 19th-century Gare du Palais in Lower Town. Trains from Montréal to Québec City and from Québec City to Montréal run four times daily on weekdays, three times daily on weekends, with a stop in Ste-Foy. Tickets can be purchased in advance at VIA Rail offices, at the station prior to departure,

through a travel agent, or online. VIA's supersaver one-way fare is C$63.24, including taxes, and must be purchased at least 10 days in advance. If you're lucky you can sometimes find web-only fares for as little as C$33.

First-class service costs C$103.48 each way, and includes early boarding, seat selection, and a three-course meal with wine. Tickets must be purchased at least 10 days in advance.

To save money, look into rail passes. But be aware that if you don't plan to cover many miles, you may come out ahead by buying individual tickets. VIA Rail offers a Canrail pass (for travel within Canada) and a Corridor Pass (for travel anywhere between Windsor, Ontario, and Québec City). Senior citizens (60 and older), children (18 and under), and students are entitled to an additional 10% discount off all rates.

Le Massif De Charlevoix, a new train system, takes you from Québec City to La Malbaie, Charlevoix for a one-day excursion. The small villages and the natural beauty along the route will wow you. There are different packages available based on the seasons. Prices start at C$249 per person.

Information Amtrak ☏ *800/872–7245*
⊕ *www.amtrak.com.*

Le Massif de Charlevoix ☏ *877/536–2774,*
418/632-5876 ⊕ *www.lemassif.com.* **VIA Rail Canada** ☏ *888/842–7245, 514/989–2626*
⊕ *www.viarail.ca.*

ESSENTIALS

■ ACCOMMODATIONS

In Montréal and Québec City you have a choice of luxury hotels, moderately priced modern properties, and small older hotels with perhaps fewer conveniences but more charm. Options in small towns and in the country include large, full-service resorts; small, privately owned hotels; roadside motels; and bed-and-breakfasts. Even outside the cities you need to make reservations before you plan to pull into town.

Expect accommodations to cost more in summer than in the colder months (except for places such as ski resorts, where winter is high season). When making reservations, ask about special deals and packages. Big-city hotels that cater to business travelers often offer weekend packages, and many city hotels offer rooms at up to 50% off in winter. If you're planning to visit Montréal or Québec City or a resort area in high season, book well in advance. Also be aware of any special events or festivals that may coincide with your visit and fill every room for miles around. For resorts and lodges, remember that winter ski season is a period of high demand, and plan accordingly.

⇨ *For more information on apartment rentals, student housing options, and B&Bs, see the Lodging Alternatives box in Chapter 8.*

APARTMENT AND HOUSE RENTALS

The *Gazette* (⊕ *www.montrealgazette. com*), Montréal's English-language daily, has a wide selection of rental listings.

BED-AND-BREAKFASTS

B&Bs, which are also known as *gîtes* in Québec, can be found in both the country and the cities. For assistance in booking these, be sure to check out B&B websites (⊕ *www.gitesetaubergesdupassant. com* and ⊕ *www.bedsandbreakfasts.ca* are good resources for B&Bs throughout the province). Room quality varies from house to house as well, so ask to see a few rooms before making a choice.

The nonprofit organization Agricotours has extensive listings of B&Bs, both urban and rural, as well as farms that take paying guests.

Reservation Services Agricotours ☎ *514/252–3138* ⊕ *www.terroiretsaveurs. com.* **BB Canada** ⊕ *www.bbcanada.com.* **Bed and Breakfast Quebec** ⊕ *www. bedbreakfastsquebec.com.* **Bed & Breakfast. com** ☎ *512/322–2710, 800/462–2632* ⊕ *www. bedandbreakfast.com.* **Bed & Breakfast Inns Online** ☎ *310/280–4363, 800/215–7365* ⊕ *www.bbonline.com.* **Montréal Reservation** ⊕ *www.montrealreservation.com.* **Stay Canada** ⊕ *www.staycanada.ca.*

HOTELS

Canada doesn't have a national rating system for hotels, but Québec's tourism ministry rates the province's hotels and bed-and-breakfasts; the stars are more a reflection of the number of facilities than of the hotel's performance. Hotels are rated zero to three stars (B&Bs, zero to four suns), with zero stars or suns representing minimal comfort and few services and three stars or four suns being the very best. All hotels listed have private bath unless otherwise noted.

■ COMMUNICATIONS

INTERNET

Most hotels—even several B&Bs—now have Wi-Fi either in-room or in-hotel. If you're looking for a cybercafé, head to the area around McGill University.

Contacts Cybercafes. Cybercafes lists more than 4,000 Internet cafés worldwide. ⊕ *www.cybercafes.com.*

LANGUAGE

Although Canada has two official languages—English and French—the province of Québec has only one. French is the language you hear most often on the streets here; it's also the language of government, businesses, and schools. Only in Montréal, the Gatineau (the area around Hull), and the Eastern Townships is English more widely spoken. Most French Canadians speak English as well, but learning a few phrases before you go is useful. Canadian French has many distinctive words and expressions, but it's no more different from the language of France than North American English is from the English spoken in Great Britain.

PHONES
CALLING WITHIN CANADA

Pay phones are becoming scarce these days as people rely more heavily on mobile phones. Phone numbers appear just as they do in the United States, with a three-digit area code followed by a seven-digit number. The area codes for Montréal are 514 and 438; in Québec City, it's 418.

CALLING OUTSIDE CANADA

The country code for the United States is 1.

MOBILE PHONES

If you have a multiband phone and your service provider uses the world-standard GSM network, you can probably use your phone abroad. Roaming fees can be steep, however: 99¢ a minute is considered reasonable. It's almost always cheaper to send a text message than to make a call, since text messages are often free or have a very low set fee (usually less than 5¢).

If you just want to make local calls, consider buying a new SIM card (note that your provider may have to unlock your phone for you to use a different SIM card) and a prepaid service plan in the destination. You'll then have a local number and can make local calls at local rates. If your trip is extensive, you could also simply buy a new cell phone in your destination, as the initial cost will be offset over time.

Contacts Cellular Abroad ☏ *800/287–5072* ⊕ *www.cellularabroad.com.* **Mobal** ☏ *888/888–9162* ⊕ *www.mobalrental.com.*

▌CUSTOMS AND DUTIES

U.S. Customs and Immigration has pre-clearance services at **Pierre Elliott Trudeau International Airport,** which serves Montréal. This allows U.S.-bound air passengers to depart their airplane directly on arrival at their U.S. destination without further inspection and delays.

American visitors may bring in, duty-free, for personal consumption 200 cigarettes; 50 cigars; 7 ounces of tobacco; and 1 bottle (1.5 liters or 40 imperial ounces) of liquor or wine or 24 355-milliliter (12-ounce) bottles or cans of beer. Any alcohol and tobacco products in excess of these amounts is subject to duty, provincial fees, and taxes. You can also bring in gifts up to a total value of C$750.

Cats and dogs must have a certificate issued by a licensed veterinarian that clearly identifies the animal and vouches that it has been vaccinated against rabies during the preceding 36 months. Certificates aren't necessary for Seeing Eye dogs. Plant material must be declared and inspected. There may be restrictions on some live plants, bulbs, and seeds. You may bring food for your own use, as long as the quantity is consistent with the duration of your visit and restrictions or prohibitions on some fruits and vegetables are observed.

Canada's firearms laws are significantly stricter than those in the United States. All handguns and semiautomatic and fully automatic weapons are prohibited and cannot be brought into the country. Sporting rifles and shotguns may be imported provided they are to be used for sporting, hunting, or competing while in Canada. All firearms must be declared to Canada Customs at the first point of entry. Failure to declare firearms will result in their seizure, and criminal charges may be made. Regulations require visitors to have a confirmed Firearms Declaration to bring any guns into Canada; a fee of C$25 applies, good for one year. For more information, contact the Canadian Firearms Centre.

Information in Montréal and Québec City
Canada Border Services Agency
✉ *2265 boul. St-Laurent, Ottawa, Ontario*
☎ *800/461–9999 in Canada, 204/983–3500,*
506/636–5064 ⊕ *www.cbsa-asfc.gc.ca.*
Canadian Firearms Centre ☎ *800/731–4000*
⊕ *www.cfc-cafc.gc.ca.*

U.S. Information U.S. Customs and Border
Protection ⊕ *www.cbp.gov.*

▌EATING OUT

French-Canadian fast food follows the same concept as American fast food, though barbecue chicken is also popular. Local chains to watch for include St-Hubert, which serves rotisserie chicken; Chez Cora, which specializes in breakfasts; and La Belle Province, Lafleur, and Valentine, all of which serve hamburgers, hot dogs, and fries. As an antidote, try the Montréal chain Le Commensal—it's completely vegetarian, and it's excellent.

MEALS AND MEALTIMES
Unless otherwise noted, the restaurants listed in this guide are open daily for lunch and dinner.

PAYING
Major credit cards are widely accepted in both Montréal and Québec City.

⇨ *For guidelines on tipping see Tipping below.*

RESERVATIONS AND DRESS
Regardless of where you are, it's a good idea to make a reservation if you can. We only mention them specifically when reservations are essential or when they aren't accepted. We mention dress only when men are required to wear a jacket or a jacket and tie.

WINES, BEER, AND SPIRITS
Beer lovers rejoice at the selection available from highly regarded local microbreweries, such as Unibroue (Fin du Monde, U, U2), Brasseurs du Nord (Boréale), and McAuslan (Griffon, St. Ambroise). You may find these and other microbrews bottled in local supermarkets

and on tap in bars. The local hard cider P.O.M. is also excellent. Caribou, a traditional concoction made from red wine, vodka (or some other liquor), spices, and, usually, maple syrup, is available at many winter events and festivals throughout the province, such as Québec City's winter carnival. Small bars may also offer the drink in season.

The province's liquor purveyor, SAQ, stocks a wide choice of wines and is also the only place you can buy hard liquor; most SAQ stores are open regular business hours. Supermarkets and convenience stores carry lower-end wines, but they can sell wine and beer until 11 pm all week (long after SAQ stores have closed). The minimum legal age for alcohol consumption is 18.

▌EMERGENCIES

All embassies are in Ottawa. The U.S. consulate in Montréal is open weekdays 8:30–noon; additionally it's open Wednesday 2–4. The U.S. Consulate maintains a list of medical specialists in the Montréal area.

In Montréal, the main English-language hospital is Montréal General Hospital (McGill University Health Centre). Many pharmacies in Montréal stay open until midnight, including Jean Coutu and Pharmaprix stores. Some are open around the clock, including the Pharmaprix on chemin de la Côte-des-Neiges.

In Québec City, the Centre Hospitalier Universitaire de Québec is the city's largest institution and incorporates the teaching hospitals Pavillon CHUL in Ste-Foy and Pavillon Hôtel-Dieu, the main hospital in Vieux-Québec. Most outlets of the big pharmacy chains in the region (including Jean Coutu, Racine, Brunet, and Uniprix) are open every day and offer free delivery.

Foreign Embassies and Consulates
U.S. Consulate General ✉ *1155 rue St-Alexandre, Montréal* ☎ *514/398–9695* ✉ *2 pl. Terrasse Dufferin, behind Château Frontenac,*

Québec City ☎ *418/692–2095.* **U.S. Embassy** ✉ *490 Sussex Dr., Ottawa, Ontario* ☎ *613/688–5335* ⊕ *www.canada.usembassy.gov.*

Hospitals Centre Hospitalier Universitaire de Québec, Pavillon CHUL ✉ *2705 boul. Laurier, Ste-Foy* ☎ *418/525–4444, 418/654–2114 emergencies.* **Centre Hospitalier Universitaire de Québec, Pavillon Hôtel-Dieu** ✉ *11 côte du Palais, Upper Town* ☎ *418/525–4444, 418/691–5042 emergencies.* **Montréal General Hospital (McGill University Health Centre)** ✉ *1650 av. Cedar, Downtown* ☎ *514/934–1934* Ⓜ *Guy-Concordia.*

■ HOLIDAYS

Canadian national holidays are as follows: New Year's Day (January 1), Good Friday (late March or early April), Easter Monday (the Monday following Good Friday), Victoria Day (called Fête des Patriotes in Québec; late May), Canada Day (July 1), Labor Day (early September), Thanksgiving (mid-October), Remembrance Day (November 11), Christmas, and Boxing Day (December 26). St. Jean Baptiste Day (June 24) is a provincial holiday.

■ MONEY

Throughout this book, prices are given in Canadian dollars. The price of a cup of coffee ranges from less than C$1 to C$2.50 or more, depending on how upscale or downscale the place is; beer costs C$3 to C$7 in a bar; a smoked-meat sandwich costs about C$5 to C$6; and museum admission can cost anywhere from nothing to C$15.

Prices throughout this guide are given for adults. Substantially reduced fees are almost always available for children, students, and senior citizens.

ATMS AND BANKS

Your own bank will probably charge a fee for using ATMs abroad; the foreign bank you use may also charge a fee. Nevertheless, you'll usually get a better rate of exchange at an ATM than you will at a currency-exchange office or even when changing money in a bank. And extracting funds as you need them is a safer option than carrying around a large amount of cash.

ATMs are available in most bank, trust-company, and credit-union branches across the province, as well as in most convenience stores, malls, and self-serve gas stations.

CREDIT CARDS

It's a good idea to inform your credit-card company before you travel, especially if you're going abroad and don't travel internationally very often. Otherwise, the credit-card company might put a hold on your card owing to unusual activity—not a good thing halfway through your trip. Record all your credit-card numbers—as well as the phone numbers to call if your cards are lost or stolen—in a safe place, so you're prepared should something go wrong. Both MasterCard and Visa have general numbers you can call (collect if you're abroad) if your card is lost, but you're better off calling the number of your issuing bank, since MasterCard and Visa usually just transfer you to your bank; your bank's number is usually printed on your card.

If you plan to use your credit card for cash advances, you'll need to apply for a PIN at least two weeks before your trip. Although it's usually cheaper (and safer) to use a credit card abroad for large purchases (so you can cancel payments or be reimbursed if there's a problem), note that some credit-card companies *and* the banks that issue them add substantial percentages to all foreign transactions, whether they're in a foreign currency or not. Check on these fees before leaving home, so there won't be any surprises when you get the bill.

Reporting Lost Cards American Express ☎ *800/528–4800 in U.S., 800/668–2639 in Canada* ⊕ *www.americanexpress.com.* **Diners Club** ☎ *800/234–6377 in U.S., 303/799–1504 collect from abroad* ⊕ *www.dinersclub.com.* **MasterCard** ☎ *800/627–8372 in U.S., 636/722–7111 collect from abroad* ⊕ *www.mastercard.com.* **Visa** ☎ *800/847–2911 in U.S., 410/581–9994 collect from abroad* ⊕ *www.visa.com.*

CURRENCY AND EXCHANGE

U.S. dollars are accepted in much of Canada, especially in communities near the border. Traveler's checks (some are available in Canadian dollars) and major U.S. credit cards are accepted in most areas.

The units of currency in Canada are the Canadian dollar (C$) and the cent, in almost the same denominations as U.S. currency ($5, $10, $20, 1¢, 5¢, 10¢, 25¢, etc.). The $1 and $2 bill are no longer used in Canada; they have been replaced by $1 and $2 coins (known as "loonies," because of the loon that appears on the coin, and "toonies," respectively).

At this writing, the exchange rate is US$1 to C$1, or par, but this is always subject to change, with the American dollar often trading as high as US$1 to C$1.40 in recent years.

Bank cards are widely accepted in Québec and throughout Canada. There are many branches of Québec's financial cooperative, La Caisse populaire Desjardins (a "Caisse Pop" as it's locally referred to), as well as bank machines (ATMs), throughout the region.

Currency Conversion
Google ⊕ *www.google.com.* **Oanda.com**
⊕ *www.oanda.com.* **XE.com** ⊕ *www.xe.com.*

∎ PACKING

If you're visiting Montréal anytime between November and May be sure to bring some warm clothes, or be prepared to purchase some while you're here. Come winter Montréal gets cold—very cold—with temperatures almost always dipping below the freezing mark from December until late March. A good winter coat, scarf, hat (locally called a "tuque"), gloves, and warm winter boots are pretty much a necessity in Québec if you want to be comfortable going outside in the winter months. In summer, however, temperatures regularly rise above 86°F (30°C) and downtown Montréal in particular can get very humid, so bring a few pairs of shorts, sandals, and warm weather clothes. While it seems unbelievable, tales abound here of hapless tourists arriving at the airport in June with their skis and snowshoes in tow, wondering where all the snow is. Also, while a large Anglophone community resides in Montréal and many of its immediate surroundings, the official language here is French, and all road signs are in this language, so having a good French/English dictionary with you is always helpful.

∎ PASSPORTS AND VISAS

All travelers will need a passport or other accepted secure documents to enter or reenter the United States. Naturalized U.S. residents should carry their naturalization certificate. Permanent residents who aren't citizens should carry their "green card." U.S. residents entering Canada from a third country must have a valid passport, naturalization certificate, or "green card."

∎ RESTROOMS

Aside from the ones in municipal parks there's a noticeable lack of public restrooms in downtown Montréal. That said, there's almost always a shopping mall or commercial establishment within striking distance should you find yourself in urgent need of relief. Most establishments won't give you much grief about coming in off the street to use their restroom, although generally the more discreet you are about it the better.

Find a Loo The Bathroom Diaries
⊕ *www.thebathroomdiaries.com.*

∎ TAXES

A goods and services tax (GST or TPS in Québec) of 5% applies on virtually every transaction in Canada except for the purchase of basic groceries. In addition to imposing the GST, Québec levies a provincial sales tax of 9.5% on most goods and services as well.

Departing passengers in Montréal pay a C$25, plus GST, airport-improvement fee that's included in the cost of an airline ticket.

Information Canada Customs and Revenue Agency ✉ *Summerside Tax Centre, 275 Pope Rd., Suite 104, Summerside, Prince Edward Island* ☎ *800/668–4748 in Canada, 902/432–5608* ⊕ *www.ccra-adrc.gc.ca.*

∎ TIME

Montréal and Québec City are both in the Eastern Standard Time zone. Los Angeles is three hours behind local time and Chicago is one hour behind.

∎ TIPPING

Tips and service charges aren't usually added to a bill in Canada. In general, tip 15% of the total bill. This goes for waiters and waitresses, barbers and hairdressers, and taxi drivers. Porters and doormen should get about C$2 a bag. For maid service, leave at least C$2 per person a day (C$3 to C$5 in luxury hotels).

∎ TOURS

DAY TOURS AND GUIDES

In Montréal, from May through October, Amphi Tour sells a unique one-hour tour of Vieux-Montréal and the Vieux-Port on both land and water in an amphibious bus. Bateau-Mouche runs four harbor excursions and an evening supper cruise daily from May through October. The boats are reminiscent of the ones that cruise the canals of the Netherlands—wide-beamed and low-slung, with a glassed-in passenger deck. Boats leave from the Jacques Cartier Pier at the foot of Place Jacques-Cartier in the Vieux-Port.

Gray Line has nine different types of tours of Montréal from June through October and one tour the rest of the year. There are also day trips to Ottawa and Québec City. The company offers pickup service

at the major hotels and at Info-Touriste (✉ *1001 Sq. Dorchester*).

In Québec City, Autocar Dupont/Old Québec Tours runs bus tours of the city, departing across the square from the Hôtel Château Laurier (✉ *1230 Pl. Georges V*); you can purchase tickets at most major hotels. The company runs guided tours in a minibus as well as tours of Côte-de-Beaupré and Île d'Orléans, and whale-watching excursions to Charlevoix. Tours run year-round and cost C$34–C$123. Call for a reservation and the company will pick you up at your hotel.

Croisières AML has day and evening cruises, some of which include dinner, on the St. Lawrence River aboard the MV *Louis-Jolliet*. The 1½- to 3-hour cruises run from May through mid-October and start at C$35 plus tax.

Contacts Amphi Tour ☎ *514/849–5181* ⊕ *www.montreal-amphibus-tour.com.* **Autocar Dupont/Old Québec Tours** ☎ *418/664–0460, 800/267–8687* ⊕ *www. oldquebectours.com.* **Bateau-Mouche** ☎ *514/849–9952, 800/361–9952* ⊕ *www. bateaumouche.ca.* **Croisières AML** ✉ *Pier Chouinard, 10 rue Dalhousie, beside the Québec–Lévis ferry terminal, Lower Town* ☎ *866/856–6668* ⊕ *www.croisieresaml.com.*

∎ TRIP INSURANCE

Comprehensive trip insurance is valuable if you're booking a very expensive or complicated trip (particularly to an isolated region) or if you're booking far in advance. Comprehensive policies typically cover trip-cancellation and interruption, letting you cancel or cut your trip short because of illness, or, in some cases, acts of terrorism in your destination.

Such policies might also cover evacuation and medical care. Some also cover you for trip delays because of bad weather or mechanical problems as well as for lost or delayed luggage.

Another type of coverage to consider is financial default—that is, when your trip is disrupted because a tour operator, airline, or cruise line goes out of business. Generally you must buy this when you book your trip or shortly thereafter, and it's available to you only if your operator isn't on a list of excluded companies.

Always read the fine print of your policy to make sure that you're covered for the risks that most concern you. Compare several policies to be sure you're getting the best price and range of coverage available.

Insurance Comparison Info Insure My Trip
☏ 800/551–1337 ⊕ www.insuremytrip.com.
Square Mouth ☏ 800/240–0369
⊕ www.squaremouth.com.

Comprehensive Insurers Access America
☏ 800/284–8300 ⊕ www.accessamerica.com.
AIG Travel Guard ☏ 800/826–4919 ⊕ www.travelguard.com. **CSA Travel Protection**
☏ 800/711–1197 ⊕ www.csatravelprotection.com. **Travelex Insurance** ☏ 888/228–9792
⊕ www.travelex-insurance.com. **Travel Insured International** ☏ 800/243–3174
⊕ www.travelinsured.com.

▌ VISITOR INFORMATION

In Montréal, Centre Info-Touriste, on Square Dorchester, has extensive tourist information on Montréal and the rest of the province of Québec, as well as a currency-exchange service and Internet café. It's open June 21 through August, daily 9–7; September through October, daily 9–6; November through March, daily 9–5; and April through June 20, daily 9–6. The Vieux-Montréal branch is open May 27 through September 5, from 9 to 7, September 6 to October 10, from 9 to 6, and October 11 to November 13, from 9 to 5.

Tourisme-Montréal, the city tourist office, doesn't operate an information service for the public, but its website has a wealth of well-organized information.

In Québec City, the Québec City Region Tourism and Convention Bureau's visitor information centers in Montcalm and Ste-Foy are open June 24–early September, daily 8:30–7:30; early September–mid-October, daily 8:30–6:30; and mid-October–June 23, Monday–Saturday 9–5, Sunday 10–4. A mobile information service operates between mid-June and September 7 (look for the mopeds marked with a big question mark).

The Québec government tourism department, Tourisme Québec, has a center open September–June 20, daily 9–5; and June 22–August, daily 8:30–7. Tourisme Québec can provide information on specific towns' tourist bureaus.

In the Laurentians, the major tourist office is the Association Touristique des Laurentides, just off Route des Laurentides 15 Nord at Exit 51 in Les Portes des Nord service center. The office is open mid-June–September, daily 8:30–8; October–mid-June, Saturday–Thursday 8:30–5 and Friday 8:30–6. Mont-Tremblant, Piedmont/St-Sauveur, Ste-Adèle, St-Adolphe-d'Howard, Ste-Agathe-des-Monts, St-Eustache, St-Jovite, and Val-David have regional tourist offices that are open year-round. Seasonal tourist offices (open mid-June–early September) are in Ferme Neuve, Grenville, Labelle, Lac-du-Cerf, Lachute, Nominique, Notre-Dame-du-Laus, Oka, St-Jérôme, Ste-Marguerite-Estérel, and St-Sauveur.

In the Eastern Townships, year-round regional provincial tourist offices are in Bromont, Coaticook, Granby, Lac-Mégantic, Magog-Orford, Sherbrooke, and Sutton. Seasonal tourist offices (open June–early September) are in Birchton, Danville, Dudswell, Dunham, Eastman, Frelighsburg, Lac-Brome (Foster), Lambton, Masonville, Pike River, Ulverton, and Waterloo. The schedules of seasonal bureaus are irregular, so it's a good idea to contact the Association Touristique des Cantons de l'Est before visiting. This association also provides lodging information.

At the Beaupré Coast Interpretation Center, in a former convent, guides in costume explain displays on the history of the region. Admission is C$6. The center is open mid-May–mid-October, daily 9:30–4:30 and mid-October to mid-May, weekdays 9:30–4:30. For information about Canadian national parks in Québec, contact Parks Canada. Contact Sépaq for information about camping and lodgings in Québec province's network of 22 "Parcs Nationaux" and 15 game reserves (*réserves fauniques*). For information on camping in the province's private trailer parks and campgrounds, request the free publication "Québec Camping," from Tourisme Québec.

Agricotours, the Québec farm-vacation association, can provide lists of guest farms in the province.

Contacts Agricotours ⊠ *4545 av. Pierre-de-Coubertin, C.P. 1000, Succursale M, Montréal* ☎ *514/252–3138* ⊕ *www.terroiretsaveurs.com.* **Association Touristique des Cantons de l'Est** ⊠ *20 rue Don Bosco Sud, Sherbrooke* ☎ *819/820–2020, 800/355–5755* ⊕ *www.cantonsdelest.com.* **Association Touristique Régionale de Charlevoix** ⊠ *495 blvd. de Comporté, C.P. 275, La Malbaie* ☎ *418/665–4454, 800/667–2276* ⊕ *www.tourisme-charlevoix.com.* **Association Touristique des Laurentides** ⊠ *14 142 rue de la Chapelle, Mirabel* ☎ *450/224–7007, 800/561–6673* ⊕ *www.laurentides.com.* **Beaupré Coast Interpretation Center** ⊠ *7976 av. Royale, C.P. 40, Château-Richer* ☎ *418/824–3677* ⊕ *www.histoire-cotedebeaupre.org.* **Canadian Tourism Commission** ☎ *604/638–8300* ⊕ *www.travelcanada.ca.* **Centre Info-Touriste** ⊠ *1001 Sq. Dorchester, Downtown* ☎ *514/873–2015, 877/266–5687* ⊕ *www.bonjourquebec.com* Ⓜ *Peel or Bonaventure* ⊠ *174 rue Notre-Dame Est, at pl. Jacques-Cartier, Vieux-Montréal* Ⓜ *Champ-de-Mars.* **Parks Canada** ☎ *613/860–1251, 888/773–8888* ⊕ *www.pc.gc.ca.* **Québec City Tourist Information** ⊠ *835 av. Wilfred-Laurier, Montcalm* ☎ *418/641–6290, 877/783–1608* ⊕ *www.quebecregion.com.* **Sépaq** ☎ *800/665–6527* ⊕ *www.sepaq.com.* **Tourisme-Montréal** ☎ *877/266–5687* ⊕ *www.tourisme-montreal.org.* **Tourisme Québec** ⊠ *1001 rue du Sq. Dorchester, No. 100, C.P. 979, Montréal* ☎ *877/266–5687, 514/873–2015* ⊕ *www.bonjourquebec.com* ⊠ *12 rue Ste-Anne, Place-d'Armes, Upper Town* ☎ *877/266–5687.*

INDEX

PHOTO CREDITS

NOTES

NOTES

NOTES

NOTES

NOTES

NOTES

ABOUT OUR WRITERS

Chris Barry is a native Montrealer and freelance journalist who has contributed to scores of publications over the years, not the least being the *Montréal Mirror* where, since 1999, his highly irreverent but hugely popular "People" column has been published every week. He's currently working on a book documenting his years as a professional rock and roll musician in the 1970s, '80s, and '90s. Chris updated the Experience, Exploring, Side Trips from Montréal, and Travel Smart chapters of this book.

Marcella De Vincenzo is a freelance writer from Montréal who specializes in all things culinary. Her keen insight and passion for food stem from the many hours she spent in the kitchen with her grandmother. She has reviewed restaurants for ⊕ *sweetspot.ca,* ⊕ *dishcrawl.com,* and ⊕ *www.where.ca.* She is currently teaching cooking classes to kids, co-authoring a cookbook, and advises people how and what to eat on her own website ⊕ *www.cucinachronicles.ca.* For this edition, Marcella updated Where to Eat.

Amanda Halm is a professional writer and near-professional wanderer. She has called Québec City, Seattle, and Chicago home. She's a frequent contributor to many travel publications. Food, travel, and spirits are her specialties. She writes about the wayfaring life with The Husband and The Dog on her travel-humor blog: ⊕ *www.ngloadventure.com.* For this book she updated the Québec City and Side Trips from Québec City chapters.

Joanne Latimer doesn't expect any sympathy, since she is tasked with grading the linens at boutique hotels, visiting new burger joints, and learning about bivalve mollusks from oysterologists. As a freelance writer—and two-time nominee for Canada's National Magazine Awards in the humor category—her work appears in *Maclean's,* the *New York Times* and the *Ottawa Citizen.* Her blog, ⊕ *sinussister.com,* is a comedy sensation, with endorsement from comics Rob Corddry, Colin Quinn, Jimmy Carr, Russell Howard, and Alonzo Bodden. Joanne is based in Montréal with her husband, Marc, and updated the Where to Stay chapter.

Vanessa Muri is a lifestyle writer and editor from Montréal, working regularly for fashion and beauty magazine *The Kit, Tourism Montréal,* and is the former Montréal editor of ⊕ *sweetspot.ca.* She loves fashion, food, wine, and travel, though not necessarily in that order. Having lived in London and Tokyo, the lures of her hometown ultimately proved difficult to resist. For this edition, Vanessa updated the Nightlife, Performing Arts, Shopping, and Sports and Outdoors chapters.

Montréal métro

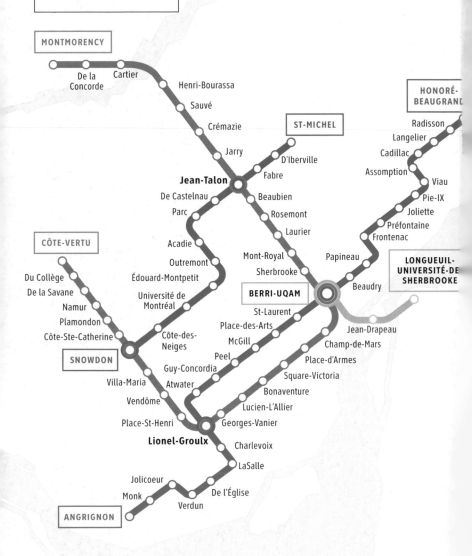